ANDREW E. TASLITZ, EDITOR

MEDIA COVERAGE IN CRIMINAL JUSTICE CASES

What Prosecutors and Defenders Should and Should Not Say

AMERICAN BAR ASSOCIATION
Criminal Justice Section

Cover design by Elmarie Jara /ABA Publishing.

Printed in the United States of America.

17 16 15 14 13 5 4 3 2 1

Library of Congress Cataloging-in-Publication Data

Media coverage in criminal justice cases : what prosecutors and defenders should and should not say / Andrew E. Taslitz, editor; Criminal Justice, American Bar Association.
pages cm
ISBN 978-1-62722-151-1
1. Free press and fair trial--United States. I. Taslitz, Andrew E., 1956- editor of compilation. II. American Bar Association. Section of Criminal Justice.
KF9223.5.M43 2013
345.73'05--dc23

2013026903

Contents

About the Editor

Professor Andrew E. Taslitz teaches at the Washington College of Law at American University, where he serves as the Director of its new Criminal Justice Practice and Policy Institute. He is a former prosecutor from Philadelphia, PA., and a graduate of the University of Pennsylvania Law School. He has, over the course of approximately the last two decades, also taught at Duke University, the University of Pittsburgh, Villanova University, and Howard University. Professor Taslitz teaches Criminal Law, Criminal Procedure, Evidence, Free Speech, White Collar Crime, and advanced courses in several of those areas. He has published over 100 works, eight of which are books, including *Rape and the Culture of the Courtroom* (1999), a book that arose from his experience as the Philadelphia prosecutor in charge of all juvenile sexual assault prosecutions, and *Reconstructing the Fourth Amendment: A History of Search and Seizure 1789-1868* (paperback ed. 2009), a work of history also sparked partly by his experiences as a prosecutor.

Recently, an increasing portion of his scholarship focuses on prosecutors' ethics, including issues of race, media contact, and innocence. Concerning prosecutor contact with the media, he has in particular published *Information Overload, Multi-tasking, and the Socially Networked Jury: Why Prosecutors Should Approach the Media Gingerly,* 37 J. LEGAL PROFESSION 89 (2012), also available at http://ssrn.com/abstract=2227118, and *The Incautious Media, Free Speech, and the Unfair Trial: Why Prosecutors Need More Realistic Guidance in Dealing with the Press,* 62 HASTINGS L.J. 1285 (2011), also available at http://ssrn.com/abstract=1864823.

He is a member of the Governing Council of the ABA Criminal Justice Section, its incoming Chair-Elect, and Editor-in Chief of its publication,

Criminal Justice, as well as being former Chair of its Book Committee. He was also the Reporter for the Uniform Law Commission's (ULC's) Uniform Code on the Electronic Recordation of Custodial Interrogations (2010) and is currently the Reporter for the ULC's Study Committee on Drafting a Uniform Statute on Eyewitness Identification Procedures. His ABA and ULC work are partly motivated by his concern for aiding prosecutors in doing justice more effectively. He has been named one of the 26 best law teachers in America in the forthcoming book, by Michael Hunter Schwartz, *What the Best Law Teachers Do* (Harvard University Press 2013).

About the Authors

Bryan L. Adamson, Associate Professor

Professor Adamson is a tenured professor with Seattle University School of Law. He joined Seattle University in 2002 as the Director of its Ronald A. Peterson Law Clinic. During his tenure as Director from 2002-2006, and interim Director in 2009, Professor Adamson established Seattle University's Predatory Lending Clinic, a Community Development and Entrepreneurship Clinic, and co-founded the Mortgage Mediation Practicum. He currently teaches Mass Media Law and Policy, Special Topics in Mass Media, Civil Procedure, and a Predatory Lending Clinic. His publications include Mass Media Law topics, Civil Procedure and judicial decision making.

Beginning in 1995, before joining Seattle University, Professor Adamson was a faculty member at Case Western Reserve University School of Law where he taught civil, criminal, and administrative law practice in Case Law's Milton A. Kramer Law Clinic Center as well as Media Law and Policy. In addition to his teaching, Bryan served as Assistant Dean for Student Services for four years at Case Law, and he directed the law school's academic enrichment program. Before teaching, Bryan practiced as a litigation attorney for Squire, Sanders, LLP in Cleveland, Ohio, and as an assistant prosecutor with the Cuyahoga County Prosecutor's Office. He holds the following degrees: B.S./Ph.B. from Miami University (Mass Communications, Interdisciplinary Studies); an M.A. from Purdue University (Mass Communications and Political Science); and a J.D. from Case Western Reserve School of Law.

Kendall Coffey

Kendall Coffey is a founding member of Coffey Burlington, PL, concentrating on complex litigation at trial and appellate levels in federal and state courts. From 1993-1996 he served as the U.S. Attorney for the Southern District of Florida, one of the nation's largest federal prosecution offices. Later, he had major litigation roles in such high profile cases as the Elian Gonzalez international custody battle, and the 2000 presidential election recount. A legal media commentator on high-profile cases, he has appeared on the Today show, Larry King Live, the O'Reilly Factor, Good Morning America, the CBS Early Show, Anderson Cooper 360, Fox & Friends, CNN International, and numerous other nationally televised programs.

Mr. Coffey has authored *Spinning the Law: Trying Cases in the Court of Public Opinion*, published by Prometheus Books, portions of which were adapted for this publication. Over the years, he has written some three dozen articles on legal topics in publications ranging from the *Yale Law and Policy Review* to the *Wall Street Journal*, and he also teaches law as an adjunct professor at the University of Miami School of Law and Florida International University School of Law.

James F. Haggerty

James F. Haggerty, President and CEO of PRCG | Haggerty LLC, is a lawyer, writer, and communications consultant with more than 20 years' experience in legal and litigation communications. With a broad background counseling corporate, nonprofit, and individual clients, Jim is frequently called upon as a trusted advisor in all manner of sensitive reputation management issues.

In the area of civil and criminal litigation, Jim is considered one of the nation's foremost experts. Over the years, he has been involved in numerous high-profile legal disputes—including the several of the largest intellectual property and antitrust cases in history, the largest lawsuit ever filed against the United States government, the largest single-family Holocaust restitution claim in history, the largest child custody and support case in history, and the largest employment class action in history. He has led the communications effort in segments of the Jonathan Pollard spy case, as well as other sensational criminal cases throughout the United States and around the world. Jim also successfully advised Consumers Union (non-profit publisher of *Consumer Reports* magazine) on two high-profile defamation cases—the infamous Suzuki Samurai rollover case, and a product disparagement lawsuit brought by The Sharper Image Corporation over the Ionic Breeze air cleaner.

Jim is the author of *In the Court of Public Opinion: Winning Strategies for Litigation Communications* (ABA Publishing, 2009). Now in its second edition, *In the Court of Public Opinion* is a groundbreaking look at the use of communications and public opinion strategies during lawsuits. *Financial Times* called the first edition of *In the Court of Public Opinion* "... the perfect handbook for this age ...." *In the Court of Public Opinion* was also positively featured in publications including the *Boston Herald*, the *New York Law Journal, American Lawyer, Law Society Gazette,* the *Washington Post, The Holmes Report, PR Week,* and *O'Dwyer's PR Newsletter.*

Jim also writes an "In the Court of Public Opinion" column for *American Lawyer's Corporate Counsel* magazine and also hosts an "In the Court of Public Opinion" radio show. In 2012 and 2013, his *Corporate Counsel* column was selected as a finalist for a Neal Award, considered business-to-business journalism's most prestigious and sought-after editorial honor. He is the only full-time public relations practitioner ever to be so honored.

From 1997–2001, Jim served as Executive Director of the International Lawyers Network (ILN), a worldwide federation of 75 law firms in 60 countries on six continents. He has also worked in public affairs for the City of New York and for U.S. Senator Daniel Patrick Moynihan.

Jim holds a B.A. in Political Science and English Literature and Rhetoric from the State University of New York at Binghamton and studied law at Fordham University in New York and Stetson University in St. Petersburg, Florida (J.D.). He is admitted to practice law in New York and Florida and is a member of the New York City and New York State Bar Associations. A frequent writer and lecturer on communications issues, Jim's articles and other writing have appeared in *USA Today*, the *New York*

Times, The National Law Journal, the *New York Law Journal, Law Practice Management,* and *PR Week.*

Peter A. Joy

Professor Peter A. Joy is the Henry Hitchcock Professor of Law and Director of the Criminal Justice Clinic at Washington University School of Law in St. Louis, Missouri, where he teaches Legal Profession, Comparative Legal Ethics Seminar, Trial Practice & Procedure, and supervises clinical students representing clients in misdemeanor and felony cases. Prior to teaching, Professor Joy litigated both criminal and civil cases in private counsel and served as appointed counsel for indigent clients in criminal cases.

He is a Contributing Editor of the ABA's *Criminal Justice* magazine, and a coauthor of *Do No Wrong: Ethics for Prosecutors and Defenders* published by the ABA. He is a former member of the *Clinical Law Review* Board of Editors, and has been a Program Director for the National Institute of Trial Advocacy (NITA). Professor Joy also serves on the Accreditation Committee of the ABA Section of Legal Education and Admissions to the Bar. Professor Joy writes primarily about criminal justice, legal ethics, and legal education issues. He has an A.B. from Youngstown State University and a J.D. from Case Western Reserve University.

Kevin McMunigal

Professor Kevin McMunigal teaches Criminal Law, Evidence and Professional Responsibility. He has held visiting appointments at the University of California (Hastings), Loyola Law School (Los Angeles), and Universidad Francisco Marroquin in Guatemala. Professor McMunigal is the co-author of *Criminal Law: A Contemporary Approach*, a criminal law casebook published by Aspen Publishing and of *Ethics for Prosecutors and Defenders,* published in 2009 by the American Bar Association. He is currently a contributing editor of the ABA Criminal Justice Section's magazine, *Criminal Justice.* Along with Professor Peter Joy of Washington University, Professor McMunigal writes a quarterly ethics column for *Criminal Justice.*

His recent publications include *Defense Counsel and Plea Bargain Perjury,* published in the Ohio State Journal of Criminal Law, *Prosecutors and Corrupt Science*, published in the Hofstra Law Review, and *Prosecutors, Ethics, and Expert Witnesses*, published in the Fordham Law Review (co-authored with Professor Paul Giannelli). Prior to teaching, Professor McMunigal served as an Assistant United States Attorney in the Criminal Division of the U.S. Attorney's Office for the Northern District of California. He also clerked for U.S. District Judge William H. Orrick in the Northern District of California.

Joshua Marquis

Joshua Marquis is the District Attorney of Clatsop County, Oregon, and is a prominent advocate of the death penalty. He contributed to *Debating the Death Penalty: Should America Have Capital Punishment?* (Oxford University Press, 2005) and has published numerous articles, some of which have been cited by U.S. Supreme Court Justice Antonin Scalia.

Marquis has been lead counsel in both the prosecution and the defense of capital cases. He has been elected to the Criminal Justice Leadership Council of the American Bar Association and is now in his fifth year on the Executive Committee of the National District Attorneys Association, of which he is also a past Vice President. He served on the Oregon Criminal Justice Commission (2005 to 2009). He has made numerous appearances in print and on television and radio, in venues such as the *National Review*, CNN, the *Los Angeles Times*, and the *Wall Street Journal*. He holds a JD from the University of Oregon.

Laurie L. Levenson

Laurie L. Levenson is the David W. Burcham Chair in Ethical Advocacy at Loyola Law School where she teaches evidence, criminal law, criminal procedure, ethics, anti-terrorism, and white collar crime. She served as Loyola's Associate Dean for Academic Affairs from 1996-1999. Professor Levenson is also the Director of the Loyola Center for Ethical Advocacy and Loyola's Project for the Innocent. Prior to joining the Loyola Law School faculty in 1989, Professor Levenson served for eight years as an Assistant United States Attorney in Los Angeles. She received the Attorney General's Director's Award for Superior Performance and commendations from the FBI, IRS, U.S. Postal Service, and DEA.

Professor Levenson received her J.D. in 1980 from UCLA School of Law and her undergraduate degree from Stanford University in 1977. In law school, she was the Chief Article Editor of the Law Review. After graduation, she clerked for the Honorable Judge James Hunter, III, of the U.S. Court of Appeals for the Third Circuit.

Professor Levenson lectures regularly throughout the country and internationally for the Federal Judicial Center, National Judicial College, international bar associations, community groups and legal societies. She also lectures for the Loyola Journalist Law School. Professor Levenson has been a legal commentator for CBS, CNN, ABC, NBC and NPR. She has commented on a wide range of high-publicity cases, including the O.J. Simpson murder trial, Rodney King beating trial, Michael Jackson molestation case, Scott Peterson murder trial, Bernard Madoff investigation, Clinton impeachment, and the Roger Clemens perjury trial. Professor Levenson is the author of numerous books and articles, including: *Ethics of Being a Legal Commentator* (1996); *The Future of Civil Rights Prosecutions: The Lessons of the Rodney King Trial* (1994); *Media Madness or Civics 101: The Lessons of "The Trial of the Century"* (1995), *"Theater of the Courtroom & Defendant's Non-testifying Demeanor"* (2007); *Witness to History: The Role of Legal Commentators in High Profile Trials* (2001); *High Profile Prosecutors & High Profile Conflicts* (2006); *Courtroom Demeanor: The Theater of the Courtroom* (2008).

Neil Vidmar

Neil Vidmar is Russell M. Robinson II Professor of Law at Duke Law School and holds a secondary appointment in the Psychology Department at Duke. Vidmar grew up in Illinois and received his Ph.D. in social psychology from the University of Illinois in 1967 and joined the Psychology Department at the University of Western Ontario in Canada after graduating. In 1973 -1974 he was a Russell Sage Resident at Yale Law School and the following year was a Battelle Fellow in Seattle, Washington. Vidmar joined the Duke Law faculty in 1987. His most recent book is Neil Vidmar and Valerie P. Hans, AMERICAN JURIES: THE VERDICT (2007). He is co-author of Valerie Hans and Neil Vidmar, JUDGING THE JURY (1986) as well as author of MEDICAL MALPRACTICE AND THE AMERICAN JURY (1995) and editor/author of WORLD JURY SYSTEMS (2000). Vidmar has written approximately 200 articles, chapters and reports in law reviews and peer reviewed social science journals and he has testified or consulted as an expert on jury behavior for criminal and civil trials in the United States as well as for criminal trials in Canada, England, Australia, New Zealand and Hong Kong. Professor Vidmar has also testified before Congress and before state legislatures on matters related to the American jury system and written briefs relating to jury matters before the U.S. Supreme Court and various state courts and legislatures.

Preface

The media plays a role in many major criminal cases. From Jodi Arias and Amanda Knox to Michael Jackson and Kobe Bryant, the media seems in a frenzy to cover criminal cases. Indeed, media coverage extends not just to salacious tales of child abuse, rape, and murder but to white collar crimes, proven and merely alleged, particularly in light of the Great Recession that began in 2008.

But lawyers need not represent the rich and powerful to find themselves with a microphone in their faces. Often a lawyer might represent a client who is but a small cog in a bigger scheme – a client who finds himself unemployed or underemployed in the wake of the larger scandal. Even more ordinary, run-of-the-mill cases sometimes make their way into the news, perhaps because the news day is slow, the town where the event occurs small, or the events highlight some category of human tragedy in which the media has recently taken an interest. Add to the mix the case commentary that arise in social media, blogs, electronic bulletin boards and the risks of media coverage affecting case outcomes become greater and all the more common.

Some lawyers find themselves frequently handling high-profile cases, developing expertise from their experience. Yet even they may have learned the media-communications trade more by trial and error rather than reflection and training. Many more lawyers will find the need for a media strategy a more unusual occurrence, but for that very reason they need guidance. No prosecutor, defense attorney, or in-house counsel overseeing or trying to fend off criminal litigation can indeed today afford to be without some sense of the rules of the media road. Few, if any, books aimed at practitioners have been designed to help the experienced and novice media-confronting attorney alike. This text aims to fill that gap.

The book's coverage is comprehensive, addressing in a relatively small space the major media issues facing criminal lawyers. The first two chapters deal primarily with strategy and tactics. Well-known criminal defense lawyer Kendall Coffey, in the book's opening chapter, fuses personal experience with precise, concrete guidelines for handling the media. He discusses such leading cases as those involving Casey Anthony and Dominique Strauss-Kahn. His position is that the modern criminal defense lawyer has an ethical obligation to be adept at media relations because cases can be lost in the press or the cyber-world before ever reaching the prosecutor's office or the courtroom. He outlines a "law-media toolbox" of instruments necessary to repair media-inflicted damage and build a media-savvy case.

Prosecutor Joshua Marquis authors a Prosecutor's Appendix to Kendall Coffey's chapter. Marquis sees Coffey's guidance as relevant to prosecutors as well as defense counsel. Marquis' worry is less about specific cases than with media images more generally. Although Marquis agrees that wrongful convictions and prosecutorial misconduct occur, he fears that the press blows both problems well out of proportion. The result may be a public (and thus a potential jury pool) that is sometimes unduly distrustful of prosecutors and police alike. Yet he acknowledges that special ethics rules limit what prosecutors can do to respond to this problem. Ultimately, he cautions prosecutors to be aware of what he sees as media bias, to counteract it where possible with truthful public statements, but to do so while strictly abiding by prosecutors' codes of ethics.

Chapter two is written by James Haggerty, a leading media consultant. Many lawyers lack the experience, expertise, or personality to engage the media effectively. Haggerty discusses the advantages of hiring a media consultant, the kinds of cases that require it, and the sorts of tasks that a consultant can complete. He also explains the proper respective roles of the lawyer, consultant, and client, and he offers hints and cautions to help in selecting the right consultant for the job. He also discusses such nitty-gritty issues as cost and the risks to the case of the lawyer getting too immersed into the media swamp in way that can detract from case preparation. He also explains why prosecutors, who rarely hire media-management consultants, are sometimes mistaken in that choice. He talks much about messages, themes, social media, rapid response, and the permanent reputational harms that clients can suffer if these things are ignored – even when a case is ultimately dropped or results in a acquittal. He too draws on well-known cases, like those involving the Duke Lacrosse team, Trayon Martin, and Martha Stewart to illustrate his main points.

Chapter three, written by Professors Peter Joy and Kevin McMunigal, two of the leading lights in the field of professional responsibility, outlines in a very practical, detailed fashion the many ethical constraints on lawyer communications with the media. The chapter broadly discusses the risks and benefits of media communication. But the chapter also addresses highly-specific questions such as what to say about concessions, confessions, false exculpatory statements, and prior inconsistent statements; fair replies to opponents' statements; the details of Model Rule of Professional Conduct 3.6; and the limits on statements by other lawyers in the principal lawyer's firm but not handling the particular case. The chapter also analyzes conflict of interest problems arising in lawyer statements to the media, book or other media deals, jury room access, the meaning of the lawyer's duty of "competence" in the context of media management, and the problem of confidentiality.

Chapter four, written by First Amendment specialist Bryan Adamson, focuses on constitutional, primarily freedom of speech, limitations on efforts of courts, prosecutors, police, and even sometimes defense attorneys to limit media access to cases or individuals and clients' access to the press. He explains the limits on using gag orders, safe harbors, and "Son-of-Sam" provisions prohibiting defendants' financially benefitting from their notoriety. He likewise discusses efforts of prosecutors or defense counsel to get information from the press, including the roles of the reporters' privilege and journalist shield laws. He additionally discusses "newsgathering crimes and defenses," such as under the Espionage Act, trespass, disorderly conduct, mail or wire fraud, and impersonating a public figure. Adamson further focuses on how the law may differ in different media, such as radio, free versus cable television, satellite, telephones, and the internet. Adamson also discusses constitutional limitations involved in accompanying civil suits, such as for defamation or under section 1983, and he reviews the special rules governing obscenity and indecency.

Chapter five is written by Professor Neil Vidmar, unquestionably a giant in the field of jury psychology. Professor Vidmar not only researches in the area of publicity's effect on jurors; he has also testified in numerous cases, particularly concerning change of venue motions on the grounds that a fair trial requires a different trial forum. Vidmar draws extensively on social science, providing background in the relevant fields in an easy, engaging style. But the chapter is no academic treatise. Vidmar's primary goal is to explain how such social science can be used in court, including via media-coverage content analyses, case-specific polls and surveys to gauge community bias, and a variety of techniques for demonstrating community attitudes as influenced by more general media effects on the jury pool, such as perceptions about racial, religious, and ethnic groups. He also discusses the purported CSI Effect and the risks from juror internet use. He further discusses the science on jury reasoning processes, particularly the "story-telling model," which focuses on the sorts of narratives that jurors create to explain an individual case. He applies these basic principles to four case studies: the American Taliban, U.S. v. al-Arian (a computer-scientist supportive of the Palestinian cause and arrested on suspicion of terrorism), U.S. v. Nacchio (the former CEO of Qwest Communications), and People v. Bolin (a marijuana-grower murder case). Vidmar continues by reviewing the social science on the relative effectiveness of various judicial remedies for feared media-induced bias. He explains with great specificity how to draft community surveys and other tools, particularly when seeking venue-change, and the value of jury questionnaires to root out bias if the change-of-venue motion is denied. Finally, Vidmar attaches as appendices to his chapter the community surveys in the American Taliban and Nacchio cases, the jury pre-trial questionnaire in the al-Arian case, and the expert declaration on habeas review in the Bolin case.

Finally, chapter six, by Loyola-Los Angeles law professor, criminal procedure expert, and frequent media voice Laurie Levenson gives hints and ethical guidelines for lawyers acting as media commentators for cases in the press. Levenson recounts the growing role of such commentators and notes the professional and societal costs and benefits of legal the legal commentariat. She particularly focuses on the social and personal benefits for, and offered by, law professors, including offering objective expert commentary to improve public debate, keeping one foot in the real world, impacting judicial decision making, fostering informed professional dialogue, and enhancing the individual's and law school's visibility. These benefits accrue, however, only if law professors are competent and ethical commentators. Levenson crafts several rules to achieve that goal, including fairness, revelation of conflicts of interest, and honing and displaying good teaching skills. Levenson closes her chapter with practical advice on how to become a commentator, how to obtain the information needed to comment wisely, when to avoid commentary entirely, how to "frame" an interview, how to speak in sound bites, what to wear, what (if anything) to get paid, and how to deal with other commentators. In doing so, she also addresses the special problems raised by Facebook, Twitter, blogs, and social media more generally.

Just as this book went to print, the Council of the Criminal Justice Section of the American Bar Association adopted the Fourth Edition of its influential Fair Trial and Free Press Standards. Recognizing the changes wrought be the internet, which make it hard to distinguish the "press" from others communicating with or via media, however, the ABA renamed its product the "Standards on Fair Trial and Public Discourse: Communication with the Public in Criminal Matters." It is highly likely that these Standards will be approved by the ABA House of Delegates at the ABA's Annual Meeting in August 2013.

These Standards are aspirational rather than designed to be a source for lawyer discipline. But the Standards have gone beyond their previous focus solely on communications risking affecting trial verdicts to discouraging also communications that "undermine[] the public's respect for the judicial process." The new Standards give more detailed advice to prosecutors and defense attorneys about what they can and cannot say and include a separate provision covering legal commentators and consultants. Further details of these Standards need not be addressed here. The main point of mentioning them is that they represent recognition by the ABA and the growing importance of criminal lawyers dealing with the media and the changes wrought by the ever-quickening change of communications technology. Moreover, although this book addresses the current state of the law on lawyer discipline, readers who seek more than simply to stay out of trouble are advised to consult these Standards for their worthy aspirations for lawyers always to do better.

Bringing together this remarkable collection of authors has been my privilege as the book's editor. But this vision of a handy, accessible, engaging source of media guidance could not have been realized without the work of Sarah Forbes Orwig, the ABA's in-house staff editor on the project, to whom I owe endless thanks.

Andrew E. Taslitz
May 17, 2013

1

Defense Perspective on Media and the Court of Public Opinion

BY KENDALL COFFEY

Introduction

Law and media are fused ever more closely in this age of YouTube, Facebook, blogs, and Twitter, as reputations are made and destroyed in a news cycle, if not in an instant. The media world not only commands our attention, it demands it—from the moment a prospective defendant retains counsel, through investigation, indictment, discovery, plea bargain, trial, and aftermath. Yet even as the court of public opinion changes its stripes to adjust to ever-more-instant technologies, any responsible defense lawyer must handle the media with awareness and caution, in ultimate service to the court of law rather than to the news cycle.

More than ever, the evolving media are subject to ever-tighter deadlines, once measured in days or hours and now in minutes, in an atmosphere in which it is better to be first than right when the truth is fluid. A courtroom blogger has 10 minutes to deliver for fear of getting scooped by another courtroom blogger, regardless of the truth, or shadings of a truth that can seem elusive under deadline pressure. As interviewer Charlie Rose so aptly says, the driving force of the media is not bias, but commerce and competition. I would also add speed. New York legal maven Benjamin Brafman likens dealing with the media to "riding a tsunami," in which one must keep one's head or drown.

If anything, the tsunami is gaining force, as what goes on the Internet stays there. Nowadays, the new media universe affects everything from jury selection to changes of venue more profoundly than ever. Yesterday's news is no longer just yesterday's news. Anyone can post a vitriolic, vindictive comment that remains online—a far cry from the days when news stories soon turned into yellowing clips in a newspaper morgue.

"It's not just one day any more. It's forever," says Roy Black, a legendary defense lawyer and veteran of many high-profile cases. "It's a new phenomenon that lawyers will have to confront."

For the defense lawyer, the best solution is to engage the media with clear eyes and discipline, with the ultimate endgame not of media approval, but of justice for the client.

A remarkable succession of cases has thrown the role of the defense lawyer in the courts of law and public opinion into focus. In recent years, the cases of O. J. Simpson, Scott Peterson, Michael Jackson, and Los Angeles Lakers point guard Kobe Bryant come to mind. Lately, the world has fixated on "Tot Mom" Casey Anthony; Conrad Murray, Michael Jackson's doctor; ex-Illinois governor Rod Blagojevich and ex-International Monetary Fund chief Dominique Strauss-Kahn. These have been some of the first celebrated cases of the social media age.

Some of these cases we will address in detail, others in passing. In short, this chapter will examine prominent criminal cases that involve the role of the media in the law and will offer strategies and suggestions on how a defense lawyer can respond, act, and create a strategy.

Criminal cases, of course, involve people, but many prominent cases directly affect the integrity of a broader enterprise, be it a leading college football program and university endowment, the International Monetary Fund, a corporation with employees and shareholders, or the Roman Catholic Church, to name just a few. This is why the legal discipline demands a broader approach in sync with corporate and crisis communications strategies. When possible and applicable, it is wise to involve seasoned, sophisticated media counselors early on in a case to lessen damage and protect individual and institutional reputations.

We will examine underlying strategies in approaching the courts, the media, and therefore the public, and then present a toolbox of tactics that can aid these strategies, from the television interview to media-friendly pleadings to news conferences. Finally, we will look to the new challenges and opportunities created by the Internet and social media. That includes dealing with "E-contamination," taking the Internet inventory, expanding E-damage control from the website to YouTube, and learning cyberstrategies for search engines. We will conclude by providing some observations on handling the ever-more-intertwined relationship between the media and the law in the new "Twitterverse."

The great undergirding principle of this discussion is that the legal and media team must emphasize strategies and tactics that overwhelmingly consider the end result of the case in a court of law while secondarily addressing the court of public opinion, always in a manner consistent with ethics and the client's best interest.

The arrest and trial of Casey Anthony is as good a place as any for launching a discussion on the new nexus between law and media.

Casey Anthony and the Media Disconnect "Tot Mom" and the Missing Child

No recent verdict has shocked more people than the July 5, 2011, acquittal of Casey Anthony, the nation's most notorious mom, on all felony counts. And no verdict better illustrates the complex relationship between the defense and the media in this new world in which Twitter, Facebook, and thei like form a deafening Greek chorus. Although some would say the acquittal was a dark day for justice, all would agree it was a dark day indeed for the pundits and commentators who all but convicted Casey Anthony of murder in the court of public opinion.

To briefly recap the heartrending, if familiar, saga: Casey Anthony's two-year-old child, Caylee, was last reported seen with Casey at the Orlando family home on June 16, 2008. Casey, then 22, did not report her daughter's disappearance for 31 days. In the meantime, she had entered a June 20 hot body contest at the Fusion nightclub, had her car towed and impounded after several days at a parking lot June 30, and on July 2, while casually chatting on the phone, received a tattoo on her back with the in-scription “Bella Vita,” Italian for “beautiful life.”

The next day, her mother, Cindy, posted a frantic MySpace message saying Casey had stolen some of her money and refused to let Cindy see her granddaughter. When Casey’s father, George, picked up her car on July 15 after more than two weeks in the tow yard, the child seat was in the back, and a pungent odor emanated from the trunk—reminding the 59-year-old ex-cop of a decomposing body. No body was found then, however—just rotting garbage. Only then did Casey Anthony report the child missing. On July 17, she was charged with child neglect, making false statements, and obstructing an investigation. The next day, she hired Jose Baez as her defense attorney.

Events cascaded in the ensuing weeks and months: $500,000 bail, felony child neglect and fraudulent check charges, a defamation suit by a sitter on whom Casey tried to pin the disappearance, bonding out of jail with an electronic tracking device, and, in October, a grand jury indictment for first-degree murder, aggravated manslaughter of a child, and four counts of providing false information to police. This time, she was back in jail with no bond.

Months later, in December, police found Caylee Anthony’s skeletal remains buried amid insects and vegetation a quarter of a mile from the family house, wrapped in a Winnie-the-Pooh blanket and bound with duct tape. The defense contended that Caylee had drowned in the Anthony family pool when she “went missing” that June 16 and that Casey and her father had frantically tried to cover up the accident. The state of Florida contended that Casey had murdered her daughter. In April 2009, the state announced it would seek the death penalty.

The Social Media Trial of the (New) Century

Over the next two years, a fast-growing, excited media commentariat smelled a story—and a cause. Cable commentator Nancy Grace, a former prosecutor, led the media charge against Casey Anthony, nightly beating the drums for her conviction, christening her “Tot Mom.” At the same time, Facebook and Twitter exploded as a media-drenched world distracted itself from depressing economic news—much as it had in the 1930s with the Lindbergh kidnapping—and turned its attention to Casey Anthony.

The 36-day trial started in May 2011, in Orlando, with great expectations of a sweeping victory for the prosecution. The case, and now the trial, had long since evolved from a big live-at-five local story to a national obsession. Scores of media trucks camped out across from the courthouse. CNN and NBC each built air-conditioned, two-story broadcast centers at a lot across the street. The *Washington Post* and the *Miami Herald* posted live streaming.

But the most reliable trial news source came from a Twitter account, NinthCircuitFL, the feed managed by the Ninth Judicial Circuit Court, with 400 reporter-blogger followers. The Ninth Circuit was the first court in the U.S. to use DNA evidence, in a 1987 rape case. It still enjoys a cutting-edge reputation. Facebook pages honoring Caylee gathered tens of thousands of friends, and Twitter accounts like CaseyJunky and OSTensCaseyAnthony, managed by the Orlando *Sentinel,* added hundreds of followers a day.

The defense team used social media inside the courtroom as well. Trial consultant Amy Singer, with the aid of other trial consultants, analyzed 40,000 opinions, both negative and positive, on social media sites and blogs and used them to help the defense craft strategy. They were particularly concerned about a volatile media's effect on seating an open and fair-minded jury.

In a highly controversial opening argument, Jose Baez contended that Caylee Anthony drowned in her grandparents' swimming pool and that Casey panicked and covered up the death after her father warned her that she could be imprisoned for life. Baez also argued that Casey was herself a victim of her own father, who allegedly had sexually abused her as a child. No evidence was presented to back up this sensational claim. The father denied it to both the defense and prosecution. Although in theory the jury could not consider it, a poisonous seed had been planted in the jury's mind that something about the father was very troubling, an impression not aided by the father's own uncomfortable testimony. The obvious goal of this remarkable strategy was to shift blame away from Casey Anthony. There is no denying the power of a specific, sensational allegation, even if unsupported by actual evidence.

More importantly, Baez, though slammed as a bumbler by commentators and seemingly chastised at every turn by the judge, did an effective job chipping away at the state's forensic evidence and highlighting patterns of mistakes and defects in the police investigation. The police had found no fingerprints, no conclusive strand of hair, and no DNA evidence pointing to Casey Anthony. In short, Baez posited assorted and, at times, legitimate questions about the sufficiency of proof to support a death-penalty offense.

Many commentators, especially after the verdict was reached, concluded that the prosecution overreached with the first-degree murder charge. They never established motive. A "wish to party" (say, at the Fusion nightclub) is hardly a compelling motive for the murder of one's own child. After all, the grandparents, however flawed, were nearby and capable of looking out for the child if Casey wished to step out. It was scandalous, awful, and tragic, surely. Yet this was not truly a death-penalty case; it was a case with enough questions to add up, at least in the jury's mind, to a reasonable doubt.

"The Devil is Dancing"

After 10 hours' deliberation, the jury acquitted Casey Anthony of the felony charges of murder, aggravated manslaughter, and aggravated child abuse and convicted her of the four misdemeanor counts she was charged with in the first place.

The court of public opinion, now viral, went ballistic.

"Somewhere out there, the devil is dancing tonight," Nancy Grace said. Traffic to news sites jumped from 2 million page views a minute to 3.3 million. ABC News reported its traffic surged to five times the normal number of visitors. One enraged Florida man started a "Boycott Casey Anthony" Facebook page on the day of the verdict and had 6,000 fans within 24 hours.

At change.org, more than 1.1 million people signed a petition calling for passage of "Caylee's Law," which would make it a felony to fail to report a child's disappearance within twenty-four hours. "I hate Casey Anthony" had 37,000 "likes" on Facebook; "Casey Anthony must die" had 1,100 "likes."

Although traditional media broke the Casey Anthony story, social media exponentially amplified it. Commentators have lately noted that during the 1995 O. J. Simpson verdict people could only scream at their TVs. With the Casey Anthony case as the first big murder trial of the social media age, people could vent their anger via blogs, Facebook, YouTube, and Twitter and reach millions.

For all the public outrage, the ever-fickle media pivoted almost instantly. Various legal commentators, who had applauded the prosecution team for its outstanding work while blistering the defense, launched a new wave of finger-pointing at the shortcomings of the prosecutors who were geniuses no more.

The Media Microscope and Casey Anthony's Lessons

The Casey Anthony case is a fascinating example in which the interests of public opinion and the courts both converge and, more importantly, diverge.

The greatest convergence was between the baying of a media bent on conviction and an intensely zealous prosecution. Public revulsion toward Casey Anthony and the widespread perception that a murder conviction was inevitable might have contributed to the prosecution's apparently crucial error: arguing almost exclusively for a first-degree capital murder conviction, which the jury—perhaps not irrationally—rejected for lack of motive, rather than a manslaughter conviction, which could have produced a 20-year sentence. It is natural for prosecutors, themselves caught up in the case in the public eye, to feel energized by the acclamations of the commentariat and the demands of the public to produce a scalp. It is also, however, the better part of wisdom to take a step back, examine the evidence, and create a strategy that is most likely to produce a successful result rather than to gamble on a spectacular one.

One other great lesson of the Casey Anthony case is that the public sees what the jury does not. The jury does not see the judge taking the prosecutor to the woodshed in sidebar or in chambers. Nor can they watch Nancy

Grace's nightly denunciations or view her web postings. They are ordered to examine evidence, avoid the media, and apply a standard of reasonable doubt. In general, with notable exceptions we will explore later in this chapter, jurors try hard to abide by the strictures of the court in a fair trial. One could argue that when jurors honor their oaths flawed forensic evidence is at least as likely to produce an acquittal as an eloquent prosecutorial closing argument is to result in a conviction.

Finally, the social media universe is beginning to figure in many aspects of defense strategy, from the retaining of counsel to jury selection, with queries into prospects' Facebook and Twitter accounts, where predispositions and prejudices are reinforced and amplified.

Prosecutors and Defense Lawyers in the Public Eye

In general, the public, which on the whole likes its society orderly, is better disposed to the prosecutors as enforcers of order than to defense lawyers as challengers of that order in the interests of a fair trial. Indeed, prosecutors set the tone, decide on the charges, call the news conferences, and are the most powerful "deciders" in the case.

Yet juries, once sequestered, take their roles seriously and base their decisions on evidence, the prosecutor's burden of proof, and the defendant's refuge of reasonable doubt. That is why prosecutors should take care in moving beyond what can clearly be proven into the more perilous, ambiguous area of what seems likely—the other lesson of the Casey Anthony case.

Defense Lawyer: The Advocate's Duty

Even if defending villains does not make defense lawyers crowd pleasers, at least they enjoy the consolation of being paid better than prosecutors. And the top defense guns often become press favorites. In cross-examinations, the great ones perform the virtuoso's solos, even while being overwhelmed by the blaring band of the prosecution's evidence. And they know that more than just jurors are watching. At times they are playing to the court of public opinion, often in defense not only of the client's legal rights but also the client's reputation before the broader public.

Inside the courtroom, defense lawyers battle the odds. While underdogs at sporting events have fans in the stands rooting for them against the big dogs, the underdog defense lawyer will likely find few cheerleaders. While attending law school, I foolishly asked one of Florida's preeminent attorneys the clichéd questions that defense lawyers invariably get from clueless law students: "Are you able to defend people even if you believe they are really guilty?" Now a highly respected judge, he guffawed. "Heck, are you kidding? Almost all my clients are guilty." So not only are defense lawyers usually climbing uphill against a mountain of evidence, their usual goal at the summit is to plant a banner proclaiming the legal innocence of someone who is factually guilty. In some cases, the defendant's conduct may be morally questionable at best, but not criminal. Where the prosecutor sees black and white, the defense lawyer by necessity must see and distinguish the grays.

The defendant's dream of acquittal may be shared only by his attorney (always), family (one hopes), and friends (both of them). Although purists extol high-minded notions about fairness and justice for all, the rest of creation often wants a guilty verdict. By the time jurors hear the case, it is no longer a game of Clue to unravel the mystery of the perpetrator's identity. Instead, the forces of law and order have already selected Colonel Mustard for his day of reckoning. The issue changes to whether he will get his just desserts. For many court watchers, the greater the defendant's fame, the greater the thrill when the mighty are felled by a conviction.

Rather than an emotional connection with lofty aspirations, such as the "presumption of innocence," the prospect of punishing the wrongdoer is far more exciting. Nor do tears help most of the time. The weeping defendant rarely does much to assuage a judge or jury, and a defense lawyer cannot do much but counsel restraint and quietly put his or her arms on the defendant's shoulder.

One of the nation's best-known defense lawyers, Miami legal superstar Roy Black, believes that "today's lawyer has an obligation to deal effectively with the media—it's a part of the job to take a proactive stance with reporters."[1] Before engaging the press, Black emphasizes the need to know the ethical rules as well as the media landscape, a perilous place for

1. Interview by telephone by author with attorney Roy Black, (January 21, 2010).

newcomers.[2] Professor Alan Dershowitz similarly emphasizes that careful judgment is needed to ascertain whether and when lawyers should enter the minefield of media communication but "sometimes it's malpractice not to change the atmosphere" created by adverse publicity.[3]

Where dealing with the media was once considered unprofessional, it now may be unavoidable, whether those dealings are direct or indirect. That does not apply only to criminal defense cases involving the prominent or notorious. Most of the concerns about the devastating impact of pretrial publicity are with future jurors. Publicity about a criminal case is almost always bad for a defendant, and there is reason to believe that bad publicity contributes to bad results. Empirical studies confirm the common-sense notion that negative publicity contributes to negative results, particularly with jurors. Even though trial judges try hard to minimize that damage through curative instructions, as one Supreme Court justice quoted a candid juror: "You can't forget what you see and hear."

But jurors are not the only decision makers who may be negatively influenced by negative news. Indeed, the vast majority of outcomes in criminal cases are resolved by plea bargains, which means that more than 90 percent of cases are decided, in effect, not by juries or judges but by prosecutors.

And prosecutors, for example, know that if they entertain low-punishment plea deals with high-profile defendants, reporters may blast them for their leniency. On the other hand, prosecutors are never skewered for being "tough" on criminals. As preeminent defense lawyer Robert Morvillo candidly acknowledges, "you get the best plea deal when no one is looking."[4] When the press is ready to second-guess, defendants often get no real deal at all.

Maximum Visibility, Maximum Time

Nor does press coverage inspire compassionate sentencing, particularly in cases that involved greater public issues, such as political, corporate, and

---

2. Interview by telephone by author with attorney Roy Black, (January 21, 2010).

3. Interview by author with attorney Alan M. Deschowitz, Professor, Harvard Law School in Miami, Florida (January 21, 2010).

4. Interview with attorney Robert Morvillo in New York, New York (Sept. 15, 2009).

investment (e.g., Ponzi scheme) corruption. When the trial participants all believe they must go by the book, the result is that judges often throw the book at defendants in deciding how many years to give. (Exhibit A: Rod Blagojevich). Post-Enron cases witnessed sentences so extreme that appellate courts have issued a string of decisions requiring reductions, including that of Enron's former president, Jeffrey Skilling. One of New York's top lawyers described the sentence imposed on fraudster Bernard Madoff as "a joke," and not because Madoff's record-setting ruthlessness deserved compassion. With the 150-year term exceeding Madoff's life expectancy sevenfold, some suggest it had more relevance to the court of public opinion than to a legal proceeding.

Michael Jackson's doctor, Conrad Murray, was convicted of involuntary manslaughter for the entertainer's June 2009 death from a fatal combination of eight tablets of the sedative Lorazepam, which the doctor administered, and the powerful anesthetic Propofol, which Jackson self-injected when the doctor left the room.

Social media also figured in this trial, too, just a few months after Casey Anthony's. Prospective jurors answered a 100-question inquiry on their social media use and blog postings.

The jury convicted Murray of involuntary manslaughter, and the judge sentenced him to four years: the maximum. Prosecutors wanted the judge to send a message that doctors cannot sell themselves to the highest bidder, and the judge delivered. But because Murray was not convicted of a crime of violence, he was able to avoid hard time in a state prison and instead serve softer time in the county jail, where he would be eligible for parole in two years. Murray can consider himself fortunate. Although the court went to the legal maximum, its hands were tied to sending a message that was more a postcard than a billboard.

Less fortunate is ex-Illinois governor Rod Blagojevich, who in December 2011 was sentenced to 14 years in federal prison—just short of what prosecutors had sought—for trying to auction off President Obama's vacated Senate seat and 17 other corruption charges. Here, too, the judge was sending a message of deterrence, this time on political corruption, by imposing a notably stiff sentence. But because it is a federal sentence, Blagojevich will likely not be eligible for release until serving 85 percent of his sentence, or nearly 12 years.

These cases tend to confirm that "sending a message" is more likely in high-visibility cases. Even before trial, critical rulings are decided by judges, many elected, who are fair enough to try to ignore the condemnation outside the courthouse but human enough to carefully follow media reports. At times, the resulting rulings can seem intended as more hospitable to the prosecution and therefore less susceptible to criticism.

Judges and the Media

It is obviously essential in any media strategy to consider the judge. The ears of judges often have chronic buzzing, particularly because they are not prohibited from following the news coverage of their cases. The law presumes that judges will ignore the media monsoons drenching the courthouse and decide every legal issue as if nary a drop had fallen. If we assume, though, that judges are real people who live in the real world—sometimes a world of judicial elections—it follows that they are acutely aware of community feelings about media-intensive cases. And judges live in more than one community. Most care deeply about maintaining respect from their peers in the courthouse and from the lawyers who practice in the same locale. Because the legal community reads newspapers much more than most, the articles that judges and lawyers will be reading should be balanced as much as possible if the playing field is to be level.

Legal icon Dershowitz recently recalled some advice he received from a local lawyer when he was handling the successful appeal for Claus von Bülow, who had been convicted of murdering his wife. "The only way you can win this appeal is if these three judges (all male back then) can explain to their wives why they let off a wife killer." Absorbing the daunting reality, Dershowitz focused not only on the legal brief but also on facts about the medical evidence that would raise questions in the minds of reasonable readers.[5]

5. Interview with Alan M. Dershowitz, Professor, Harvard Law School, in Miami, Fla. (Jan. 20, 2010).

Step One: Assemble the Team, Temper Expectations

Good press is a form of damage control with juries, prosecutors, and even judges. It is also a recruitment poster for lawyers, experts, and even fact witnesses. Winnability magnetizes cases. Lawyers and experts may be mercenaries, but even hired guns prefer to be retained by winners. For the top professionals who can pick and choose their cases, many prefer a cause that is acclaimed to one being defamed. Even fact witnesses, the main determinant of most cases, can be more effective if they believe their testimony will be featured in a success story. Just as many prefer to join the team with all the cheerleaders, horrible publicity can impair recruitment efforts. (Note: large up-front payments to lawyers and experts can make even beastly cases seem beautiful.)

Because the court of public opinion can impact the court of law in so many ways, legal and media strategy starts the moment the client retains a defense lawyer, often long before an indictment or even an investigation. The best strategy, at this earliest stage, is to respect the client's confidentiality and screen media phone calls. If there is any doubt about the wisdom of commenting publicly, the best advice is to say nothing on the record. Unless there is a specific strategy, it is often best to let the public record speak for itself.

If one can afford it, public relations counselors with sophistication in crisis management, the legal system, and the media are recommended and can be vital. Their job is to be neither a "friend" nor an "enemy" to the media, but to see the case objectively. Lawyers themselves gain enormously in direct proportion to the amount of media coverage that quotes or mentions counsel. When media consultants coordinate public comments, these temptations are controlled.

"A crisis PR counselor needs to take a hard and detached look at the situation, make recommendations quickly, and be the 'fact doctor,' not the spin doctor," says Ray Casas of Miami, a public relations professional and crisis counselor for more than 30 years.

Media professionals can also appreciate other dynamics, in some cases, involving, for example, stockholders, university endowments and athletic programs, vendors and contractors, employees, and any entity or institution that stands to be affected by the criminal case. Such work often involves deciding whether to sever ties with a client's employer (Dominique Strauss-Kahn and the International Monetary Fund, with 187 nations as members) or to handle the departure with more subtlety (Martha Stewart as prime mover of Martha Stewart Enterprises, who submerged rather than departed).

Incidentally, a public relations crisis counselor is NOT the same thing as a publicist. Excellent publicists and promoters have been retained in legal cases leading, at times, to disastrous results. The vast majority of a crisis communicator's work is away from the media, with your client's interest—not the media's—paramount. Some of the best of counselors, if not all, have extensive experience as reporters and editors and understand the mindset. They may be friends with old colleagues, but they know the rules of engagement and can be trusted not to share privileged communications. Indeed, prosecutors can hold all the news conferences they want, presenting your clients, of course, in the worst possible light. Meanwhile, defense lawyers may be ill advised to respond in kind in their own press conference way without sufficient ammunition and—in evolving situations—in which they may not yet have full command of the facts.

Any counselor retained should hold your client's long-term interest paramount.

"There are short-term techniques to handling a crisis and defusing negative media," Casas says. "But the overriding perspective is the long-term viability of the client. A short-term fix can be a long-term death sentence. The public tends to judge people and companies not so much as to the fact they are in crisis, but by how they handled the crisis." Bluffing and BS are not options, and the lawyer and PR consultant should unite against counseling against such "spin" in its worst form.

"One of my clients tried bluffing during a highly-charged press conference on the advice of his lawyer and against my PR advice," Casas says, "and he's now a fugitive in hiding somewhere out of the country."

Important as media crisis communication and litigation support consultants are, they can only do so much. L.A. public relations guru Elliot Mintz agrees. He has had dozens of celebrity clients over the years. Among other things, Mintz is credited with helping to turn Paris Hilton from an Internet video controversy to an international celebrity.[6] Although he regularly advises lawyers, his advice includes recognition that at the end of the day, he says, "it's not a media game—the gavel comes down in the courtroom."

For that reason, expectations need to be realistic. And realism may not come easily to high-profile defendants. Savaged by the hostile coverage that follows arrests or nasty lawsuits, some believe if they simply find the right PR person with the right connections, harsh publicity can be transformed into puff pieces. Such magicians do not exist in the real world. Even the best media consultants cannot put a happy face upon a federal indictment. Benjamin Brafman summarizes the importance of circumspection in this way: If a case has a good outcome, no one will remember a bad press day. If it has a bad outcome, no one will remember a good press day.

Dominique Strauss-Kahn and the Virtue of Saying Little

The world remembers the arrest of International Monetary Fund Managing Director Dominique Strauss-Kahn on seven counts of sexual assault of a 32-year-old African-born housekeeper at his room in the midtown Manhattan Hotel Sofitel on May 14, 2011. Newspapers and television networks everywhere ran the televised images of a disheveled, tieless, and unshaven Strauss-Kahn paraded before the cameras for arraignment in a Manhattan courtroom. His evident shabby treatment in public caused a greater furor in his native France, where he was—and is no more—a leading candidate for the presidency in April 2012.

Strauss-Kahn quickly retained Brafman, who had represented Sean "P. Diddy" Combs, Michael Jackson, and Jay-Z, among others, and William Taylor of Zuckerman Spaeder. Brafman and Taylor interviewed Strauss-Kahn and quickly concluded that he was not guilty of a crime, despite his undisputed reputation as a roué. Brafman told interviewer Charlie Rose in February 2012 that even Strauss-Kahn's wife, experienced journalist Anne Sinclair, "got it" and was on board with the team. (The New York Review

6. Interview with Elliot Mintz, [title], [institutional affiliation], [location of interview if done in person] (Sep. 29, 2009).

of Books' Edward Jay Epstein raised serious questions about the case in December 2011, suggesting it was a politically motivated setup, and at least three French journalists at this writing are working on books.)

What was undisputed was that sexual contact had occurred in the hotel room over six or seven minutes. Strauss-Kahn said it was consensual; the accuser said it was forced. She reported the incident an hour later, after Strauss-Kahn had checked out.

Brafman and Taylor quickly assembled a Murderers' Row of high-powered, low-profile crisis management investigators and counselors to keep the media at bay and, presumably, later rebuild his shattered reputation. The *Atlantic* identified one as TD International, a Washington firm involved in "strategic consulting," "commercial intelligence," and "security services." Two of its employees are former CIA officers, and Strauss-Kahn had retained them in 2007 to help him get his IMF job. The *Atlantic* also reported that the Strauss-Kahn team also included Guidepost Solutions, a New York private investigation firm, and current or former top executives at Euro RFSCG public relations firm's Paris operation.

With the team working behind the scenes and under the radar, Brafman quietly presented the flaws in the prosecution case to the prosecution. Along the way, the team supplied the media with 30-second sound bites, nothing too substantive, but just enough to slake the media's 24-7 thirst. The key was to avoid, in Brafman's words, the four-minute "soundbite of death."

Assembling the team was imperative, with the case on the front page of every major newspaper in the world. The reverberations of the case quaked through France and the global financial community. Under the circumstances, Strauss-Kahn had little choice but to step down from the IMF on May 18; he was replaced a month later by Christine Lagarde, highly regarded as the French Minister of Economic Affairs and former chair of the global law firm Baker & McKenzie.

Over time, as stories presented flaws in the prosecution's evidence, Manhattan District Attorney Cyrus Vance dropped the case for lack of evidence, and Strauss-Kahn was sprung from house arrest.

Today, Strauss-Kahn's political prospects are dashed and his reputation is in tatters. His rehabilitation in the court of public opinion will be arduous.

But he is, as of this writing, a free man. The goal in his case was not to establish him as an angel or model example of fidelity. By his own admission, he is not. The point was to rescue him from the clutches of the criminal justice system, and this was done.

Throughout his legal ordeal, Strauss-Kahn wisely kept his counsel and his head. The approach was disciplined, and experts were hard at work early.

As the crisis management team goes to work under pressure, the relationship between the defense lawyer and the client often grows personal. You are holding a client's fate in your hands. The mission is often to reassure your client, who may be depressed—some even become suicidal. When accused of crimes, personal despair may overwhelm a client facing already-frightening legal hazards. It is not easy to help the client conduct himself or herself with grace, courage, and especially discretion through a humiliating ordeal in the media's spotlight, but it is important to buffer the client from the media's pressures as much as possible.

Speaking and Leaking: Perils and Pitfalls

Silence can seem like a straitjacket at first, but, as Ben Brafman notes, "The avalanche of adverse publicity is so difficult that trying to level the playing field is as difficult as the case itself."[7] Recognizing that defendants are also human beings who need to survive professionally in the outside world, Brafman believes that judges will tolerate press strategies so long as any "gag orders," described below, are strictly obeyed and "nothing is done to undermine the integrity of the process." But good press, he notes, "does not mean anything if you're guilty."

With legal news, as with diets, some of the most delicious tidbits are off-limits. In fact, some laws make it a federal crime to disclose confidential information about especially sensitive subjects. In cases with national security implications governed by the Classified Information Procedures Act (CIPA), a leakster could potentially face criminal prosecution. Grand jury proceedings are also confidential, and prosecutors and government

7. Interview with attorney Ben Brafman, New York, New York (Aug. 25, 2009).

agents could be prosecuted themselves for disclosing those secrets. Significantly, the witnesses are under no such restraints, and some are surprisingly talkative.

In ordinary circumstances, the rules prohibit lawyers from creating publicity that they know or should know will have a "substantial likelihood of materially prejudicing" the judicial proceedings.

Publicity hounding early in a case is more tolerable, but, as the trial draws near, the risk skyrockets that publicity reaching future jurors will influence their later decisions. Judges understandably perceive that the likelihood of prejudice is greater with publicity that is near the time of trial as opposed to negative stories much earlier that are mostly forgotten by the average juror.[8] Moreover, for prosecutors at least, extensive chest thumping about their case is rarely a good idea. Especially if defense lawyers are seeking to move the case to a different city, they will pounce upon press-happy prosecutors as purveyors of excessive pretrial publicity that prejudices potential jurors.

The "gag order," of course, produces even greater restriction on press communication. The term is often used loosely to describe an assortment of limitations. In its extreme form, a true gag order prohibits virtually any communication about a pending case by the litigation team or courthouse personnel. Ordinarily disfavored due to concerns for rights of the press and the public, gag orders were imposed in the Scott Peterson and Michael Jackson trials because nothing else could adequately protect the defendants from barrages of relentless news coverage.

However, this is not always the case. The media's penchant for conflict means that although generally indictment and guilt are more newsworthy than innocence, nothing is better than newsworthiness. In the case of George Zimmerman, prosecuted for the alleged second-degree murder of African-American teenager Trayvon Martin, at times the prosecution found itself on the losing end of news coverage and became the party requesting the gag order.

When Mark O'Mara came on board as George Zimmerman's defense

8. State v. Avery, 374 S.C. 524, 649 S.E.2d 102 (Ct. App. 2007) (venue change denied where a vast majority of potential jurors recalled nothing about defendant and could remember only that crime had been committed).

attorney, he took control of his client's press strategy. With a continual pummeling by the media and the inherent advantages of the prosecution, O'Mara opted not to try to calm the waters but instead chose to dive in to the new storm. O'Mara apparently shut down all of Zimmerman's websites and social profiles. This included a website entitled "therealgeorgezimmerman.com" and opening a new one called gzlegalcase.com. These measures served the purpose of controlling the message that is presented to the public from the defense and to build a seawall against the tsunami of adverse media coverage his client was receiving.[9]

A quick trip to the website shows a prominent link bar with links to press releases, legal documents, media requests, and a defense fund. Every post contains links that automatically tweet, "like" on Facebook, or post to Google+—almost everything in a media strategy's arsenal. On the right side of the website, a running feed of the defense's Twitter account is ever present.[10]

On April 20, 2012, the same day that the prosecution and defense teams argued before the court in George Zimmerman's bond hearing, an unnamed source gave ABC News a photograph that shows George Zimmerman with cuts and a possible contusion on the back and crown of his head, respectively. This led some in the media to wonder whether perhaps Zimmerman's version of the events had some legitimacy after all.[11]

The defense's more focused media strategy, coupled with apparent leaks from unknown sources, lent more credibility to Zimmerman's case. Indeed it was the prosecution, not the defense, that requested a gag order to stop the press barrages. Not once but twice the prosecutors attempted to gag the parties and their counsel. Both times, the judge ruled against the prosecution but allowed the possibility of future motions on the issuance of a gag order.[12]

---

9. George Zimmerman Legal Case, Mark O'Mara PA, http://gzlegalcase.com/ (last visited Dec. 21, 2012).

10. George Zimmerman Legal Case, Mark O'Mara PA, http://gzlegalcase.com/ (last visited Dec. 21, 2012).

11. Matt Gutman, *George Zimmerman Tells Trayvon Martin's Parents 'I Am Sorry,'* ABC News (Apr. 12, 2012), http://abcnews.go.com/US/george-zimmerman-tells-trayvon-martins-parents/story?id=16177849#.UOtGgKU6cyE (last visited Dec. 21, 2012).

12. Frances Robles, *Judge Denies Gag Order in George Zimmerman Murder Case*, The Miami Herald (Oct. 29, 2012), http://www.miamiherald.com/2012/10/29/3073159/judge-denies-gag-order-in-george.html (last visited Dec. 21, 2012).

Some confidentiality orders are less drastic, even routine. For example, in cases about business trade secrets, courts frequently prohibit the disclosure of confidential processes, patents, or formulas. Perhaps because these restrict access to technical tedium rather than to courtroom dramas, they are often agreed to by all parties and raise fewer objections from the media.

The Sound Bite and the Judge

During the trial of the superstar rapper Sean "P. Diddy" Combs for a nightclub shooting, Brafman confronted not only a phalanx of prosecution witnesses but the public's "sinister picture of the rap music world." Media obsession with the case included newspapers pummeling Combs's lopsided accounts of the trial and exaggerated portrayals of the guns and bling culture. Although an array of advisors continually clamored for defense ammunition to combat the bad press, the courtroom counsel were essentially muted by an unofficial gag order. Moreover, despite the temptation to come out swinging rather than keep taking punches in the press, Brafman emphasized the need to avoid revealing key evidence and strategies to reporters so that lawyers keep "bullets in the gun belt" for the critical moments during the trial itself.[13]

And so Brafman developed a television sound bite to provide some voice for his client's cause without provoking judicial displeasure. He secured almost daily coverage with variations of, "While there's a lot I would like to tell you, we are under orders not to, but I hope you are following closely today's testimony, and if the jury pays close attention, we believe we will be fine."[14]

Brafman won the trial, no doubt due to trial factors such as his highly effective and humanizing presentation of defendant Combs on the witness stand. But, as Brafman acknowledged, getting better coverage on the outside never hurts with the verdict delivered inside the courtroom.[15]

---

13. Interview with attorney Ben Brafman, New York, New York (Aug. 25, 2009).
14. Interview with attorney Ben Brafman, New York, New York (Aug. 25, 2009).
15. Interview with attorney Ben Brafman, New York, New York (Aug. 25, 2009).

Press Strategies in "Self-Defense"

With experience in dealing with reporters, Roy Black only deploys press strategies "in self-defense" because "news focuses on the controversy, and the controversy is the accusation, not the defendant's claim of innocence."[16] Because news coverage is usually hazardous to a defendant's legal health, Dershowitz's advice about speaking on the record to reporters is, "when in doubt, don't do it."[17]

Lying low is an undervalued position. It is often the best prescription for minimizing a news overdose in the early stages of an investigation, before any court papers are filed or public action taken. Reporters who have no one credible to quote may have nothing that they can credibly write about the client. Lawyers need to avoid press when their client's interests require it. Some lawyers, though, are drawn to reporters like moths to flames—and it may be the client who gets burnt.

Even after an arrest is made or a lawsuit is filed, it is better to give no comment than blast the adversary if an out-of-court resolution is the goal, as is the general case. Occasionally, some civil settlements may thrive on press warfare, but usually, once the bullets have left the gun, the damage is done. Once the adversary has been thoroughly trash-talked in the press, there may be less, rather than more, incentive for the opponent to settle.

Mark Geragos, whose high-profile clients have included Whitewater defendant Susan McDougal, actress Winona Ryder, and hip-hop artist Chris Brown, sometimes chooses not to speak to the press based, for example, upon a "calculated decision looking to plea bargain out the case."[18] In fact, when a public official was exposed to high levels of publicity despite low levels of criminal exposure, Geragos's only public comments were expressions of regret about the leaks. Some battles are better fought behind the scenes, and Geragos won the best kind of victory for a client when no criminal charges were pursued by the district attorney.

---

16. Interview by author with attorney Roy Black in Miami, Florida (January 21, 2010).
17. Interview by author with Alan M. Dershowitz, Professor, Harvard Law School.
18. Interview with attorney Mark Geragos, Los Angeles, California (Sep. 29, 2009).

The Jerry Sandusky Example

Penn State provides an object lesson in what not to do. Former Penn State defensive coordinator Jerry Sandusky was arrested on November 5, 2011, on 40 counts of child sexual abuse between 2004 and 2009. Penn State's legendary coach, the late Joe Paterno, had apparently heard of the allegations and, although conveying information to university officials, did not report them to police authorities. On the night of November 8, after speaking at a rally in front of his house with a group of students supporting him, Paterno was relieved of his coaching duties later that night by the Board of Trustees, effective immediately.

One would think that Sandusky, facing an indictment on charges of sexual abuse of children, would stay far away from the media while coping with horrific charges that also happened to imperil a major university's footing. Although even savvy lawyers approach the press warily in high-stakes cases, the risks can soar off the charts when the clients themselves speak publicly. Interviews given by defendants on television[19] as well as radio[20] can and will be used against that defendant.

Sandusky's mystifying encounter with Bob Costas is a strong contender for worst defense interview in recent years. The following excerpt speaks for itself:

> **BOB COSTAS:** Mr. Sandusky, there's a 40-count indictment. The grand jury report contains specific detail. There are multiple accusers, multiple eyewitnesses to various aspects of the abuse. A reasonable person says where there's this much smoke, there must be plenty of fire. What do you say?
>
> **JERRY SANDUSKY:** I say that I am innocent of those charges.
>
> **COSTAS:** Innocent? Completely innocent and falsely accused in every aspect?
>
> **SANDUSKY:** Well I could say that, you know, I have done some of those things. I have horsed around with kids. I have showered after work-

---

19. United States v. Tate, 821 F.2d 1328 (8th Cir. 1987); People v. Massie, 66 Cal. 2d 899, 59 Cal.Rptr. 733, 428 P.2d 869 (1967).

20. Britt v. Embry, 202 Fed.App. 774, 782 (10th Cir. 2008) (radio interview); Allen v. State, 662 So.2d 323 (Fla. 1993).

outs. I have hugged them and I have touched their leg, without intent of sexual contact. But—so if you look at it that way—there are things that wouldn't—you know, would be accurate.

COSTAS: Are you denying that you had any inappropriate sexual contact with any of these underage boys?

SANDUSKY: Yes, I—yes I am.

COSTAS: "Are you sexually attracted to young boys, to underage boys?"

SANDUSKY: "Am I sexually attracted to underage boys?"

COSTAS: "Yes."

SANDUSKY: "Sexually attracted, you know, I enjoy young people. I love to be around them. But no I'm not sexually attracted to young boys."[21]

There is little to add. The video, easily Googled and YouTubed, is even more damning. In answering whether you are sexually attracted to children, an instant no is the only answer. Sandusky took too long, and his delays in denial sealed his already precarious fate in the court of public opinion.

Some puzzling finishing touches to Sandusky's puzzling press strategies were provided by his defense lawyer Joseph Amendola on June 22, 2012. While the jury was still deliberating, he said publicly, "I would die of a heart attack—shocked—if he was acquitted on all the charges." Perhaps shocking best describes the comments of a defense lawyer who openly predicted his own client's conviction in a world where nosey jurors sometimes cannot resist Googling the latest about their cases.

But Amendola was not finished with the day's work of ill-advised press comments. After the conference, he acknowledged "the overwhelming amount of evidence against Jerry Sandusky" and also tossed bouquets to the prosecutors ("The prosecution handled the case in an exemplary manner . . .") and then proceeded to lavish praise upon the judge's trial performance:

---

21. Jessica Hopper, *Jerry Sandusky to Bob Costas in exclusive 'Rock Center' interview: 'I shouldn't have showered with those kids,'* NBC News (Nov. 14, 2011), http://rockcenter.nbcnews.com/_news/2011/11/14/8804779-jerry-sandusky-to-bob-costas-in-exclusive-rock-center-interview-i-shouldnt-have-showered-with-those-kids?lite.

> The judge in this case was marvelous. Judge Cleland was the ultimate jurist, he was firm, he was reasonable. He would give the defendant and give counsel a fair shake and a fair trial. We believe he did an outstanding job.[22]

Because appeals are often based on insufficiency of the evidence, improper arguments, conduct by prosecutor, or harmful error by the judge, Amendola's comments publicly undermined all of these usual suspects for a defendant's appeal. Ultimately, when Sandusky's briefs are written, such unhelpful comments will presumably not be part of the record. Still, even if a case is legally hopeless, one should stick to predictably safe words ("Jerry Sandusky continues to maintain his innocence") or bland words ("we will be reviewing appellate options"), rather than adding the defense counsel's own defeatism in the court of public opinion to a horrendous defeat in the court of law.

Sandusky would eventually be convicted and sentenced to 30 to 60 years in prison. For lawyers, the interview of Jerry Sandusky drives home an unforgettable lesson: In all criminal cases, keep your client away from the media. You almost never win, and you—and your client—will usually lose big time. And for lawyers who want to give interviews, this strange episode underscores the need to protect, within ethical bounds, the client's interests, which must always override any personal temptations to score points with reporters, prosecutors, or even judges.

Knowing Your Audience

If a decision is made that media exposure in the form of an interview is warranted to try to rehabilitate a client's image for prospective jurors, understanding that what may be beneficial in the trial by jury may convict you in the trial by viewers is a necessary requisite.

After a barrage of crushing news coverage, George Zimmerman, having been accused of murdering a 17-year-old African-American teenager, the Zimmerman legal team decided to give an interview to Sean Hannity

22. Fox News, August 9, 2012. www.foxnews.com/on-air/oreilly/2012/08/10/Sundsky-Lawyer-we-werent-given-enough-time.

of Fox News. When Hannity asked if Zimmerman felt any regret about the night he killed Martin, this exchange ensued:

> **ZIMMERMAN:** No, sir.
> **HANNITY:** Do you regret that you had a gun that night?
> **ZIMMERMAN:** No, sir.
> **HANNITY:** Do you feel you wouldn't be here for this interview if you didn't have that gun?
> **ZIMMERMAN:** No, sir.
> **HANNITY:** You feel you would not be here?
> **ZIMMERMAN:** I feel it was all God's plan and for me to second-guess it or judge it—[23]

Although such rigidly defensive and unrepentant positions may have been generally consistent with his "Stand Your Ground" hearing or his trial, his lack of any regret insensitivity toward the family of Martin, who was still grieving the loss of their family member. After the interview, it did not take much deliberation for the Nielson Ratings Jury to lose any sympathy they may have had toward Zimmerman.[24]

Risky Business

In opposition to the above examples of what not to do during an interview stands Gary Condit. For a period of months, Condit became virtually a household name during the investigation into the disappearance in May 2001 of an intern for the Federal Bureau of Prisons, Chandra Levy. During the investigation, Condit lied to investigators about his relationship with Levy, leading to increasing negative portrayals in the media and in the court of public opinion. However, Condit steadfastly maintained his innocence. Although he refused to submit to a police polygraph, his lawyer stated that Condit had passed a polygraph administered by a private company. So far,

---

23. Sean Hannity, *Exclusive: George Zimmerman breaks silence on 'Hannity,'* Fox News (July 18, 2012), http://www.foxnews.com/on-air/hannity/2012/07/18/exclusive-george-zimmerman-breaks-silence-hannity?page=5#ixzz2FxjwPUk9.

24. Hal Boedeker., *George Zimmerman's interview: How big a mistake?* ORLANDO SENTINEL (July 19, 2012), http://blogs.orlandosentinel.com/entertainment_tv_tvblog/2012/07/george-zimmermans-interview-how-big-a-mistake.html (last visited Dec. 28, 2012).

so good—the lawyer's statements actually helped Condit. But press-wise, Condit took a huge gamble when he decided to give a primetime interview to Connie Chung. The interview was a disaster for Condit's political career as Chung hammered repeatedly and effectively on the infidelity issues.

At least with the transcendent question of Levy's disappearance, though, Condit fared much better.

Clear, concise, and convincing. When your mistress disappears and you're a congressman, there is no chance of remaining out of the spotlight, but being used to the limelight gave Condit the experience necessary to handle himself with composure on the homicide question. It also helps if you are innocent; in 2010, Ingmar Guandique, who had admitted to assaulting two women in the same park where Levy's remains were found, was convicted of Levy's murder.

Knowing The End-Game Early

Geragos believes that media planning requires a calculated decision in the beginning about the likely result in the end. "You can usually tell about a case," Geragos observes and recommends that lawyers assess whether a media strategy is warranted and "try to calculate early on, get into the first news clip or damp it down" if the case is a likely plea deal.[25]

Whatever magic a consultant may have is often centered upon particular media, and so identifying the target audience for the campaign is vital. In the 2000 case of Elian Gonzalez, rescued at sea and brought to Florida when his mother died escaping from Cuba, we prioritized local Miami radio and national television. As a result, the administration's spin machinery had a virtual monopoly on America's major newspapers, which remain to this day the principal news source for the federal judiciary. There may not be enough resources to launch a press strategy upon every station, newspaper, magazine, and blog in the state. For that reason, the target audience should be identified, and media priorities should be assigned. A longtime New Yorker who still rides the subways, Charles Stillman rarely sees his travel companions reading newspapers—they are more likely reading their

25. Interview with Mark Geragos, *supra* (Sep. 29, 2009).

Droids, BlackBerries, or iPhones. He concludes that for jury purposes newspapers are far less important than in times past. Judges, on the other hand, read newspapers.[26]

Even apart from the key decision making at the end of the case is a defendant's reputation while the case is pending. Stillman represented one of the nation's great law firms in a discrimination case brought by lawyers formerly employed by the firm. Despite consistent success in the legal proceeding, the defense was supposedly striking out according to some of the buzz within the legal community—a prime determinant of a firm's reputation. Stillman, therefore, recommends that media plans need to consider not only the ultimate decision makers at trial but also the reputation makers along the way.[27]

Press-Wise or Publicity-Foolish

Some press-friendly lawyers not only try to extract advantages for the client, but in some instances for the press-friendly lawyer. Many in the media are troubled by publicity seekers who carry a law license. PR expert Elliot Mintz refers to a "greed factor" among publicity-hungry lawyers. Self-promotion, more benignly referenced as marketing, has escalated dramatically since the Supreme Court decided in a Virginia case that lawyers have a right to advertise. The profession has never been the same, and the legal world's ever-increasing enthusiasm for legal marketing often targets the free advertising that comes when lawyers' names and faces appear in news stories about their cases.

Many Lawyers Worry That Some Self-Aggrandizers Go Too Far

Philadelphia's Richard Sprague is one of the nation's preeminent trial lawyers; his career includes the epic prosecution of labor leaders for murdering rival Joseph Yablonsky along with his wife and daughter in the 1970s. In recent years, Sprague won a stunning dismissal of criminal charges against basketball superstar Alan Iverson. Over time, Sprague has wit-

26. Interview with attorney Charles Stillman, N.Y.C., N.Y. (Sep. 14, 2009).
27. Interview with attorney Charles Stillman, N.Y.C., N.Y. (Sep. 14, 2009).

nessed a troubling trend by lawyers who grab ink by tipping off the reporters who hold the pens. "Disgusting" is Sprague's word for lawyers who push themselves into the limelight at the expense of clients who might be better served by dimming the lights.[28] To his dismay, news stories have appeared with information about the ongoing investigation, and some items just happened to mention the names of lawyers.

Naturally, the article might, in identifying the lawyer, report a refusal to comment. But savvy veterans like Sprague are not fooled by lawyers who hand out tidbits off the record to get their names in the news and then purport to decline comment to keep their fingerprints off the story. Sprague has been making a list of such lawyers and will not have to check it twice to remember not to refer cases to those lawyers again.

The Dating Game for the Legal Climber

One barrister who may have competed for worst offender in the court of public opinion is the former lawyer for convicted wife-killer Drew Peterson.

After Peterson's fourth wife, Staci Peterson, disappeared, police exhumed the body of Peterson's third wife, Kathleen Savio, who had been found dead in her bathtub years earlier. Her death had been ruled accidental, but police believe that many supposedly first-time offenders are actually repeat offenders who simply were not caught on prior occasions. And so Savio's death may have been no accident at all. Following a medical examination of the body that concluded that Savio's death was a homicide made to look like an accident, prosecutors charged Peterson with her murder.

But even before the indictment, Peterson's lawyer, Joel Brodsky, had already begun his unconventional media strategy. Peterson participated in numerous interviews and even hired a publicist to negotiate selling the rights to his story. However, Brodsky's masterpiece was his suggestion to the hosts of the "Steve Dahl Morning Show" that they offer listeners a chance to participate in a "Win a Date with Drew Peterson" contest. Mr.

28. Interview by author by telephone with Richard Sprague (Sep. 28 2009).

Peterson quickly accepted his chance to choose from a trifecta of bachelorettes, noting that "Dahl could chaperone the date as long as there wasn't any 'three-way stuff.'"[29]

Although Brodsky's surrealist defense may have increased his hits on Google, it made his client appear like a care-free bachelor ready for wife number five—some would say victim number three.

Although Staci Peterson's murder is unsolved as of this writing, Drew Peterson was eventually convicted of the murder of Kathleen Savio. Many would say, "with the help of his counsel," and, in fact, that is exactly what Peterson's current lawyers are saying as they seek to overturn his conviction:

> Attorney Brodsky expected that Drew Peterson would be his ticket to the legal elite [...] Regrettably, he was poorly equipped to try a case of this magnitude, resulting in hornbook errors and a smorgasbord of ethical violations. Individually and cumulatively Brodsky singlehandedly deprived Drew of his right to effective assistance of and conflict-free counsel.[30]

The legal process continues as of this writing, but whatever may be the legal outcome, the reality will remain that Joel Brodsky's press strategy appeared to be more of a lawyer's reach for fanfare than for a client's welfare.

The Law-Media Toolbox: Part One

Strategies for the Court of Public Opinion

The late Dwight Eisenhower, former president and megageneral, once explained famously that planning is everything but that often plans become useless due to the onrush of unexpected surprises. Despite the frequent uselessness, media planning can help create some certainty in an uncertain process, and it should rely on a toolbox that includes PR strategies and tactics as well as legal devices.

---

29. "Radio Station Cancels Contest to Win a Date with Ex-Cop Drew Peterson," Fox News, Jan. 23, 2008. www.foxnews.com/story/2008/01/23/radion-station-cancels-contest-to-win-date-wtih-ex-cop-drew-peterson.

30. "Peterson Lawyers Slam Ex-Lead Attorney in Filing to Overturn Conviction," Chicago Tribune, Dec. 12,2012.

Use Helpful Hooks to Formulate Your Message

The late Kurt Cobain, founder of the 1990s rock phenomenon Nirvana, once attributed his success to writing songs with "hooks," melodic phrases or lyrical segments that would catch on and stay with a listener as soon as they were heard. Like music, the best media strategies rely on themes that can be reduced to a single thought that will play to the game plan in court. Not many of us have forgotten Johnnie Cochran's, "If it doesn't fit, you must acquit!" Many experts believe that the most effective litigation messages should take ten seconds or less to deliver.[31]

Unless it targets human feelings, though, the message will not hook human beings. In litigating the battle to keep Elian Gonzalez in this country, we saw the case as centering upon his best interests and having those interests determined by a family court—the usual judicial forum for a child's needs—rather than by the chronically insensitive immigration bureaucracy. Those legal issues drowned, however, under waves of emotional reactions to the so-called battle between the rights of the natural father and the anti-Castro sentiments of the Cuban-American community. No amount of information about legal issues could overcome the lifetime of feelings people have about age-old issues such as parental rights. In the end, winning themes for media—and law—need to be as human and simple as possible. One father reclaiming his son (Elian Gonzalez) overwhelms legal issues, just as a single dead voter (Miami-Dade vote fraud) can symbolize an entire election case.

Although some favorite themes are recent innovations (the client is now in rehab), most media messaging relies on the retreaded ghosts of trials past—the accusers are lying scoundrels (sometimes true); it's a political vendetta (even if true, rarely provable or relevant); just going after the defendant because he or she is rich and famous (sometimes true, but riches and fame rarely score sympathy points); the witness is psychotic (occasionally true, but not always relevant); my client is mentally unbalanced (often true, but almost never suffices as legal insanity); someone else did it (preferably with at least threads of supporting evidence); and

34. Interview ["by" and interviewer name if not the author] with Laurie Levenson, Professor, [institutional affiliation], [location of interview if done in person] (Jan. 12, 2010).

the client was somewhere else (better have video or at least documents to prove it).

Avoid Inconsistency, the Hobgoblin of Legal Minds

Lawyers are trained in court to present alternative theories, even when they are completely incompatible positions. But in the court of public opinion, there is zero tolerance for contradictory positions. In the 2000 presidential recount litigation, the Democratic lawyers' message for the public was reported early and often: "count all the votes." In fact, legal maneuvers at odds with counting every vote—such as trying to invalidate absentee ballots in Republican counties—were avoided by the Gore/Lieberman legal team. With media-intensive cases, speaking to the press means speaking out of only one side of your mouth—if you want to have it your way, do not try to have it both ways.

Show Your Adversary's Deficiencies and Inconsistencies

High-profile cases attack an accuser's credibility by putting the alleged victim on trial before the court of public opinion as well as with juries. This venerable strategy has countless antecedents, such as the case of Captain Bligh. When he returned to England, he was initially acclaimed as the heroic victim of the famous Mutiny on the Bounty, who miraculously navigated an open longboat filled with the loyal crew members across thousands of miles of open seas to safety in Indonesia. Later, however, Bligh was portrayed as a tyrant through a defendant's shrewdly crafted publicity campaign, when the accused mutineers were brought to a well-publicized trial in eighteenth-century London. These tactics can be risky—one of the mutineers against Bligh skated with a royal pardon, but three were hanged. Still, whenever believing the accuser means convicting the alleged abuser, the battle plan becomes an all-out attack on that witness's credibility.

Prior inconsistent statements of accusers are the gold standard for negating accusations in any venue. Michael Jackson's defense team struck a gold mine that included documented instances of the allegedly abused boy previously denying Jackson's wrongdoing. Even when the public may have empathy for an alleged double-talker, the fact of the inconsistency is almost always more powerful than the excuses.

Court-Weak Messages Can Still Be Media Strong

Some messages may never reach the court of law but still register big time with public opinion. For example, a jury will not hear evidence about a witness's psychological problems unless the conditions are severe enough to impair the ability to recall events and tell the truth. But even if legally harmless, a wide variety of mental issues can send the witness's credibility crashing with the public. When Los Angeles Lakers guard Kobe Bryant was accused of the sexual assault of a hotel employee in 2003, his legal team repeatedly scored points with the public by disclosing his accuser's past hospitalizations for depression, which a judge almost assuredly would not have allowed to reach a jury.

Other facts that may be press worthy but not court worthy may include some of the more appalling allegations about a witness's past. With the latest O. J. Simpson case prosecution—for the dumb-and-dumber souvenir hunt in a Las Vegas hotel room and resulting 33-year sentence for kidnapping and armed robbery—his past arrest for murder would officially be excluded from jurors (which could have indeed mattered to the only three adults in Nevada who did not already know). To counteract the nuclear fallout from Simpson's past, his lawyer proclaimed publicly that the sketchy prosecution witnesses had enough baggage to provide a defense lawyer's "dream." To be sure, when codefendants make sweetheart deals to "turn state's evidence," defense counsel can indeed pummel the past of the cooperator to portray him as a rat lying to save his own hide. Apart from cooperating witnesses, though, a lot of baggage gets checked outside the courtroom. Most misdeeds and even misdemeanor convictions of witnesses are not discussed in court. Felony convictions are usually revealed but not described in detail.

Although some of the spiciest menu items may never be served to a jury, they can be routinely fed to the press because some themes that never appear in trial transcripts will splash hugely in newsprint transcripts.

The law-media toolbox: Part Two—Tactics

The Press Conference

There is no sure antidote for toxic publicity during ongoing cases. In certain discrete instances though, well-crafted press conferences sometimes balance the bad news, particularly when conducted with sophisticated media counselors (again, if they are not exclusively or primarily publicists). Geragos provided press briefings almost daily—during trial—when President Clinton's friend Susan McDougal was tried in Arkansas in a case that sprang from the Whitewater investigation. Along with highlighting any episodes from the trial in which the defense was beating the prosecution, Geragos's media messages kept beating the drums that asserted a politically inspired vendetta on the part of the Special Counsel, Kenneth A. Starr.[32]

Geragos, while representing Michael Jackson following his arrest on child molestation charges, immediately launched a counteroffensive to attack the salacious charges: Jackson was "greatly outraged by the bringing of these charges," Geragos declared, and the charges were categorically untrue and "a big lie."[33] To shift the focus from alleged abuser to accuser, Geragos added, "Anybody else who knows anything about the history of these accusers, anybody who knows anything about the history of the investigators and the axes they have to grind, know [sic] that these charges are not only categorically untrue, but they're driven, driven by two things: money and revenge."[34] In putting the alleged victims on trial, Geragos was trumpeting the theme that Jackson was the real victim. Geragos said: "Michael Jackson is not going to be abused. Michael Jackson is not going to be slammed. He is not going to be a piñata for every person who has financial motives."[35]

Geragos not only knew how to score quotability points, his stock with the media was high enough so that the message he crafted got drafted by reporters.

---

32. Interview with attorney Mark Geragos, Los Angeles (Sep. 29, 2009).

33. John M. Broder, *Michael Jackson Is Booked on Molesting Charges That He Calls Lies*, N.Y. Times, Nov. 21, 2003, at A18.

34. John M. Broder, *Jackson Is Formally Charged With Child Molesting*, N.Y. Times, Dec. 19, 2003, at A24.

35. David Carr, *Persistent New Leaks Fuel Coverage of Jackson Case*, N.Y. Times, Nov. 29, 2003, at A9.

Defense press conferences are not always well attended because reporters see prosecution charges as news and a defendant's denials as a snooze. Even when reporters respond, they are usually predisposed toward skepticism rather than enthusiasm for predictable deniability. After all, there is no presumption of innocence in the court of public opinion. Moreover, the press will select a few quotations from the many, and lawyers can only hope they will use the best rather than the least of their comments. For that reason, some high-profile veterans repeat their key themes repeatedly to multiply the likelihood that the press will quote the armor-piercing bullets rather than select a weaker pellet from a shotgun.

Another big-league lawyer wise in the media's ways is San Francisco's Harlan Braun, who has represented American Taliban John Walker Lindh as well as Robert Blake, the former actor accused of killing his wife. Soon after Blake was arrested, the prosecution held a press conference about Blake's murder charges. Braun did not sit back with a bland denial, but instead lunged forward, repeating the key theme for the defense, "The woman had an extensive history, and there are people in her past who have made threats to her . . . ." To ensure that his main theme would get the most steam, he restated it in different ways, such as everyone "who ever came into contact with her had a motive."[36] Putting the victim on trial seemed risky, especially one's dead wife. But unless the defense could show that others wanted her gone, her accused husband would be the only viable suspect for the jury. Focused on his message, Braun knew it did not need a low-watt transmitter and turned up the dial. " . . . I'm not trying to besmirch [the late wife], but the woman had an extensive history and there are people in her past that have made threats to her, people with motives."[37]

In the rare case when a press conference is greeted by a sea of cameras for a live broadcast, the lawyer's every word may actually be heard. As a result, a more complete message may reach the viewers.

In the Kobe Bryant case, defense lawyer Pamela Mackey opted to address

36. Gary C. King, *Who Murdered Bonny Lee Bakley? Blake Arrested*, TruTV, http://www.trutv.com/library/crime/notorious_murders/family/bakley/20.html (last visited Jan. 12, 2010).

37. *Blake behind bars after arrest in wife's slaying*, CNN.com (Apr. 20, 2002), http://archives.cnn.com/2002/US/04/19/robert.blake.case/index.html (last visited Jan. 12, 2010).

not only her client's denial but also his explanation of the encounter as consensual. The points she made included chastising the Eagle County sheriff for his leaks and the district attorney for filing weak criminal charges. In conclusion, she repeated that she would "not try this case in the press" but before "a Colorado jury."[38]

Because Kobe Bryant was a major sports celebrity and the charges had just been filed, public fascination was sky-high, and all of her points reached a national audience. Usually, though, lawyers need to pick and choose their themes selectively because, otherwise, reporters will select the quotation for them.

Although many advocate press conferences so long as they are planned carefully and delivered by press-savvy lawyers, two of the biggest names in the business are reluctant to use them. Nationally renowned defense attorney Roy Black does not summon reporters for a press conference. "The only time I have a press conference is when there are a lot of reporters and photographers already standing and waiting outside the courthouse and it is easier to speak to make a statement at the same time to all the press."[39] Nationally renowned defense attorney Alan Dershowitz believes that organizing a press conference is usually a mistake and will be seen by media "as a sign of weakness that creates an artificial situation."[40] Rather than pursue reporters to get them to come to a "transparently manipulative" press conference, Dershowitz recommends "letting them come to you" when there is real news to discuss and especially when one-on-one discussions and off-the-record comments would benefit the client.[41]

The Television Interview

Television interviews can be a great forum for a lawyer's getting a message to the public. But they sometimes offer pain as well as gain because, in many ways, the broadcast venue is less forgiving than a judge and jury, particularly in this viral YouTube world of 2011–2012.

---

38. Bryant, Wife and Lawyer Profess His Innocence in Statements, L.A. Times (July 19, 2003), http://articles.latimes.com/2003/jul/19/sports/sp-excerpts19 (last visited Jan. 12, 2010).

39. Interview with Roy Black, *supra*.

40. Interview with Alan Dershowitz, *supra*.

41. Interview with Alan Dershowitz, *supra*.

During the Elian Gonzalez case, I appeared in dozens of national news interviews during a four-month period in 2000. As I discovered immediately, each interview required the same intense level of preparation that lawyers require for a closing argument, except that closing arguments rarely occur between 7:00 and 7:30 a.m.—that is, when network morning shows were starting their day with Elian. The time of day was manageable; no one on our team was sleeping much. As I soon learned, however, other factors made television interviews and court appearances about as similar as Oz and Kansas.

Superficially, a reporter's interview consists of questioning lawyers about the client's case just as judges question them in a regular courtroom. And, like good judges, good reporters typically ask thoughtful questions that intellectually challenge the attorney's position, especially in high-profile cases during which reporters can take the time to study the issues.

Judges and juries, though, while holding the actual power of decision, are almost always a more hospitable venue than the networks. In a courtroom, judges and juries actually want lawyers to do their best and, conversely, are often uncomfortable, even frustrated, over courtroom stumbles. As judges and jurors watch them walk across the legal tightrope, they want to see the lawyer safely reach the other side even if they do not agree with that lawyer's side of the case.

In high-profile cases, television interviewers, on the other hand, might just as soon see the lawyer stumble precariously on the tightrope with arms flailing, perhaps hanging on by a finger or maybe even falling. Legal missteps, like other unexpected twists, are simply more newsworthy.

And the court of law is more forgiving of mistakes than the court of public opinion. When lawyers misspeak during court proceedings, their corrections are routinely accepted. With damage control for televised mistakes, however, there is usually more damage and less control. In contrast to ongoing court proceedings, there is no second chance for correction after the interview is concluded. And although all judges know that smart lawyers are capable of saying dumb things, neither the media nor the public seems sympathetic when ill-advised mouthings come from professional mouthpieces.

Also crucially different is the appetite for conflict. Judges and jurors rarely enjoy contentiousness between opposing lawyers. To the contrary, when judges ask questions, they often look for areas of agreement between lawyers and are usually gratified when opposing lawyers seem to agree on significant issues.

Talk shows, however, do not stage lawyers for a group hug. Conflict is the spice of legal life for television. From the standpoint of many news producers, the more contentious the interview, the better the segment. As a result, rather than a judge's question exploring concurrence between parties, news shows can be a relentless search for conflict in which reporters try to accentuate existing disagreements or provoke new disputes. During one of my interview tapings for *Good Morning America*'s Diane Sawyer, she confronted me with the statement by an unnamed member of Elian's own legal team who said there was no chance of winning our appeal. Although I still stuck to my position that the asylum statute's phrase "any alien" included a child, I was caught off guard and was relieved when that exchange was not used in the actual news story. Whenever inconsistencies were made by a team's lawyers, the press pounced to hammer about any apparent discrepancies. Through such experiences, we learned about the importance of weekly message consistency even if, at times, the message necessarily must evolve over the course of litigation.

Be Careful about Overt Operations

Calls from obvious media handlers may be resented, especially when reporters feel they are being walled off from the real sources. That being said, the high-profile case is no place for amateurs. A media-savvy member of the legal team may be able to assume a prominent role, although even veterans of the practice have scars to show from reporters' words. Most emphatically, lawyers with slim media experience should not handle media relations without professional help. At a minimum, press experts should be consulted at the inception of a problem with the media, even if the team cannot afford continuous involvement. At times, a client's regular spokesperson may be able to take the lead, but some public relations professionals are effective in times of peace yet struggle with the intense questions that strike at a blinding pace during legal wars.

Commitment to professionalism in this process is critical because lawyers often mistake a reporter's seeming friendliness for a guarantee that stories will be friendly. Bear in mind, though, that communications with a press specialist may not be privileged from subpoenas and care should be exercised, particularly when exchanging correspondence and e-mail.

Pitching the Press

Calls to reporters, seemingly friendly as well as the patently hostile, are critical except in circumstances of the Invisible Client, who is hoping to have no profile in a high-profile controversy that is ensnaring others. Before making calls that could wind up on the front page, careful planning is needed to craft the public message points as well as for any private lobbying tactics that rely on "background" comments, which remain off the record. Often, the most important function of background discussions is simply to clarify the client's position and assure that the main issues are understood. Even when bad stories are unavoidable, a confusion-infected disaster may be preventable by providing legitimate clarifications to reporters before even worse damage is done.

Finding the right person to pitch can be easy in frenzied cases because the reporters are calling the lead lawyers anyway. Veteran AP reporter Brian Skoloff recommends that lawyers "know your reporter and learn about their work in the past."[42] In lower-profile matters, lawyers, the client, or an outside PR agent may have existing relationships with the media. If not, simply identify the newspaper and television reporters assigned to the courthouse and make a cold call.

Although reporters usually do not mind the sales pitches, the pitcher should establish any ground rules concerning what is "background" at the front end. Without an explicit agreement, all comments are fair game and the consequences can be an unfair story. Local reporters generally honor such agreements, especially if they plan on continuing to work effectively in the same community. Skoloff points out that just as lawyers are trying to

42. Telephone interview with Brian Skoloff, [title], Associated Press (Jan. 20, 2010).

identify reporters to speak to about their cases, journalists are trying to develop a network of sources. Even if reporters take what lawyers say with the proverbial "grain of salt," Skoloff advocates a collegial relationship and believes that mutual trust is a legitimate goal, even as reporters and lawyers see each other as tools of their respective trades.[43] Caution should nonetheless be exercised, though, especially when dealing with unknown, out-of-town reporters who may not care about a future relationship with the local legal team. Dershowitz points out that a common mistake for the would-be legal spinmeister is to assume that because a reporter seems friendly to counsel the news will be kind to the client.[44] In all events, even background comments should be judicious, all the more so when they are discussions about a judge.

File Press-Friendly Pleadings

Courthouse files largely immunize their contents from the laws of defamation so reporters rely overwhelmingly upon court papers and hearings. As a result, press-savvy lawyers craft court papers that not only nourish procedural requirements but also feed the press.

The graphically detailed indictment of Atlanta Falcons star quarterback, Michael Vick, on federal charges of involvement in an interstate dog-fighting ring in 2007 is a striking example of prosecutorial sophistication in stating a case to the public. Even though the rules for federal indictments do not require all the details of a crime, the Vick indictment included devastating specifics, stating that codefendants and "Vick, and two others known and unknown to the Grand Jury 'rolled' or 'tested' additional 'Bad Newz Kennels' dogs by putting the dogs through fighting sessions at 1915 Moonlight Road to determine which animals were good fighters." Reading more like the opening statement of a trial than the bland boilerplate of most indictments, the charges by themselves were enough to appall readers who returned an immediate guilty verdict in the court of public opinion.

Because a litigant's best facts can be launched aggressively and with legal immunity in court papers, the party who files first has a huge advan-

---

43. *Id.*
44. Interview with Alan M. Dershowitz, Professor, Harvard Law School, Miami, Florida (Jan. 20, 2010).

tage over an adversary with no papers in the courthouse. Even litigation weaklings can appear muscle bound when they are juiced by a "court document" with "facts" that go unanswered. Although defending parties will file detailed written responses down the road, they may become media's roadkill while they wait. With few exceptions, reporters demand same-day service in responding to the day's breaking news. In the highest profile cases, the defense's response, even weeks later, may generate a story by itself. But the later story about the defendant's denial gets much less ink and often no airtime.

Some legal strategists anticipate the initiator's huge advantage by preparing their own legal document with their key facts. Although the defense will rarely have enough time to fully respond in writing to the just-filed accusatory document, first responders should consider something as basic as a motion for a status conference—a request to discuss general issues about court scheduling—loaded with the defendant's best facts. Given the critical nature of securing balanced coverage on day one, legal papers readied for almost immediate filing may help to balance the news cycle that will otherwise be owned by the other side. As maestros such as Alan Dershowitz and Roy Black note, being late for the news cycle means being too late to have an impact on the public's initial reactions—the first impressions that often become lasting ones.[45]

On a cautionary note, as former Durham, North Carolina, district attorney Michael Nifong learned in the Duke lacrosse team case, when public statements go beyond the public record, misinformation can result in suits for defamation. Had Nifong stuck to the script of the court papers containing the false rape allegations, he likely would have escaped being sued because even the most unjust prosecutions do not, in general, allow victims to sue for damages.

Speak Loudly in Hearings When Reporters Are Listening

Court hearings, traditionally the centers for legal advocacy, have increasingly become the center stage for press strategies. Although preliminary

45. Interview with Alan M. Dershowitz, Professor, Harvard Law School, Miami, Florida (Jan. 20, 2010); telephone interview with attorney Roy Black (Jan. 21, 2010).

hearings are typically limited in scope, they can become mini-trials, as the cases of Scott Peterson, Kobe Bryant, and the O. J. souvenir caper demonstrated. They have become important centers of information for the press, and the need to control the message that is sent is key. In fact, in a recent community service progress hearing for Chris Brown's 2009 battery of Rihanna, Mark Geragos, Brown's lawyer, shut his client down before he could answer the judge's question by saying, "I don't dance, you don't talk."

Media-friendly prosecutors are also part of the prosecution business. In the Liberty City Seven case of alleged terrorists, rather than the usual executive summary, the prosecution provided an abundance of specific evidence including excerpts from the defendants' intercepted telephone conversations. Those details may not have been necessary for purposes of the bond hearing, but they were certainly impressive. The evidence also demonstrated to a skeptical press corps that the alleged terrorists were not just "punks from the hood" but were perhaps indeed far more lethal than laughable.

That's What Friends Are For

Clients with bad facts need good quotations to achieve balanced press coverage. Reporters will occasionally accept suggestions about other sources to contact for quotations, and when they ask for names to call you should have a list ready. The best choices are people whose opinions are client reliable and publicly credible, as reporters dislike overt manipulation. Some strategists send talking points to their allies, especially recognized experts who are regularly quoted by the media. Other methods include getting friends to write Op-Ed pieces as well as letters to the editor. Today's spinners will also most assuredly hit the blogging circuit, and most use their Facebook, LinkedIn, and Twitter accounts.

Although pitching to allies is risk free, care should be exercised in dealing with opposing viewpoints. During the Michael Jackson child sex abuse case, a press handler for District Attorney Tom Sneddon contacted Professor Laurie Levenson following her critical legal commentary to try to get her to "go easy" on Sneddon. She was decidedly unimpressed. Correspondingly, when I was doing commentary on the Rush Limbaugh prescription drug case and received a memorandum with legal points concerning the controversy, the materials were helpful and appreciated.[46]

Spinning the Unspinnable: The Shocking Allegation

As the ultimate news vampire, the Shocking Allegation (often involving sex, molestation, and, recently, animal cruelty) sucks up all of the attention devoted to a subject, making it virtually impossible to tell the rest of the story because many people only care about the headline. As a result, the defense spin is often of little help in such cases. The only defense worth promoting is complete denial, and the only distraction may be another Shocking Allegation, preferably involving someone else's client. As at least one former governor experienced, it becomes very difficult to use a litany of past good deeds to humanize the client who is being demonized by sensational allegations, such as alleged sex with prostitutes.

To insist that the Shocking Allegation about a sex scandal is overstated (it was twice, not three times) or that the media are exaggerating about the embezzlement from a children's charity (it wasn't nearly that much) confesses to infinitely more than it denies. If the proof is undeniable—video recordings are especially bothersome—it may be a convenient time to revise one's philosophy about a media campaign and minimize press interaction, insisting, for example, that your client does not believe in trying his or her case in the press. Sometimes, the only exit from an unrelenting press onslaught is the miraculous arrival of someone else's disaster to replace your client's disaster with new headlines above the fold.

Even so, the Shocking Allegation at times can be met with another Also Sensational Allegation. After ex-congressman Mark Foley abruptly resigned from office, he was being battered by horrific publicity due to overly friendly e-mails to underaged congressional pages. His lawyer, David Roth, softened the blistering coverage by convening a press conference to announce that Foley had been abused as a boy by a Catholic priest. Although irrelevant in legal terms, it was interesting enough to generate significant press coverage because the Also Sensational Allegation was apparently true.

---

46. Interview with Laurie Levenson, Professor, [institutional affiliation], [location of interview if done in person] (Jan. 12, 2010).

Scott Peterson was accused of an even more Shocking Allegation—murdering his wife and unborn son—and so lawyer Mark Geragos captured some badly needed attention for the defense by suggesting that a satanic cult might have committed the murder. Taking the offensive in a seemingly indefensible case, Geragos also proclaimed that the defense had evidence to "totally exonerate" Peterson. Within weeks, commentators were suggesting that reasonable doubt about Peterson's guilt might not be as unreasonable, with such articles as "From 'Why Did He?' to 'Did He?' in 28 Days." Although the press coverage became more balanced, winning some battles in the media does not mean it is possible to win the war in the courtroom—as Peterson now sits on California's death row.

The Ambush: When to Speak Softly or Not at All

When the truth is too ugly for cosmetics and too obvious for denials, there may be nothing useful to say. Specific denials that are demonstrably false accomplish little and can sacrifice any remaining scraps of credibility that should be saved for the remorse and repentance phase of the case that comes later. Moreover, bogus denials can fuel more counterpoints that give more life to a story that might otherwise spin itself off the front pages. Fortunately, even the most lamentable culprits are allowed to make general denials with the obligatory "We look forward to the opportunity to develop the real facts at the proper time in a court of law." For the client who is ambushed walking out of the home, office, or rehab clinic, the only possible response may be, "It is a legal matter, and my lawyers have directed me not to discuss it." Less may not be more, but it may be all there is.

No tried-and-true formula was available for Michael Vick. Lying low and silent, pleading guilty, and entering prison even before prison is ordered may prove to be the only long-shot hope for eventual rehabilitation. After his release from 21 months in federal prison, he was signed by the Philadelphia Eagles, a return accepted by the National Football League. Public acceptance may prove more elusive. Sometimes a symbolic return to the scene of the crime is needed. Perhaps charitable support for abused animals or working at or contributing to shelters could help convince skeptics that Vick is sincere in his remorse rather than just glad to be out of prison. Of course, for NFL fans, throwing plenty of touchdowns while staying out of legal trouble may be rehab enough.

Roger Clemens and the Samurai Strategy

As the baseball steroid scandal unraveled, one wonders whether Roger "the Rocket" Clemens, the greatest baseball pitcher of his generation, should have hunkered down quietly, taken some short-term press hits, and reappeared after the worst of the storm subsided. Instead, Clemens launched an astonishing publicity offensive. In a strident attack against the ex-trainer who accused him of using steroids, Clemens sued for defamation and even tape-recorded an ambiguous telephone conversation between them that Clemens then proclaimed to be clear proof of his innocence. After rocketing himself to the center of the steroids controversy, Clemens's adamant congressional testimony was contradicted not only by his former trainer but also by statements of Clemens's longtime friend, pitcher Andy Pettite. Clemens's Samurai strategies not only stole all the negative attention, they won him a congressional referral to the Justice Department concerning possible charges of perjury.

Like others, I had advised another baseball player about the joys of invisibility. When high-profile legal problems are casting about for potential actors, the best role for a client may be the "Invisible Man." Scores of other baseball players hoping to vanish from the press radar must have silently thanked Clemens's show-stopping tactics that stole the thunder and acid rain of a media downpour. Whatever may be the truth of the Clemens controversy, the criminal charges were brought and later dropped, and the results included a battered reputation and a long and expensive legal ordeal.

Avoid the Press with E-ducking

Sometimes, there is no helpful answer to inevitable questions, and even saying "no comment" could seem incriminating. When asked specific questions about appalling allegations (why so much greed and child abuse?), rather than leave a client completely mute and unprotected, you can avoid phone discussions by e-mailing or faxing a brief statement to the press. Although ducking behind an e-mailed statement invariably leads to a punishing story, it usually ensures that some portion of your response will appear among all the painful paragraphs.

Taking the Offensive by Rattling the Saber

For most clients, the worst media nightmare is an imminent, extremely damaging story fraught with inaccuracies. Understandably, when the client's war cry demands ballistic counterattacks, canceling one's subscription to the offending newspaper hardly seems sufficient. Many, including the guiltiest, demand that counsel write every misbehaving media and threaten every manner of lawsuit against reporters, editors, producers, and even the maintenance crew. Despite the obvious therapeutic value, such threats may not have much legal force.

If publicly filed court records are fueling the news engines, the media are versed enough in their craft to know that those documents can be used for devastating news reports that avoid legal exposure. When bad news is arriving before judicial proceedings are commenced, the immunity shield surrounding the story may be more fragile, but it is still imposing. With celebrities and politicians, even cub reporters know that the law has declared open season on public figures except in the most extreme cases of blatant falsehoods. To be effective, counterpunchers should concentrate on the media's most reckless allegations, those that are contradicted by clear evidence or based on sources with giant credibility gaps.

Threatening lawsuits and even making good on those threats can be legitimate weapons to protect reputations. Few clients, though, will endure the years of tribulations required to pursue even a strong defamation lawsuit all the way to trial. One prominent leader who was falsely called a "mobster" eventually settled a suit against a national magazine for a charitable contribution after enduring days of depositions that were anything but charitable.

Because such suits become a costly ordeal for the defamation victim, they are occasionally filed not for litigation recoveries but for message deliveries. The event of suing for defamation is by itself a proclamation of innocence to the public. George Zimmerman has recently decided to sue

NBC Universal for defamation, claiming that an edited sound clip made Zimmerman sound like he was racially profiling Trayvon Martin instead of responding to a 911 operator's request to describe the man Zimmerman was observing. It is also a warning to other reporters. Using lawsuits as a publicity stunt may stand on a dubious footing ethically. Still, such filings occasionally have a deterrence effect; even the most zealous reporters do not relish the prospect of being sued and having to explain the lawsuit to every future employer. As a result, lawsuits, as well as the threats of litigation against reckless media, can be necessary tools for lawyers who recognize that reputation can be as important as a client's legal rights.

When to Speak to the Reporter's Boss

If reporters persist in unjustified attacks on a client, there may be a limited opportunity for an informal appeal to their editors or news directors as long as there is enough time before a news deadline. Requests for such meetings should be highly selective and not a generalized gripe session so that they will be seen as rare indignation rather than chronic complaining. Usually, only provable mistakes in the facts or clear failures to consider contrary information are worth raising. Most stories cannot be killed in their entirety, and the best hope is usually for a more balanced story that avoids glaring falsities. When getting stonewalled by the newsroom, grievances concerning over-the-top stories can also be directed to senior management, the ownership, and even the news organization's counsel.

Taking Your Marbles Away and Quitting the Game

Perhaps the least effective strategy in damage control is to threaten to stop speaking to an organization's reporters if they persist with brutal coverage. The desire to never speak again to a news abuser is understandable, but it rarely helps. A reporter may surface on the phone someday concerning a different news story for a different client. Only clients with exceptional importance to the media—police agencies and professional sports teams seem to have juice—create real problems for reporters. For instance, if a courthouse reporter faces retaliation from the district attorney because allegedly unfair coverage has embarrassed prosecutors, the cutoff in access to a key news source could even require the reassignment of the reporter to a different news desk. In general, though, threats are neither advisable nor necessary. Of course, reporters already know that positive stories promote cooperation, just as they know that negative stories can leave some news sources frozen like the tundra.

Also uncool, but potentially serious and also occasionally effective, are threats from clients who spend major advertising dollars to punish newspapers and television stations by refusing to buy ads from offending media. As with the joys of being sued, no rational news director enjoys the prospect of angering one of the sales department's biggest customers. When aggressive business people menace the media where it really counts, harmful media coverage is occasionally reduced. Plainly, though, lawyers should not go near these heavy-handed tactics. Threatening to pull ads from a television station or newspaper is hardly a proper or ethical function of lawyers, and, apart from serious professionalism concerns, any lawyer who issues such threats can expect reporters to retaliate some day.

Bad News Bears

Bad press can become a self-fulfilling prophecy. In the early stages of an investigation before the targets of an investigation are fully defined, it is crucial to keep hot water from boiling over into scathing publicity. When possible, steer the media toward a more tantalizing subject, and occasionally their focus may veer away from your client. A case based on the law of nature illustrates the strategy. As a bear abruptly appeared in the meadow charging at the two hunters, the first hunter began running. Standing flat-footed, the second hunter told the first that trying to outrun the faster and more powerful bear was a complete exercise in futility. As the first hunter yelled back to the second, it was not necessary to outrun the bear—the only need was to outrun the second hunter.

Be careful, though, about going to a seemingly friendly reporter to plant a news story about an adversary. Surprises may grow from such plantings because news sources (especially self-serving lawyers) do not control the direction of news. Once a case kicks into high gear, reporters doing their job will hear the adversary's version of the facts—a version detailing all the reasons why your own client is the real culprit. More than a few investigations (by police as well as media) were initially launched in one direction but then boomeranged back against the original complainant.

Life Beyond Trial

Although winning at trial is paramount, defendants care deeply about the attitudes of their professional and personal constituency. When there is a happy ending to a case, good press along the way contributes to a more complete vindication of the falsely accused rather than a perception of a lucky defendant who beat the rap.

No matter how well the media messages are spun, though, the vast majority of criminal cases result in guilty verdicts. In federal prosecutions, 97 percent or more of indictments ultimately lead to either a guilty plea or a jury conviction on at least one of the charges. With state cases, the conviction rates vary but still range from 80 to 90 percent. As far as the press is concerned, once found guilty, continued denials compound the original crime with a succession of lies that would "insult the intelligence" of a Michael Corleone and most everyone else.

In recent years, the formula for cushioning the enormous disaster of guilt focuses on remorse, repair, and attempted rehabilitation. To be effective, remorse generally requires an unqualified acceptance of guilt for the crimes that have been proven. Also to be included are deep expressions of shame, apology to all the injured parties, and a stated willingness to take personal responsibility for all the consequences.

Although remorse often follows a largely predictable script when guilty pleas are entered, it becomes difficult, almost impossible, for a defendant to seek forgiveness for crimes in cases that are going to be appealed. Inevitably, defendants who seek to appeal their convictions will fail to exhibit remorse, much less acceptance of responsibility. They are, after all, continuing to maintain their innocence. This complicates the scenario at sentencing, often the final chapter for the court of public opinion, which counts on tearful apologies to begin the road back to redemption. Because nothing can be admitted when appealing the verdict, the sentencing strategy is limited to words about the defendant's past good deeds as well as sympathy for the victims with words that sidestep any complicity. At Martha Stewart's sentencing, neither apologies nor tears were offered, and she instead pursued an appeal. By choosing to serve her prison sentence while the appeal was being taken, however, she accepted the court's punishment even if she never accepted her own guilt.

Martha Stewart is the most spectacular example of losing at trial but winning enough public support to keep a career alive and thriving. Even for the less rich and famous, getting convicted against a backdrop of positive press allows the remaining supporters (sometimes only a spouse and family dog) to argue that the conviction was the product of flaws in the legal system ("politically motivated," "set up," "sweetheart deals with lying witnesses") rather than the flawed character of the defendant ("he was actually guilty as sin").

Apart from the human importance of promoting more favorable reactions within one's personal universe of family and friends are the economic consequences with respect to future livelihood. News coverage that is sympathetic can create attitudes that are empathetic and see a conviction as an isolated, even overblown mistake in an otherwise honorable life. There is usually life after trial for convicted defendants, and once the prison sentence is completed, a difficult but critical chapter of that life is still to be written.

It's the Internet, Stupid: Marthatalks.com

Alongside Robert Morvillo's courtroom defense of Martha Stewart was a pioneering use of a website for her public defense. Although he gives credit for the innovation to her media strategists, Morvillo viewed the website as a great asset. In addition to posting defense pleadings, press statements, and fan mail, the website included "the few positive pieces" written in newspapers about the most famous defendant in the post-Enron prosecution wave.

It may not have been the first defendant's website, and years have passed, but it remains a model example of a defendant's reputation building. Others such as the late Michael Jackson made modest use of a defense website to present a personal letter to the public and some press releases. But Stewart's pioneering site launched a full-fledged media campaign. By the time of her trial, more than 6 million visitors had seen its tasteful green-and-light-blue color scheme.[47] Loaded with supportive letters and selected e-mails from the over 80,000 sent to the site, the website also included photos of the defendant for Martha's fans.[48]

As Stewart described it, the Internet was her means to "stay in direct touch with her public." Launched immediately after her indictment, Stewart fired back with an electronic appeal to the public through an open letter saying, "I want you to know that I am innocent—and I will fight to clear my name."[49] In its first day, the site received a million hits. Best of all were friendly e-mails soon posted to the site, such as "somebody's grandstanding and using you to get their name with the press."[50] The site occasionally included statements from her lawyers, who criticized "frequent errors" in media coverage. [51] They answered the indictment with a statement saying, "Even though insider trading was the subject of the criminal investigation she supposedly obstructed, the insider trading charge is included only in the civil complaint."[52] It also included Stewart's court pleadings.

Most experts praised the strategy, including L.A.'s megastrategist Elliot Mintz. Some even suggested it should have been used sooner.[53] Lawyers know, however, that prior to an indictment, it is never wise to tug on Superman's cape or otherwise annoy prosecutors with press strategies—at least as long as there is any hope for a nonindictment.

Throughout the proceedings, press reports about the site were almost universally positive, some describing it as "brilliant," even as some diagnosed its none-too-subtle ulterior motives. On the eve of trial, the *Wall*

47. Erin McClam, *Martha Stewart Says 6 Million Have Visited Web Site She Set Up to Tell Her side of Story*, Washington Post (June 9, 2003), http://www.washingtonpost.com/wp-dyn/articles/A35783-2003jun9.html. [ED: Article no longer exists on website; cannot verify title.]

48. Martha Stewart Appeals To Supporters on Personal Web Site, Wall Street Journal (Jan. 11, 2004), http://online.wsj.com/article/0,,BT_CO_20040111_000521,00.html.

49. Constance L. Hays, *Martha Stewart Uses Web to Tell Her Side of Story*, N.Y. Times (June 6, 2003), http://www.nytimes.com/2003/06/06/business/media/06ADCO.htmal?ex=1055897387&ei=1&en=5c7e5858db721b6a.

50. *Id.*

51. *Martha's lawyers hint at defense*, CNNMoney (June 10, 2003), http://money.cnn.com/2003/06/10/news/companies/martha_defense/index.htm.

52. *Id.*

53. Constance L. Hays, *Martha Stewart Uses Web to Tell Her Side of Story*, N.Y. Times (June 6, 2003), http://www.nytimes.com/2003/06/06/business/media/06ADCO.htmal?ex=1055897387&ei=1&en=5c7e5858db721b6a.

Street Journal described it as "stylish" (would one expect anything less?) and reported that experts deemed it "remarkably thorough." The *Journal* further explained, "Image consultants say the site is an attempt to hold on to supporters believing she was being targeted as a woman."[54]

It also provided a way to initiate a media offensive without being too offensive. One strategist described the analysis as searching for a "middle ground" between hiding in the background and being too up-front and visible. As another expert noted for the *Journal,* "The Internet gives you the freedom to talk right to your audience without filtered interpretation."

YouTube: Going Public with No Questions Asked

With state and federal investigators searching his offices and home, Dr. Conrad Murray's role as the doctor for the late Michael Jackson brought him vastly more blame than acclaim. Numerous reports identified him as a target of criminal inquiries into whether his treatment of Jackson with high-powered sedatives caused the death of the King of Pop. Although Dr. Murray generated vast amounts of media interest, he was much too endangered legally to be answering a reporter's questions. As a result, he appeared publicly—with no questions asked—by posting a video statement on YouTube. The statement said little, but a testimonial that cannot be cross-examined assures that there is little risk of making things worse than they already are. In addition to thanking friends for their support, he assured them that "I have done all I could do, I have told the truth and I have faith the truth will prevail."[55] Such a statement is better than no comment at all, according to L.A. media guru Elliot Mintz, and is the best strategy available under obviously difficult circumstances.

Naturally, some skeptics posted several rebuttals on YouTube. One posting featured a spoof by a speaker posing as Dr. Murray who essen-

54. Martha Stewart Appeals To Supporters on Personal Web Site, WALL STREET JOURNAL (Jan. 11, 2004), http://online.wsj.com/article/0,,BT_CO_20040111_000521,00.html. [ED: Article no longer exists on website; cannot verify title.]

55. *Dr. Conrad Murray Thanks Supporters*, YouTube (Aug. 18, 2009), http://www.youtube.com/watch?v=x1bjDWRJx9I&feature=related.

tially fessed up and whined about going to prison. Still, by last count, the real doctor's own video had five times more traffic than all the imposters combined. For a target wearing a bull's-eye on his back, those numbers may be better news than a spike in the Dow Jones average. Most assuredly, his innovative use of YouTube to provide a presence and voice to an otherwise faceless and notorious target of a criminal investigation will not be the last, despite his ultimate conviction and four-year sentence.

Making the News—Having It Your Way

In California, some people who are in the news are creating their own news. Relying on their own websites to communicate to the public, they are hiring ex-reporters to write the articles. The Los Angeles Kings as well as the Consumer Attorneys of California, a trial lawyers association, say the articles they post on websites will offer journalistic merit rather than self-serving press releases.[56] Although the website writers insist that they are not doing public relations (of course they are!), some skeptics may conclude that you don't have to have a six-shooter to become a hired gun.

Juries, E-Contamination, and the Media

As we have reviewed cases, potential defense pitfalls, and judicious press strategies for a defense lawyer's toolbox, we now come to the issue of picking juries in a media-saturated age. Google, Wikipedia, Facebook, and Twitter penetrate not only jury selection but also deliberations.

"Social media has given jurors new opportunities to disobey court rules and has given them many avenues for doing this," says Dallas jury consultant Mary Griffitts. "Now some judges are banning jurors from going on Facebook, Twitter, and LinkedIn during the trial. It's almost as if social media gives some jurors a false sense of anonymity, saying what you might not even say to your friend or your spouse."

Even prior to trial, legal blogs chat about ongoing cases, sometimes never aiming at the truth. In fact, some strategists hire bloggers to bombard a small but focused audience with e-shilling for one side of a con-

---

56. James Rainey, *A new spin on inside stories*, L.A. Times, Sep. 30, 2009.

troversy. The few, the anonymous, and the bloggers may represent only a fraction of the reaction but a majority of Internet content on many subjects. Internet messages do not die, and, unlike old soldiers, they do not even fade away. Years after a case is closed, the ill tidings can remain in the ocean of news to be found by a Google search engine.

"Information is power, but bad information is even more powerful," Griffitts says. With unverified, unsourced "information" so commonplace, there is little if any opportunity for recourse, and the potential for e-contamination of potential jurors amid the avalanches of misinformation seriously imperils the right to a fair trial is extremely troubling.

Defense lawyer Roy Black argued that this was exactly the case after wealthy Palm Beach polo club founder John Goodman was arrested for DUI manslaughter when he crashed his Bentley into a Hyundai Sonata driven by Scott Wilson, who drowned after his car overturned in a canal.

In a 92-page change of venue motion, Black argued that media coverage, especially in the *Palm Beach Post* and its website, had tainted a potential jury pool. He also argued that such coverage fanned prejudice and even hatred toward Goodman.

"I know exactly what it takes to get on a jury," said one online commentator on the *Palm Beach Post* website. "So do a lot of bored people like me .... Pray I don't get a summons John ... PRAY." Other comments called Goodman names like "low life garbage," "scum of the earth," "punk," and worse.

As it happened, the trial judge turned down Black's request for a venue shift, citing a Florida Supreme Court ruling in another case saying the charge was not "extreme or unusual enough to warrant a change of venue." Black says, however, that such comments are facts defense lawyers must deal with as they work as advocates for their clients.

Internet contamination is a relatively new phenomenon, and research studies have not fully analyzed the issue. The anecdotes, however, are troubling. In the super-sized trial of Scott Peterson, the judge dismissed a juror, Francis Gorman, because she had done her own research.[57] In fact, Gorman had gone fishing on the Internet to explore a perceived dis-

57. Carolyn Marshall, *Peterson Judge Dismisses Juror for Misconduct*, N.Y. TIMES (Nov. 10, 2004), http://www.nytimes.com/2004/11/10/national/10peterson.html.

crepancy in the testimony regarding a website that Peterson had visited.[58] The defense had argued he had visited a fishing website to determine currents in the San Francisco Bay *before* Amber Frey's best friend confronted him about being married. The prosecution asserted he had checked it afterward—suggesting evidence of premeditation.[59] Although Gorman was dismissed, it is increasingly clear that others are conducting their own surreptitious e-research using many unsubstantiated and irrelevant sources.

In a complex federal conspiracy case involving the allegedly illegal sale of prescription drugs, a juror after eight weeks of trial admitted to the federal judge that he had undertaken his own investigation of the case using Internet tools such Google and Wikipedia. When the judge questioned other jurors, it turned out that eight more admitted to doing cyberresearch on the case. The judge properly declared a mistrial.[60] What the judge could not declare, though, is a guarantee that nosey jurors in the next trial would not be nosing around the Internet.

Some judges are taking jurors' phones at the beginning of the day, and keeping them until they leave the courthouse. Some are even fining jurors for violating instructions. Griffitts says the lawyer's best recourse is to form an alliance with the judge and encourage the court to enforce its instructions.

Reports about such juror misconduct show that the virus is becoming highly contagious. Because people are naturally curious, the problem is typically juror research:

- A juror in South Dakota Googled the defendant and passed along that the defendant had never been sued before to five other jurors.[61]
- In Bartow, Florida, a juror investigated the defendant online, pulled up his "rap sheet," and informed the other jurors in the case.[62]

---

58. Diana Walsh, Stacy Finz, et al., *Behind Closed Doors*, SAN FRANCISCO CHRONICLE, Dec. 16, 2004, ["at" and page on which article appears].

59. *Id.*

60. Fred Grimm, *Juries without Web junkies? Impossible*, MIAMI HERALD, May 19, 2009, ["at" and page on which article appears].

61. Ralph Artigliere, Jim Barton, and Bill Hahn, *Reining in Juror Misconduct: Practical Suggestions for Judges and Lawyers*, 84 THE FLORIDA BAR JOURNAL, 9 (2010).

62. *Id.*

- In a Riverside, California, murder trial, two jurors were dismissed after searching the Internet for information on the death penalty and bringing the research into the deliberations.[63]
- In a Maryland trial of a homeless man's murder, a mistrial was declared after a juror looked up the word *lividity* on Wikipedia.[64]
- In the trial of the Taser-induced death of a Kentucky man, the jury foreman researched the case on the Taser manufacturer's website and used that information to convince other jurors that Tasers are "nonlethal" and cannot cause fatal injuries.[65]

At other times, jurors are engaged in e-chatter about the ongoing trial:

- In a Philadelphia public corruption case, jurors were posting trial updates on Twitter and Facebook.[66]
- In San Diego, jurors admitted they were reading about their fraud trial on a local legal blog.[67]
- A juror in New York City sent a Facebook friend request to a witness during deliberations.[68]
- In a Maryland trial involving the alleged corruption of Baltimore's first female mayor, jurors friended each other on Facebook despite the judge's instructions not to communicate with each other outside the jury room.[69]
- In an Arkansas case, a juror in a $12.6 million judgment sent Twitter messages during the trial such as "oh and nobody buy

63. Associated Press, *Jurors Tossed For Using Web*, CBS News (May 5, 1998), http://www.cbsnews.com/stories/1998/05/07/tech/main8948.shtml (last visited Jan. 30, 2010).

64. Del Quentin Wilber, *Social networking of jurors is trying judges' patience*, Washington Post (Jan. 9, 2010), http://www.washingtonpost.com/wp-dyn/content/article/2010/01/08/AR2010010803694.html (last visited Jan. 30, 2010).

65. United Press International, Lawyer: Juror used Internet info in case, United Press Int'l (Jan. 10, 2010), http://www.upi.com/Top_News/US/2010/01/10/Lawyer-Juror-used-Internet-info-in-case/UPI-51351263163800/ (last visited Jan. 30, 2010).

66. Teresa Baldas, *Juries gone wild*, Daily Business Review (May 18, 2005), https://www.dailybusinessreview.com/archive/purchase_article.html?news_id=35061. [ED: Article cannot be found online; cannot verify.]

67. *Id.*

68. Hillary Hylton, *Tweeting in the Jury Box: A Danger to Fair Trials?* Time Magazine (Dec. 29, 2009), http://www.time.com/time/nation/article/0,8599,1948971,00.html (last visited Jan. 30, 2010).

69. Brendan Kearney, *Despite judge's warning, Dixon jurors went on Facebook*, Daily Record (Dec. 2, 2009), http://mddailyrecord.com/2009/12/02/despite-judge's-warning-dixon-jurors-went-on-facebook/ (last visited Jan. 30, 2010).

> Stoam [company]. It's bad mojo and they'll probably cease to exist, now that their wallet is 12m lighter" and "So Johnathan, what did you do today? Oh nothing really, I just gave away TWELVE MILLION DOLLARS of somebody else's money."[70]

Some episodes result in new trials while others do not. In confronting this perplexing new retrofit of an ages-old problem, the courts are still struggling to find consistent responses to the e-taint that creeps into jury deliberations. At this writing, a California appellate court is preparing to consider whether the court can compel a former juror to turn in all the Facebook entries he posted during trial for the court to review. Expect to see more such cases. At the beginning of 2012, it became illegal for jurors in California to tweet, use the Internet, or go on Facebook to give or get information about an ongoing trial. Although potential solutions are being explored, the reality remains that jury adherence to the rules remains largely an honor system, and today's temptations pose greater challenges than ever before.

The "Web" of Lawyers

The Internet, for all its perils, creates new opportunities in mounting an advocate's side of the story. In the age of newspapers, only the publisher could dictate the news coverage. Today, the lawyers themselves can launch their own coverage over the Internet. Increasingly, lawyers use websites to tout their ongoing accounts of ongoing cases. At least lawyers hawking their positions on their own websites are not hiding anything. A California defense lawyer, without disclosing who hired him, blogged about the trial concerning the financial collapse of San Diego's Peregrine Systems.[71] And he, at least, was not an unidentified blogging missile. Others prefer to fire from the shadows by using anonymous bloggers to attack the adversary. Needless to say, secret cybersnipers are resented, but recourse is limited. To date, bar associations have not writ-

---

70. John Schwartz, *As Jurors Turn to Web, Mistrials Are Popping Up*, N.Y. Times (Mar. 17, 2009), http://www.nytimes.com/2009/03/18/us/18juries.html?pagewanted=2&_r=2 (last visited Jan. 30, 2010).

71. Teresa Baldas, *Tainted Talk*, Daily Business Review, May 9, 2008, ["at" and page on which article appears].

ten rules that specifically address Internet bashing of a client. The existing rules amount to general prohibitions concerning public dissemination of statements where there is a "substantial likelihood" that they will interfere with a fair trial or otherwise prejudice the due administration of justice.[72] Although a useful guidance for scrupulous lawyers, this is not a sharp sword against misbehavior.

Whatever may be the prohibitions, the overriding concern is that like the rest of us most jurors are Internet junkies who will be unable to resist Google, Wikipedia, Facebook, or Twitter during a trial. The irresistible Internet creates grave concerns that the right to a fair trial, based only on the evidence inside the courtroom, will suffer serious but invisible damage. The usual measures to control traditional forms of publicity—careful questions from lawyers during jury selection and strong warnings from judges through the trial—will help some in treating this increasingly common problem. But for cases that demand more, some will consider combating jury poisoning with some cybermedicine of their own.

Cyberstrategies for Search Engines

Most of us are addicted to Internet search engines, and most addicts traffic in Google. Currently, Google has captured between 65 to 70 percent of Internet users compared to 17 percent who use Yahoo and 9 percent for Bing.[73] Often turning to Google, Internet-savvy jurors with inquiring minds may want to know more. Unless they are sequestered without computers or handheld devices, they enjoy instant access to research about a defendant, a lawyer, a judge, or almost any issue that could arise in a trial.

Defendants and other litigants can do little to affect the newspaper story, much less the headline or the placement of the article. The Internet, though, has given birth to a cottage industry of tech companies that specialize in search engine optimization (SEO). Normally, SEO companies provide a marketing function by utilizing tactics to elevate a client's website to a high-

---

72. *Id.*

73. Juan Carlos Perez, *ComScore: Google Gains More Ground Than Bing in September*, PC World (Oct. 14, 2009), http://www.pcworld.com/businesscenter/article/173690/comscore_googl e_gains_more_ground_than_bing_in_september.html.

er ranking. If, for example, a local company wants to be seen by Internet searchers, they want to appear, if possible, on the first page of Google and of other search engines and as close to the top as possible. In promoting a business, appearing way in the back of a search is an e-bummer. Many millions of dollars are spent by companies who strategize with SEO marketers to brainstorm their way up the ladder of a search engine's ranking so that a distant, essentially invisible position on page 10 is replaced by a listing on the first page. For defendants in ugly lawsuits or facing never pretty criminal charges, however, an elevated ranking is the last thing they desire. In fact, if publicity-battered litigants could get Google and Yahoo to banish their name from the Internet entirely, they would, no doubt, be thrilled to do so.

No such erasure, though, is possible. Instead, what SEO companies can provide are a strategy and a campaign for improving the first few pages of search engine results by trying to boost favorable or neutral items ahead of the unkindnesses. The naysayers will never go away, but hopefully they can be pushed from the front door to the back of the room.

Because reputation is everything for most successful people and because today's reputation is increasingly defined by the Internet, SEO strategies can be as vital to repairing a tattered image as they are to boosting a new product.

One specialist in SEO strategies for combating Internet toxicity is Rebecca Bilbao, who explains that the first step in improving Internet health is a thorough checkup. Upon examining the existing search results, an assessment is made of the existing positive content so that these pieces can be pushed up to higher positions in order to effectively push down the ranking of the unfriendly pieces. Once the basic diagnosis is completed, a strategy is developed to use links to other sites to move up as many neutral or favorable pieces as possible. In some instances, SEO companies help build websites to create items that will rank higher in a client's search engine results. Moreover, a client's existing or additional websites can be linked to other Internet sources.

By all accounts, Google, Yahoo, and other search engines prioritize articles that are heavily linked to other legitimate Internet pieces. Although links are emphasized by search engine optimizers, the actual algorithms used by the major search engines are not disclosed publicly. The formulas for rankings are a secret because so many Internet subjects are inevitably trying to improve their good news and push down the bad stuff. (By the way, do not bother having friends click the favorable sites because hits do not determine placement.) Although some trade secrets are a single set of unchanging ingredients, the search engines change their algorithms regularly in order to stay ahead of the experts who are constantly studying the systems in order to manipulate them for better rankings. Coca-Cola's recipe would be easier to find.

In a random sampling taken recently, the first five pages of Martha Stewart's Google search contained no articles about her arrest, conviction, and prison sentence. This was a remarkable achievement considering the thousands of negative pieces that had accumulated about those obviously newsworthy subjects. No doubt her own marketing strategies contributed to the rise of the trouble-free pages. Within a few weeks, though, bad news arrived about her company's stock price, and Stewart's first page suddenly included one of the old stories about the lying and obstruction charges. As Bilbao notes, "The court of public opinion is never completely out of session online."

Search engine optimization may or may not be an optimal use of a client's finite resources for litigation. Superstar lawyers like Dick Sprague recognize the jury problems created by bloggers and Google searches but are not inclined to develop strategies for Google placement or counter-blogging to neutralize Internet hostility. For Sprague, a lawyer's job is winning inside the courtroom. Although there are disquieting concerns about the Internet, and some thoughtful advocates believe in aggressive Internet strategies, all agree that the surest way to winning in the court of public opinion is winning in the court of law.

The Advocate's Duty in an Imperfect World

We do not live in a perfect world. We live in a world in which lawyers, litigants, and media alike relentlessly pursue their own interests and in which the public hungers for the details of the famous and their trials.

In large part, it is the job of lawyers to seek every legitimate advantage, which sometimes drives them near the often-shifting borders of permissible conduct. Still, our system is based on an adversarial principle, and it is the defense lawyer's obligation to present the client's case as compellingly as possible.

For journalists, every high-profile case creates a potential for more viewers and readers and greater market share and profits, under ever-greater time pressure and competition, all of which push some (but certainly not all!) reporters and commentators to relax the standards of objective journalism. Dramatically compounding the already-daunting issues of the mainstream media are the dizzying new challenges of Internet-driven coverage that can be created by anyone who can type on a keyboard.

In this chapter, we have reviewed the media-drenched, deadline-driven minefield through which today's defense lawyer must navigate. We have attempted to illustrate the temptations and hazards a dedicated, resourceful lawyer needs to resist while in ultimate service to the court rather than the media. And we have offered a toolbox of strategies and tactics to consider when the media comes calling. Finally, we have attempted to shine a light on how the Internet has affected so many aspects of trying a case today, challenges that will increase dramatically in the future.

Above all, we have emphasized that the lawyer's primary consideration is to serve the court of law while remaining mindful of the court of public opinion, which can influence the client's future welfare and ultimate chances of rehabilitation. Maintaining our ethical standards while focusing on the client's best interest requires that media strategies remain merely tools to be utilized thoughtfully and selectively and should never be the prime determinant of a lawyer's conduct.

In a free society, extending access and understanding to the public about constitutionally protected processes is the way to deal with these issues. The defense lawyer has a duty to promote that access and understanding as well as the public's of constitutional protections in a media-saturated world. As that world changes, the best course is for everyone on all sides to understand as fully as possible not only the way things are supposed to work but also the way they really work—while vigorously upholding the strictures and the values of the Constitution that was conceived to ensure a fair process, a free press, and a democratic society.

***Editor's Note**: The below addendum to this chapter is written by Joshua Marquis, a well-known elected prosecutor in the state of Oregon. Marquis does not express sharp disagreement with most of the tactical advice that Kendall Coffey offers defense lawyers, much of which may be relevant to prosecutors as well. But Marquis notes a crucial and sweeping exception: Prosecutors communicating with the media should generally limit themselves to the matters expressly permitted by ethics codes. Indeed, Marquis similarly urges prosecutors to do their best to limit police press statements because they may sometimes be chargeable to the prosecution. Marquis also makes an extended argument, however, that these appropriate ethical limitations, combined with incomplete and unbalanced media coverage of prosecutor behavior, handicap the prosecutors' image in the public mind and that of juries. Marquis thus takes issue with the idea that slanted media coverage in fact routinely unequally harms the defense. Additional concerns specific to prosecutors are addressed in later chapters, including the chapter devoted solely to ethics.*

ADDENDUM TO CHAPTER 1:
A Prosecutor's View

BY JOSHUA MARQUIS

If we measured the role of the prosecutor by what appears in popular culture, we—or someone watching from overseas or another planet—might think that prosecutors in America get frequent flyer miles for putting people in prison—extra ones if they are factually innocent—and that it is common for a district attorney in a trial to fabricate evidence to frame an innocent suspect. The prosecutor is usually displayed as extremely prosperous, as contrasted with the threadbare but plucky public defender. If there is an opportunity, the prosecutor is usually the actual perpetrator of the crime or at least ignores clear evidence.

For those who think that this is a paranoid or fantastical view, each of the above scenarios comes from major American television series or movies, respectively, *True Believer* (starring James Woods), *True Crime* (starring Clint Eastwood), *The Judge* (starring Edward James Olmos), the ABC series *Injustice*, and, more recently, the hit TV series *The Good Wife* (from the husband/wife producers who brought us *Injustice*).

Many professions complain that popular culture distorts their profession and creates unrealistic expectations. Doctors used to complain about *Marcus Welby, M.D.* or, more recently, *House*, because patients expected either regular house calls or incredible diagnostic powers every time they showed up at a clinic.

But unlike in medicine, Americans participate very directly in the legal system as members of juries, as well as less frequently victims and, even less often, as defendants.

Some say that the public is able to differentiate popular fiction from reality, but television has further blurred that division. Many popular television stories carry enough reality to inform but also create unrealistic expectations. One prime example is the profusion of CSI shows, which portray actual forensic science but make it appear instantly accessible and available to police officers on the street and to line prosecutors. By the same token, the incredible winning streak of fictional defense lawyer Perry Mason made some viewers expect a lawyer to reduce witnesses to confess to perjury or, better yet, leap to their feet from the audience and confess to the crime. One has to wonder how Mason's adversary, District Attorney Hamilton Burger, kept his job after losing over 250 consecutive murder trials.

Documentary films can illuminate real injustice, such as Errol Morris's *The Thin Blue Line*, but more often are being used as what can most politely be called "advocacy journalism." Two prominent examples include the *Paradise Lost* documentaries about the so-called "Memphis 3" (three young men convicted of murdering three boys in rural Arkansas who recently were released after entering Alford pleas to first-degree murder) and the many PBS *Frontline* films of Ofra Bikel, who is severely critical of law enforcement handling of child abuse cases.

As a prosecutor, I frequently teach courses on both trial practice and also on the proper way to communicate with the media without violating ethical rules or prejudicing a defendant's right to a fair trial.

As an example of how strongly influenced Americans can be by popular media, I often use polls measuring support for capital punishment that often show broad support for the death penalty but, at the same time, a fairly widespread belief that there are a very significant number of innocent people sentenced to death (in excess of 10 percent).[1] Douglas Berman, who writes and blogs on sentencing, notes that even the belief that as many as 34 percent of those supporting capital punishment think innocent people have been executed.

The measurement of wrongful convictions is a highly controversial subject. My work has been cited by both Justice Antonin Scalia in his concurrence in *Kansas v. Marsh* and by detractors of Scalia and myself who have called my estimate of a 99.27% accuracy rate in serious felonies to be callous and inaccurate.[2]

My argument is set forth in both a *New York Times* editorial motivated by outrage over the TV series *Injustice*,[3] and a much longer article called "The Myth of Innocence" that was published after a symposium in Northwestern University Law School's *Journal of Criminal Law*.[4]

While of greatest interest in selecting impartial juries in capital cases, prosecutors—and anyone involved in the justice system—should be concerned about both the reality and perception of wrongful convictions.[5] There are some commentators who have suggested that as many as 3 to 5 percent of those convicted are factually innocent. As a lawyer of thirty years and a prosecutor for twenty-five, I find such a number chilling, and, if I thought it were true, I would not be able to continue in my chosen profession.[6]

To claim that wrongful convictions do not occur would be sheer folly,

---

1. *See* http://www.gallup.com/poll/123638/in-u.s.-two-thirds-continue-support-death-penalty.aspx; http://sentencing.typepad.com/sentencing_law_and_policy/2009/10/latest-gallup-poll-showing-support-for-death-penalty-reamins-strong.html.
2. *See* http://www.theatlantic.com/national/archive/2012/05/yes-america-we-have-executed-an-innocent-man/257106/; http://papers.ssrn.com/sol3/papers.cfm?abstract_id=931454; http://www.nytimes.com/2008/03/25/us/25bar.html.
3. http://www.nytimes.com/2006/01/26/opinion/26marquis.html
4. *See* Joshua Marquis, *The Myth Of Innocence*, __ J. Crim. L. & Criminology __ (2005).
5. *See* http://www.cato-unbound.org/2012/03/07/joshua-marquis/rightful-convictions.
6. *See* http://reason.com/archives/2011/06/07/wrongful-convictions/singlepage.

but their frequency can best be described as episodic, not epidemic.

A similar description could also be used for the instances of serious prosecutorial misconduct. But once again, popular media insistence on widespread abuses, including studies such as the Center for Public Integrity's *Harmful Error,* which claimed to chronicle widespread misconduct by state and local prosecutors, is still available online.[7] *Harmful Error*'s claims were repeated frequently in mainstream media, such as in an article from CBS News.[8] As a former reporter, I know well the maxim that "it isn't news to report how many planes landed safely." By extension, the fact that a guilty person was convicted is not news, but the imprisonment of an innocent person is very much news. If that is compounded by gross misconduct of the person charged with being a "minister of justice," it is even more newsworthy.

In recent history, one of the biggest stories was the egregious misconduct by then-Durham, North Carolina district attorney Mike Nifong, who proceeded with the prosecution of several Duke University lacrosse players despite scientific evidence of their innocence.[9] Nifong's conduct is rare but not unheard of. I myself have been elected five times to the post of district attorney in Astoria, Oregon, after first being appointed in 1994 after the arrest, indictment, and later felony conviction and disbarment of my predecessor.[10] Unfortunately, she was not the first nor last elected prosecutor disbarred for misconduct in Oregon in my professional lifetime. Somehow neither my predecessor nor any of the other cases from my state were initially picked up by researchers who prepared the *Harmful Error* report.

In 1980, the long-time and powerful district attorney in the state capital, Salem, Gary Gortmaker, was convicted of multiple crimes and permanently suspended as a lawyer.[11] In 1999, the district attorney of one of Oregon's most populous counties in the suburban Portland area,

---

7. *See* http://www.iwatchnews.org/accountability/harmful-error.

8. *See* http://findarticles.com/p/articles/mi_go1613/is_9-10_12/ai_n9232040/.

9. *See* http://photo.pds.org:5012/cqresearcher/document.php?id=cqresrre2007110900; http://abcnews.go.com/US/LegalCenter/story?id=2760232#.T8QudcU8U1I; http://durhamwonderland.blogspot.com/2007/04/marquis-clarifies.html.

10. *See* http://community.seattletimes.nwsource.com/archive/?date=19931022&slug=1727449.

11. *See* http://news.google.com/newspapers?nid=1243&dat=19831013&id=uY9TAAAAIBAJ&sjid=nYYDAAAAIBAJ&pg=2226,4881479.

Clackamas County, was indicted and later disbarred.[12] However, missing from the current online version of the story is the one-page "correction" that the Center for Public Integrity (CPI) invited me to write. Misreporting about prosecutorial behavior or one-sided reports of prosecutorial wrongdoing that ignore the great good that the vast majority of prosecutors do all the time thus poses a danger to accurate public perceptions of the justice system. My published response to CPI's report on alleged prosecutorial misconduct sought to fire back:

> Dear Center for Public Integrity:
>
> The study entitled "Harmful Error" claims that prosecutorial misconduct is epidemic among the thousands of state and county prosecutors. The truth is that such misconduct is better described as episodic, those few cases being rare enough to merit considerable attention by both the courts and the media. There is no question that given the critical role of gatekeeper the district attorney holds in our legal system, the men and women who work as prosecutors should continue to be held to the highest standards of conduct. In the criminal justice system, there is an elaborate system of checks and balances designed to protect both the innocent and the guilty. Alone among the legal profession, a prosecutor's sole allegiance is to the truth—even if that means torpedoing the prosecutor's own case.
>
> When trial judges make mistakes, appellate courts will reverse or remand those cases. We call these cases "judicial error." When defense attorneys fail to properly represent their clients, the accused's conviction is frequently set aside because of "inadequate assistance of counsel." Yet when a prosecutor makes an error, it's called "prosecutorial misconduct," a term that summons up images of a district attorney hiding evidence, lying to a jury, or framing an innocent suspect. The reality is that the overwhelming majority of prosecutorial errors are indeed "harmless," not "harmful," meaning that there was no malice on

12. *See* http://news.google.com/newspapers?nid=1310&dat=19991110&id=_0xWAAAAIBAJ&sjid=9esDAAAAIBAJ&pg=6634,2547232.

the part of the D.A. and that there was no unjust result. Keep in mind that only the defense has the right to appeal misconduct, and therefore there is no judicial review of misconduct by a defense attorney.

How pervasive are instances of true misconduct by prosecutors? Because record keeping varies so much from one state to another, it would be unwise to draw any sweeping conclusions across the country. The statistics on this website about my own state of Oregon show that in the last 33 years Oregon's appellate courts have raised issues of prosecutorial error 44 times, but in only 8 of those instances the prosecutor's conduct was found to be prejudicial. Comparing those numbers against the thousands of criminal appeals rendered during this same time provides a rate of prosecutorial misconduct of less than one tenth of 1 percent. It is even more instructive to look at what kind of misconduct was deemed "prejudicial"—in one of those eight cases it was the exasperated description of a professional defense witness in a drunk driving case as a "pimp." The prosecutor never should have made the comment, but it is hardly in the same class as concealing evidence.

The study implies that in those rare cases where prosecutors get caught little more than a slap on the wrist is given. The researchers missed no less than two cases in the past 10 years in Oregon, where elected prosecutors were permanently disbarred for misconduct in office. I should know—I have been three times elected District Attorney of Clatsop County where I was originally appointed by the governor to replace the previous District Attorney, who was indicted, convicted, jailed, and disbarred.

Prosecutors continue to be subject to the harshest sanctions on those truly rare occasions where they violate their oaths. No human endeavor is error free, and the only way to achieve even lower error rates is simply to avoid prosecutions altogether.

Editors' Note: *The Center thanks District Attorney Joshua Marquis for his thoughtful response. We agree that prosecutorial misconduct is episodic, not epidemic. We never said—or meant to imply—otherwise. We also thank Mr. Marquis for pointing out that we did not cite two cases in Oregon of elected prosecutors who were* *permanently disbarred for misconduct in office. We have made the corrections in our database and posted some of them on our website.*

Many defense lawyers anguish about whether publicity is bad or good for their clients, and it is becoming increasingly common for high-profile defendants to hire not just a defense lawyer but a PR firm. The ethical issues that arise from someone issuing statements specifically calculated to affect the possible triers of fact is of concern, to say the least. Usually there is a Chinese wall erected between the defense firm and the PR firm, and although the PR firm's principal may be tried or once licensed as lawyers, they claim not to be acting as lawyers. The degree to which defense lawyers can "respond" to negative publicity, often engendered by horrific acts by their client, has been greatly expanded by cases like *Gentile*, which is discussed in a later chapter of this book.

For a prosecutor sanctioning anything like this would be unthinkable. Although the prosecutor cannot control an angry family who decides to take its message public, *any* involvement or participation by a prosecutor's office in such an endeavor would have potentially catastrophic consequences.

One common trope among the defense bar is that the prosecution has the direct and, in theory, limitless resources of all state and federal law enforcement, and that because the popular press often sensationalizes the initial arrest and information released by police, an inherently unfair playing field exists. Although some of this is true, the 24/7 media stream is always looking for the "man bites dog" story, and if they are provided a story that says, "Police frame wrongly accused man," "Lab director implicated in scandal endangers cases," or, better yet, "Innocents crowd our prison," all these are much more attractive stories than "Police arrest guilty man."

Nonetheless, ethics rules clearly make prosecutors responsible for public comments made by police, and ABA Special Rule for Prosecutors 3.8(f) says that

> except for statements that are necessary to inform the public of the nature and extent of the prosecutor's action and that serve a legitimate law enforcement purpose, [prosecutors must] refrain from making extraju-

> dicial comments that have a substantial likelihood of heightening public condemnation of the accused and [must] exercise reasonable care to prevent investigators, law enforcement personnel, employees or other persons assisting or associated with the prosecutor in a criminal case from making an extrajudicial statement that the prosecutor would be prohibited from making under Rule 3.6.

This is complicated by the fact that, although the media often refer to the district attorney or U.S. attorney as the "top cop," that is not in fact the proper role of the prosecutor in America; and although different states give the usually popularly elected chief prosecutors (called variously district attorneys, state's attorneys, commonwealth attorneys, county attorneys, and a few other names) differing powers, they rarely (except in New Jersey, where prosecutors are appointed by the governor) have any direct control over police investigators.

Yet in Illinois, rules were established to the great consternation of prosecutors and the media that made clear that prosecutors would be held directly responsible for police comments. Many state's attorneys in Illinois responded by directing the police to say nothing to the press. But even in states without such draconian rules, courts from trial to appellate level have held prosecutors accountable for police comments if the court finds they endanger the defendant's right to a fair trial. This can range from theoretically prophylactic gag orders to threats to dismiss a case for outrageous governmental misconduct.

Again, although the defense bar sees the police and prosecutors as a unified bloc, the reality is that the police often see their primary job as keeping order, providing direct protection to the public, and arresting people for whom probable cause exists. It is the prosecutor's job to take the case from there.

The safest thing for a prosecutor to do is to direct police to turn over all public statements about a case to their office once a formal charge is lodged in court. From that point, the prosecutor is best served by stating those matters generally agreed to be appropriate for release to the press as set out in ABA Rule 3.6:

Rule 3.6 Trial Publicity

(a) A lawyer who is participating or has participated in the investigation or litigation of a matter shall not make an extrajudicial statement that the lawyer knows or reasonably should know will be disseminated by means of public communication and will have a substantial likelihood of materially prejudicing an adjudicative proceeding in the matter.

(b) Notwithstanding paragraph (a), a lawyer may state:

(1) the claim, offense or defense involved and, except when prohibited by law, the identity of the persons involved;

(2) information contained in a public record;

(3) that an investigation of a matter is in progress;

(4) the scheduling or result of any step in litigation;

(5) a request for assistance in obtaining evidence and information necessary thereto;

(6) a warning of danger concerning the behavior of a person involved, when there is reason to believe that there exists the likelihood of substantial harm to an individual or to the public interest; and

(7) in a criminal case, in addition to subparagraphs (1) through (6):

(i) the identity, residence, occupation and family status of the accused;

(ii) if the accused has not been apprehended, information necessary to aid in apprehension of that person;

(iii) the fact, time and place of arrest; and

(iv) the identity of investigating and arresting officers or agencies and the length of the investigation.

(c) Notwithstanding paragraph (a), a lawyer may make a statement that a reasonable lawyer would believe is required to protect a client from the substantial undue prejudicial effect of recent publicity not initiated by the lawyer or the lawyer's client. A statement made pursuant to this paragraph shall be limited to such information as is necessary to mitigate the recent adverse publicity.

(d) No lawyer associated in a firm or government agency with a lawyer subject to paragraph (a) shall make a statement prohibited by paragraph (a).

In the accompanying chapter, noted lawyer Kendall Coffey discusses one very high-profile case that seemed to be tried more in the media than in the courtroom: *State of Florida v. Casey Anthony*, aka the "Tot Mom" case, which shocked many people when the jury acquitted the defendant of all the most serious charges. In a case like that, the prosecutor is pretty much between the devil and the deep blue sea. In the Anthony case, the lead defense attorney, Jose Baez, engaged in an extremely aggressive extrajudicial campaign designed to cast doubt on the state's case long before it ever saw the inside of a courtroom. The media quickly gravitated to the utterly unproven (even after the trial) allegations that the defendant, accused of killing her young daughter, had been the victim of sexual molestation at the hands of her father. Although it may have been that if the prosecutor had responded in kind that the ultimate result might have been different—and, in the view of many, more just—it would have been at the expense of the ethical duties of the prosecutor.

Americans are fascinated by the modern-day morality tales of criminal cases, and the result has been streams of "lawyer shows" on television, ranging from hits from sixty years ago like *Perry Mason* to modern-day successes like *The Good Wife,* in which the producers eschew traditional fictionalizing of locations and make the current Cook County state's attorney a crack-smoking, unfaithful husband to the title character.

The majority of these programs make the defense lawyer the conquering hero. Even those of us who ended up devoting our careers to prosecution, despite, as Coffey correctly points out, the decided financial disincentives, were often inspired by characters like Atticus Finch from Harper Lee's *To Kill a Mockingbird.*

The public would be better served, however, by understanding the real but usually unacknowledged roles of defense and prosecution lawyers.

The media version is that the courtroom is that of modern-day gladiators, each bringing his or her own version of the truth to the arena, which is now a courtroom for the jury to decide, after the intellectual combat of a trial, which version of the truth is correct.

The reality is that only one side has the ethical duty to turn over all evidence, particularly that which might undermine their case. Only one side has the burden of proof, as it should have.

The system works best when the prosecution is confronted by clever and aggressive defense lawyers who do everything they can, short of suborning perjury, to cast doubt on the prosecution's case. If a jury decides that the state's case can withstand all that a good defense lawyer can throw at it, or not, then justice will triumph either way.

2

Working with Public Relations Experts in High-Profile Criminal Cases

BY JAMES F. HAGGERTY

There is a certain type of lawyer out there all defense counsel know: media savvy, telegenic, and comfortable before the microphone. The type who sends you a press release before you actually receive a copy of the complaint. The type who leaks key pieces of evidence to the media to increase public pressure to settle—sometimes before any sort of formal legal action has been filed. The type who trots out potential victims in front of the cameras before a packed press conference when announcing the commencement of legal action—ethics and potential jury prejudice be damned. The type who uses all of the tools of the modern media age to coax big settlements out of unwary defendants.

I'm not talking about flashy plaintiffs lawyers here. I'm talking about prosecutors.

Welcome to the new age of criminal defense, in which properly representing your clients sometimes requires effectively waging a battle in the court of public opinion as well as in a court of law. Criminal defense lawyers of all stripes need to understand that prosecutors have learned to expertly use—and misuse—the media and other public audiences in pursuit of their goals. They do it at least as effectively as the most accomplished plaintiffs lawyers in America. Defense counsel need to rise to this challenge, and often this involves retaining public relations expertise as a case moves forward. This chapter will look at when and why outside public relations expertise may be needed in criminal cases, what is really important in working effectively with your expert, the different types of public relations firms and practitioners available to assist in your efforts, and the cost and value of having such a consultant as a member of your team.

The reality is this: With instantaneous, widespread access to media coverage and other information about your case, through the Internet, social media, and other means, criminal lawyers need to understand that what happens outside the courtroom can often impact the ultimate resolution of their case far more quickly and decisively than anything that happens before a judge or jury. In this modern era, defense lawyers who understand this and arm themselves to wage this battle will succeed on behalf of their clients. Those who do not, most assuredly, will not.

Why Use an Expert?

I often tell people you need a license to practice law, but any lawyer who has been interviewed once or twice in the media thinks they are qualified to handle public relations in high-profile cases. Sometimes it's true, no doubt; many times, it is not.

Now, I'm certainly biased because, despite my legal pedigree, the bulk of my work is as a public relations consultant to high-profile litigation. So, to be fair, I can tell you that some lawyers, in fact, are very good at working with the media during cases and can move seamlessly between the set of skills needed to communicate in court to those needed for communicating with extrajudicial audiences, including media and other stakeholders.

But many lawyers are not so good at it. And—more dangerously—many lawyers, including criminal defense lawyers, think they are good at it when they aren't. Indeed, it has been my experience that some of the biggest mistakes in communication during litigation are perpetrated by those lawyers who underestimate the particular skills and mindset needed to operate in the media arena—those who believe that dealing with the media is easy. That it is just an extension of the communicating they do throughout their case to judges, prosecutors, and the jury. These are the lawyers who inevitably screw it up.

Conversely, it is the lawyers who take the process seriously—those who understand the importance of being prepared, who work hard to understand what the media needs (in terms of both story and logistics)—who not only ultimately succeed in managing the media aspects of their cases in a manner that limits the damage wrought by overly aggressive prosecutors, but who actually help advance the ball in a manner that leads to a more positive resolution of their case. In the end, I argue, public communication during a high-profile court case is a litigation management function that must be handled with the same seriousness and care as any other element of the case.

So, if the case is going to involve anything other than the most rudimentary contact with media during its course, it may be advisable to have qualified—repeat *qualified*—public relations counsel close at hand.

What Kind of Case Warrants Outside Public Relations Assistance?

It is true that outside public relations counsel is probably not needed to augment existing capabilities in many, or even most, of the criminal cases most lawyers will face over the course of their careers. There are some cases that are just not interesting enough to warrant media attention and others in which media attention will be minimal throughout the course of the proceeding. In these instances, a little knowledge and critical thought as to message and themes, as well as reliance on key background resources (such as those contained in this book, for example), may be enough.

But there are other cases that will warrant more public attention, and at times it may not be readily apparent to counsel at the outset of the case when concern is more immediately focused on issues of investigation, indictment, arrest, or arraignment. To systemize the process and get counsel to more effectively focus on the potential for public exposure, I often encourage those I work with to run their case through what I call a "Media Litigation Checklist." If you consider some of the questions below at the outset of a criminal case, it may help to crystallize your thinking as to the level of media interest, and therefore whether outside help is needed.

Some of the checklist elements we focus on at the outset of a litigation assignment include the following:

- ❑ Does the case involve sensational facts?
- ❑ Does the case involve a large sum of money?
- ❑ Are the parties to the suit well known or otherwise high profile?
- ❑ Is the lawsuit unique, out of the ordinary, or otherwise "man bites dog"?
- ❑ Is it a case that will merit attention in regional or trade media?
- ❑ Does the case make new law?
- ❑ Does the case involve a new application of old law?
- ❑ Is the area of the law considered "hot" by the media right now?
- ❑ Does the case have a compelling "human face"?
- ❑ Is the case indicative of a trend?
- ❑ Is there a political or regulatory aspect that will attract interest in the case?
- ❑ Does the other side have a history of publicizing his or her cases?
- ❑ Does the other side play it close to the vest or fast and loose when dealing with the reporters who cover his or her cases?

There may be other questions as well that you can think of that will help you make the determination, but the key point is this: If you have a system of running cases through such a checklist, you are more than likely to come to the right conclusions as to whether you need an outside consultant to assist you in your efforts early on in the process—which can only help in ensuring a consistency and cohesion of approach as a high-profile criminal case moves forward.[1]

So let's assume that you've looked at the facts and circumstances surrounding a case and come to the conclusion that outside help may be warranted. Depending upon the type of criminal matter at hand, outside public relations consultants can provide a variety of services to support the litigation. Some of the more important services may include the following:

1. James F. Haggerty, In the Court of Public Opinion: Winning Strategies for Litigation Communications (2d ed. 2009) (more information regarding the Litigation Media Checklist).

Strategy and counsel regarding communications options: Some of the most value-added services a skilled communications consultant brings to the team relate to their skill in knowing *what* to say and *when* to say it, and in *what order* and in *what format*. Remember that nearly anyone can find a podium for a press conference or write a rudimentary press release. The true skill lies in knowing when to hold the press conference, if at all, or when to issue that press release—again, if at all.

There are nuanced decisions to be made related to such issues as these: At what point do you bring your complete argument to the public? When should you highlight publicly available evidence? How do you react when the prosecutor attacks? Which arguments do you counter, and which do you just ignore?

And when you've decided to refute an argument or launch your own, do you bring the story to a single reporter or to several media outlets at the same time? How about the mix between television and print media? When do you begin to enlist bloggers and other social media into your campaign? Where does Twitter fit in? These are the types of high-level, strategic questions that will mean far more to your litigation than mere press releases and media lists. And a skilled public relations practitioner should have the ability to help you find answers to these questions. Ideally, therefore, you want to hire the type of consultant who does this every day—and has done it in a variety of criminal cases—and who understands the nuances of effective litigation communications strategy and planning.

Development of messages and themes: I tell lawyers and their clients that proper messaging is the foundation of every effective public relations program. Even the best media contacts, written materials, and tools of dissemination will not turn a weak argument into a strong one or make a muddled message or theme clear. *Message, then medium* is my mantra.

It has been my experience that criminal lawyers know this better than most other lawyers because in preparing their cases theories and themes are critical. But messaging and themes in the public context can vary considerably from those that are used in the courtroom, and a skilled public relations practitioner at your side can refine your courtroom messages in a manner that will help them resonate fully with the broader public.

For example, some of your pretrial arguments will be tailored to persuade one specific audience: the judge to whom your case has been assigned. Such messages may resonate with broader audiences as well, but likely not. Indeed, some may actually turn off media and public audiences without proper refinement for context and "big-picture" applicability. A skilled public relations consultant will be adept at tailoring arguments made in the courtroom to broader audiences who may ultimately have as great—or a greater—an impact on the ultimate disposition of the case.

Press releases and other written materials: Again, the foundational aspects of litigation communications work—strategy, messages and themes, and so on—are critical to public relations during criminal proceedings, but do not underestimate the importance of proper materials in summarizing your case. Public relations specialists can create materials that are sharp, coherent, and—perhaps most critically—perfectly targeted to media and other nonlegal audiences (we'll talk about what reporters really need further along in the chapter). Lawyers who spend most of their day writing may feel that a press release is just another document to be written for the case, no different than any motion or brief. But this is not really true, and a good public relations writer will create material in support of your case—including press releases but also written statements, case summaries, and media briefs—in a manner that meets the needs of the media in question.

What are the differences between good legal writing and good public relations writing? Well, here's just one: Lawyers are trained to build arguments, point by point, to an inescapable conclusion. There is an assumption that your audience will stick with you, page by page (pulled along by the strength of your prose and the cogency of your argument), until they fully understand the argument you are making and why you are right and the other side is wrong. Public relations writing is the opposite. To be effective, media materials are written in journalistic style—most significantly with reliance on the "inverted pyramid" model: *who, what, where, when* and *why* up top, with details supporting your conclusion following, generally in descending order of importance.[2] This is the way reporters write, and it is the way they read and think as well. I always assume I have about five seconds or so of reporters or producers' time before they make a decision about the strength of my clients' argument and their case. If I haven't sold them by then, I've probably lost them. Even the most skilled writers among practicing lawyers sometimes have difficulties adapting their style to the vagaries of the media mind.

Rapid response: Legal matters can unfold over months and years, but some of the individual events—an arrest, a raid at a client's offices, a hastily called press conference to reveal newly discovered evidence—can literally explode onto the scene, leaving both your legal and communications strategies in disarray. Public relations practitioners with experience in crisis communications and crisis response will have developed what I call a *rapid response* component to their work to allow for immediate coordination of effective communications responses. Some of the elements of this can include pre-event scenario planning that ensures that lawyer and client are adequately prepared for common eventualities; a crisis alert mechanism to bring the appropriate members of a team together at a moment's notice; and a secure, virtual war room for the transmission of appropriate documents and exchange of information from far-flung locations. Most good legal public relations practitioners will be skilled at rapid response, but it makes sense to ensure that this is a real part of their tool kit before retention.

Websites and social media: It is becoming increasingly common for criminal defendants in high-profile cases to develop websites supportive of their cause. This can be done either directly through their

---

2. *Inverted Pyramid*, Wikipedia, http://www.poynter.org/how-tos/newsgathering-storytelling/chip-on-your-shoulder/12754/writing-from-the-top-down-pros-and-cons-of-the-inverted-pyramid/ (visited by the author 6/21/2013).

legal counsel or by so-called "third parties" who are enlisted to help make the defendant's case in the public arena. One of the first to do this was Martha Stewart, whose website went live just after her indictment in 2003.[3] More recent examples include Mark Cuban, billionaire businessman and owner of the NBA's Dallas Mavericks, who pressed his case quite publicly—including by blogging about it—when faced with SEC allegations of insider trading;[4] and Rajat Gupta, former director of Goldman Sachs and head of consulting giant McKinsey, who lined up some well-heeled friends to fight back in 2012 against charges of insider trading by launching a website entitled friendsofrajat.com. According to an article discussing the site, "the roster of endorsers reads like a guest list from the World Economic Forum's annual meeting in Davos, Switzerland, which Gupta once frequented."[5] George Zimmerman, the defendant in the Trayvon Martin murder trial in Florida that had made news throughout 2012, also launched his own website shortly before his indictment that, among other things, raised more than $200,000 online to support his defense.[6]

Let's face it: Such tactics may not work for everyone or for every case that comes your way. But a skilled public relations counselor can assist in the risk assessment surrounding so high profile a tactic. A PR firm will also have the technical design and communications skills needed to prepare a website that helps further your communications message.

So, too, in the area of social media—including Facebook, Twitter, and the like—which are just now coming into their own as communications vehicles. Counsel might think the use of such media to convey litigation communications messages is far-fetched and perhaps overreaching for any legitimate lawyer to consider. But please remember

3. *See, e.g.*, Constance L. Hays, *Martha Stewart Uses Web to Tell Her Side of Story*, N.Y. Times, June 6, 2003, http://www.nytimes.com/2003/06/06/business/the-media-business-advertising-martha-stewart-uses-web-to-tell-her-side-of-story.html.

4. Amir Efrati, *SEC's Insider Trading Suit Against Mark Cuban Is Dismissed*, Wall Street Journal, July 17, 2009, http://blogs.wsj.com/law/2009/07/17/secs-insider-trading-suit-against-mark-cuban-is-dismissed/.

5. Patricia Hurado, *Gupta's Davos-Worthy Friends Praise 'Other Rajat' Online*, Business Week, May 25, 2012, http://www.businessweek.com/news/2012-05-21/gupta-s-davos-worthy-friends-praise-other-rajat-online.

6. Hayley Tsukayama, *George Zimmerman raised just over $200K online, lawyer says*, Washington Post, Apr. 27, 2012, http://www.washingtonpost.com/business/technology/george-zimmerman-raised-200k-online-lawyer-says/2012/04/27/gIQApX4hlT_story.html.

that we were saying the same thing 10 years ago about websites and the same thing twenty years ago about animation and other cutting-edge graphics presentation in the courtroom. Times change, and technology along with it. PR practitioners with their fingers on the pulse of new media technologies can give lawyers a key advantage in communicating effectively in the crowded informational marketplace of the modern age.

One final value a public relations practitioner or firm can bring to your criminal case: Time! That is, the time to devote to these activities in order to make your communications program a success. As I've said, public relations techniques are not as simple as just jotting off a press release in your spare time or calling a reporter back when all the "real" work is done at the end of the day. In high-profile court cases, communications is not an add-on or an afterthought. It can sometimes be central to the overall case, a key component of the defense of an individual or organization. As I often say, effective communications during high-profile litigation is not the "icing on the cake" —in many cases, it *is* the cake.

Consider the comments of Joseph Cheshire of Cheshire Parker Schneider Bryan & Vitale of Raleigh, North Carolina, one of the lead lawyers in the Duke lacrosse rape case that unfolded in 2006–2007. In an interview, he stated that part of the reason they were able to stem the media feeding frenzy that had already convicted their clients in the public eye was through sheer hard work in bringing the media over to their side.

"It took an enormous amount of work to get [the media] to turn," Cheshire said, adding that at the height of the case he was working "four or five" hours a day solely on media relations activities.

"Most of the other lawyers were very hesitant to take on the media," Cheshire said, "but I thought it was critical and believe it was a big reason we were ultimately successful."[7]

To do the job well in high-profile litigation takes an enormous amount of time—including strategy, messaging, media relations, and preparing to counteract the arguments of the other side. Even counsel as skilled at litigation communications as any public relations counselor in his or her area would be wise to consider supplementing their activities with additional resources, lest the core of the client's criminal defense suffer.

Public Attention Has Changed the Way Prosecutors Do Their Jobs

So why is all this important now? It is important to understand that the ways prosecutors use media to persuade have changed considerably over the past few decades. Indeed, there may actually have been a time when prosecutors and regulators didn't regularly use the media to leak evidence, poison jury pools, or otherwise use the court of public opinion to coerce a guilty plea. Older criminal defense lawyers tell me they remember a time when criminal prosecutors, although always self-promotional, kept the bulk of their real fighting to the courtroom rather than to the courthouse steps.

Renowned defense lawyer Theodore "Ted" Wells, for example, cohead of the litigation practice at powerhouse New York law firm Paul Weiss Rifkind Wharton & Garrsison, highlighted the change as follows:

> Someone should go back twenty, twenty-five years, and review prosecutors' indictments over that time. What they'd find is that today's indictments have become little more than press releases with legal cap-

---

7. James F. Haggerty, In the Court of Public Opinion: Winning Strategies for Litigation Communications 262 (2d ed. 2009). To be fair, in my 2009 interview with Cheshire, he had little good to say about the public relations firm he worked with at the time:

> The public relations folks we worked with didn't have a clue . . . . It's like they were living in the 1950s. Their advice was always to not say anything . . . . Most PR-types engage in corporate-speak that doesn't seem to have any relationship to what I do for my clients. Criminal law and litigation is not rocket science, but there is an awful lot of psychology involved.

> *Id.* at 264.

His criticisms may well be valid, but they appear to reflect the particular public relations advice he was receiving, which was from a large international public relations firm that was perhaps more comfortable dealing with large corporations than individual criminal defendants and their counsel, which is important to consider as well when contemplating the type of public relations firm or practitioner to add to your team.

tions. Twenty-five years ago, an indictment was legal document. You read an indictment these days—that's the prosecution's press release right there. It has a huge negative impact on a defendant's ability to get a fair trial.[8]

In addition, prosecutors have a distinct advantage that even the flashiest of plaintiffs lawyers do not: the imprimatur of governmental authority. This sometimes brings credence to even the most wild-eyed accusations against your client or clients—allegations without even a scintilla of evidence to back them up. Consider this recent exchange I had with a reporter regarding such a dubious government indictment:

> "You have to understand that the government says there are thousands of instances of fraud in that complaint, but they only document a dozen or so instances," I said. "How can you print *thousands*?"
>
> "This is an official legal document," the reporter replied. "If the government didn't have some basis for believing it, they wouldn't have put it in there."
>
> "But if a private lawyer made such an unsupported statement in a complaint, with absolutely nothing to back it up, you'd see right through it."
>
> "Yes, but prosecutors have to hold themselves to a higher standard."

This is exactly the problem. There is this vestigial notion that prosecutors are working on the truth. In my experience, they may want the truth, but they also sometimes want (a) to please their constituencies, (b) to further their careers, and (c) headlines that make defendants rush to accept a plea.

Is this cynical? Perhaps. But in this media age, there are practical impacts of the court of public opinion on the judicial system that are just

8. James F. Haggerty, In the Court of Public Opinion: Winning Strategies for Litigation Communications 275 (2d ed. 2009). *Id.* at 275.

too big to be ignored. The most important is this: The primary mission of prosecutors appears in certain cases to be to make sure they are not perceived as taking the *wrong* action in response to a set of facts presented to them. It doesn't necessarily mean they are looking to take the *right* action. And that's a big difference.

Hence the increasing need for a qualified resource at your disposal when your case is clearly going to play out in the court of public opinion as well as in a court of law.

What *Not* to Look For in a Public Relations Consultant

We've looked at some of the skills that an effective outside public relations consultant can bring to a lawyer facing high-profile litigation. Now let's consider what you shouldn't necessarily look for. Given the lack of professional credentials and the diverse nature of the work, there are many misconceptions that have developed about what PR is and what it isn't. Some people think that public relations is all parties and products, or representing celebrities and athletes, or political consulting. These are subspecialties to be sure, but they don't necessarily have anything to do with the type of public relations expertise you need to help you with your case.

Some things to consider in this regard are the following:

1. The myth of contacts

I know a lot of reporters, particularly those who cover the legal beat. I can tell you one thing though: They all hang up on me if I don't have a story to tell.

I call this the "myth of contacts," or "who do you know" syndrome. A lawyer looking to hire my firm will say, "Just get me in front of a reporter you know. I'll know what to say when I get there." Bad idea.

Some PR practitioners are all too willing to play to this erroneous notion that somehow contacts are what make the difference. They do not. Contacts are fine (and I must confess that after more than 20 years doing this kind of work my contacts are likely among the best in the industry), but—as discussed above—it is the *message* that lies at the foundation of any good litigation communications campaign. If my client doesn't have your story down tight, the best contacts in the world aren't going to help me. Conversely, if I have a good enough story to tell, I can get it in front of any reporter in the country.

So, look for the ability of your outside public relations consultant to package messages and themes that will resonate with your target audience(s). Then, worry about the types of contacts that will help get you there.

2. Public relations as solely being press releases

Another point that lawyers should understand when working with public relations practitioners during court cases is that PR is not solely about press releases.

Unfortunately, the perception of public relations—and the training offered at many schools (and, indeed, on the job at many PR firms) —feeds into this erroneous sense of what effective public relations support is in the legal context. Indeed, there is a type of public relations practice that I call the "Lather, Rinse, Repeat," in which all PR assignments are handled as follows:

1. Write the press release.
2. Prepare the media list.
3. Send the press release to the media.
4. Repeat steps one through three.

Unless you are publicizing a simple product like shampoo, it usually doesn't work that well, and communications during court proceedings is definitely not simple.

In fact, these sorts of cookie-cutter tactics often do more harm than good by sending the *wrong* message to the *wrong* audience at the *wrong* time. Reporters feel they are getting a sales pitch, so they react the way everyone reacts when getting a sales pitch: Their eyes glaze over, and they look elsewhere for news about a particular case.

Focusing On Media Needs

So mass-produced, cookie-cutter press releases don't usually work in court cases. So what skills should your outside consultant have?

When communicating with the media about your dispute, it is vitally important that lawyers and their consultants work backward from what the media really needs rather than forward from what you want to give them. This is so important a concept that it requires further elaboration, in the interest of ensuring that both lawyer and retained consultant are on the same wavelength.

In any story, but particularly in a legal story, there is an enormous amount of information. All of it may be relevant to you, your client, and to the court, but much of it will be entirely irrelevant to the media with which you're attempting to communicate. Conversely, you'll find that many reporters are more interested in elements of a legal case that you find mundane or off point. This is particularly true in legal disputes in which you are usually dealing with reams of facts and legal theories that need to be "distilled" for a reporter who has 500 to 1,000 words to write a story or—if we're talking television—three minutes for a news segment.

So rather than focusing on contacts and press releases, your outside media consultant should be working with you to develop a laserlike focus on giving reporters what they want, not what you think they should want. This is often a hard point for a practicing lawyer to understand. In most cases, the parties and their lawyers not only want to give reporters what is needed to write the story, they want to convert them to their cause. I can't tell you how many times I've spoken to the legal team or to the parties and have heard something like, "If I just lay out all the case documents in front of the reporter, I'm sure they'll see how right we are in this dispute."

Perhaps, but at an elemental level, this reflects a misunderstanding of the role a reporter plays as an objective conveyor of the facts of a legal case.

Put simply, on some level, reporters don't care. They don't care about your case, about how your rights have been violated, or about the way the other side has been acting.

Okay, that may be a little harsh. They do care in certain ways. Particularly if you have been wronged, as many parties to criminal proceedings have been. But reporters are also professionals. As professionals, the media (or at least what we used to call the "mainstream" media) attempts to maintain a certain distance from most of the stories it covers. The idea of the crusading reporter, the ardent pursuer of right who is going to take your case and run with it until justice is served . . . . Well, let's just say that that sort of ideal probably never existed, and it certainly doesn't exist today in the era of 24-hour news, the Web, social media, and other sources of information.

So, a threshold in seeking outside public relations help is finding a consultant who truly understands what a reporter wants, and needs. Understanding this is essential to working with the media during the course of a criminal case. Remember that any legal proceeding by its very nature runs counter to the immediacy and brevity of modern communication. It unfurls over months and even years—hardly in keeping with the rhythm of our times. So, knowledge of how to fit this square peg into the round hole of modern media coverage is a key value added that your public relations consultant can bring to the case.

Here are my "threshold" guidelines on what reporters want based on what I've observed of reporters from all manner of media, at all levels, for more than 20 years:

1. Reporters want the truth.
2. They want it now.
3. They want it in a form they can use.

Seems simple, doesn't it? But it is deceptively difficult, particularly as these rules apply in the context of the modern criminal trial.

1. Reporters want the truth

In a world of high-priced spin doctors and focus-grouped media messages, this is a point often forgotten. All reporters want the truth. Which is to say they want to get the story right, and they don't want to be misled.

As you describe your case or legal matter to a reporter, you can usually hear what they're thinking in the tone of their questions. They're thinking, *Are these people leveling with me? What aren't they telling me? Is this the truth or just one version of the truth?* Every reporter's greatest fear is to be duped, to be taken in, convinced of something that turns out not to be the case. So virtually everything reporters do is informed by this interest in getting the story right.

Now, particularly in the context of a legal proceeding during which there can be hundreds (or thousands) of pages of legal filings and thousands (or hundreds of thousands) of documents produced during discovery, there are shades of meaning that can be assigned to facts. But when presenting the "truth" of a story, facts are facts, and if you start playing fast and loose with the facts—and this includes omission of factual elements of your case that are perhaps unfavorable—you risk damaging your entire relationship with the reporter. In other words, bend the truth too much and it breaks. Spin too much, and your reporter will be dizzy. Nothing kills your credibility with the media more than a lie, or even a half-truth.

2. Reporters want it now

Even in the most contentious of legal disputes, I often confront circumstances similar to the following: A reporter calls my office, let's say around 10:15 a.m., regarding a particular case. I am on the phone with the legal team by 10:30.

We quickly review what the reporter is looking for and the main message points we want to get into the resulting coverage.

Confident in our response, I give the lawyer the reporter's number.

"So you'll call her," I say.

"I'll call her right now."

At 3:30 p.m., I receive another call from the reporter; the lawyer hasn't gotten around to calling back yet.

Here's the point: Reporters work on a very different schedule than you or me. Calling the reporter back immediately, therefore, is imperative. Now means now.

Lawyers, of course, often work on a far different timetable. Responses to pleadings, for example, are usually due in days or weeks. This mindset begins to affect the way they respond to telephone calls, including calls from the media. So much so that attorneys sometimes pledge on their websites and in their promotional materials that "all calls will be returned within 24 hours."

In the media world—particularly with the advent of the Internet and social media—24 hours is a lifetime. Reporters have deadlines, and, in the age of the Internet, that deadline is usually "as soon as I can post the story."

But some lawyers ask me, "Why don't they just read everything I send them, if they really want to do their job right? Are they lazy?" Well, some of them are lazy, I suppose, just like some lawyers are lazy. But think for a moment about the job reporters have to do, particularly when reporting on complex legal matters. They have to take information contained in a 50- or 100-page complaint (or other legal filing or document), find the areas of relevance, get to the heart of the issues at hand, and then condense that information to the 500 or 1,000 words (on average) that will convey the story to their usually nonlegal audience.

And they have to do it instantaneously. Not an easy job. A good public relations consultant working at your side will force you to view the realities of the situation from this perspective. And, as a result, more phone calls will be returned promptly, and more stories will be written with your client's arguments adequately represented.

3. Reporters want it in a form they can use

Building on the above, lawyers just can't expect reporters to read all the legal documents regarding a case. Send along everything you have, but there's no guarantee it will be read. Sometimes I imagine a pile of documents—12 inches thick or more—arriving on a reporter's already-cluttered desk, usually with a terse cover note that says something like, "Per our discussion, enclosed are the documents you requested regarding *Smith v. ABC Corporation*. Please let me know if you have any questions."

This follows the faulty premise that like a judge or opposing counsel reporters are somehow obligated to read what you send them. But it doesn't work that way. The truth of the matter is that reporters need things in a format they can use. Not in 10,000 pages, but in the proverbial 10 words or less. Do not rely on a reporter digesting all of the relevant documents surrounding a case. Again, it's not that they're lazy, unintelligent, or incapable of accurately understanding the nuances of your case. They just don't have the time.

This is not in any way to suggest that clients and their lawyers should hide the actual case documents from a reporter. There is no reason why a reporter shouldn't see everything (and in the age of PACER and other electronic filing systems for federal and state pleadings, they will). But clients and their lawyers should not rely solely on the pleadings and other documents to give reporters information regarding the case. It's just too much detail, too much information. There has to be a distillation of the information so that the reporter can easily come to terms with the key question: "What's the story here?"

How "Level of Immersion" Threatens Effective Communication during Court Cases

Another key reason why external public relations counsel may be useful to your high-profile criminal case is inherent in a communications concept I call "level of immersion." The following will illustrate what I'm talking about.

Imagine you are in the midst of a criminal case that has just been filed. You are back at your desk plowing through legal theory and strategy that will best protect your client's interest. The phone rings and it is an Associated Press reporter. He'd like to ask a few questions. What should you do?

Inevitably, I advise the following: Don't take the call. Refer it to your outside consultant if you have one, or simply take the reporter's name and number, find out what the deadline is, and then call back.

The reason is simple: You need a moment to take a breath and to think about what you're going to say before responding. Whether it's five minutes or five hours, every interview subject needs some time to think about his or her message and how to convey it properly to media covering a case.

Even a lawyer who is the most skilled communicator to the media and other nonlegal audiences often has an "immersion problem"—that is, he or she is at most points in the day hip deep in the complexities of some element of the legal or factual argument that is most pressing. Perhaps preparing for an upcoming hearing, perhaps responding to a subpoena. The phone rings and it's a reporter asking about the case. If the lawyer doesn't take a step back and think about what to say—what the case message really is—he or she is likely to start speaking about the particular issue of the moment, in the same "voice" as in the brief or argument being prepared. In other words, the response will be laden with complexity and great specificity about a very specific element of the case, with the detailed legal arguments foremost in his or her mind at that moment, discussing precedent and the application of precedent to the facts of this particular aspect of the case before the court.

Any core message the legal and communications team has considered regarding the case is out the window.

The ramifications of such immersion should be readily apparent. Reporters need information in a form they can use, and, given the complexity of most legal actions, if you're not prepared with your message before the interview begins, you're doing a grave disservice to the case and ultimately your client. If a lawyer or client is speaking to a reporter the way he or she speaks to a judge or to the other side about a small sliver of the case, the message is likely not getting across. The focus is all wrong.

Hence the need to take a short breather, to coordinate your thoughts, and to refocus your attention on your core message before responding to the reporter's call.

There are a few exercises I use in training lawyers that make this point. Try this one now. Hold a piece of blank white paper up to your eyes about two inches or so away, and stare at it for a full minute. Now lower the paper and stare out across the room.

See how looking at something that closely screws up your focus?

It's the same thing with lawsuits. As a lawyer for a part in a criminal proceeding, you are, figuratively speaking, two inches away from the details of your case all day. It's natural that you need a little decompression—even if it's just a few minutes—before you begin looking at the case from another perspective: that of the media and the general audience for whom the media is writing.

In fact, when training lawyers, I often pull an unsuspecting volunteer from the audience and ask him or her to stand facing the wall (again, about an inch or two away) and tell me what they see.

Depending on the wall, I usually get a response like the following:

> "I see paint . . . I see a few cracks . . . There appears to be a pen mark . . . ."
>
> Then, standing on the other side of the room, I ask, "Now . . . ask me what I see."
>
> "What do you see?"
>
> "I see a wall."

That's the point. Lawyers and their clients are looking at the cracks, the pen marks, and the paint chips. Reporters want to hear about the wall.

Hence the importance of telling the reporter you'll call back, or relying on the perspective of your outside consultant to handle the call and media response. I usually say, "Look, I'm in the middle of something right now. Let me put it aside and call you back. What's your deadline?" This is no lie, by the way. I'm always in the middle of something. I'm sure you are as well. There's nothing devious about this. You just need a moment to put aside what you're doing and focus on the reporter and his or her questions.

Combating "level of immersion" problems is another key value added that a skilled public relations practitioner can bring to your legal team as a criminal case moves forward.

Who do you choose?

So you've made the decision to add a public relations consultant to your legal team. Now it's just a question of who, and at what price.

The prior sections of this chapter were designed to give you a sense of what skills are most valuable to add to your team, by providing a sense of how media work, what they need, and how a skilled PR consultant or public relations firm can bring both strategic and practical expertise to the task(s) at hand.

But there are as many types of public relations firms out there as there are law firms. How do you decide which one to use?

Again, I will start by revealing my own biases: I run a small specialist firm in New York City that deals primarily with litigation and other complex legal crises. We handle both civil and criminal work and operate across the nation (and internationally—we have consulted with clients in Europe, Asia, South America, and Australia, for example). I have been handling high-profile cases for more than 20 years and am also a lawyer who has occasionally handled legal work as well.

Thus, quite naturally, I believe the ideal candidate to provide most public relations services to lawyers in criminal cases should

- specialize in legal issues, litigation, and other forms of crisis communications;
- be small enough to provide the type of senior-level attention that will ensure understanding of the very complex issues and facts that are often presented in modern criminal litigation;
- have a thorough understanding of the law—and perhaps even be lawyers themselves;
- have years of experience with a variety of cases and how they are reported.

Again, however, I am biased. Some of my best competitors practice their trade with some of the largest public relations firms in the nation. But, much like what is said about law firms, you are hiring the PR professional, not the firm, and if you are going to go the big PR firm route, I suggest you confirm that the skilled practitioner you hire is the one who will be assigned to work on your case on a day-to-day basis.

The reality is this, however: The economics of such a retention may not work for many larger public relations firms, who tend to like to push things down to the least experienced account executive possible to handle most of the work. Again, that may work with products and parties, but it most certainly does not work with complex legal communications matters.

So ask the question upfront: Will you, dear counselor, be working on the PR elements of my client's case day in and day out and be my primary contact for this assignment? Any good PR pro has too much business to lie; they'll tell you if they are too busy to bring senior-level attention to your case because, presumably, their dance card is quite full to begin with. In other words, work with someone who doesn't need the work, but rather *wants* the work, and is configured to provide the kind of senior-level attention to your case that will do it justice.

One other point regarding specialization: For all the reasons described in this chapter, communication during legal proceedings is very different from other forms of public relations, so whomever you choose, make sure they are skilled and adept at working on legal issues on a day-to-day basis. You simply can't have a PR pro at your side who is handling a product launch on Monday, a real estate opening on Tuesday, and a high-profile lawsuit on Wednesday. The skill set is just not transferable, any more than a corporate lawyers' skills are transferable to criminal defense work. So regardless of the size of the firm, look hard to ensure that you choose a public relations consultant whose experience, skills, temperament, and interest match the proceedings at hand.

How much should it cost?

> The first thing I ask a new client is "Have you been saving up for a rainy day? Guess what? It's raining." —Richard Gere as a criminal defense lawyer in the 1996 movie *Primal Fear*

Ah, there's the rub. Assuming a legitimately skilled litigation public relations consultant can be found for your upcoming high-profile criminal case, who wouldn't want his or her assistance? It is cost that is the issue, particularly in cases in which most criminal defendants can barely afford the legal team and experts needed to mount an adequate defense.

And public relations fees in the heat of a high-profile court case can add up quickly. In many instances, PR professionals bill the way lawyers do—in big cities, hourly rates can be upward of $500 or more. Indeed, it is not unheard of in very intense high-profile cases for monthly public relations fees to run in excess of $25,000.

But it's quite less than that in many other cases, and the intensity of the effort tends to ebb and flow with the courtroom action as the case progresses toward trial. Therefore, it is highly advisable to devise a fee structure with your PR firm or consultant that effectively accounts for the unpredictability of litigation and the public attention that various elements of the case will attract.

This ebb and flow and unpredictable nature of litigation can sometimes make it difficult to come up with a fee system that fits into traditional public relations models. Although most public relations fees are theoretically based on time, some firms will charge a flat monthly retainer for a certain level of work for a certain stated period of time. An initial fee of $10,000–$15,000 per month might be a common baseline retention for a smaller PR firm in a mid-level market. In order for such a flat fee retention to work, however, both sides must feel comfortable that they will not be taken advantage of by the other as the intensity of the effort changes as the case progresses.

At my firm, we have attempted to recognize the unpredictable nature of litigation work by being flexible and tailoring our fees accordingly. We tend to bill hourly against an evergreen retainer that must be replenished each month. We require no minimum length of contract or extended notice of cancellation (some PR firms have traditionally required 60 to 90 days notice before ending a retention). We also have no minimum, although in most cases there is a minimum level of fees incurred each month just to stay current on the latest developments in the case and general media interest in similar cases and issues.

This flexibility doesn't necessarily mean we're cheap. We are not a low-end provider by any means, and, when involved in a real firefight, the public relations fees can add up rather quickly. Rather, we aim to be cost effective with our time and our fees to ensure the maximum return on investment in the litigation context.

In the end, I suggest that the best defense counsel can do is negotiate a public relations retention that bears in mind the unpredictable nature of the litigation process and prices the consultant's time and expertise accordingly. Know that it is not cheap to bring on highly qualified consultants, and the work is just too complex and nuanced to bring on an unqualified consultant. But also know that the quantum leap in skills, expertise, and knowledge you will gain by retaining the right consultant will probably save your client money in the long run (and perhaps even his or her reputation and freedom as well).

As to whether it is ultimately worth it, this will likely vary depending on the case and what is at stake. In some criminal cases, the best you can do is sometimes to protest your client's innocence and look forward to vindication in the courtroom. When facing an aggressive opponent, however, one who seems hell-bent on poisoning the jury pool, turning the tide of public opinion against your client, and shattering faith in the impartiality of the criminal justice system, the costs of retaining experienced public relations counsel to bring the fight to the court of public opinion may be the best money a criminal lawyer ever spends.[9]

9. Portions of this chapter originally appeared in James F. Haggerty, In The Court of Public Opinion: Winning Strategies for Litigation Communications (2d ed., 2009).

3

Ethics: Criminal Practice and the Media

BY PETER A. JOY AND KEVIN C. McMUNIGAL

Introduction

Prosecutors and defense lawyers often seek to use the media to shape public opinion and to help their client's causes. Even the alleged victim may retain counsel for advice and help in dealing with the media. Each lawyer attempting to advance a client's position must work within ethical constraints when speaking with and using the media. Courts may also step in and impose legal constraints on the lawyer's use of the media. Both ethics rules and court orders regulating publicity balance the competing values of a fair trial against free speech and the public's right to be informed. Before answering a reporter's questions, calling a press conference, or having other dealings with the media, a lawyer should know the ethical boundaries as well as the potential risks and benefits to the client.

This chapter discusses the history and current contours of ethics rules concerning public comment by lawyers. It addresses press conferences and speaking with the media, media access to clients, and media deals. It also identifies areas of ambiguity in the ethics rules regulating lawyers advocating in the court of public opinion where lawyers need to proceed with caution. To help illustrate some of these issues, we begin with some examples of the ways lawyers have used the media in recent years.

Uses of the Media

Media scrutiny of criminal trials is commonplace. Local newspapers and television news programs frequently feature stories about criminal trials, and local news reporters often ask prosecutors and defense lawyers to comment on cases. National newspapers and television give extensive coverage to charges against such high-profile personalities as Dominique Strauss-Kahn and Martha Stewart, as well as to cases against those accused of terrible crimes, such as Jeffrey Dahmer. Television, through TruTV (formerly Court TV), provides coverage and commentary on criminal trials of more obscure defendants whose trials never make the nightly news. Occasionally, the media propels a defendant, such as Casey Anthony, into national and international news.

In the 2011 case against Dominique Strauss-Kahn, the prosecution, the defense, and a lawyer for the alleged victim all called press conferences. The defense employed public relations consultants. Undisclosed sources close to the police investigation leaked information to the press that was at first highly damaging to Strauss-Kahn and later cast doubt on the credibility of his accuser. The lawyers involved actively engaged with the media to shape public opinion—they sought to try the case in the press.

In addition to press conferences and speaking with the press, media campaigns to protect public images and fend off criminal liability are becoming increasingly popular. Martha Stewart, for example, agreed to be interviewed on television and created a website providing information about her trial. The accounting and consulting firm Arthur Andersen used a website as well as newspaper advertisements to counter prosecution charges of wrongdoing. The firm even posted a background paper prepared by its lawyers asserting "factual and legal errors" in the government's case.[1] Richard Scrushy, former CEO of HealthSouth, not only had a website entitled "News Source: Setting the Record Straight" on which he frequently posted statements by his trial counsel, he was a frequent guest on radio talk shows and cohosted with his wife a weekly

1. The paper was inaccurate and misleading on a number of points. Kathleen F. Brickey, *Andersen's Fall From Grace*, 81 Wash. U. L.Q. 917 (2003).

television program called "Viewpoint" in Birmingham, Alabama, where he faced trial. In other instances, clients and their lawyers have allowed the media access to case preparations and discussions of defense strategies before trial.

Potential Benefits and Risks of Engaging with the Media

Criminal defense lawyers regularly warn clients against discussing their cases with anyone other than their lawyer. Why do some clients under criminal investigation or who are criminally charged and their lawyers reject this conventional wisdom and choose to engage with the media?

Potential Benefits

Engagement by the lawyer or the client with the media may produce a number of potential benefits. One is reducing damage to the client's personal and professional reputation. Being criminally charged with, or even investigated for, criminal activity can have a devastating impact on a client's reputation, even if the client is ultimately acquitted. For this reason, a client may believe that the best defense is to go on the offense—at least when it comes to how the media portrays the client.

Our criminal justice system presumes innocence, but human beings rarely do. Many reason that someone being investigated for or charged with a crime is probably guilty. Such an inference is especially likely if the person charged makes no public denial of guilt. A client's silence in the face of accusation or even suspicion of a crime is likely to be viewed as a tacit admission of guilt. If the client has a high profile, that fact is likely to compound the instinct to respond publicly in the face of public suspicion or accusation.

Engagement with the media through a press conference or a media campaign might produce a number of other rewards directly connected to the outcome of the case. If it succeeds in generating public sympathy for the client during an investigation, it might help convince a prosecutor not to seek a charge, grand jurors not to indict, or a preliminary hearing judge not to bind the client over for trial. If the prosecutor does seek a charge, public sympathy might influence the prosecutor to seek a lesser charge than he or she might have pursued otherwise.

If the client is charged, publicity might produce postcharge benefits as well. The publicity and public reaction to it, such as public skepticism about the factual or legal basis of or the motivation behind the prosecution, might influence the prosecutor to be more generous in guilty plea negotiations than he or she might be otherwise. Despite judicial efforts to insulate jurors from publicity prior to and during trial, statements made by the defense might nonetheless influence jurors to be inclined toward the client and against the government. Finally, such publicity and any public sympathy it generates might influence the trial judge to be more favorable to the client in rulings made prior to, during, and after the trial as well as more lenient at sentencing.

Risks

Despite the potential rewards engagement with the media might produce, such a campaign also poses serious risks, many of which are not intuitively obvious, especially to one not trained in law or experienced in criminal litigation. Criminal defense lawyers have good reasons for routinely counseling clients to avoid making statements, especially public statements, about a pending case. If the client is used to dealing successfully with the media and the public, it may be difficult for the client to fully appreciate these risks.

One risk is that a press conference or media campaign might generate negative rather positive reactions to the client by the public, victim, prosecutor, judge, or jury. A client or a client's spokesperson might, for example, come across as evasive or arrogant in an interview or press conference. The prosecutor and trial judge might resent what they may view as an inappropriate attempt to manipulate the legal system in favor of a client with the resources to conduct a media campaign. In addition to the risk of generating unsympathetic reactions, public statements by a client might reveal confidential information and tip off the prosecutor to the defense's trial strategy. Public statements by the defense might also prompt negative statements by the prosecution or the victim.

Public statements aimed at influencing an ongoing investigation or upcoming trial may be made prior to the client and defense counsel being fully informed of the strengths and weaknesses of the prosecution's case. If the case is still in the investigative stage, even the general contours of the potential charges may be unclear. The defense's own investigative efforts may be far from complete. Even after charging, the full strengths and weaknesses of the government's proof may not be known until its witnesses testify at trial. The restricted nature of criminal discovery in many jurisdictions exacerbates this uncertainty for defense counsel. In the federal system and in a majority of state systems, for example, prosecution witnesses are not normally deposed prior to trial. Nor will they typically testify at a preliminary hearing, which federal prosecutors and many state prosecutors routinely avoid by using a grand jury to indict.

A press conference or media campaign that addresses the factual and legal dimensions of prospective or pending charges thus may require client and counsel to take strategic positions based on imperfect information. The dilemma of making a strategic decision on imperfect information is a common one for defense lawyers, though one they typically seek to avoid. Take, for example, a decision about whether or not to rely in an opening statement on self-defense in a homicide case. Making the factual concessions implicit in reliance on self-defense—that is, that the client killed the victim and did so with purpose regarding the death—at the outset of trial would prove to be a strategic error if the prosecution was unable at trial to establish convincingly that the client was the killer. Defense counsel might seek to mitigate the dilemma of choosing a strategic position based on imperfect information by delaying the defense opening statement until after the prosecution witnesses have testified and have been cross-examined. In short, the defense might delay the strategic decision about reliance on self-defense until more information is available. An early media campaign, by contrast, does just the opposite. It exacerbates this dilemma for the defense by pressuring counsel and client to commit to a strategic position, such as reliance on self-defense, much earlier than the start of the trial, at a time during which the defense typically has even less information than it does at the beginning of trial.

Concessions, False Exculpatory Statements, Prior Inconsistent Statements

Statements based on imperfect information made by a client, a public relations spokesperson, or even by the client's lawyer may prove helpful to the prosecution in a number of ways. First, a statement might concede, either purposefully or inadvertently, a factual issue the prosecution might have difficulty proving without the statement. A media campaign aimed at establishing that a client acted justifiably in self-defense in shooting someone, for example, might include a statement conceding that the client was the shooter while the government might have difficulty proving that point. Such a statement by a client qualifies as a personal admission under the law of hearsay.

Statements that do not concede any factual issues the prosecution seeks to prove may be useful to the prosecution in other ways. If a client says something in a press conference or media interview that later turns out to be false, such as an alibi or a denial that the client was acquainted with the victim of a rape or homicide, the statement can later be introduced as a false exculpatory statement showing consciousness of guilt, even if the client never testifies and the defense concedes the truth at trial.

If the client takes the stand at trial, the prosecutor may use client statements made during a media campaign for impeachment as prior inconsistent statements. The prosecutor may use inconsistency or even the appearance of inconsistency between testimony at trial and a prior statement made during a media campaign to great advantage during cross-examination. If the potential damage to the client's credibility from a prior inconsistent statement is severe enough, it may even discourage the client from testifying.

Disqualification of Counsel

Another risk arises if defense counsel makes statements during a press conference or media campaign. Such statements qualify as authorized admissions under the hearsay rule. If such a statement by defense counsel is sought to be introduced at trial by the prosecution as an authorized admission, the prosecution might also seek to have defense counsel disqualified under the advocate witness rule.

Returning to the self-defense example previously considered, imagine that defense counsel at a press conference conceded that the client had shot the victim but that the client did so in self-defense. Imagine also that by the time of trial, due to the granting of a pretrial suppression motion and the discovery of some serious credibility problems on the part of prosecution witnesses, the defense at trial wishes to contest the government's proof that the client was the shooter. The prosecution might well attempt both (1) to introduce defense counsel's press conference admission that the client shot the victim and (2) to disqualify defense counsel under the advocate witness rule.

Current Model Rule 3.6 and Its History

Of the ethics rules that bear on a lawyer's interactions with the media, none is more significant than Model Rule 3.6 and its state counterparts. It is the logical starting point for understanding how ethics rules restrict lawyers in dealing with the media.

To understand current Model Rule 3.6, it helps to know a bit of its history. Two Supreme Court cases, *Sheppard v. Maxwell*[2] and *Gentile v. State Bar of Nevada*,[3] figure prominently in that history. The facts in these cases shed light on the policy objectives of MR 3.6 and the meaning of its specific provisions. We highly recommend reading both cases.

In *Sheppard*, the Supreme Court considered Dr. Sam Sheppard's habeas corpus petition challenging the constitutionality of his murder conviction for the bludgeoning death of his pregnant wife. The case caused a national media sensation and inspired both a television series[4] and a movie.[5] In the words of Justice Clark, "bedlam reigned at the courthouse."

The Supreme Court granted Sheppard's habeas petition, finding that the trial judge's failure to protect Sheppard from "massive, pervasive and prejudicial publicity" denied Sheppard a fair trial. The Court stated that "[c]ollaboration between *counsel and the press* as to information affecting the fairness of a criminal trial is not only *subject to regulation*, but is *highly*

2. 384 U.S. 333 (1966).
3. 501 U.S. 1030 (1991).
4. The Fugitive (United Artists Television 1963–1967).
5. The Fugitive (Warner Bros. 1993)

censurable and worthy of discipline."[6] The Court listed the most egregious public statements made during the *Sheppard* trial, such as those regarding Sheppard's refusal to take a lie detector test, the identity of prospective witnesses and their probable testimony, and allegations never proven at trial. The reversal of Sheppard's conviction along with the Court's admonition that statements by counsel were "worthy of discipline" prompted the ABA to include in its 1969 Model Code an ethics rule explicitly aimed at curtailing trial publicity generated by lawyers.[7] That rule, the precursor of MR 3.6, contained a list of prohibited statements paralleling the *Sheppard* Court's list of egregious statements. Comment [5] to MR 3.6 currently contains that same list.

Twenty-five years later in *Gentile*, the Court for the first time reviewed the constitutionality of the ethics rule it had nudged the bar to adopt in *Sheppard*. Gentile, a prominent Nevada criminal defense lawyer, represented a client under investigation. During the investigation, the police provided the press with a great deal of information damaging to Gentile's client. Six months prior to trial, Gentile held a press conference to respond to the negative publicity. His client was acquitted at trial, but the Nevada Bar disciplined Gentile under Nevada's version of MR 3.6 for the press conference. The Supreme Court upheld the constitutionality of bar disciplinary rules curtailing lawyer trial publicity. It also upheld the constitutionality of the risk formula at the heart of MR 3.6—its "substantial likelihood" test. It nonetheless overturned the Nevada Bar's discipline of Gentile, finding that parts of MR 3.6 that have since been changed were impermissibly vague.

A quick look at the architecture of Model Rule 3.6 reveals four components: (1) a rule, (2) a list of illustrations, (3) an exception, and (4) a provision extending the rule to all lawyers associated in a firm or office. We address each in detail.

Section (a): The Basic Rule

MR 3.6(a) sets forth MR 3.6's foundational rule:

---

6. 384 U.S. 363 (emphasis added).

7. The rule the ABA adopted was ABA Code of Professional Responsibility DR 7-107 (1969).

> (a) A lawyer who is participating or has participated in the investigation or litigation of a matter shall not make an extrajudicial statement that the lawyer knows or reasonably should know will be disseminated by means of public communication and will have a substantial likelihood of materially prejudicing an adjudicative proceeding in the matter.

Substantial risk. A key feature of Section (a) is its "substantial likelihood" formula. The rule prohibits only statements that create "a substantial likelihood" of material prejudice. Prior to *Gentile*, this aspect of MR 3.6 was a focal point of debate over its constitutionality. The defense argued in *Gentile* that this standard was too restrictive of free speech, that the First Amendment demanded that lawyer speech be curtailed only when it created a higher risk, a "clear and present danger" of prejudicing the proceeding. The *Gentile* court rejected this argument and approved the "substantial likelihood" formula.

Adjudicative proceeding. Criminal cases involving jury trials, such as the O.J. Simpson and Casey Anthony cases, often attract media attention. Accordingly, such cases may come most readily to mind when discussing the dangers of trial publicity. But MR 3.6 is not limited to criminal cases. Nor is it limited to cases involving jury trials. The language of MR 3.6—"adjudicative proceeding" —makes this clear, as does Comment [6], which states that MR 3.6 places limitations on civil trials, nonjury hearings, and even arbitration proceedings. Whether the case is criminal or civil and whether the fact finder is a judge or jury, though, are factors taken into account in assessing the risk of prejudice, with criminal jury trials being treated as the "most sensitive to extrajudicial speech."

Participating lawyers. MR 3.6(a) restricts only lawyers who have participated or are participating in the investigation or litigation of a case. Accordingly, the legal experts whom cable news programs so often feature do not fall under the rule, even though their statements in some cases might create a risk of prejudicing a trial by, for example, discussing inadmissible evidence or expressing an opinion about a defendant's guilt. Despite this restriction in Section (a), the vicarious liability component of MR 3.6, found in Section (d), makes the rule applicable to lawyers associated with participating lawyers even though those lawyers may not personally have participated in the investigation or trial of a case.

Extrajudicial statements. MR 3.6 applies only to extrajudicial statements. It does not apply to oral statements made in open court or to written statements made in court filings, even though the press may be present in court and have access to the filings.

Although the contours of MR 3.6, as described in the previous paragraph, appear fairly straightforward at first glance, the rule does pose practical challenges for a lawyer interacting with the media. Comment [5], for example, lists "any opinion as to the guilt or innocence of a defendant" as a statement that is "more likely than not to have a material prejudicial effect . . . ." A lawyer pressed in an interview or press conference with questions about the client's guilt may, for example, find it difficult not to express his or her opinion that the client is innocent. What if a reporter asks the lawyer publicly, "Do you think your client is innocent?"

MR 3.6 also presents interpretative challenges. One is the task of assessing under MR 3.6(a) whether or not a particular statement will have a substantial likelihood of creating material prejudice. Another is whether under MR 3.6(c) a lawyer's public reply to a prior public statement is required to protect a client from substantial undue prejudice. Terms such as *substantial, material*, and *undue* may require fine judgments by the lawyer concerning issues of degree, judgments with which later disciplinary authorities may disagree.

Section (b): The Permitted List

MR 3.6(b) gives a list of illustrations of typically permitted statements—ones that will not ordinarily violate Section (a). These are fairly straightforward and include

> (1) the claim, offense or defense involved and, except when prohibited by law, the identity of the persons involved;
> (2) information contained in a public record;
> (3) that an investigation of a matter is in progress;

(4) the scheduling or result of any step in litigation;
(5) a request for assistance in obtaining evidence and information necessary thereto;
(6) a warning of danger concerning the behavior of a person involved, when there is reason to believe that there exists the likelihood of substantial harm to an individual or to the public interest; and
(7) in a criminal case, in addition to subparagraphs (1) through (6):

(i) the identity, residence, occupation and family status of the accused;
(ii) if the accused has not been apprehended, information necessary to aid in apprehension of that person;
(iii) the fact, time and place of arrest; and
(iv) the identity of investigating and arresting officers or agencies and the length of the investigation.

Comment [5]: The Impermissible List

Comment [5] sets forth the following list of impermissible topics that contrasts with Section (b)'s list of permissible topics:

(1) the character, credibility, reputation or criminal record of a party, suspect in a criminal investigation or witness, or the identity of a witness, or the expected testimony of a party or witness;
(2) in a criminal case or proceeding that could result in incarceration, the possibility of a plea of guilty to the offense or the existence or contents of any confession, admission, or statement given by a defendant or suspect or that person's refusal or failure to make a statement;
(3) the performance or results of any examination or test or the refusal or failure of a person to submit to an examination or test, or the identity or nature of physical evidence expected to be presented;
(4) any opinion as to the guilt or innocence of a defendant or suspect in a criminal case or proceeding that could result in incarceration;
(5) information that the lawyer knows or reasonably should know is

> likely to be inadmissible as evidence in a trial and that would, if disclosed, create a substantial risk of prejudicing an impartial trial; or (6) the fact that a defendant has been charged with a crime, unless there is included therein a statement explaining that the charge is merely an accusation and that the defendant is presumed innocent until and unless proven guilty.

The two "do's" and "don'ts" lists found in Section (b) and Comment [5] have a sort of symmetry. Together they provide concrete details that help lawyers discern where Section (a) draws the line between permissible and impermissible statements.

Comment [5]'s impermissible list tracks the list of egregious statements in the *Sheppard* case. It is a "laundry list" of problematic publicity from that case. The statements in the *Sheppard* case that inspired the Comment [5] list are useful in remembering and understanding that list. Comment [5], for example, includes a statement likely to be prejudicial about "the refusal or failure of a person to submit to an examination or test." In *Sheppard*, the press publicized Dr. Sheppard's refusal to take a lie detector test and treated that refusal as indicative of his guilt. Comment [5] also lists statements typically impermissible about "information . . . likely to be inadmissible at trial." In *Sheppard*, the press publicized a number of allegations that in Justice Clark's words were "never heard from the witness stand." These included claims that Sheppard had purposely impeded the investigation and that his wife had called him a "Jekyll-Hyde" and "a barefaced liar." Two jurors in the case admitted to having heard that "a prison inmate claimed Sheppard as the father of her illegitimate child," though no evidence of that was admitted at trial.

Section (c): The "Fair Reply" Exception

Section (c) of MR 3.6 creates what may be called its "fair reply" exception, the only exception found in MR 3.6. It provides the following:

> (c) Notwithstanding paragraph (a), a lawyer may make a statement that a reasonable lawyer would believe is required to protect a cli-

> ent from the substantial undue prejudicial effect of recent publicity not initiated by the lawyer or the lawyer's client. A statement made pursuant to this paragraph shall be limited to such information as is necessary to mitigate the recent adverse publicity.

The fair reply exception does not limit a lawyer to responding to publicity generated by an opposing lawyer or client. Negative publicity from a third party, such as a newspaper or television news program, can trigger the exception.

There are two important limitations on this right of fair reply. The first is a sort of contributory fault or "unclean hands" component. The text of Section (d) states that neither the lawyer using it nor his or her client can have initiated the publicity. Comment [7] adds another limitation: A lawyer using the fair reply exception is limited to attempting to redress prior negative publicity. In the words of Comment [7], a "responsive statement" should "contain only such information as is necessary to mitigate undue prejudice created by the statements of others."

Section (d): Other Lawyers in a Firm or Office

Section (d) of MR 3.6 addresses application of the rule to lawyers in a firm or government agency who are not personally involved in a case. It states the following:

> No lawyer associated in a firm or government agency with a lawyer subject to paragraph (a) shall make a statement prohibited by paragraph (a).

Section (d) thus eliminates the possibility that a lawyer might evade MR 3.6's restrictions by having another lawyer in his or her office or firm make public statements prohibited by Section (a). One might plausibly view statements made by lawyers not participating in a trial as less prejudicial than those made by participating lawyers because the press and public may treat such statements as less credible and authoritative than those made by participating lawyers. MR 3.6(d) clearly rejects this view.

Imputed disqualification is commonly associated with conflict of interest. MR 1.10 provides that "[w]hile lawyers are associated in a firm, none of them shall knowingly represent a client when any one of them practicing alone would be prohibited from doing so" by conflict of interest rules. This idea is sometimes simply stated as, "If one lawyer in a firm can't do it, no lawyer in the firm can do it." Similarly under MR 3.6(d), if one lawyer in a firm or agency can't make a particular public statement, no lawyer in the firm or agency can make that statement.

Pre-1994 versions of MR 3.6 and its Model Code predecessor lacked this "other lawyers" provision. A number of states do not include it in their versions of MR 3.6.[8] It would be unwise, though, to view the absence of this specific provision in a state's version of MR 3.6 as exempting associated lawyers from MR 3.6's restrictions. The Model Rules have other widely adopted provisions outside MR 3.6 that can be and frequently are used to extend the reach of ethics rules beyond a particular lawyer. For example, MR 8.4(a) makes it misconduct to "violate . . . the Rules of Professional Conduct, knowingly assist or induce another to do so, or do so through the acts of another." A lawyer participating in a trial who asked a non-participating lawyer in the firm to make a public statement prohibited by MR 3.6(a) would commit misconduct under MR 8.4(a). MR 8.4(d) makes it misconduct for a lawyer to "engage in conduct that is prejudicial to the administration of justice." A nonparticipating lawyer who assisted a participating lawyer in attempting an end run around MR 3.6(a) could easily be held to have violated Section 8.4(d).

Responsibilities of a Prosecutor

MR 3.6's obligations, discussed in the prior section, apply to prosecutors just as they do to criminal defense lawyers and civil litigators. MR 3.8(f), though, also imposes responsibilities on a prosecutor regarding publicity. It provides that a prosecutor in a criminal case shall

> (f) except for statements that are necessary to inform the public of

8. Such jurisdictions include Alabama, the District of Columbia, and New Jersey.

> the nature and extent of the prosecutor's action and that serve a legitimate law enforcement purpose, refrain from making extrajudicial comments that have a substantial likelihood of heightening public condemnation of the accused and exercise reasonable care to prevent investigators, law enforcement personnel, employees or other persons assisting or associated with the prosecutor in a criminal case from making an extrajudicial statement that the prosecutor would be prohibited from making under Rule 3.6 or this Rule.

MR 3.8(f) has two focal points: statements that could increase public condemnation and the exercise of reasonable care to control public statements by others working with the prosecutor.

Public Condemnation. MR 3.8(f) incorporates the "substantial likelihood" formula found in MR 3.6. Although MR 3.6(a) prohibits statements that create "a substantial likelihood" of material prejudice to an "*adjudicative proceeding*," MR 3.8(f) goes further and prohibits statements that create a "substantial likelihood of *heightening public condemnation of the accused*." Does this language create a restriction on prosecutor statements beyond what MR 3.6 already restricts? In other words, does MR 3.8(f)'s public condemnation language create a "special" responsibility of a prosecutor? Or is this language simply redundant of the responsibilities that MR 3.6 already places on prosecutors and other lawyers? The legislative history of MR 3.8 sheds no light on this question. Courts, ethics authorities, and commentators have yet to clarify if and how MR 3.8(f)'s public condemnation language restricts statements not also restricted by MR 3.6.

When a disciplinary authority finds that a prosecutor violated a state's version of MR 3.8(f), it also routinely finds a violation of the state's versions of MR 3.6. These findings suggest that statements by prosecutors that create a "substantial likelihood of heightening public condemnation of the accused" also create "a substantial likelihood" of material prejudice to an "adjudicative proceeding." The vagueness of both MR 3.6 and MR 3.8(f), a frequent point of criticism among commentators, makes it difficult to determine if MR 3.8(f) reaches statements not prohibited by MR 3.6.

Reasonable care. MR 3.8(f) also imposes a responsibility on a prosecutor to "exercise reasonable care" to prevent others, including law enforcement personnel and employees "associated with the prosecutor in a criminal case," from making statements a prosecutor may not make under Rule 3.6 or Rule 3.8(f). According to Comment [6], the reasonable care obligation is satisfied if a prosecutor issues "appropriate cautions to law-enforcement personnel and other relevant individuals."

MR 3.8(f)'s "reasonable care" provision raises redundancy questions similar to those raised by MR 3.8(f)'s public condemnation language. Does its reasonable care language create restrictions on prosecutors beyond what MRs 5.1 and 5.3 already impose? Does MR 3.8(f)'s reasonable care language create "special" responsibilities of a prosecutor? Or is it redundant of the responsibilities that MRs 5.1 and 5.3 already place on prosecutors and other lawyers? Again, the legislative history of MR 3.8 sheds no light on this question. Courts, ethics authorities, and commentators have yet to clarify if and how MR 3.8(f)'s reasonable care language imposes obligations not already imposed by MRs 5.1 and 5.3.

Comment [6] to MR 3.8 explains that prosecutors, like other lawyers, are subject to MR 5.1 and MR 5.3. MR 5.1 addresses the responsibilities of lawyers in firms and government agencies for actions by other lawyers in the firm or agency. MR 5.3 deals with the responsibilities of such lawyers for the actions of nonlawyers "employed or retained by or associated with a lawyer." Though a prosecutor clearly does not employ or retain police officers, they certainly are "associated with" the prosecutor. The comment to MR 3.8 states that Section (f) "reminds the prosecutor of the importance of these obligations [under MR 5.1 and 5.3] in connection to the unique dangers of improper extrajudicial statements in a criminal case." MR 3.8(f) thus creates a duty that is redundant of the obligations a lawyer has under MRs 5.1 and 5.3 to take reasonable measures to ensure that other lawyers and nonlawyers working with the lawyer conform their public statements to what MRs 3.6 and 3.8 allow.

Model Rule 3.6 after *Gentile*

How have courts and ethics authorities applied MR 3.6 since *Gentile*? How have prosecutors and defense lawyers approached their obligations under the ethics rules when speaking with the media? There are not many cases or advisory ethics opinions applying and clarifying the text of MR 3.6. This section discusses those that do exist and provides some guidance to lawyers engaging with the media.

Substantial Risk

As discussed in the preceding section, a key feature of MR 3.6(a) is its "substantial likelihood" standard. The rule prohibits only statements that create "a substantial likelihood" of material prejudice to the proceedings. How have courts and ethics authorities applied this standard?

Perhaps the most notable case since *Gentile* involving a lawyer's statements that violated MR 3.6(a) has been the Duke lacrosse team prosecution. District Attorney Michael Nifong made numerous statements to the media in that case that contributed to his later disbarment. An exotic dancer reported that three men had raped her during a party hosted by the Duke lacrosse team members. Among Nifong's statements found to have met the substantial likelihood of material prejudice standard were repeated statements that the lacrosse team members "were not cooperating with authorities," had put up a "stonewall of silence," and had "refused to speak with investigators." Nifong expressed his personal views that a rape had occurred, that there was "a deep racial motivation" for the rape, that "racial slurs" and "racial hostility" were present, and that it was "essentially a gang rape." He referred to members of the team as "hooligans." He also criticized team members for getting lawyers and stated that "one would wonder why one needs an attorney if one was not charged and had not done anything wrong."[9]

The North Carolina disciplinary panel found that these and other statements had a substantial likelihood of prejudicing the criminal adjudicative proceeding and constituted a violation of North Carolina's Rule 3.6(a). The disciplinary panel also found that these statements violated Nifong's additional obligation as a prosecutor under Rule 3.8(f) because the statements "had a substantial likelihood of heightening public condemna-

---

9. The North Carolina State Bar v. Michael B. Nifong, O6 DHC 35 (July 10, 2007), http://www.newsobserver.com/content/media/2007/7/12/NIFONGFINDINGS.pdf.

tion of the accused."[10]

In another case, *In re Litz*,[11] the Indiana Supreme Court publicly reprimanded a defense lawyer who represented a woman charged with neglect of a dependant resulting in serious bodily injury. A jury convicted his client. On appeal, the lawyer won a reversal, and the case was remanded to the trial court because the lower court had erred in determining that evidence of battered women's syndrome was irrelevant. When the prosecutor decided to retry the case, the defense lawyer sent letters to various newspapers stating that his client had spent time in jail "for a crime she did not commit." He also stated that she had passed a lie detector test and called the prosecutor's decision to retry the case "abominable." After the newspapers published these letters, the defense lawyer filed a motion for change of venue citing prejudicial pretrial publicity. In issuing a public reprimand of Litz, the court found his statements to be a purposeful attempt to gain an unfair advantage in the retrial of his client.

The *Nifong* and *Litz* cases illustrate how courts apply the substantial likelihood of prejudice standard. When statements to the media include subjects specifically identified in Comment [5] as "more likely than not to have a material prejudicial effect on a proceeding," disciplinary authorities will usually find a violation of the ethics rule. For example, Nifong stated that the suspects were not cooperating with the police, and Litz stated that his client passed a lie detector test, both types of information that would be inadmissible at trial and that Comment [5] states are "more likely than not to have a material prejudicial effect on a proceeding." Both Nifong and Litz also rendered opinions about guilt or innocence, again statements Comment [5] identifies as impermissible.

The type of interaction with the media may also play a role in finding an ethics violation. For example, a lawyer might issue a press release or hold a press conference at which the lawyer refuses to respond to questions. Or the lawyer might decide to engage in a question-and-answer exchange either during a press conference or an interview. There is some authority that a lawyer engaging in a question-and-answer format press

10. *Id.*
11. 721 N.E.2d 258 (Ind. 1999).

conference or interview may violate the ethics rule. In response to inquiry by a prosecutor, the Pennsylvania Bar Association Ethics Committee issued an ethics opinion that states that a lawyer may not be interviewed in a question-and-answer format "since matters would almost certainly be addressed which would be beyond the permissible areas outlined in the rules and the prosecutor's refusal to answer such questions would appear as withholding information and thus have a substantial likelihood of prejudicing the proceeding."[12] This ethics opinion counseled the prosecutor not to participate in a question-and-answer format press conference or interview but couched its advice to apply more broadly to all lawyers. The concern here appears to be that a "no comment" response by a lawyer may prompt listeners to infer that the lawyer has damaging information he or she cannot reveal.

A recent Indiana disciplinary action, *In re Brizzi*,[13] makes clear that MR 3.6 focuses on risk of harm rather than actual harm. The Indiana Supreme Court approved the discipline of a lawyer under MR 3.6 even when evidence suggested there had been no actual prejudice. In the *Brizzi* case, the court found violations of Rules 3.6(a) and 3.8(f) and issued a public reprimand to a prosecutor for making public statements in which the prosecutor stated that the "evidence is overwhelming." The prosecutor also stated that there were "several aggravators present, any one of which would merit the death penalty" and "[t]o do otherwise would be a travesty." In issuing the reprimand, the court rejected the findings of the disciplinary hearing officer who had examined jury questionnaires and other evidence and determined that because no actual prejudice to the proceedings against the defendants had occurred there was no violation. The court reasoned that each statement must be considered "at the time made, not whether it actually worked to the detriment of a defendant."[14] In deciding *Brizzi*, the court emphasized that "substantial likelihood" of prejudice is distinct from actual prejudice.

The discipline of Nifong, Litz, and Brizzi suggests that statements that

---

12. Pa. Ethics Op. 92-70 (1992).
13. 962 N.E.2d 1240 (Ind. 2012).
14. *Id.* at 1245.

go beyond those expressly permitted in MR 3.6 run the risk of meeting the substantial risk of prejudice standard if they appear calculated to gain strategic advantage by bolstering one's case, casting doubt on the merits of the opposing party's case, or otherwise attempting to influence or prejudice the proceeding.

Adjudicative Proceeding

The nature of the proceeding, especially whether it is a jury trial, can be key to determining the likelihood of prejudice. In *Gentile*, the Court observed that the "substantial risk of material prejudice" test "will rarely be met where the judge is the trier of fact, since trial judges often have access to inadmissible and highly prejudicial information and are presumed to be able to discount or disregard it."[15]

In *United States v. Scarfo*,[16] the district court granted a gag order based on New Jersey's Rule 3.6 while a suppression motion was pending after a defense lawyer commented to the press about the propriety of law enforcement surveillance of his former client charged with illegal gambling. In reversing the gag order, the appellate court held that the risk of material prejudice would not be present while a suppression motion was pending because "[j]udges are experts at closing their eyes and ears to extraneous or irrelevant matters and focusing only on the relevant in the proceedings before them."

The *Restatement (Third) of the Law Governing Lawyers* notes that the concern that a lawyer's comments about a pending matter will prejudice a proceeding is "largely irrelevant in matters to be decided by judges."[17] Thus, a lawyer's statements to the media before a bench trial will not likely be prejudicial to the proceedings. Nor would a lawyer's statements to the media before a preliminary hearing or a hearing on pretrial motions, unless, as we discuss below, the statements occur close in time to a jury trial of the matter.

15. 501 U.S. at 1077.
16. 263 F.3d 80 (3d Cir. 2001).
17. Restatement (Third) of the Law Governing Lawyers § 109 cmt. b (2007).

Timing

When there is a jury trial, the timing of the lawyer's statements to the press is an important factor in assessing potential prejudice. The U.S. Supreme Court addressed the importance of timing in *Sheppard v. Maxwell*,[18] in which shortly before and during a jury trial the prosecution leaked inadmissible evidence to the press.

In *United States v. Bingham*,[19] a federal district court ordered disciplinary authorities to investigate whether defense counsel representing street gang members should be disciplined. In interviews the night before jury selection, the lawyer criticized the trial judge's decision to impanel an anonymous jury. The court reasoned that because the statements were made the evening before trial they posed a serious threat to the proceeding. In *Iowa Supreme Court Bd. of Prof'l Ethics & Conduct v. Visser*,[20] the Iowa Supreme Court refused to discipline a lawyer for impermissible statements made almost two years before the trial, reasoning that the statements would have no impact on the trial.

How large a time lapse between a statement and a trial is required to make the risk of prejudice less than "substantial"? The answer is not clear. In *Commonwealth v. McCullum*,[21] the court of appeals rejected a criminal appeal based, in part, on a trial court's denial of a motion for change of venue where there had been information in the press about the defendant's prior record and an alleged confession to the crime nine months before the trial. In affirming the trial court's decision, the appellate court reasoned that nine months was a sufficient "cooling off" period between the statements and the start of a trial to reduce potential prejudice.

Extrajudicial Statements

MR 3.6 applies to "extrajudicial statements," which are statements made outside of court and court filings. MR 3.6 places no restrictions on what a lawyer may say in a court proceeding or filing.

For example, a prosecutor or defense lawyer may include in pretrial

18. 384 U.S. 333, 360–61 (1966).
19. 769 F.Supp. 1039 (N.D. Ill. 1991).
20. 629 N.W.2d 376 (Iowa 2001).
21. 602 A.2d 313 (Pa. 1992).

motions information specifically enumerated in Comment [5] of MR 3.6 as being "more likely than not to have a material prejudicial effect on a proceeding." Such matters include information relating to the "character, credibility, reputation or criminal record of a party, suspect in a criminal investigation or witness, or the identity of a witness, or the expected testimony of a party or witness." This type of information may appear in a suppression motion, motion in limine, or other pretrial motion. If the press obtains copies of court filings containing statements not permitted by MR 3.6, there would not be a violation of the ethical rule if the press publicized them because they are part of the case's public record and not "extrajudicial statements."

There is case and ethics authority that a lawyer may repeat to the press something stated in court or point the press in the direction of newsworthy court filings. An Ohio court refused to sanction a prosecutor for statements made in open court where he named an individual under grand jury investigation and stated that he expected the person to be indicted.[22] A Pennsylvania ethics opinion found that a lawyer may inform the media of the docket number of a newsworthy case because it is public information.[23]

The 2004 sexual assault case against basketball star Kobe Bryant illustrates how statements that would otherwise violate MR 3.6 may be made in court filings. Due to the publicity surrounding the Kobe Bryant case, the trial judge imposed a sweeping gag order. Mindful that lawyers might make allegations that could create a substantial risk of prejudicing the proceedings, the judge required all court filings to be under seal. In some of the filings under seal, defense lawyers raised the alleged victim's mental stability and her sexual activity in the days after the alleged rape. They also referred to DNA evidence suggesting that the alleged victim had sex with someone soon after her encounter with Bryant. One or more court clerks accidentally posted the filings on the court's website, and the media quickly publicized the information. After the accidental posting, the judge lifted the gag order so that the prosecution and the alleged victim

---

22. *In re* Grand Jury Investigation, 492 N.E.2d 459 (Ohio Ct. App. 1985).
23. Pa. Ethics Op. 2005-185 (2005).

could respond. The woman denied having sex after the alleged rape, and the prosecutors maintained that the DNA evidence may have been contaminated. During jury selection, Bryant's accuser informed the prosecution that she was unwilling to testify. The prosecutors dismissed the case.

Permissible and Impermissible Statements

MR 3.6(b) provides a list of typically permitted statements, or safe harbors, which will not ordinarily violate Section (a). Comment [5] to MR 3.6, which also appears previously, lists various types of information that are usually impermissible topics for public statements. Together, the two lists provide guidance about what a lawyer may and may not say when speaking with the media.

Although MR 3.6 phrases its prohibition in terms of "extrajudicial statements," it also has been read to prohibit dissemination of prejudicial information about a case without a lawyer making any public statement at all. *In re Duncan*[24] is such a case. The South Carolina Supreme Court indefinitely suspended a defense lawyer for, among other reasons, releasing a tape to the media of him talking with his client that law enforcement officials had surreptitiously recorded. After the tape was broadcast, Duncan filed an affidavit with the court stating that his client could not receive a fair trial in the county. The court found that releasing the tape to the media was an attempt to influence his client's trial and that it constituted an "extrajudicial statement about a case that the lawyer would expect to be disseminated by the media knowing that it will have a substantial likelihood of materially prejudicing an adjudicative proceeding."[25]

What happens if information a lawyer is typically barred from speaking about, such as the results of a test or a person's criminal record, is already in the public record? MR 3.6(b) specifically permits "information contained in the public record," but it does not define public record. Some courts have addressed this question.

In *Attorney Grievance Commission v. Gansler*,[26] the Maryland disci-

24. 533 S.E.2d 894 (S.C. 2000).
25. *Id.* at 896.
26. 835 A.2d 548 (Md. 2003).

plinary authority brought proceedings against a prosecutor for making numerous comments at press conferences concerning three cases. These included comments about a defendant's confession, a decision to offer a plea bargain, his opinion as to the guilt of two defendants, the results of some tests apparently linking one of the defendants to a crime, and the criminal record of one defendant. The Maryland Supreme Court found the statements about the decision to offer a plea bargain and the prosecutor's personal opinion about guilt impermissible.

The prosecutor argued that the results of the tests and the confession of one defendant were already in a "public record" because they had been reported in the press before he confirmed the information. He argued that the criminal record was also a public record. So does the phrase "contained in a public record" cover information that has been reported in the news? Or should the phrase be read more literally to cover only information in a governmental record of some sort? The court found that there was no settled definition of "public record" in this context. Because of the lack of guidance in Maryland's ethics rule, the court found for purposes of the *Gansler* case only that information in the public record included "anything in the public domain, including public court documents, media reports, and comments made by police officers."[27] Therefore, the prosecutor's statements about the confession, the test results, and the criminal record were found permissible.

The Maryland Supreme Court, however, adopted a narrower definition for future cases. It ruled that in the future "[t]o receive the protection of the 'public record' safe harbor, the lawyer must not provide information beyond quotations from or references to public government records." It reasoned that without this narrow definition a lawyer could avoid the rule whenever someone not bound by the ethics rules leaked information or made statements to the press that the lawyer later repeated.[28] Some jurisdictions have adopted Maryland's definition of public record. In others, it remains undefined.

27. *Id.* at 567.
28. *Id.* at 569.

Fair Reply

MR 3.6(c) contains a fair reply clause that permits a lawyer to "make a statement that a reasonable lawyer would believe is required to protect a client from substantial undue prejudicial effect of recent publicity not initiated by the lawyer or the lawyer's client" provided the statement is "limited to such information as is necessary to mitigate the recent adverse publicity."

This fair reply doctrine is closely associated with the *Gentile* case, which is discussed previously in this chapter. Gentile tailored his comments carefully to include only admissible evidence and to steer clear of potentially inadmissible evidence. Gentile took questions after his brief remarks and several times refused to answer questions because his view of his ethical obligations prohibited a response. As discussed earlier, at least one state bar ethics committee has stated that the simple act of engaging in an interview or press conference with a question-and-answer format may violate MR 3.6.[29]

Gentile's measured approach, limiting information he disclosed, exemplifies how one can use the fair reply provision of the ethics rule to protect a client from the undue prejudice of negative publicity.

Nonparticipating Lawyers Inside a Firm or Agency

MR 3.6(d) addresses application of Section (a) to lawyers who are not participating in an investigation or trial but who are within the same firm or agency as a lawyer who is participating. It states, "No lawyer associated in a firm or government agency with a lawyer subject to paragraph (a) shall make a statement prohibited by paragraph (a)." This provision makes clear that if one lawyer in a defense firm, a prosecutor's office, or a public defender's office is barred from making a particular statement by MR 3.6, then all lawyers working in that firm or office are similarly barred.

Nonparticipating Lawyers Outside a Firm or Agency

MR 3.6(a) states that it is applicable to lawyers who are participating or have

29. *See* note 12 and accompanying text.

participated in the matter and their associates. Comment [3] of MR 3.6 explains that the rule does not apply to a lawyer not participating in the proceeding and not associated with a lawyer participating in the proceeding, reasoning that "the likelihood of prejudice to a proceeding by the commentary of a lawyer who is not involved in the proceeding is small . . . ." Hence, legal commentators who have become a regular feature of news coverage of noteworthy cases who have not participated in the case and who are not associated with any participating lawyer, do not violate MR 3.6.

Such legal commentators, though commonplace and allowed by MR 3.6, have not escaped criticism. A former ABA president criticized lawyer commentators in the O. J. Simpson case and other cases by comparing them to "$2 hookers" who "pimp their dubious talents and hustle the public" with their observations.[30] Some academics have called for a set of ethical guidelines to prevent commentators from misleading the public by predicting trial outcomes and from rating lawyer performance.[31]

Nonlawyers: Police and Clients

Prosecutors have an additional responsibility under MR 3.8(d) to "exercise reasonable care to prevent investigators, law enforcement personnel, employees or other persons assisting or associated with the prosecutor in a criminal case from making an extrajudicial statement that the prosecutor would be prohibited from making under Rule 3.6 or this Rule." This responsibility to exercise "reasonable care" to ensure that others associated with the prosecution comply with the ethics rules limiting comments about cases is aimed at curbing public statements or leaks that would likely heighten public condemnation of the accused. Comment [6] to MR 3.8 explains that a prosecutor will ordinarily satisfy the "reasonable care standard . . . if the prosecutor issues the appropriate cautions to law-enforcement personnel and other relevant individuals."

Lawyers must also be careful in passing on information to a client that the client may release to the press. MR 8.4(a) prohibits a lawyer from vio-

---

30. Gail D. Cox, *Bushnell: O.J. Commentators are '$2 Hookers,'* NAT'L L.J., June 12, 1995, at A4.

31. *See* Erwin Chemerinsky & Laurie Levenson, *The Ethics of Being a Commentator*, 69 S. CAL. L. REV. 1303, 1309 (1996); Jean Hellwege, *No Comment: Professors, Legal Groups Consider Ethical Codes For Legal Commentators*, 34 TRIAL, July 1998, at 16.

lating the ethics rules through the acts of another. If a lawyer directs a client in making extrajudicial comments to the press that the lawyer could not make, the lawyer may be found to have violated the ethics rules.

Media Access to the Client

The use of a media campaign as part of a defense strategy has become increasingly common in high-profile cases. Examples include the prosecutions of both Martha Stewart and the Arthur Andersen accounting firm.[32] A client media campaign raises a number of potential ethical issues for defense counsel.

False Statement

MR 4.1(a) provides that "In the course of representing a client a lawyer shall not knowingly . . . make a false statement of material fact or law to a third person[.]" Two factors can generate a serious risk of a false statement in the context of a media campaign. First, when a media campaign is undertaken, pressure from the client to put an exculpatory "spin" on the relevant facts and law is likely to be intense, especially if the client has a high public profile. Second, the lawyer's access to information at the time the media campaign is undertaken may be quite limited because the defense investigation may not have progressed far and knowledge of the prosecution's evidence will often be scant.

The Arthur Andersen media campaign provides an example of the sort of behavior that raises potential MR 4.1(a) issues. As part of its media campaign, Arthur Andersen posted on a website a background paper prepared by its lawyers "billed as an analysis of the 'factual and legal errors' in the government's case."[33] Professor Kathleen Brickey, in a detailed examination of the Arthur Andersen case, including its use of the media, concludes that the Arthur Andersen paper was "replete with misleading assertions."[34]

Defense counsel may attempt to defend against an allegation of violation of MR 4.1(a) by relying on lack of the required mental state of knowl-

32. *See* Brickey, *supra* note 1.
33. *Id.* at 943.
34. *Id.*

edge of a statement's falsity. Even if ultimately successful, such a strategy would, at best, prove awkward due to the likelihood that it would require defense counsel to reveal confidential information in order to demonstrate lack of knowledge.[35]

What if false statements of fact or law are made by either the client or a nonlawyer spokesperson for the client during a media campaign during which defense counsel provides advice and assistance? In such a situation, even if defense counsel is not making the false statements at issue, the lawyer's involvement with the media campaign could expose the lawyer to a charge of misconduct under either MR 8.4(a), which prohibits violating a Model Rule "through the acts of another," or MR 8.4(c), which states that "it is professional misconduct for a lawyer to . . . engage in conduct involving dishonesty, fraud, deceit, or misrepresentation[.]"

Prohibited Trial Publicity

MR 3.6 regulates public comment by lawyers participating in the investigation or trial of a criminal case. MR 3.6 prohibits a lawyer participating in the investigation or litigation of a case from making a public statement that "will have a substantial likelihood of materially prejudicing" the trial or any other "adjudicative proceeding" in the case. If defense counsel acts as a client's spokesperson during a media campaign by, for example, holding a press conference or granting an interview with a print or television reporter, the lawyer must abide by MR 3.6.

Vicarious Violation of Model Rule 3.6

The interaction of Rules 3.6 and 8.4(a) raises a less obvious ethics issue for a lawyer whose client engages in a media campaign. In an attempt to avoid MR 3.6's restrictions, the lawyer and client might decide not to have the lawyer act as public spokesperson for the client in a media campaign, instead choosing to have the client or another nonlawyer act as spokesperson. What if the client or nonlawyer client spokesperson makes a state-

35. Model Rule 1.6(b)(5) allows a lawyer to reveal confidential information "to establish a claim or defense on behalf of the lawyer . . . to respond to allegations in any proceeding concerning the lawyer's representation of the client."

ment that would be barred by MR 3.6 if made by defense counsel? What if, for example, the client or client spokesperson held a press conference to inform the public of a rape complainant's inadmissible sexual history? If the client makes statements that would violate MR 3.6 if the lawyer made them, does the lawyer violate MR 8.4(a) by advising, encouraging, or assisting the client in the public relations campaign?

MR 8.4(a) states that "It is professional misconduct for a lawyer to . . . violate . . . the Rules of Professional Conduct, knowingly assist or induce another to do so, or do so *through the acts of another*." There is scant authority on what MR 8.4(a)'s "through the acts of another" language prohibits. What sort of conduct is required? What sort of mental state is required? The answers to these questions are unclear. If the lawyer were to direct a nonlawyer public relations person hired by the client to make statements that violate MR 3.6, such as a statement about the sexual history of a rape complainant, there is little doubt that the lawyer would violate MR 8.4(a). But what if the client or client spokesperson informs the lawyer that he plans to make such a statement and the lawyer fails to object? Or what if the lawyer consciously avoids being informed about the content of such public statements in order to avoid a vicarious violation of MR 3.6?

Consider the following scenario. The defense's investigation finds damaging information about the character and credibility of a government witness. However, the lawyer concludes that he or she is barred from making a public statement about it because of MR 3.6(a)'s general prohibition and Comment [5]'s listing of "the character, credibility, and reputation . . . of a witness" as subjects that are more likely than not to create prejudice. But the lawyer and client together decide to have the client hold a press conference at which the client will disclose the damaging information about the witness. Has the lawyer violated MR 3.6 through the acts of another and thus violated MR 8.4? A Massachusetts lawyer who was asked to assist a client in drafting an advertisement that the lawyer thought would likely materially prejudice a pending proceeding asked for guidance. The Massachusetts Bar in response stated that "[a] lawyer who drafts an advertisement for a client to place under its own name runs a substantial risk of violation of Rules 3.6 and 8.4(a) of the Massachusetts Rules of Professional

Conduct ('MRPC') when the lawyer concludes that placing the same advertisement under her own name would violate Rule 3.6."[36]

In *State v. Grossberg*,[37] the Superior Court of Delaware entered a gag order restricting the prosecutors, defense lawyers, law enforcement officers, and other persons assisting or associated with counsel from publicly commenting on two capital murder cases involving the death of an infant. The court exempted from the gag order statements allowed by Delaware's Rule 3.6. Subsequent to the gag order, one of the defense lawyers arranged for his client and her parents to be interviewed by Barbara Walters for an ABC News *20/20* broadcast. During the interview, the defense lawyer directed his client to answer questions about how she felt concerning the death of her infant, her mourning the loss of her baby, and what she would say "when the Delaware prosecutors say that you are a baby-killer." The client responded to the "baby-killer" question by stating, "It's the furthest thing from the truth. The furthest thing. I wouldn't hurt anybody or anything, especially something of mine."

The court held that the lawyer's preparation of his client and her parents "should have been limited to those areas [on] which he himself would have been permitted to comment. Otherwise, Rule 3.6 is meaningless." Because of the lawyer's attempt to circumvent Rule 3.6 through his client and the lawyer's own statements to the media relating to his client's character, the court revoked the lawyer's *pro hac vice* admission and removed him from the case.

A Pennsylvania ethics opinion[38] states that Rule 8.4 limits a lawyer's preparation of a client for media interviews to areas about which Rule 3.6 permits the lawyer to comment. The ethics opinion notes, however, that Rule 3.6 does not apply to the client and "the only restriction on the client's comments are those which stem from the client's own conscience."

Conflict of Interest

MR 1.7 on concurrent conflict of interest requires a lawyer to avoid a situa-

36. Mass. Op. 03-2 (2003).
37. 705 A.2d 608 (Del. Super. Ct. 1997).
38. Pa. Ethics Op. No. 96-45 (June 21, 1996).

tion posing "a significant risk that the representation of . . . [a] client [] will be materially limited . . . by a personal interest of the lawyer." Does a media campaign create a significant risk to a client based on a personal interest of the lawyer? If so, how?

Lawyers have a powerful interest in receiving and generating publicity about themselves and their cases. The lawyer may find such publicity an enticing source of ego gratification. It might also lay the foundation for a future career in politics or as an author, a consultant for movies, or a "talking head" legal commentator on television. But the primary reason lawyers find publicity attractive is as a means of attracting future business.

These personal and economic interests of the lawyer in garnering publicity pose a danger of distorting the lawyer's judgment and advice regarding the advisability of a media campaign and how such a campaign should be conducted. The lawyer's self-interest may lead her to favor a media campaign that will bring the lawyer and the case notoriety when the risks to the client substantially outweigh the potential rewards. One of the advantages of MR 3.6's restriction of lawyer speech regarding pending cases is that it reduces the opportunities for lawyer self-interest to distort lawyer decisions about what the lawyer says publicly about a pending case.

Who Decides?

Does defense counsel have the legal and ethical authority to decide whether or not a client should conduct a media campaign? Or is this decision for the client to make? MR 1.2 states that the objectives of the representation are for the client to decide but that the means for achieving them are generally for the lawyer to decide in consultation with the client. A media campaign is certainly a means that may advance the objectives of limiting damage to the client's representation, shielding the defendant from criminal punishment, or minimizing the punishment imposed on the defendant. Thus, the question of whether the client should engage with the media prior to and during a trial certainly seems at first glance to be a means or strategy decision for the lawyer. But both the Model Rules and Supreme Court authority give the client final say over means or strategy decisions that have a significant constitutional dimension, such as whether or not to waive a jury trial or to testify. Because a client's decision to speak with the media implicates the client's First Amendment rights, one may argue that this decision should ultimately be the client's to make.

Even if the lawyer does have the authority to decide this question, the lawyer has little, if any, practical means to keep a client from making a public statement in most cases. The lawyer can control the arguments raised in an appellate brief because the lawyer writes and files the brief. Similarly, the lawyer has ultimate control over matters raised in cross-examination because the lawyer asks the questions during cross-examination. By contrast, there is typically no way for defense counsel to control whether a client, especially one not in custody, speaks to the media.

Even if the decision whether or not to conduct a media campaign is the client's to make under MR 1.2, most clients are likely to defer to their lawyers on questions of how to interact with the media and effectively cede to them the power to make such decisions. A wise lawyer may avoid confronting the issue of whether lawyer or client has the ultimate authority to decide whether to pursue a media campaign by talking the matter over with the client and reaching a decision upon which both agree.

Competence

A lawyer must provide a client with competent representation. Perhaps the most basic of ethical obligations, the mandate of competence appears in MR 1.1 at the very outset of the Model Rules. Regardless of whether counsel or client makes the decision about waging a media campaign, to act competently the lawyer must assess the risks and potential rewards such a campaign presents. If the lawyer makes the decision about whether to engage with the media, such weighing is obviously necessary. But even if the client makes the decision, the lawyer should advise the client about that decision. Weighing the risks and rewards of a media campaign is equally necessary for the lawyer to act competently either in the role of advisor or the role of decision maker.

How does a lawyer competently decide whether the benefits of a media campaign outweigh the risks? Competent handling of this decision requires a good deal of legal knowledge concerning such things as the admissibility and potential prosecutorial uses of statements made during such a campaign and the availability and effectiveness of alternative means for responding to negative pretrial publicity, such as a change of venue and pretrial challenges to jurors. When making such assessments, as pointed out above, the lawyer and client will typically have quite limited information.

Assessing the risks and potential rewards of a media campaign also involves factual questions that may be complex and difficult to resolve. It may, for example, be hard to predict how a client will respond to the pressure of an interview or a press conference; what questions will be asked; and how the public, jurors, witnesses, judges, and prosecutors will react to what the client says or how the client appears. Some clients may be able to afford public relations experts to help the lawyer in making such predictions, but many will not.

With a wealthy, high-profile, or corporate client, it may be a challenge for the criminal lawyer to get the client to appreciate the risks of a media campaign. Some clients, especially ones with large egos who are used to receiving positive press, may be strongly inclined to defend themselves publicly after being publicly attacked. A client's business advisors and business lawyers may reinforce a client's inclination to speak publicly because they may be more concerned about containing business damage than minimizing the client's risk of conviction. The defense lawyer may need to work hard to get the client to understand the risks posed by public comment, most of which are not readily apparent to someone who lacks criminal trial experience.

The Ethics of Media Deals

A lawyer negotiating a personal media deal in relation to a criminal case is not uncommon. Marcia Clark, lead prosecutor in the O. J. Simpson case, entered into a million-dollar contract to write a book, *Without a Doubt*, about the case. One of the defense lawyers in that case, F. Lee Bailey, had negotiated years before a contract to write a book about his representation of millionaire heiress Patricia Hearst that gave rise to a claim of conflict of interest.[39] A New York ethics opinion found that it would be an ethics

39. United States v. Hearst, 638 F.2d 1190 (9th Cir. 1990).

violation for a prosecutor in a high-profile homicide case to sell media rights to her life story until after the case was concluded because of a possible conflict of interest between "the lawyer's economic motivation" and her "undivided loyalty to her client."[40]

Every jurisdiction, except California, has adopted a form of ABA MR 1.8(d), which states, "Prior to the conclusion of representation of a client, a lawyer shall not make or negotiate an agreement giving the lawyer literary or media rights to a portrayal or account based in substantial part on information relating to the representation." Comment [9] to MR 1.8(d) explains the conflict by noting that "[m]easures suitable in the representation of the client may detract from the publication value of an account of the representation."

The rationale for the rule focuses on the risk that financial incentives arising from a media deal may distort a lawyer's judgment about critical decisions that might impact public interest in the case and thus its media value, such as acceptance of a guilty plea or choice of defense strategy. A media contract may also entice a lawyer to breach the duty of confidentiality owed to the client. One commentator has observed that the incentives of a media deal can persuade a lawyer to present the "most sensational, drawn-out, selectively proved, and ultimately unsuccessful defense that can be managed."[41]

The prohibition against acquiring an interest in literary or media rights in a case before ending the representation may not be waived by the client, except in California. In California, a prospective or current client may waive the conflict of interest and agree to the lawyer profiting from the client's story.[42]

After the representation is over, all states permit the lawyer to enter into a media deal without any requirement of client consent. As a practical

40. N.Y. State Bar Op. 606 (1990).

41. Charles Wolfram, Modern Legal Ethics 524 (1986).

42. California's equivalent of MR 1.8 is California Rules of Professional Conduct Rule 3-300, which does not have a counterpart to MR 1.8(d). California courts have stated that a defendant may waive the conflict if it is the client who does it "knowingly and intelligently." Maxwell v. Superior Court, 639 P.2d 248, 254 (Cal. 1982). In *Maxwell*, the court found that defense counsel's agreement with the defendant outlining possible conflicts and prejudices to the client agreeing to give to his lawyer the literary rights to his case story as a fee had sufficiently informed the defendant of the risks so that waiver was knowing and intelligent. *Id.* at 251–253.

matter, waiting until the representation is over may not necessarily insulate the lawyer from the perverse incentives such media deals create. The lawyer's conduct before and during a trial in a high-profile case may be distorted simply by the prospect of later entering into a media deal.

Client Media Deals and Lawyer Ethics

Lawyers are not the only ones who may enter a media deal; the client may do so too. What if a filmmaker contacts a client to document the client's trial story as it unfolds or to film jury deliberations? What are the ethical implications? Two cases, *Echols v. Arkansas*[43] and *Texas v. Poe*,[44] address these issues and raise an interesting set of ethical questions for lawyers.

Interviews With Clients and Recording Defense Preparation

In *Echols*, Arkansas prosecuted Echols and several codefendants for the gruesome murders of three young boys. The boys were found hog-tied in a drainage ditch. All had been sexually abused, and one was severely mutilated. Prior to trial, filmmakers under contract to HBO entered an agreement with Echols and his two codefendants to interview them and film their trials in return for payments of $7,500 each. The defense lawyers did not receive any payments.

Echols was convicted and sentenced to death. In challenging his conviction, Echols raised an interesting argument that his contract with the filmmakers created a conflict of interest for his trial lawyer that entitled him to a new trial. First, he argued that the lawyer sacrificed time meeting the needs of the filmmakers that should have been spent preparing for trial. Second, he argued that his lawyer chose to use the funds from HBO to pay for investigation and expert witnesses rather than applying to the court for such funding, which might have been more ample. Finally, Echols argued that in order to accommodate the filmmakers' broadcast date, his lawyer failed to seek a continuance that could have helped the case.

The appellate court rejected each of these arguments because Echols

43. 127 S.W.3d 486 (Ark. 2003).
44. 98 S.W.3d 194 (Tex. 2003).

failed to demonstrate an adverse impact on his lawyer's performance as required by *Strickland v. Washington*.[45] The court also pointed out advantages Echols received from the HBO agreement. For example, by using his own money rather than court funds for investigation and experts, his lawyer was able to prevent notifying the prosecution of the defense strategy, which inevitably would have happened had defense counsel applied for court funds.

Access to the jury room

The state of Texas charged Cedric Harrison with murder and sought capital punishment. Prior to trial, Harrison consented to the PBS documentary series *Frontline* videotaping the jury deliberations in his case for later broadcast. Though Harrison waived the right to use the video recording in any later challenge to a conviction, the prosecutor in the case opposed the recording. The trial judge held a hearing and questioned both Harrison and his lawyer about Harrison's decision to consent and then ruled to allow the recording. Jurors were to be screened, and only those who consented to the taping were to sit on Harrison's jury.

The prosecutor sought immediate appellate review, and a Texas appellate court granted mandamus prohibiting the videotaping.[46] The court found that videotaping the jury would violate a Texas statute providing that "No person shall be permitted to be with a jury while it is deliberating." The cameras and microphones were to be remotely operated, so no person other than the jurors would have actually been in the jury room. The text of the statute simply did not address recording jury deliberations. Nonetheless, the court ostensibly adopted a textualist approach to this exercise in statutory interpretation and found that the plain language of the statute "clearly and indisputably" barred the recording.[47] According to the court, television viewers who would later watch the recording would be "with the jury while it is deliberating."[48] A more plausible rationale for the result reached by the court is one based on legislative purpose, that the

45. 466 U.S. 668 (1984).
46. Texas v. Poe, 98 S.W.3d 194 (Texas Crim. App. 2003).
47. *Id.* at 202.
48. *Id.* at 201.

policy behind barring any person from being in the jury room would likewise dictate barring videotaping of the jury.

Should the recording of jury deliberations be allowed? There are a number of persuasive arguments on both sides. We insist that criminal trials be public but then shroud what is arguably the most crucial phase of the trial, the jury deciding the defendant's fate. Why doesn't the ideal that democratic government should be open dictate exposing jury deliberations to public view? Recording and broadcasting jury deliberations could help educate the public, legislators, and legal reformers about how juries operate and help us craft better procedure and evidence rules. It could also reveal and remedy jury misconduct, which in turn would arguably deter misconduct.

But how might public exposure negatively affect the way jurors function? Jurors who conclude that the government has failed to prove the guilt of an unpopular defendant might nonetheless convict for fear of reprisal. They might also feel inhibited in freely expressing their views or in voting to nullify. Publicity might prompt some jurors to "act" for the cameras to gain notoriety for themselves, as do participants in reality television shows. The publicity resulting from such recording and broadcasting could also discourage potential jurors from serving, shrinking and possibly skewing the jury pool.

The debate about recording criminal jury deliberations has yet to be resolved. Though the Texas court in the *Harrison* case barred recording, Arizona, Ohio, Maine, and Wisconsin have allowed it.[49] How other states will handle the issue remains to be seen.

Who Decides?

Who makes the decision when a client enters into a media deal? MR 1.2 addresses the allocation between client and lawyer of the authority to make decisions concerning the representation. The client has final authority to

---

49. The Arizona and Wisconsin cases are not published, but they have been discussed by student commentators. *See* William R. Bagley, Jr., Note, *Jury Room Secrecy: Has the Time Come to Unlock the Door?*, 32 SUFFOLK L. REV. 481, 485 (1999); Clifford Holt Ruprecht, Comment, *Are Verdicts, Too, Like Sausages?: Lifting the Cloak of Jury Secrecy*, 146 U. PA. L. REV. 217, 224 (1997). In 2004, the Ohio Supreme Court approved ABC News's recording and televising jury deliberations in a Cleveland criminal trial. Debra Rosenberg, *Cameras Report, the Jury Decides*, NEWSWEEK, Aug. 9, 2004, at 8.

make decisions concerning the objectives of the representation, while the lawyer has final authority over the means for pursuing those objectives. MR 1.2 specifically states that what plea to enter, whether to waive jury trial, and whether to testify are questions for the client to resolve.

Are questions such as those faced by Echols and Harrison—whether to agree to a recorded interview or to have jury deliberations recorded—ultimately for the client or the lawyer to decide? Do these decisions concern objectives or strategy? In the *Echols* and *Harrison* cases, both the lawyers and the courts appear to have assumed that these were client decisions. But are they? One could easily characterize both as questions of strategy. If the client and lawyer disagree on the strategic wisdom of enhanced media scrutiny, is the lawyer ethically allowed to veto a client's decision to agree to recording jury deliberations or granting an interview? Is the lawyer required to do so if the lawyer is convinced the publicity will hurt the client's case?

The lawyer may have little if any practical means of vetoing a client's decision to allow increased media access. The lawyer's veto power probably depends on the type of media exposure and whether or not the client is in custody. Clearly the lawyer could act to veto the recording of jury deliberations by opposing it in court. By contrast, the lawyer would be hard pressed to keep a client who is not in custody from granting an interview to a television crew.

Competence

MR 1.1 requires a lawyer to provide competent representation to a client. How does a lawyer go about deciding whether or not enhanced media scrutiny will help or hurt the client? The lawyer confronts this issue regardless of whether the lawyer or the client makes the ultimate decision. If the decision is the client's to make, the lawyer nonetheless has to advise the client about which course is preferable. If the decision is the lawyer's to make, he or she similarly must determine which course is in the client's best interest.

Predicting whether and how enhanced media involvement will affect a client's case is likely to be a challenging and hazardous task. For example, how is the lawyer to know whether recording jury deliberations will make the jury more or less likely to convict? Is a lawyer able to predict whether a jury pool screened of potential jurors uncomfortable with being taped will be more receptive or more hostile to the lawyer's arguments than an unscreened jury pool? The debate about recording jury deliberations reveals that questions such as these are hotly contested and not easily resolved. The fact that both sides make plausible claims suggests that such questions will be difficult for lawyers in individual cases to resolve. The *New York Times*, for example, ran a story detailing the testing done and the many experts consulted by Martha Stewart's legal team in planning a media campaign coordinated with her trial.[50] How many lawyers will have access to such resources in deciding whether and how to have a client interact with the media?

Confidentiality

The taping of jury deliberations poses no apparent risk to client confidentiality. But an agreement such as the one in *Echols* poses serious risks to client confidentiality. The most obvious arises from the client being interviewed. Anything the client says is a potential admission, even if the client chooses not to testify at trial. And if the client does testify, statements made during the interview could be used for impeachment during cross-examination. Even if the interview is not broadcast until after the trial is over, the filmmakers and camera operators will know about the client's statements. If the prosecution is aware of the taping of such an interview, it might subpoena the film crew to testify and produce its film or videotape. If there is a mistrial or a retrial after a reversal on appeal, the broadcast version could provide admissions and material for cross-examination at the retrial. If the filming includes defense strategy sessions, such as one mentioned in *Echols* about whether or not to call a certain witness, the film crew and its film or videotape provide potential avenues for such strategic information reaching the prosecution.

---

50. Constance L. Hays, *Selecting Stewart Jury: How Much Publicity Is Too Much?*, N.Y. Times, Jan. 23, 2004, at C5.

Conflict of Interest

The prohibition against a lawyer acquiring media rights concerning the representation of a client prior to concluding the representation recognizes the conflict between the interests of the client and the personal interests of the lawyer. Comment [9] to MR 1.8 explains, "Measures suitable in the representation of the client may detract from the publication value of an account of the representation." Are the risks posed by scenarios such as the one in *Echols*, in which the client enters into the media deal, serious enough to warrant a prophylactic approach? Or should courts simply look for evidence that such risks resulted in actual impairment of the lawyer's conduct or harm to the client's case?

As with lawyers themselves entering into media deals, the incentives here are mixed, and courts will likely continue to take the second option and look for evidence that perverse incentives negatively affected the lawyer's conduct or harmed the client. But lawyers who find themselves in such situations should be aware of the risks those situations pose in order to guard against them.

Prosecutorial Objections

The prosecutor might have a number of reasons to object to enhanced media exposure in the form of recording jury deliberations for broadcast or a media deal by a defendant. First, the prosecutor may conclude that enhanced exposure would create a strategic disadvantage for the government. Second, the prosecution has an interest in eliminating grounds for possible appeal. The prosecutor also has an ethical duty to ensure that proceedings are fair to the defendant. Comment [1] to MR 3.8 explains that the prosecutor has a "specific obligation to see that the defendant is accorded procedural justice, [and] that guilt is decided upon the basis of sufficient evidence . . . ." Finally, concern that perverse incentives created by a media deal may influence the defense lawyer's conduct may motivate the prosecutor to object.

A court is likely to give the prosecutor standing to object to the recording of jury deliberations, as the Texas trial and appellate courts did in the *Harrison* case. In fact, the prosecutor eventually prevailed and prevented the recording of jury deliberations in that case. It is less certain that a court would give a prosecutor any voice concerning media deals involving a defendant.

4

A Criminal Practitioner's Guide to the Media in Client Representation

The First Amendment and Related Constitutional Limits and Mandates

BY BRYAN L. ADAMSON

Introduction

The United States Constitution, federal and state statutes, and common law set forth obligations and rights that impact the criminal practitioner and the media in myriad ways. Whether representing or prosecuting a criminal defendant, a media defendant alleged to have committed a crime, or a media member seeking access to information of public interest, the criminal practitioner should be aware of the legal and ethical contours of mass media law. The Fourth, Fifth, and Sixth Amendments are not the only relevant constitutional boundaries; the First Amendment also contains provisions vital to the criminal practitioner's work. Furthermore, federal and state codifications impose additional mandates and limits on the criminal practitioner. Finally, state common law figures prominently in several areas of media and communications crimes and torts.

Overview: The First Amendment

The First Amendment, relevantly, directs that "Congress shall make no law . . . abridging the freedom of speech, or of the press[.]"[1] The intent behind this provision is to ban any law that tends to suppress, or chill, the expression of ideas whether directly or indirectly. First Amendment provisions, of all amendments, have been seen by the Supreme Court as holding a "preferred position;" that is, the ideals enshrined are so fundamental in a free society and consequently are entitled to more judicial protection than other constitutional values.[2] Although the First Amendment most explicitly applies to federal legislation, it also applies to the states through the Fourteenth Amendment's due process clause.[3] Moreover, although by its own terms the First Amendment seems absolute, both federal and state law have carved out exceptions. It is important to note that state constitutions, and judicial interpretation of its state's First Amendment provisions, may provide greater protections for speech and the press, but not less.[4]

The United States First Amendment applies only to government infringements and only to private actors in a few specific circumstances. One instance is when a private actor is effectively serving a public function traditionally performed by the state, and then that private party is engaged in "state action," and thus would be constrained by First Amendment obligations.[5] A second instance is when a strong nexus exists between government through its exercise of coercive powers or in its provision of significant encouragement, and the private party; under that scenario, First Amendment obligations would apply to that party as an effective state actor.[6]

"Freedom Of Speech"

Appreciation of what might constitute speech is a foundational requisite for prosecuting or defending individuals or institutions that allegedly

1. U.S. Const. amend. I.

2. Murdock v. Pennsylvania, 319 U.S. 105, 115 (1943).

3. Gitlow v. New York, 268 U.S. 652 (1925). "U.S. Const. amend XIV (No State shall make or enforce any law which shall abridge the privileges...of citizens...nor...deprive any person of life, liberty, or property, without due process of law...nor deny...the equal protection of the laws[.]" (emphasis added); Gitlow v. New York, 268 U.S. 652 (1925).

4. Cooper v. California, 386 U.S. 58, 62 (1967).

5. Jackson v. Metropolitan Edison Co., 419 U.S. 345 (1980).

6. Rendell-Baker v. Kohn, 457 U.S. 830 (1982); Lugar v. Edmonson Oil Co., 457 U.S. 922 (1982); Blum v. Yaretsky, 457 U.S. 991 (1982).

run afoul of laws proscribing what may or may not be communicated. "Speech," for First Amendment purposes, has been defined broadly and entails expression of ideas, thoughts, or opinions. Most commonly, it is the spoken word heard live, on television, or on radio (along with understood paralinguistic characteristics of tone, pitch, pace, or rate); visual images fixed or moving; words written in a newspaper, blog, on a placard, a T-shirt, or a billboard (along with semiotic conventions such as punctuation); or combination of words and images that constitute our most basic understanding of speech.

However, in its most expansive sense, "speech" constitutes messages understood by any (or some combination) of our most basic senses—sound, sight, touch, taste, or smell—such as the following examples: a speech act such as a hand clap, a wink or a nod, or a music note; a "thumbs-up" hand gesture, how one is dressed (or not dressed); a caress or a punch; a scoop of ice cream on the tongue; or smoke wafting from a lighted fire. Each is a kind of expression that communicates an idea, thus fairly considered "speech."[7] Moreover, communication of an idea can occur frequently from what is *not* expressed. A statement that demands the making of inferences from what is expressed adds meaning to what is said. Consequently, it is important to appreciate that "speech" might incorporate an array of what is said, what is done, and/or what is said and done (or *not* said or done) by the communicator.

It should be apparent that freedom of speech and the press is by no means absolute. Certain categories of speech, in any form, enjoy no absolute First Amendment protection:

- Obscene speech[8]
- Child pornography[9]

---

7. Some of the earliest Supreme Court cases interpreting the First Amendment's freedom of expression provision arose in the context of antidraft expression during times of war. *See* Schenck v. United States, 249 U.S. 47 (1919) (printed circulars discouraging citizens from registering for the draft found to violate the Espionage Act); Abrams v. United States, 250 U.S. 616 (1919); Whitney v. California, 274 U.S. 357 (1927).

8. Roth v. United States, 354 U.S. 476 (1957); Miller v. California, 413 U.S. 15 (1973).

9. New York v. Ferber, 458 U.S. 747 (1982).

- Speech considered "fighting words"[10]
- Speech creating a "clear and present danger of imminent lawless action"[11]
- Purposefully made or recklessly made false statements such as defamation or fraud[12]
- Commercial advertising[13]

The Press

It has long been understood that the drafters of the Constitution, in a rare example of citing a specific institution, saw a free press as essential to a free and functioning democracy.[14] Of course, we are a far cry from "the press" as it existed in 1787. Beginning with readers, pamphlets, and books, and through the evolution of modes of communication, the "press" organizations have existed in myriad forms: record, magazine, broadcast (radio, television, and satellite), wire-line and wireless, text, cable, and Internet. With that evolution, defining who exactly is a member of the press has transformed dramatically; reporters, editors, newsreaders, bloggers, opinion givers, and citizen reporters might each to some degree claim the mantle of fourth-estate membership. This fact becomes critical to the criminal practitioner—especially when it impacts local news and court reporting.

Freedom of Association

Freedom of association emerges out of the First Amendment right of assembly[15] and entails the expressive association—i.e., "the right to associate for the purpose of speaking"—or to petition the government for redress of

---

10. Chaplinsky v. New Hampshire, 315 U.S. 568 (1942) (but not "hate speech"); *see* R.A.V. v. City of St. Paul, Minn., 505 U.S. 377 (1992).

11. Brandenburg v. Ohio, 395 U.S. 444 (1969).

12. Zauderer v. Office of Disciplinary Counsel, 471 U.S. 626 (1985); Gertz v. Robert Welch, Inc., 418 U.S. 323 (1974); Beauharnais v. Illinois, 343 U.S. 25 (1952).

13. Valentine v. Chrestensen, 316 U.S. 52 (1942); Pittsburgh Press Co. v. Pittsburgh Comm'n on Human Relations, 413 U.S. 376 (1973); Virginia State Bd. of Pharmacy v. Virginia Citizens Consumer Council, Inc., 425 U.S. 748 (1976).

14. New York Times Co. v. Sullivan, 376 U.S. 254, 274 (1964).

15. U.S. Const. amend. I. ("Congress shall not abridge . . . the right of the people peaceably to assemble, and to petition the Government for a redress of grievances.")

grievances.[16] Freedom of association, like the freedom of speech, is a right that proscribes governmental interference (as distinguished from a right that the government must facilitate).[17]

The criminal practitioner may confront this constitutional claim when an individual or several members of organizations established on affinity-related grounds (based, for example, upon race, religion, or social cause) are said to be targeted by state or federal law enforcement actors because of or through membership within that group.[18] The legal contentions arise when the government pursues crimes of general application but have the impact of targeting individuals who are members of groups based on common affinity.

For example, an undercover investigation into money laundering within the Ismaili community raises due process concerns of targeting individuals based on their religious association. Courts, however, are reluctant to uphold claims of association violations in which otherwise valid laws of general applicability are sought to be enforced. Most forcefully, courts have said that no citizen has a right to be "free of investigation."[19] If it is shown that investigation targets a specific religious group incidentally to the law that is enforced generally, the investigation would not violate the First Amendment.[20]

The First Amendment and the Legal Standard

The First Amendment guarantees are a "fundamental element of liberty."[21] Consequently, legislative enactments or government actions that place content-based conditions upon speech or the press are not only disfavored but, when challenged judicially, undergo strict scrutiny analysis.[22] The first ques-

16. NAACP v. Alabama, 357 U.S. 449, 462 (1958) ("compelled disclosure of affiliation with groups engaged in advocacy may constitute as effective a restraint on freedom of association as the forms of governmental action in the cases . . . were thought likely to produce upon the particular constitutional rights there involved").

17. *See, e.g.*, Rust v. Sullivan, 500 U.S. 173, 198–200 (1991); Christian Legal Soc'y v. Walker, 453 F.3d 853, 873 (7th Cir. 2006) (Wood, J., dissenting) ("The Supreme Court has often drawn a line between rules that compel conduct and rules that merely withhold benefits."); Eugene Volokh, *Freedom of Expressive Association and Government Subsidies,* 58 STAN. L. REV. 1919, 1944 (2006).

18. *See, e.g.*, United States v. Jacobson, 916 F.2d 469 (8th Cir. 1990)

19. *Id.* at 467, 469 (8th Cir. 1990) (en banc), *cert. granted in part,* 111 S. Ct. 1618 (1991).

20. United States v. Allibhai, 939 F.2d 244 (5th Cir. 1991).

21. Gitlow v. New York, 268 U.S. 652 (1925).

22. *See, e.g.*, Federal Election Com'n v. Mass. Citizens for Life, Inc., 479 U.S. 238 (1986).

tion to answer is whether the restriction is content based—that is, whether the restriction relies upon the substance of the expression. If yes, the second question to answer is whether the condition imposed serves a compelling government interest and does so in the least restrictive manner.

In the face of constitutional challenge, states (and by extension state actors) can advance arguments that particular acts are within their "legitimate interests." Moreover, the federal government has compelling interests where matters of national security are concerned. As a baseline, it has been well established that states may pursue acts in accordance with their inherent police powers interests in safeguarding safety and health and impose reasonable time, place, and manner restrictions. Those interests may outweigh direct or incidental infringement upon expression provided that any restrictions are "justified without reference to the content of the regulated speech," that they are "narrowly tailored" to serve a significant or substantial governmental interest, and that they "leave open ample alternative channels for communication of the information."[23] "Narrow tailoring" requires a showing that "the means chosen do not burden substantially more speech than is necessary to further the government's legitimate interests[.]"[24]

The Criminal Practitioner and Managing the Media

Criminal Practitioners and Gag Orders

The criminal practitioner must always be mindful of the impact statements outside the courtroom may have upon a particular case. Rules of Professional Conduct provide important guidance for defense lawyers and prosecutors. Rule 3.6 of the Model Rules of Professional Conduct prohibits a lawyer from making "an extrajudicial statement that the lawyer knows or reasonably should know will be disseminated by means of public communication and will have a substantial likelihood of materially prejudicing an adjudicative proceeding in the matter,"[25] although the revealing of certain basic information is permitted.[26] Similarly, Rule 3.8 lists the spe-

---

23. Clark v. Community for Creative Non-Violence, 468 U.S. 288, 293 (1984). *Accord* Members of the City Council v. Taxpayers for Vincent, 466 U.S. 789, 807 (1984).

24. Ward v. Rock Against Racism, 491 U.S. 781, 802 (1989).

25. *Id.*

26. Model Rules of Prof'l Conduct Rule 3.8.

cial obligations of prosecutors, notably 3.8(f), which prohibits statements to the public beyond those "that are necessary to inform the public of the nature and extent of the prosecutor's action and that serve a legitimate law enforcement purpose[.]" Rule 3.8 also holds the prosecutor to the same requirements as those for a lawyer listed in 3.6.[27] Moreover, prosecutors must take reasonable care to ensure law enforcement, investigative officers, or others who assist in the process do not violate Rule 3.6.

Commentary under the Model Rules cites specific types of extrajudicial statements that could have a prejudicial impact on trial proceedings. Those include

- references to character, credibility, or reputation or expected testimony of a suspect or witness or identity of a witness;
- the existence or comments of a confession or refusal to make a statement;
- reference to the possibility of a guilty plea;
- reference to test results or the refusal to submit to an exam or test;
- any opinion about the guilt or innocence of a criminal defendant or suspect;
- the identity or nature of physical evidence;
- information that a trial participant "knows or reasonably should know would be inadmissible at trial"; and
- the fact of being charged with a crime without a corresponding caution that the defendant is presumed innocent "until or unless proven guilty."

Safe Harbors

The Model Rules contain safe harbors that are recognized by courts. Rule 3.6(b) allows lawyers to respond extrajudicially to "recent publicity" that might prejudice the client if the publicity was not initiated by the lawyer or the client and only to the extent needed to "mitigate recent adverse publicity." Criminal prosecutors may make statements to "inform the public of

---

27. Model Rules of Prof'l Conduct Rule 3.8.

the nature and extent of the prosecutor's action" and those which serve a legitimate law enforcement purpose.[28]

Out-of-court speech restrictions attempt to balance the interests of the public, the litigants, and the judicial process. The public interest lies in ensuring an informed citizenry about litigation, the law, and the court system. In meeting that interest, criminal practitioners and the media play a vital role for the public in accessing court proceedings. Litigants may often wish to place a dispute before the public to call attention to their plight or perceived systemic biases. The freedom to speak about the judicial process also serves to facilitate critique of and, if warranted, correction of government corruption, ineptitude, or malice. Litigants may also wish to publicize information that will counteract or mitigate public perceptions about the litigant or the legal matter.

However, information regarding details of particular cases can have an adverse effect on the ability to achieve Sixth Amendment assurances of a fair trial. Extrajudicial comments can have a very real impact on potential or actual jurors, potential or actual witnesses, or even the judge by tainting the evidence or shaping the impressions of the case and participants.

As demonstrated by the Duke men's lacrosse team scandal, abuse of authority by the prosecution can be hugely problematic. Prosecutors or other governmental lawyers' extrajudicial statements may be subject to greater controls in circumstances in which they are involved as advocates.[29] Particularly in jurisdictions in which prosecutors are elected, there is a heightened public interest to curtail speech that could be construed as currying favor for a constituency or for votes.

Other speech restrictions depend on the status of the person involved in the litigation. For example, the names or other matter that could lead to the identity of juvenile offenders or sexual assault victims may not be communicated. In addition, confidentiality provisions of the Rules restrict communication that may be adverse to a client, such as trade secrets or other proprietary information.[30]

---

28. Model Rules of Prof'l Cond. R. 2.8(f).
29. Id., Comments.
30. Restatement (Third), The Law Governing Lawyers, 6(a).

Balanced against the press freedom and the right of the citizenry is the governmental interest of ensuring a fair and equitable justice system and the public interest in ensuring effective measures of safety and security. Faced with potential abuse by a media entity in the case of ongoing litigation or a criminal trial, there are several available options, but nearly all must be exercised at the discretion of the court. The court can issue gag orders and close portions of the trial to the public and the media; however, any such decision must withstand First Amendment scrutiny.

In *Nebraska Press Ass'n v. Stuart*,[31] the Supreme Court established three factors to be considered before placing a restriction on the press: (1) the "nature and extent of publicity," (2) the ability of other methods such as efforts to control jury access to media information to be effective to mitigate the effects of publicity, and (3) whether the restriction itself would actually be effective.[32] Courts can also hold media representatives in contempt for failure to comply with an order.

Lower courts are split on the standard for applying gag orders,[33] with the Second, Fourth, and Tenth Circuits at the most lenient end of the spectrum requiring a reasonable likelihood of prejudice;[34] the Third and Fifth requiring a substantial likelihood of prejudice;[35] and the Sixth, Seventh, and Ninth with the strictest standard requiring a clear and present danger of material prejudice.[36] Following a trial, a convicted defendant can appeal under a claim that the trial was unfair due to excessive media involvement, as demonstrated in the famous case of *Sheppard v. Maxwell*.[37] In that case, the Supreme Court overturned Dr. Sheppard's murder conviction due to the lack of a fair trial following a media-induced "carnival atmosphere"[38] in the courtroom.

---

31. Nebraska Press Ass'n v. Stuart, 427 U.S. 539 (1976).
32. *Id.* at 562.
33. Jonathan Eric Pahl, *Court-Ordered Restrictions on Trial Participant Speech*, 57 DUKE L.J. 1113 (2008).
34. *Id.* (citing *In re* Morrissey, 168 F.3d 134 (4th Cir. 1999); United States v. Cutler, 58 F.3d 825 (2d Cir. 1995); *In re* Application of Dow Jones, 842 F.2d 603 (2d Cir. 1988); United States v. Tijerina, 412 F.2d 661 (10th Cir. 1969)).
35. *Id.* (citing United States v. Scarfo, 263 F.3d 80 (3d Cir. 2001); United States v. Brown, 218 F.3d 415 (5th Cir. 2000)).
36. *Id.* (citing United States v. Ford, 830 F.2d 596 (6th Cir. 1987); Levine v. United States, 764 F.2d 590 (9th Cir. 1985); Chicago Council of Lawyers v. Bauer, 522 F.2d 242 (7th Cir. 1975)).
37. Sheppard v. Maxwell, 384 U.S. 333 (1966).
38. *Id.* at 358.

The Press and Trial Publicity

Discussion of the criminal practitioner's extrajudicial statements is incomplete without considering the role of the press in disseminating those statements. Above all, the balance that is being struck is the right to a fair trial against the public's "right to know," that is facilitated by the press. Pretrial and trial coverage can have very real effects on potential jurors and witnesses, the criminal defense lawyer, the prosecutor, the judge, and especially the defendants.

Generally speaking, prejudicial publicity may arise in two contexts. The first involves attempts to influence judicial behavior by writing articles or reporting on pending cases. The second involves the institution of the jury and the imperative that jurors be impartial. Media reports potentially impact jurors and trials if they focus on matters that, by rule and law, cannot come into consideration in determining guilt or innocence. An accused's prior conviction record is generally inadmissible in evidence unless the defendant chooses to testify, which, as a constitutional matter, the defendant may refuse to do. The concern is that jurors, having heard, seen, or read reports of the prior convictions, would be more inclined to convict even though the prosecution has failed to prove its case beyond a reasonable doubt.

In addition, pretrial confessions are not admissible in trial unless they have been made voluntarily and the accused has been properly Mirandized. Media reports of confessions may also unduly influence jurors; even if other evidence shows the confession to be accurate, law enforcement is not discouraged if the confession was in fact defective or coerced.

Finally, inadmissible evidence seized in an unlawful search is not admissible in court. As with confessions, the goal is to discourage the state from engaging in unconstitutional behavior. Because under these circumstances the evidence reported would be inadmissible, the courts seek to keep jurors from gaining access to the information.

To prevent prejudicial information from reaching the public, courts have developed a number of remedies. In addition to admonishments to trial participants and assistants regarding extrajudicial statements, courts attempt to shield witnesses from the press, caution journalists about potential dangers, and encourage adoption of bench-bar-press guidelines.[39]

Other remedies are pursued in an effort to find unbiased jurors and include granting a change of venue, a change of venire, granting a trial delay or continuance request, or simply relying upon a rigorous *voir dire* process.

Some remedies seek to ensure that jurors remain unbiased by instructions against reading or listening to reports or other comments about the case, and even sequestration. None of these remedies directly restrict the press. Yet gags on police and lawyers may be challenged on First Amendment rights of expression. That said, to the extent those remedies adversely impact the news-gathering process, they give rise to First Amendment press challenges.[40]

More dramatic remedies include closing the courtroom to the press and public during pretrial hearings, closing the courtroom to the press and public during trials, imposing conditions on those allowed into the courtroom, barring cameras or recording devices out of the courtroom, or ordering the press not to publish or report certain information. These latter remedies, especially when imposed on the press, raise important First Amendment considerations.

Consequences

Court restrictions on speech can take a variety of forms, enforced through the contempt powers of trial courts. First, courts may place an outright ban on extrajudicial statements remotely relevant to the proceedings.[41] Other restrictions may be qualified by language that track the Model Rules or codes, by restricting speech that has a "reasonable likelihood," "substantial likelihood," or "clear and present danger" of materially impacting the proceedings.[42] Courts may also issue orders that explicitly incorporate the court rules and rules of professional conduct, and remind the trial participants of the ability and intent to enforce those rules.

A final type of restriction involves no notice to the parties at all. Conse-

---

39. T. Barton Carter, Marc A. Franklin & Jay B. Wright, The First Amendment and the Fourth Estate: The Law of Mass Media 502–03 (Foundation Press 10th ed. 2008).

40. *See, e.g.*, Richmond Newspapers v. Virginia, 458 U.S. 555 (1980).

41. Pahl, *supra* note 34 at 120.

42. *Id.*

quences for violations may include contempt sanctions and result in fines or even imprisonment through the court's inherent powers. However, the lack of notice and the substance of the extrajudicial comment may be directly challenged on First Amendment and due process grounds.[43]

Regardless of the form of speech restriction, the punishment can go beyond a contempt citation. In the most egregious circumstances, consequences could even result in a mistrial or reversal on appeal.

Criminal prosecutors specifically may expose themselves to federal or state civil rights violations for improper comments to the media. Lawyers, however, should always explore remedies when subject to sanction. For example, if a gag order is vague, or overbroad, lawyers subject to violations may argue the order or that its enforcement is unconstitutional.

The Criminal Practitioner and Profiteering: Son of Sam Laws

Introduction

Named after the serial killer David Berkowitz, "Son of Sam" laws restrict the ability of convicted criminals to capitalize financially on their stories. Since their inception, they have had a bit of a tortured history. The first such law was passed in New York in reaction to fear that Berkowitz was going to sell his story to the media, thus making a killing from his, well, killings.[44] The law had two goals: "to prevent criminal authors from profiting from their criminal notoriety and to promote crime victim compensation."[45] Dozens of other states followed suit by passing similar versions of the law.[46]

In the early 1990s, New York's law reached the Supreme Court following a contract between Simon and Schuster and ex-Mafia member Henry Hill for a book detailing Hill's experiences in organized crime.[47] The Court first found that the law was content based and then applied strict

---

43. Bridges v. California, 314 U.S. 252 (1942).

44. Orly Nosrati, Note and Comment, *Son of Sam Laws: Killing Free Speech or Promoting Killer Profits?*, 20 Whittier L. Rev. 949 (1999); *Id.* at 953. Ironically, Berkowitz was never subjected to the law because the court found him mentally incompetent to stand trial.

45. Kathleen M. Timmons, *Natural Born Writers: The Law's Continued Annoyance with Criminal Authors*, 29 Ga. L. Rev. 1121, 1128 (1995).

46. *Id.* at 1131.

47. The book later became the foundation for the movie *Goodfellas.*

scrutiny, finding that although the state had a compelling government interest in compensating crime victims by the perpetrators the law was not narrowly tailored in that it was overinclusive both as to who was subject to the statute and which works fell within its scope.[48] Following the Court's decision, the New York legislature amended its Son of Sam law to remove the overinclusive elements, and many other states followed suit.[49]

Current Son of Sam Laws

In spite of the amendments, the issues surrounding Son of Sam laws are constantly in tension. Additionally, although not technically Son of Sam law, similar laws have been promulgated in an effort to prevent general profiting from crime.

Modern Son of Sam laws vary somewhat from state to state, so this discussion will be kept quite general. A conviction is now required, thus limiting the problem of overinclusiveness. However, it has been frequently argued that overinclusiveness is still a problem because the statute can still be applied to works with only incidental references to crimes.[50] Underinclusiveness is also argued to be a problem due to the failure of the statutes to adequately compensate victims as per their intended purpose.[51] For one thing, they do not distinguish between assets generated from the expression and general assets.[52] For another, the profits are returned to the criminal author after five years in escrow.[53]

Arguments are also made that such laws are ineffective for several reasons, including the ability of a criminal to profit and spend prior to conviction and the requirement that a victim go to the trouble of obtaining a civil judgment in order to receive any compensation.[54] Finally, arguments exist that Son of Sam laws are unfair due to inherent vindictiveness because their application may vary depending on the level of public sympa-

---

48. Simon & Schuster, Inc. v. Members of N.Y. State Crime Victims Bd., 502 U.S. 105 (1991). For example, the law did not require a conviction and did not make any qualifications as to what sort of works could be included. Following this rationale, myriad authors would fall under the statute's shadow, from Malcolm X to St. Augustine.

49. Timmons, *supra* note 45 at 1136.

50. *Id.* at 1139.

51. *Id.* at 1141.

52. *Id.*

53. *Id.*

54. This appears to be the situation in Florida. *Id.* at 1145.

thy for the criminal in question.[55]

Alternate methods that resemble but are technically outside the realm of Son of Sam laws include the imposition of fines, orders of restitution, and probation conditions prohibiting financial gain.[56] The idea behind these methods is based on the anticipation of profits received from the sale of the criminal defendant's story.[57] Of course, the defendant may never actually sell his or her story, and this requires the judge to guess at the market value of such story in the case that the defendant should choose to sell it.[58] Proponents of such arguments maintain that tort law is much better suited to addressing these sorts of problems.[59]

There are also questions regarding the relationship between Son of Sam laws and other aspects of the Constitution, including the Fifth, Sixth, and Eighth Amendments. The Fifth Amendment is implicated because of its guarantee of due process, and yet Son of Sam laws frequently freeze assets in spite of the presumption of innocence.[60] The fact that a defendant may have to forego payment for a story that could pay for adequate legal defense implicates the Sixth Amendment.[61] Meanwhile, the Eighth Amendment is a concern due to the prohibition on excessive fines.[62]

Variations

It is not just criminal defendants who must consider the consequences of profiting from the story of a crime. Lawyers, witnesses, and jurors also face restrictions. Lawyers are frequently in a position to know extraordinary (and potentially profitable) details about their clients' stories. Thus far, legislatures have not attempted to directly legislate in this particular area, leaving such regulation to professional disciplinary organizations and the courts. For example, Model Rule of Professional Conduct 1.8(d)

55. *Id.* at 1146.
56. *Id.* at 1148.
57. *Id.*
58. *Id.*
59. *Id.*
60. Nosrati, *supra* note 44 at 982–83.
61. *Id.* at 985–86.
62. *Id.* at 985.

provides that "[p]rior to the conclusion of representation of a client, a lawyer shall not make or negotiate an agreement giving the lawyer literary or media rights to a portrayal or account based in substantial part on information relating to the representation."[63]

It is not possible to describe all the potential considerations at issue here, but one example is when a client may need to present a diminished capacity defense while the lawyer attempts to show the client's capacity to enter into a literary contract.[64] Rule 1.6(a) is also implicated,[65] and there are plenty of arguments for a host of other rules as well. There is ongoing debate as to the extent of clients' ability to give informed consent in such matters. The Supreme Court has not had a great deal to say on the subject, although it did hold that in the case of the First Amendment, "state-imposed restrictions on attorney speech are subject to less stringent review than state-imposed restrictions on other speakers."[66]

In the wake of the O. J. Simpson fiasco, California enacted a law limiting the ability of both jurors and witnesses to profit from their interactions with the media. In relation to jurors, California's law prohibits jurors from discussing the trial during the time of the trial or within 90 days of discharge.[67] Witnesses face a similar prohibition.[68] This idea has produced much criticism, however. One argument is that the law only affects lay witnesses,[69] while ignoring concerns about expert witnesses and other defendants who obtain a favorable plea bargain in exchange for their testimony.[70] Most importantly, of course, free speech issues are also

---

63. Model Rules of Professional Conduct Rule 1.8(d).

64. Ría A. Tabacco, Note, *Defensible Ethics: A Proposal to Revise the ABA Model Rules for Criminal Defense Lawyer-Authors*, 83 N.Y.U. L. Rev. 568, 575–76 (2008).

65. Model Rules of Professional Conduct Rule 1.6(a) states, "A Lawyer shall not reveal information relating to the representation of a client unless the client gives informed consent."

66. Tabacco, *supra* note 64 at 596. *See* Gentile v. State Bar of Nevada, 501 U.S. 1030 (1991).

67. James R. Cady, Note, *Bouncing "Checkbook Journalism": A Balance Between the First and Sixth Amendments in High-Profile Criminal Cases*, 4 Wm. & Mary Bill Rts. J. 671, 679 (1995).

68. Chrysanthe E. Vassiles, *Checkbook Journalism: It May Involve Free Speech Interests But it is Not Free; Can Witnesses Be Prohibited From Selling Their Stories to Media Under the First Amendment?* 56 Ohio St. L.J. 1619, 1630 (1995). California's statute includes anyone who "has witnessed or has personal knowledge of a criminal event or occurrence in the state of California, whether or not that person is a material witness." *Id.*

69. Marcy Strauss, *From Witness to Riches: The Constitutionality of Restricting Witness Speech*, 38 Ariz. L. Rev. 291, 301 (1996).

70. Vassiles, *supra* note 68 at 1640.

implicated,[71] including issues of prior restraint.[72]

Conclusion

Current Son of Sam laws and their progeny appear to be balanced on the precipice of constitutionality left by the Supreme Court's decision in *Simon & Schuster*. It is likely that until such time as the Court chooses to revisit this issue they will remain in effect, although subject to ongoing debate in the tug-of-war between the First Amendment and other considerations.

The controversy surrounding these kinds of laws is not going to go away and will likely be sharpened by the powers of the Internet. So-called "murderabilia" websites have sparked outrage and controversy,[73] although it is usually not the criminal defendant who profits from such an enterprise. Current Son of Sam laws are not equipped to deal with such issues, and the Internet is a vast thing to subject to regulation. It will be interesting and challenging to see how this front develops.

The Criminal Practitioner and Knowing the Media Issues: Courts and Trials

Reporter's Privilege and Shield Laws

Reporters are frequently placed in the position of observers of the legal institutions in which criminal practitioners work. Whether in the courts or reporting on events, journalists as observers have unique access to information that potentially impacts court or law enforcement processes. A corollary to the federal government's obligation not to abridge the "freedom of the press" in reporting information is the obligation that government not unduly infringe upon the right of the press to *gather* information. Yet, constitutional guarantees of a free press may conflict with Sixth Amendment guarantees of trial by an impartial jury.

The Sixth Amendment reads:

---

71. Strauss, *supra* note 69 at 307.

72. Vassiles, *supra* note 68 at 1624.

73. Suna Chang, Note and Comment, *The Prodigal "Son" Returns: An Assessment of Current "Son of Sam" Laws and the Reality of the Online Murderabilia Marketplace*, 31 RUTGERS COMPUTER & TECH. L.J. 430, 432 (2005). Oddly enough, the original Son of Sam himself, David Berkowitz, has been a vocal critic of online sales of crime memorabilia. *Id.*

> In all criminal prosecutions, the accused shall enjoy the right to a speedy and public trial, by an impartial jury of the State and district wherein the crime shall have been committed, which district shall have been previously ascertained by law, and to be informed of the nature and cause of the accusation; to be confronted with the witnesses against him; to have compulsory process for obtaining witnesses in his favor, and to have the Assistance of Counsel for his defence.

Information obtained by a reporter in the course of reporting may compromise the panoply of Sixth Amendment rights of an accused. When such a circumstance arises, a reporter or a news organization may be subpoenaed to testify or turn over information obtained in the course of news gathering and reporting. A point arises when a decision must be made as to when a reporter must reveal sources (or the information provided by those sources) to further ensure Sixth Amendment rights are preserved or that law enforcement or national security interests are served.

Fourth Amendment concerns arise when government actors, through warrants, act to seize documents or instruments of news gathering, writing, and reporting (such as computers, audio or video recordings, telephone logs, reporter's notes). As with Sixth Amendment provisions, search and seizure attempts run headlong into First Amendment protections for the press.

"Shield laws," sometimes referred to as the "reporter's privilege," are designed to protect reporters from being compelled to reveal confidential sources. Reporters might be compelled to reveal confidential information sources in the context of third-party criminal prosecutions, their own prosecution, or in civil cases. In addition to being compelled to reveal information sources, reporters have also been commanded to submit investigative notes, documents, travel or telephone records, or photographs, or submit to wholesale newsroom searches or other evidence (whether or not such evidence was ultimately used in or for a story).

For purposes of the reporter's privilege, the First Amendment presumes the right, above all, of the public to information provided by the press to best facilitate the public's participation in a democracy. Confidential sources, even nonconfidential sources, provide the public with information vital to this press function. On one hand, the argument is made that forcing reporters to reveal confidential sources creates a chilling effect, discouraging those with important information from sharing such information with reporters out of fear of being revealed.[74] The effect of such a chill, it is said, is to deprive the public of such vital information. Furthermore, proponents of the privilege assert that to compel the identity of a confidential source would expose the source to serious personal, professional, and perhaps legal consequences.[75]

Opponents of the reporter's privilege assert that such laws prevent vital information from a trier of fact[76] and present a danger to national security, as we saw advanced in the Judith Miller/*New York Times* and WikiLeaks sagas.[77] Moreover, opponents argue that it is far from certain whether in fact the absence of a privilege discourages sources from sharing information with reporters.[78]

Criminal practitioners needing to litigate shield laws must begin with *Branzburg v. Hayes*,[79] a 1972 case in which the Supreme Court first considered whether the First Amendment supported a privilege claimed by reporters who were being compelled to respond to a grand jury subpoena and to answer questions relevant to a criminal investigation.[80] Justice White, writing for the 5–4 majority, stated that the First Amendment did not grant newspaper reporters a testimonial privilege for confidentiality agreements made with informants.[81] However, Justice White did allow that Congress and state legislatures could nonetheless codify a privilege delimited by First Amendment proscriptions.[82] What remains is that fed-

---

74. *Id.* at 808.
75. Mary-Rose Papandrea, *Citizen Journalism and the Reporter's Privilege*, 91 MINN. L. REV. 515, 536 (2007).
76. Randall D. Eliason, *Leakers, Bloggers, and Fourth Estate Inmates: The Misguided Pursuit of a Reporter's Privilege*, 24 CARDOZO ARTS & ENT. L.J. 385, 417 (2006).
77. Yochai Benkler, *A Free Irresponsible Press: Wikileaks and the Battle over the Soul of the Networked Fourth Estate*, 46 HARV. C.R.-C.L. L. REV. 311 (2011); Jason A. Martin, Mark R. Caramanica, & Anthony L. Fargo, *Anonymous Speakers And Confidential Sources: Using Shield Laws When They Overlap Online*, 16 COMM. L. & POL'Y 89 (2011).
78. Eliason, *supra* note 76 at 416.
79. Branzburg v. Hayes, 408 U.S. 665 (1972).
80. *Id.* at 708.
81. *Id.* at 682–83.
82. *Id.* at 706.

eral law gives reporters no absolute privilege to refuse to testify or give over names of sources or information when subpoenaed for grand jury proceedings. Critically, a qualified privilege articulated in Justice Stewart's *Branzburg* dissent has proven to be profoundly influential.

Some federal circuits such as the Second, Third, and the Eleventh have interpreted *Branzburg* narrowly and thus have recognized a qualified privilege.[83] As far as the states are concerned, however, shield laws are pervasive. When *Branzburg* was decided in 1972, 18 states had shield laws that protected reporters from forced disclosures of confidential sources.[84] In response to *Branzburg*, dozens of states passed new shield laws. Currently, 49 states recognize some type of reporter's privilege.[85] The shield statutes in 35 of those states and the District of Columbia have codified the reporter's privilege,[86] while the others have implemented the privilege through common-law judicial interpretation.[87]

Whether in the federal circuits, state statutes, or state common law, the existence of a reporter's privilege is made on a case-by-case basis. The test in virtually all circumstances applies the standard announced in Justice Stewart's *Branzburg* dissent, or the merest variation of the same:[88] When

83. See, e.g., Chevron v. Berlinger, 629 F.3d 297 (2d Cir. 2011); Titan Sports, Inc. v. Turner Broad. Sys. (In Re Madden), 151 F.3d 125 (3d Cir. 1997); Price v. Time, Inc., 416 F.3d 1327 (11th Cir. 2005).

84. Caroline Lynch Pieroni, Comment, *Staying Out of Jail . . . Sometimes: Maintaining a Free Press Through Journalist Shield Laws Requires Changes not at the Federal Level, but also Among the States*, 47 U. Louisville L. Rev. 803, 809 (2009).

85. *Id.* (Wyoming is the only state that does not recognize some type of reporter's privilege.)

86. *See, e.g.*, Ala. Code § 12-21-145 (2005); Ariz. Rev. Stat. Ann. 12-2237 (2003); Ark. Code Ann. § 16-85-510 (2005); Cal. Evid. Code § 1070 (2009); Colo. Rev. Stat. Ann. § 13-90-119 (2008); Conn. Gen. Stat. Ann. § 52-146t (2006); Ga. Code Ann. § 24-9-30 (1995); 735 Ill. Comp. Stat. Ann. 5/8-901 to 5/8-909 (2003); Ind. Code Ann. § 34-46-4-2 (2008); Ky. Rev. Stat. Ann. § 421.100 (2006); La. Rev. Stat. Ann. § 45:1452 (1999); Md. Code Ann., Cts. Jud. Proc. § 9-112 (2006); Mich. Comp. Laws Ann. § 767.5a (2000); Mont. Code Ann. §§ 26-1-901 to 903 (2009); Neb. Rev. Stat. § 20-146 (2007); Nev. Rev. Stat. Ann. § 49.275 79-h (2009); N.C. Gen. Stat. § 8-53.11 (2007); N.D. Cent. Code § 31-01-06.2; Ohio Rev. Code Ann. §§ 2739.04, 2739.12 (2006); Or. Rev. Stat. § 44.520 (2007); 42 Pa. Cons. Stat. Ann. § 5942 (2000); R.I. Gen. Laws §§ 9-19.1-2 to 19.1-3 (1997); S.C. Code Ann. § 19-11-100 (2008); Utah R. Evid. 509 (2008); Wash. Rev. Code. Ann. § 5.68.010 (2009).

87. *See, e.g., In re* Contempt of Wright, 700 P.2d 40, 44 (Idaho 1985); Winegard v. Oxberger, 258 N.W.2d 847, 850 (Iowa 1977); State v. Sandstrom, 581 P.2d 812, 814 (Kan. 1978); State v. Hohler, 543 A.2d 364, 366 (Me. 1988); *In re* Promulgation of Rules Regarding the Protection of Confidential News Sources, 479 N.E.2d 154, 156, 158 (Mass. 1985); Eason v. Federal Broad. Co., 697 So. 2d 435, 437 (Miss. 1997); State ex rel. Classic III, Inc. v. Ely Stone, 954 S.W.2d 650 (Mo. Ct. App. 1997); CBS Inc. v. Campbell, 645 S.W.2d 30, 33 (Mo. Ct. App. 1982); State v. Siel, 444 A.2d 499, 503 (N.H. 1982); Hopewell v. Midcontinent Broad. Corp., 538 N.W.2d 780, 782 (S.D. 1995); State ex rel. Healey v. McMeans, 884 S.W.2d 772, 775 (Tex. Crim. App. 1994); State v. St. Peter, 315 A.2d 254, 256 (Vt. 1974); Brown v. Commonwealth, 204 S.E.2d 429, 431 (Va. 1974); Philip Morris Co. v. American Broad. Co., 36 Va. Cir. 1, 15 (Va. Cir. Ct. 1994); State ex rel. Hudok v. Henry, 389 S.E.2d 188, 192–93 (W. Va. 1989); State v. Knops, 183 N.W.2d 93, 99 (Wis. 1971).

88. *See* discussion, *infra*.

a reporter is asked to appear in a court proceeding and reveal confidences or other information obtained in the course of the reporter's work and invokes the privilege (through, for example, a motion to quash the subpoena compelling the reporter's testimony), the government must (1) show that there is probable cause to believe that the reporter has information that is clearly relevant to a specific probable violation of law, (2) demonstrate that the information sought cannot be obtained by alternative means less destructive of First Amendment rights, and (3) demonstrate a compelling and overriding interest in the information.[89]

Absolute or Qualified Privilege

States differ in the extent to which the reporter's privilege is recognized.[90] Some states recognize an absolute privilege, meaning a reporter's sources and news-gathering materials will remain confidential regardless of the circumstances of the proceedings.[91] Arizona, for example, recognizes an absolute privilege against being compelled to testify "before any jury, inquisitorial body or commission, or before a committee of the legislature, or elsewhere" about any information "procured or obtained by him for publication."[92] However, it is more common for states to codify a qualified privilege, which allows a party to compel the disclosure of confidential information when it can demonstrate (1) that the desired

89. Branzburg v. Hayes, 408 U.S. at 743.

90. Papandrea, *supra* note 75 at 546.

91. *See, e.g.*, ALA. CODE § 12-21-142 (stating that a reporter has an absolute privilege as long as the information from the source has been published, broadcast, or televised); ARIZ. REV. STAT. ANN. § 12-2237 (recognizing an absolute privilege against being compelled to testify "before any jury, inquisitorial body or commission, or before a committee of the legislature, or elsewhere" about any information "procured or obtained by him for publication"); Cal. EVID. CODE § 1070(a) (providing a privilege against being held in contempt "by a judicial, legislative, administrative body, or any other body having the power to issue subpoenas" for refusing to disclose a source or unpublished information); D.C. CODE §§ 16-4702(1), -4703(b); IND. CODE ANN. § 34-46-4-2 (providing an absolute protection for the identity of a source); KY. REV. STAT. ANN. § 421.100 (recognizing an absolute protection for the identity of a source); MONT. CODE ANN. § 26-1-902 (providing for an absolute privilege for a source's identity or information obtained in the course of gathering, receiving, or processing news); NEB. REV. STAT. §§ 20-144 to -147 (providing an absolute protection for a source's identity and for all unpublished information); NEV. REV. STAT. § 49.275 (providing an absolute protection for a source's identity and all unpublished information); OR. REV. STAT. § 44.520(1) (creating an absolute privilege in all proceedings for the source of published or unpublished information and for any unpublished information, except when a person claiming privilege is believed to have committed or is about to commit a crime); 42 PA. CONS. STAT. ANN. § 5942. *But see* Diaz v. Eighth Judicial Dist. Court, 993 P.2d 50, 59 (Nev. 2000) ("[A]lthough the [Nevada] news shield statute provides an absolute privilege to reporters engaged in the newsgathering process, there may be certain situations, e.g., when a defendant's countervailing constitutional rights are at issue, in which the news shield statute might have to yield so that justice may be served.").

92. ARIZ. REV. STAT. ANN. § 12-2237.

information is important to the suit, (2) that other means of obtaining the information have proven inadequate, and (3) that the balance of interests disfavors disclosure.[93] Importantly, regardless of the juridical breadth of the privilege, the exemptions created by states apply only to state proceedings.

In advance of arguing the applicability of the reporter's privilege and the balancing test courts deploy, the criminal practitioner needs to know (1) who qualifies for the privilege; (2) the types and sources of information to which the privilege applies; and (3) the type of proceeding in which the privilege, if it exists, can be invoked. Only after such an assessment is it useful to assess the elements of arguing for or against the privilege and the evidentiary burdens applied.

Who Is A "Journalist"?

Importantly, state laws vary greatly as to who qualifies as a journalist or what qualifies as journalism.[94] For example, Louisiana's privilege statute applies to "any *person* . . . in the *business* of collecting, writing, or editing news for publication through the news media."[95] New York's shield statutes, for example, include and define the "newspaper," "news organiza-

---

93. *See, e.g.*, Colo. Rev. Stat. § 13-90-119(3) (setting out a three-part test); Ga. Code Ann. § 24-9-30 (same); 735 Ill. Comp. Stat. Ann. 5/8-906 to -907 (same); La. Rev. Stat. Ann. § 45:1459 (requiring an inquiry in cases seeking unpublished information); Md. Code Ann., Cts. & Jud. Proc. § 9-112(d)(1) (same); Mich. Comp. Laws § 767.5a (providing for a qualified privilege before a grand jury when an inquiry is for a crime punishable by life in prison); Minn. Stat. § 595.024 (setting forth conditions necessary for overriding the privilege); *In re* Contempt of Wright, 700 P.2d at 44-45(recognizing a qualified privilege under the First Amendment, the Idaho Constitution, and common law, and applying a balancing test); Lamberto v. Bown, 326 N.W.2d 305, 308-09 (Iowa 1982) (recognizing a qualified privilege subject to a three-factor inquiry); State v. Sandstrom, 581 P.2d 814 (Kan. 1978) (recognizing a qualified privilege); State ex rel. Classic III, Inc. v. Ely, 954 S.W.2d 650, 653 (Mo. Ct. App. 1997) (recognizing a qualified privilege under the First Amendment); *cf.* In re Letellier, 578 A.2d 722, 726 (Me. 1990) (holding that a case-by-case balancing test, rather than a three-factor test, applied); New Hampshire v. Siel, 444 A.2d 499, 503 (N.H. 1978) (recognizing a three-part test for overcoming a qualified privilege). Other state statutes provide more simply that the privilege applies unless nondisclosure "will cause a miscarriage of justice" or will be "contrary to the public interest." *See, e.g.*, Alaska Stat. § 09.25.310(b) (providing that a court may deny a privilege if withholding testimony would "result in a miscarriage of justice or the denial of a fair trial to those who challenge the privilege" or "be contrary to the public interest"); La. Rev. Stat. Ann. § 45:1453 (requiring a finding that "disclosure is essential to the public interest"); N.D. Cent. Code § 31-01-06.2. One state statute provides that the privilege applies in all proceedings unless it can be shown that the publication was made "in bad faith, with malice, and not in the interest of the public welfare." Ark. Code Ann. § 16-85-510 (2005). Although the statute specifically mentions only grand juries, the Supreme Court of Arkansas has construed the statutory language "to any other authority" to include civil proceedings as well. *See* Saxton v. Arkansas Gazette Co., 569 S.W.2d 115, 117 (Ark. 1978).

94. Pieroni, *supra* note 84 at 812–13.

95. La.R.S. § 45:1451 (emphasis added).

tion," "magazine," and "news agency" as "broadcaster."[96] Kentucky's statute applies to any person who obtains and publishes information "in a newspaper or by a radio or television broadcasting station by which he is engaged or employed, or with which he is connected."[97] California's shield law extends its protection to a "publisher, editor, reporter, or other person connected with or employed by a newspaper, magazine, or other periodical publication, or by a press association or wire service," as well as to a "radio or television station news reporter or other person connected with or employed by a radio or television station."[98] North Carolina's statute covers any person, company, or entity engaged in the "business of gathering, compiling, writing, editing, photographing, recording, or processing information for dissemination via any news medium."[99]

It is important to determine how broadly or narrowly a state defines those who might seek the protection of the privilege. Virtually all statutes recognize the coverage to include news organizations and entities in the business of publishing or broadcasting news. If an individual is seeking the privilege, coverage may turn upon the individual's connection with a news organization (employee, agent, freelance) or the question of whether the individual engages in information gathering and dissemination on a regular basis or for compensation. Note that many state shield laws have not yet explicitly incorporated relatively modern news dissemination mediums such as the Internet, and so it remains uncertain whether the blogger, citizen-reporter, or writer otherwise unaffiliated with a bona fide news organization could find safety in the reporter's privilege.

Questions frequently arise as to whether the reporter's privilege can be invoked by nonreporters. Maryland, New York, Indiana, Ohio, and New Jersey shield statutes have been interpreted to make clear that the privilege belongs to the journalist, not the informant.[100] In other words, the statute seeks to protect the reporter, not the source who wishes to remain anonymous. As a result, courts in those states have held that the informant at-

---

96. N.Y. Civ. Rights Law § 79-h(a)(1)-(8).

97. Ky. Rev. Stat. Ann. § 421.100.

98. Cal. Evid. Code § 1070 (a) & (b).

99. N.C. Gen. Stat. § 8-53.9.

100. Matthew Bender, Chapter 17, State Shield and Federal Codifications, 2-17 Newsgathering and the Law § 17.02[1][b].

tempting to block information communicated does not have standing to challenge disclosure through the shield law.[101]

Sources and Types of Information

Are Only Confidential Source Disclosures Exempt?

A majority of states with shield laws explicitly exempt compelled disclosure of confidential sources and information that could lead to the revelation of confidential sources.[102] Indiana, for example, provides an absolute privilege against identifying confidential sources,[103] as does Kentucky.[104] Minnesota extends privilege to the identity of a person from which information was obtained and to any unpublished information, whether or not it would tend to identify the person from which the information was obtained.[105] Furthermore, based upon a determination that the privilege belongs to the reporter, some courts have interpreted their statutes to hold that a source's subjective expectations as to whether the information will be disclosed is irrelevant, thus the privilege applies regardless of whether the source is a "confidential source" or not. That said, some states such as New York give less protection to nonconfidential information.[106]

When the subpoena recipient is engaged in journalistic activity—formally or informally—the media has increasingly attempted to defend against a subpoena seeking an anonymous poster's identity by asserting a journalist's privilege. Depending on the jurisdiction, the privilege may be grounded in the First Amendment, common law, court rules, or a shield law. Indeed, state shield laws have precluded the unmasking of anonymous posters in a number of states. On the other hand, several courts have held that its particular shield law could not reasonably be read to apply to protect the compelled disclosure of the identities of anonymous website posters.[107]

States also differ when applying the privilege in circumstances in

101. *Id.* at footnote 56, citing Lipps v. Indiana, 258 N.E.2d 622, 626 (Ind. App. 1970); Ohio v. Ventura, 720 N.E.2d 1024, 1028 (Ohio C.P. 1999). *See also* Gastman v. North Jersey Newspapers Co., 603 A.2d 111, 112 (N.J. App. 1992); Torah Soft Ltd. v. Drosnin, 2001 U.S. Dist. LEXIS 18614, **6-13 (S.D.N.Y. Nov. 14, 2001).

102. Bender, *supra* note 100 at § 17.02[4][a].

103. Ind. Code Ann. § 34-46-4-2.

104. Ky. Rev. Stat. Ann. § 421.100.

105. Bender, *supra* note 101 at § 17.02[4][a].

106. Id. at § 17.02[4][c].

107. Id. at § 17.02[2][a].

which the reporter is an eyewitness to an event—for example, a crime. California's statute has been interpreted to shield reporters from testifying to such accounts. The same is true in Colorado, Florida, and Alabama. However, in states such as Kentucky, New Jersey, and Maryland, reporters witnessing crimes can be compelled to give testimony, even when publishing stories based upon the reporter's eyewitness account.

Types of Information Protected

In addition to protecting human sources of information, most shield laws go further to protect other types of information and instrumentalities of the news-gathering process. Common targets of subpoenas and warrants such as photographs, notes, telephone or dining logs, schedule books, outtakes, audio and video tapes, and film and negatives may be covered in shield statutes, or under common law. The District of Columbia exempts from disclosure notes, outtakes, photographs or photographic negatives, video or sound tapes, film, or other data "irrespective of its nature, not itself communicated in the news media."[108] Colorado includes in its statute "knowledge, observation, notes, documents, photographs, films, recordings, videotapes, audiotapes, and reports, and the contents and sources thereof[.]"[109] The state of Washington includes "notes, outtakes, photographs, video or sound tapes, film, or other data of whatever sort in any medium now known or hereafter devised," but not physical evidence of a crime.[110] Some states make no reference to whether inanimate sources of information can be shielded.[111]

Proceedings In Which The Privilege Can Be Invoked

Though some federal courts follow *Branzburg*'s refusal to recognize the

108. D.C. Code, § 16-4702.
109. Colo. Stat. § 13-90-119.
110. Wash. Rev. Code § 5.68.010.
111. Bender, *supra* note 100 at § 17.02[4][a].

reporter's privilege in the context of a grand jury proceeding,[112] circuit courts are split as to whether such a privilege exists in criminal and civil proceedings. The Second, Third, and Eleventh Circuits have held that *Branzburg* applies only to grand jury proceedings but extend a First Amendment privilege to civil and other types of criminal proceedings.[113]

The practitioner should note that state shield laws might not apply in all governmental proceedings. States such as Arkansas apply their shield laws broadly to "any Grand Jury or any other authority." Arizona's shield law applies in civil and criminal proceedings.[114] Other states cover legal or quasilegal proceedings before judges or administrative bodies, or even the legislature.[115] Other states are more restrictive. The Colorado shield law, for example, does not include hearings "conducted by, before, or under the general assembly."[116] Michigan's shield law applies only in the grand jury context.[117]

It is most often in the criminal proceeding context that the reporter's privilege is invoked.[118] The more challenging instance is when a defendant wishes to compel testimony or evidence from a journalist for defense purposes.[119] California courts have said that a reporter's statutory privilege must give way upon a defendant showing that "nondisclosure would deprive the defendant of his federal constitutional right to a fair trial."[120] Upon the reporter making a prima facie showing that he is entitled to

---

112. *In re* Grand Jury Subpoena, Judith Miller, 438 F.3d 1138, 1147–49 (D.C. Cir. 2006) (holding that no First Amendment privilege exists in the grand jury context); Storer Communications, Inc. v. Giovan (*In re* Grand Jury Proceedings, 810 F.2d 580, 583–86 (6th Cir. 1987) (noting that the majority in *Branzburg* rejected the existence of a First Amendment privilege before a grand jury); Lewis v. United States, 517 F.2d 236, 238 (9th Cir. 1975) ("The First Amendment does not afford a reporter a privilege to refuse to testify before a federal grand jury as to information received in confidence.").

113. Papandrea, *supra* note 75 at 556 (citing Price v. Time, Inc., 416 F.3d 1327, 1343 (11th Cir. 2005) (recognizing a privilege in civil cases); United States v. Caporale, 806 F.2d 1487, 1504 (11th Cir. 1986) (recognizing a privilege in a criminal case); United States v. Burke, 700 F.2d 70, 77 (2d Cir. 1983) (recognizing a privilege in both criminal and civil cases); United States v. Cuthbertson, 630 F.2d 139, 147 (3d Cir. 1980) (recognizing a privilege in criminal cases); Riley v. City of Chester, 612 F.2d 708, 715 (3d Cir. 1979) (recognizing a privilege in civil cases); Baker v. F&F Inv., 470 F.2d 778, 784 (2d Cir. 1972) (recognizing a privilege in a civil case).

114. Ariz. Rev. Stat. Ann. § 12-2214.

115. *See, e.g.*, Ala. Code § 12-21-142; Ky. Stat. § 421.100; Nev. Stat. § 49.275.

116. Colo. Stat. § 13-90-119(1)(e).

117. Mich. Comp. Laws § 767.5a.

118. In civil proceedings in which a journalist or news organization is not a party, the First Amendment does not yield as forcefully to protect reporters. The protections are even less when the journalist or news organization itself is a party in a civil proceeding.

119. *In re* Farber, 394 A.2d 330 (N.J. 1978).

120. Delaney v. Superior Court, 50 Cal.3d 785 (1990).

withhold the information, the defendant must make a threshold demonstration that there is "a reasonable possibility that the information will materially assist" the defendant's case.

To be sure, states like California, Colorado, and Illinois apply a test akin to the *Branzburg* test: (1) whether the information is in fact confidential or sensitive, (2) whether the goals underlying the shield law will be thwarted by disclosure, (3) whether the information sought is important or material to the defendant's case, and (4) whether less intrusive measures can be used to obtain the same information. Some states require the defendant to exhaust other avenues to obtain the information before seeking to invoke a privilege exception.[121]

Other states deploy a less rigid balancing test. With a balancing test, the court is to weigh, on a case-by-case basis, the "freedom of the press and the obligation of all citizens to give relevant testimony with respect to criminal conduct."[122] This approach is the favored approach in states such as New Jersey, Ohio,[123] and Idaho.[124] Still other state shield laws such as those in Alaska provide simply that the privilege may be overcome if withholding the sought-for information would result in a "miscarriage of justice,"[125] or, conversely, as is provided for in Louisiana, "disclosure is essential to the public interest."[126] Virtually all shield laws provide no protection if the informant has committed a crime or the reporter is an eyewitness or has evidence of a crime.

Burdens of Proof

Whether balancing the constitutional issues at stake or applying a multifactor test, a majority of states require a defendant to demonstrate the need for the shielded information by a preponderance of the evidence. Florida,[127]

121. New Jersey v. Boiardo, 416 A.2d 793 (1980).

122. *In re* Letellier, 578 A.2d 722, 726 (Me. 1990).

123. *In re* McAuley, 408 N.E.2d at 709–10.

124. *In re* Contempt of Wright, 700 P.2d 40, 44 (Idaho 1985) (recognizing a qualified privilege under the First Amendment, the Idaho Constitution, and common law, and applying a balancing test).

125. Alaska Stat. § 09.25.310(b).

126. La. Rev. Stat. Ann. § 45:1453 (requiring a finding that "disclosure is essential to the public interest").

127. Ulrich v. Coast Dental Servs., Inc., 739 So. 2d 142 (Fla. App. 1999).

Colorado,[128] Kansas,[129] Maine,[130] New Jersey,[131] Ohio,[132] New York,[133] New Mexico[134] and, Wisconsin[135] are just some states that apply this standard. As a matter of process, that determination would only follow when a subpoena has been served upon a newspaper, a reporter, or other media representative who has challenged the subpoena.

The person seeking it must apply in writing, with specific detail of the reporter, the subject, the medium, the relevance, and the specific information sought. Some states will require that the applicant affirm that he or she has exhausted all other avenues to obtain the sought-after information along with the subpoena.

Appropriately, the party served would then respond with a motion to quash. If the status of the movant was not conceded, then proofs would be taken to a determination that the movant did or did not qualify for the statutory privilege. *In camera* review may be a prerequisite to a final determination. If, by a "fair preponderance of the evidence" or a "preponderance of the evidence" there was a "legitimate need" for the information, a "reasonable probability or likelihood that the information sought" was material and relevant, a "reasonable, not speculative" possibility that the information would "materially assist" the movant and could not be had from another source, a reporter may be compelled to turn over information and offer testimony if necessary.

The First Amendment and the Press

News-Gathering Crimes and Defenses

Given the broad prescription the First Amendment affords the news media, there exists the long-standing proposition that "if a newspaper lawfully obtains truthful information about a matter of public significance then [the state] may not constitutionally punish publication of the information, absent

128. Colo. Rev. Stat. § 13-90-119(3).
129. Kan. Stat. § 60-482.
130. Me. Code § 61(2).
131. *In re* Farber, 394 A.2d 330 (N.J. 1978).
132. *In re* McAuley, 63 Ohio App. 2d 5 (Ohio App. 1979).
133. People v. Marin, *86 A.D.2d 40 (1982).*
134. N.M. Stat. § 11-514.
135. State ex rel. Green Bay Newspaper Co. v. Circuit Court, Branch 1, 113 Wis. 2d 411 (1983).

a need to further a state interest of the highest order."[136] The caveat, however, rests in the word "lawfully." Since *Branzburg v. Hayes*,[137] established 40 years ago, the Supreme Court made clear that the First Amendment does not exempt the press from criminal laws and criminal liability.[138]

Perhaps obviously, media engagement in theft, bribery, or burglary can result in criminal indictment. On those matters, the media has absolutely no privilege different from all citizens to not engage in such acts. For other acts ostensibly performed in the course of news-gathering activities, the interests balanced among media defendants is that First Amendment jurisprudence firmly recognizes the vital role of news gatherers in which the right of the public to know must mean, by extension, the right of access to information deemed to be in the public interest. On the other hand, the Supreme Court has never construed the First Amendment to accord news gatherers absolute immunity from liability for crimes or torts committed while gathering news.

Generally applicable criminal laws do not offend the First Amendment because their enforcement against the press has incidental effects on its ability to gather and report the news. It has been firmly established that the First Amendment does not guarantee the press a constitutional right of special access to information that is not generally available to the public.[139] "Crimes and torts committed in news gathering are not protected. There is no threat to a free press in requiring its agents to act within the law."[140]

Furthermore, important distinctions are drawn between public and private property, the latter never being regarded as a traditional forum such as a sidewalk, street, or park where a constitutional guarantee of access can be compellingly argued. Courts have even held that news gatherers are not immune to criminal prosecution for crimes committed on government-owned

136. Smith v. Daily Mail Publishing Co., 443 U.S. 97, 103, 61 L. Ed. 2d 399, 99 S. Ct. 2667 (1979).

137. 408 U.S. 665 (1972).

138. *See, e.g.*, Dietemann v. Time, Inc., 241 F.Supp. 925 (C.D. Cal. 1968), *aff'd*, 449 F.2d 245 (9th Cir. 1971) (two reporters gained entry into home under false pretenses to investigate occupant's claims surrounding his success as a physician).

139. Food Lion Inc. v. Capital Cities/ABC Inc., 194 F.3d 505 (4th Cir. 1999).

140. LeMistral v. Columbia Broadcasting System, 61 S.D.2d 491 (1978).

property.[141] However, conduct by media actors in the news-gathering context can pit First Amendment rights against Fourth Amendment proscriptions. The Fourth Amendment constitutionalizes the "right of the people to be secure in their persons, houses, papers, and effects, against unreasonable searches and seizures[.]"[142] Particularly as it regards private homes, efforts to gather news through surreptitious acts or concealed devices are disdained and are the most common bases for criminal prosecutions.

A journalist's potential criminal liability for news gathering and publication is prosecuted under any one of a myriad of statutory prohibitions: aside from the more obvious ones mentioned before (theft, burglary, bribery), federal or state laws that sanction espionage, trespass, disorderly conduct, impersonation of a law or public officer, and mail or wire fraud.

Espionage Act

Perhaps the most notable case on the criminalization of using classified information is *New York Times Co. v. United States*.[143] The *New York Times* and *Washington Post* published the Pentagon Papers on June 13, 1971, which chronicled roughly three decades of U.S. involvement in Vietnam. The document revealed, among other things, that the executive branch "followed a pattern of deception against the public regarding its intentions to commit troops to Vietnam" and ultimately served to raise public sentiment against the war effort.[144] Of the 7,000-page study commissioned by the government, three pages of the material appeared in different sections of the newspapers. The top-secret document had been leaked to the press by Daniel Ellsberg. Ellsberg was a Defense Department analyst who helped author the study, which was how he had authorized possession of the document. Ellsberg was authorized to keep the document in his home, but it was removed and copied by Anthony Russo. The Nixon administration sued in New York and District of Columbia federal courts to enjoin the publication.

The Nixon administration attempted to enjoin the *Times* and the *Post*

141. *See* Greer v. Spock, 424 U.S. 828 (1976); Adderley v. Florida, 385 U.S. 39 (1966).
142. U.S. Const. amend. IV.
143. 403 U.S. 713 (1971).
144. *Id.*

from publishing the excerpts of the study. They sought a prior restraint rather than postpublication prosecution and therefore did not rely on the Espionage Act or other statutory or regulatory authority, as no statute or regulation authorized prior restraints. Instead, the administration argued that it had inherent authority to request, and courts had inherent authority to grant, a prior restraint based on the national security dangers that publication could cause.[145]

The Supreme Court held that no injunction should issue and directed the Second Circuit to lift the injunction. The case was decided not on the constitutional issues of the punishing of Ellsberg and Russo for communicating information relating to government policy making but on whether the government could enjoin reporting news that was obtained through the unauthorized transfer of secret documents. The Court found that prior restraints against publication of information, classified or not, even if illegally obtained, are presumptively invalid unless the government meets its "heavy burden" of justification for the injunction.[146] Justice Stewart wrote:

> [We are being asked] to prevent the publication . . . of material that the Executive Branch insists should not in the national interest, be published. I am convinced that the Executive is correct and with respect to some of the documents involved. But I cannot say that disclosure of any of them will result in direct, immediate, or irreparable damage to our Nation or its people.[147]

The case, however, left open the possibility that the press may be punished criminally after classified information is published. Six of the nine justices wrote that Ellsberg and Russo could be charged under the Espionage Act, 18 U.S.C. § 793(e).[148]

---

145. Heidi Kitrosser, *Classified Information Leaks and Free Speech*, 2008 U. Ill. L. Rev. 881, 897 (2008).

146. Mitchell J. Michalec, *The Classified Information Protection Act: Killing the Messenger or Killing the Message?*, 50 Clev. St. L. Rev. 455, 459–460 (2003).

147. Geoffrey R. Stone, *Secrecy and Self-Governance*, 56 N.Y.L. Sch. L. Rev. 81, 92 (2011).

148. 18 U.S.C. § 793 states, "Whoever having unauthorized possession of, access to, or control over any document, writing . . . or information relating to the national defense which information the possessor has reason to believe could be used to the injury of the United States or to the advantage of any foreign nation, willfully communicates . . . the same to any person not entitled to receive it . . . [s]hall be fined not more than $10,000 or imprisoned not more than 10 years, or both."

Trespass

Trespass is classically defined as the unauthorized entry onto a person's land that interferes with the owner's possessory interest.[149] It matters not whether harm or damage ensues; the violation rests in the mere fact of entry without authorization. In the news-gathering context, this crime arises when a news gatherer trespasses onto private homes or businesses either explicitly without consent, by exceeding consent, or through misrepresentation. As one court noted, the "First Amendment has never been construed to provide immunity from either tortious or criminal conduct committed in the course of news-gathering; it provides no license to trespass, steal or surreptitiously intrude into another's home or office."[150]

Examples include entering a fenced yard with a visible "No Trespassing" sign to interview the subject of a criminal investigation[151] or entering onto a cooperative's property with protesters who occupied the property despite warnings not to do so.[152] Consent as a defense to an action in trespass must be given by the owner or possessor of the premises. Although consent may be implied from custom, usage, or conduct, it may not be extended by inference to justify the unlicensed entry of others. Although a trespass may be legalized or justified by lawful authority, as by a police officer acting in the performance of his duty, such authority does not extend by invitation, absent an emergency, to every and any other member of the public, including members of the news media.[153]

At first, if a journalist seeks to challenge the prosecution, the journalist bears the burden of demonstrating more than simply that the goal of the trespass was to gather news for a story that was of "public concern." The most common and best defense is authorization by the owner or possessor of the property. If a privilege to enter upon property existed, and the journalist did not exceed that privilege and only engaged in acts consistent

149. *See* Restatement (Second) of Torts § 158 comments i and j (defendant need not personally enter property, but may be liable for simply causing the wrongful entry).

150. Hornberger v. American Broadcasting Companies, Inc., 351 N.J. Super. 577, 630 (N.J. 2002).

151. Arizona v. Wells, 2004 WL 1925617 (2004).

152. Stahl v. State, 665 P.2d 839 (1983).

153. *But see* Florida Publishing v. Fletcher, 340 So.2d 914 (Fla. 1976) (journalist had implied consent to enter home and take pictures when invited by on-site coroner).

with that privilege, then no liability attaches.[154]

On that score, defenses such as implied permission, lack of knowledge, or scienter of the private nature of the property may negate criminal liability. Other potentially dispositive issues include whether the subject of the invasion had a reasonable expectation of privacy, and whether the journalist's conduct was highly unreasonable.[155]

Disorderly Conduct

It is easy to envision a news gatherer at a crime scene, attempting to capture a story that by circumstance is arguably in the public interest. However, a journalist may run headlong against the competing interest of the imperative of safety and security, broadly writ as state police powers. Even if admonished or warned by law enforcement, a journalist may nonetheless broach the "do not cross" line and/or ask questions of law enforcement, investigators, or material witness to the crime. If taken too far, a journalist might find himself or herself cited for disorderly conduct.

States, cities, municipalities, townships, or other government subdivisions are considered to have police powers to maintain order or to quell interference with the law enforcement or investigative process.[156] Government bodies have statutes, codes, or ordinances with goals to regulate or prevent situations that may likely instigate violence, result in breaches of the peace, or interfere with the proper investigation of law enforcement. Prototypically, a statute would charge a journalist with being "in a public or private place" and engaging in "violent, abusive, indecent, profane, boisterous, unreasonably loud or otherwise disorderly conduct under circumstances in which the conduct tends to cause or provoke a disturbance[.]"[157]

Situations in which a news gatherer has refused to move away from an accident site, has refused to exit a building to a public sidewalk, or has interfered with a police officer's witness questioning after a direction

---

154. *Cf.* Dietemann v. Time, Inc., 449 F.2d 245, 249 (9th Cir. 1971) ("one who invites one into his home does not and should not be required to take the risk that what is heard and seen will be transmitted[.]").

155. *Cf.* LeMistral, *supra* note 140.

156. New Jersey v. Lashinsky, 404 A.2d 1121 (1979).

157. Wis. Stat. Ann. §§ 940.20(2).

from a police officer to quit the area or cease interference have given rise to claims of disorderly conduct. Relevant evidentiary facts in the calculus, on one side, are considered explicit and implicit rights and obligations of the press to report on matters of public interest or concern. On the other side, there are the questions as to whether there was in fact material interference, physical intrusion, or the requisite intent to interfere. Moreover, the question as to whether a law enforcement officer's request to quit the scene or desist with the intrusive acts were reasonable and the defendant-journalist's response was unreasonable, is a jury question.[158]

Impersonating A Public Official

State and federal laws[159] prohibit citizens from assuming false identities. Media actors have been prosecuted for impersonating public officials for the purpose of gaining access to newsworthy events or facts.[160] If there are penal codes in place, reporters can be found guilty if they have, beyond reasonable doubt, impersonated officers such as police, criminal investigators, or other public officials.[161] In such cases, the First Amendment provides no safe harbor, as false identity laws apply to the public generally. Furthermore, courts have uniformly declined to append an "actual malice" standard to false identity laws in which a journalist or reporter was the defendant. [162]

Mail Or Wire Crimes

The news media has been subject to claims arising under state and federal wiretap and mail statutes in which journalists either record conversations without the consent of one or more of the participants or receive and thereafter disseminate the content of such conversations when they have been unlawfully recorded by someone else. Although such statutes

---

158. *See, e.g.*, New Jersey v. Lashinsky, 404 A.2d 1121 (1979).

159. *See, e.g.*, 18 U.S.C. § 912 (2012); Ala. Code, § 13A-10-10 (2012); Cal. Penal Code § 146a (2012); D.C. Code § 22-1406 (2012); Fla. Stat. § 843.08 (2012); N.J. Stat. Ann. 2C:28-8; N.Y. Penal Code § 190.25 (2012); Ohio Rev. Code § 2913.44 (2012); 3 Pa. Cons. Stat. § 4141 (2012); R.I. Gen. Laws § Gen. Laws 11-14-1 (2012).

160. Bender, supra note 100 at § 15.01-15.04.

161. *Cf.*, State v. Cantor, 534 A.2d 83 (N.J. App. Div. 1987) (in which a journalist was indicted for impersonating the mother of a decedent crime victim in order to access the morgue).

162. *Id.*

often differ from each other in some respects, they typically impose criminal penalties.[163]

The 1986 Electronic Communications Privacy Act makes it a crime for "any person who, unless authorized, intentionally intercepts, uses or discloses any wire, oral, or electronic communication[.]"[164] That act prohibits not only the unlawful interception of a communication covered by its terms, but also the subsequent "use" or "disclosure" of the contents of such a communication.[165] Section 1341 of the United States Code, Chapter 18, makes it a crime to use the mails as part of a scheme or device to commit fraud or deprivation of property or money by false pretenses, representations, or promises.[166] Instances arise under which a reporter has violated state or federal wiretap statutes or violated a person's Fourth Amendment rights by working in concert with state actors.

News Gathering Under Color of State Law

Traditionally, only government actors have been held liable for violating an individual's constitutional rights under 42 U.S.C. § 1983, but private parties such as media actors can also be held liable if they are found to have acted under color of law.[167] Whether a private party acted under color of state law is subject to a two-prong test, which the Supreme Court established in *Lugar v. Edmondson Oil Co.*[168] First, the deprivation must result from the exercise of a right or privilege emanating from state authority.[169] Second, the party charged with the violation must be a state actor, but this can include will-

---

163. 18 U.S.C. §§ 2511(4)-(5), 2520. *See also, e.g.*, Cal Pen Code § 631 (2012); Fla. Stat. § 934.03 et.seq. (2012); N.C. Gen. Stat. GS §14-155, et seq. (2012); Ohio Rev. Code §2933.51, et seq. (2012); Or. Rev. Stat §165.535, et seq. (2012); Pa. Cons. Stat. 18 Pa.C.S § 5701, et seq. (2012); Wyo. Stat. §7-3-701(2012). Many statutes also grant a civil right of action for damages.

164. 18 U.S.C. § 2511(a).

165. 18 U.S.C. § 2511(1)(b)-(d).

166. 18 U.S.C. § 1341 (applies to anyone who places such material with said intent "in any post office or authorized depository for mail matter, any matter or thing whatever to be sent or delivered by the Postal Service, or deposits or causes to be deposited any matter or thing whatever to be sent or delivered by any private or commercial interstate carrier, or takes or receives therefrom, any such matter or thing, or knowingly causes to be delivered by mail or such carrier according to the direction thereon, or at the place at which it is directed to be delivered by the person to whom it is addressed, any such matter or thing[.]").

167. Sheila M. Lombardi, *Media in the Spotlight: Private Parties Liable for Violating the Fourth Amendment*, 6 Roger Williams U. L. Rev. 393, 395 (2000).

168. *Id.* at 395.

169. *Id.* at 395, 396.

fully participating in a joint activity with the state or state agents.[170]

It is possible that a media defendant might be held liable for violating a victim's Fourth Amendment rights if found to be acting jointly or conspiring to do so with a police officer. Several cases have considered this topic in recent years. The case of *Dennis v. Sparks*[171] recognized the right of an individual to sue a private party for the violation of their Fourth Amendment rights, noting that a defendant did not have to be an officer of the state to be considered acting "under color of state law."[172]

In contrast, the Second Circuit court held a federal officer liable for violating a person's Fourth Amendment rights by permitting the media to accompany him on a search.[173] Although that court did not "expressly hold that CBS was acting under color of law," the court concluded that CBS violated a clearly established Fourth Amendment right and denied CBS the right to invoke a qualified immunity defense because it was not a government official.[174] In *Wilson v. Layne*,[175] the Supreme Court held that it was "a violation of the Fourth Amendment for police to bring members of the media . . . into a home during the execution of a warrant when the presence of the [media] in the home was not in aid of the execution of the warrant."[176]

In *Berger v. Hanlon*,[177] the Ninth Circuit held CNN liable as state actors for violating a couple's Fourth Amendment rights after CNN contracted with the U.S. Fish and Wildlife Service to participate in a raid on a ranch. In its opinion, the court stated, "Considering the 'inextricable involvement of [CNN] with both the planning and execution of th[e] search,' Service's active involvement with CNN's news gathering activities, and the mutual benefits derived by CNN and the Service were 'more than enough' to conclude that CNN's actions were those of a state actor."[178]

However, it appears that in order for a private party to hold a media defendant liable for a Fourth Amendment violation the connection to law en-

170. *Id.* at 396.
171. 449 U.S. 24 (1980).
172. *Id.* at 28.
173. Ayeni v. Mottola, 35 F.3d 680 (2d Cir. 1994).
174. Lombardi, *supra* note 167 at 399.
175. 526 U.S. 603 (1999).
176. *Id.* at 614.
177. 129 F.3d 505 (9th Cir. 1997).
178. *Id.* at 515.

forcement activity must be extremely strong. For example, in *Brunette v. Humane Society of Ventura County*,[179] the Ninth Circuit held that media that had been invited to a raid on a woman's ranch were not state actors and therefore not liable for violating the woman's constitutional rights. In its analysis of the facts, the court considered three tests for determining whether a private party is engaged in state action.[180]

"First, the 'joint action' test examines whether private actors are willful participants in joint action with the government or its agents."[181] Second, "the 'symbiotic relationship' test asks whether the government has so far insinuated itself into a position of interdependence with a private entity that the private entity must be recognized as a joint participant in the challenged activity."[182] Third, "the 'public functions' test inquires whether the private actor performs functions traditionally and exclusively reserved to the States."[183] The Ninth Circuit concluded that none of the tests were applicable to the facts of the case and noted that the reporter's "only role during the search was to gather information as a reporter and a photographer. He rendered no assistance to the Humane Society and in no way facilitated its ability to search the premises."[184]

Whether acting alone or in concert with federal officials, reporters are subject to both state and federal wiretap laws. State laws differ on whether recording conversations requires only one party, or two-party consent. For the media defendant, the issue turns on either consent (expressed or implied), or the extent of the media defendant's participation in the interception or use of the device intercepting the ostensibly private communication. For example, the state of Washington's privacy law requires parties to consent to recording.[185]

Some states provide disclosure exceptions for media actors. If a reporter is acting in the scope of news-gathering duties, consent to record and divulge is presumed if the consent is expressly given or the recording or

179. Brunette v. Humane Soc'y of Ventura Co., 294 F.3d 1205 (9th Cir. 2002).
180. *Id.* at 1210.
181. *Id.*
182. *Id.*
183. *Id.*
184. *Id.* at 1208.
185. RCW § 9.73.030.

transmitting device is apparent or obvious. The reporter is still privileged to divulge the communication even if the second party subsequently withdraws consent.[186]

Journalists have engaged in those proscriptions, and the criminal practitioner can rely upon traditional statutory and common law principles to prosecute or defend against such allegations.[187] Two reporters got into a plaintiff's home to determine if he was a "medical quack." One reporter took pictures with a hidden camera, and conversation was transmitted to outside confederates by a hidden transmitter. As one court put it, "one who invites one into his home does not and should not be required to take the risk that what is heard and seen will be transmitted. Especially in cases where privacy is most valued."[188]

The Criminal Practitioner Prosecuting or Representing Clients on Media-Related Issues

It is important to keep in mind that whether for clearly protected speech or speech enjoying no absolute First Amendment protection, the degree and kind of legal protections and proscriptions of media members, court actors, or criminal practitioners engaged in speech frequently depend upon the medium used to communicate the speech. For that reason, it is useful to describe the most common media and their relative constitutional rights and burdens. This is especially important given that the 1996 Telecommunications Act enacted pervasive provisions regarding the scope of federal preemption of state law regulations of certain media and speech.[189]

"Traditional Media": Print

Traditional print media has arguably shaped more than any media our First Amendment jurisprudence. Thus, the earliest Supreme Court decisions on issues of censorship, news gathering, sedition, obscenity, and indecency were made in the context of the print media. Importantly, the doctrine of prior restraint was established in the context of states imposi-

---

186. *See, e.g.*, Wash. Re. Code § 9.73.030(4).
187. 18 U.S.C.A. § 641 (theft of government property).
188. Dietemann v. Time, Inc., 449 F.2d 245 (9th Cir. 1971).
189. 47 U.S.C. §253.

tion of prepublication conditions upon the press. The prior restraint doctrine was most famously reaffirmed in *Near v. Minnesota*,[190] in which the Supreme Court declared unconstitutional a Minnesota law that permitted continued injunction against a publication if in the first instance a particular edition was found to be a "malicious, scandalous and defamatory newspaper, magazine or other periodical[.]"[191] The law's defect was its practical effect of allowing a continuous injunction that served to prohibit any future publication without a need for determining whether that future publication ran afoul of the law.

The Supreme Court has made clear that laws that punish speech *after* it has been communicated are not *per se* unconstitutional. Although prepublication restraints like the law at issue in *Near* are proscribed, publishers may still be liable for the effects that flow from the publication. So, a speaker may be sanctioned subsequently to the communication or publication of matters that might be, for example, considered private, libelous, or of national security import.[192]

Radio and Television Broadcast

Radio and television industries, in general, have lessened First Amendment protections than print media have. The electromagnetic spectrum utilized to broadcast is allocated by the federal government and licensed to industries as a public trust. The Communications Act of 1934 grants powers to the Federal Communications Commission (FCC) to oversee television and radio broadcast to ensure operation in the "public interest, convenience, and necessity."[193] The primary reason for lessened First Amendment privilege for radio and television broadcast is based upon what is popularly described as the "scarcity rationale." Because the spectrum is a finite resource, heightened burdens are imposed upon those granted use of spectrum frequencies

---

190. 283 U.S. 697 (1931).

191. *Id.* at 701.

192. Alexander v. United States, 509 U.S. 544, 550–51 (1993); Southeastern Promotions, Ltd. v. Conrad, 420 U.S. 546, 558–559 (1975).

193. 1934 Communications Act, Communications Act of 1934, Pub. L. No. 416, Act of June 19, 1934, ch. 652, 48 Stat. 1064, codified at 47 U.S.C. §151 et seq. Other federal agencies have important roles in the regulation of mass communications in addition to the FCC. The National Telecommunications & Information Administration, the Federal Trade Commission, and the Department of Justice, Antitrust Division are the primary examples.

to ensure that licensees use those frequencies to optimize the public interest, convenience, and necessity.[194] Although indecent or even obscene material may be published in a magazine, there are severe prohibitions upon broadcasters for transmitting the same.[195] Laws or regulations that could be seen as content based and unconstitutional if imposed upon a print entity would not necessarily be unconstitutional as applied to broadcast due to the longstanding acceptance of the scarcity rationale and the FCC authority granted by Congress. A prime example is the constitutional power of the FCC to evaluate broadcaster's program content—including news—in prelicensing and renewal evaluations.[196]

Cable Television

Cable television is a type of multichannel audio and video system. In contrast to radio and television, which transmit over the air, cable programming is transmitted through coaxial or hybrid coaxial networks. But like radio and broadcast, cable television is regulated by the FCC.[197] Congress has granted the FCC authority to regulate cable broadcast as "reasonably ancillary" to its responsibility for radio and television.[198] Consequently, cable operators, networks, and producers are afforded less First Amendment protection than print media but greater protections than radio and broadcast. For example, cable operators are obligated under "must carry" rules to transmit certain programming (e.g., that of local over-the-air networks),[199] but cable networks and cable content producers have greater leeway to broadcast indecent or obscene expression.[200] Also, cable operators, because their media transmission architecture does not impinge

---

194. Federal Communications Comm'n v. League of Women Voters of California, 468 U.S. 364 (1984).

195. *See, e.g.*, Federal Communications Comm'n v. Pacifica Foundation, 438 U.S. 726 (1978).

196. National Broadcasting Co. v. United States, 310 U.S. 190 (1943). Also, compare Miami Herald Publ. Co. *v. Tornillo*, 418 U.S. 241 (1974), in which the Court held unconstitutional Florida's Right of Reply statute, to Action for Children's Television v. Federal Communications Comm'n, 59 F.3d 1249 (1995), *cert denied*, 516 U.S. 1072 (1996), which sanctioned the FCC's ability to "consider the extent to which a [broadcast] licensee . . . has served the educational and informational needs of children[.]"

197. 1934 Act, 47 U.S.C. §601–641.

198. 47 U.S.C. §152(c); United States v. Southwestern Cable Co., 392 U.S. 157 (1968).

199. Cable Television Consumer Protection and Competition Act of 1992, Pub. L. No. 102-385, 106 Stat. 1460 (1992) (1992 Cable Act or 1992 Act); H. Rep. No. 628, 102d Cong., 2d Sess. (1992) (*House Report*"); *Senate Report*. *See also* 47 U.S.C. § 534; Turner Broadcasting System, Inc. v. Federal Communications Comm'n, 520 U.S. 180 (1997).

200. *See, e.g.*, United States v. Playboy Entertainment Group, 529 U.S. 803 (2000); 47 U.S.C. § 561 of Communications Act held unconstitutional as applied to cable operators; Cruz v. Ferre, 755 F.2d 1415 (1985).

upon a finite resource such as the electromagnetic spectrum, are not constrained by the same degree of public interest regulatory imperatives that cover traditional broadcasters.

Satellite

Another type of multichannel video provider, satellite television, also comes within the ambit of FCC regulation.[201] Signal transmission originates from an earth station to a satellite and back to earth, where the signal is captured by a dish and then decoded for viewing and listening. Regulation of direct-to-home satellite operators such as DirectTV and DISH and satellite radio owners, programmers, and producers is more akin to cable regulation.[202] Both media forms are subscription services—that is, information services to which a consumer affirmatively opts into by paying a fee. Yet there are significant differences. In contrast to cable "must carry" requirements, for example, satellite carriers are not required to carry television stations if they do not rely on the statutory license but instead privately negotiate for the copyright license.[203] Nor are satellite carriers generally required to carry a station if its programming is duplicative of the programming of another station carried by the local satellite operator.[204]

Telephony

Telephone communication is regulated under the 1934 Act's "common carrier" provisions.[205] Telephone services, like a public utility, are a "common carrier" in that providers offer services, though for a fee, to the general pub-

---

201. 1934 Communications Act, 47 U.S.C § 601–641; Cable Television and Consumer Protection Act of 1992, Pub. L. 102-385; Satellite Home Viewer Improvement Act of 1999, Pub. L. 106-113 Stat. 1501, (Nov. 29, 1999); 17 U.S.C. § 119.

202. Federal Communications Comm'n v. Beach Communications, 508 U.S. 307 (1993).

203. Satellite Home Viewer Extension and Reauthorization Act of 2004 (SHVERA), Pub. L. No. 108-477, 118 Stat. 2809 (2004). *See also* Implementation of the Satellite Home Viewer Extension and Reauthorization Act of 2004 to Amend Section 338 of the Communications Act, MB Docket No. 05-181, 20 FCC Rcd 14242 (2005) (Section 338(a)(4) supersedes carry-one, carry-all by mandating analog and digital carriage in Alaska and Hawaii).

204. 47 U.S.C. § 338(c)(1).

205. The primary distinction between a "common carrier" and "broadcaster" is that the former is a conduit with no legal capacity to control the content. In other words, they must provide, without discrimination, the facility for message transmission. 47 U.S.C. § 153(h) [now 47 U.S.C. § 153(10)].

lic indiscriminately.[206] Although common carriers are bound to operate "in the public interest," there is limited criminal liability to the carrier for communication transmitted through its lines.[207] However, telephonic communications, especially wireless, represent a burgeoning field of issues surrounding bona fide news gathering and reporting, third-party intermediaries, and Fourth Amendment considerations of search, seizure, and subpoena.[208]

Telephone communications can be made through wire line or wireless transmission. Wireless telephone communications allow for much greater flexibility and communications features than traditional landline phones and, as a result, allow for more acts that may give rise to traditional and new criminalized behavior and defense. Aside from crimes of telephone harassment, impersonation, stalking, libel or defamation, unwanted texting, bullying, or transmission of indecent or obscene matter adds to the scope of possible issues of interest and need of criminal practitioners.

Internet

Just as imperative as modern telephony and criminal law, the legal contours of Internet communication are crucial for the modern criminal practitioner to appreciate. The Internet is essentially an interconnected global computer network on which data is transmitted over networks using Internet protocols. The Internet system is comprised of end users, Internet service providers, and backbone providers.[209] The FCC is authorized to regulate Internet communications as a source of "information services" or "enhanced services."[210] Consequently, the regulatory regime of Internet communication is distinct from satellite, cable, broadcast, and certainly print.

---

206. 47 U.S.C. § 201(a) ("It shall be the duty of every common carrier engaged in interstate or foreign communication by wire or radio to furnish such communication service upon reasonable request therefor; and, in accordance with the orders of the Commission, in cases where the Commission, after opportunity for hearing, finds such action necessary or desirable in the public interest, to establish physical connections with other carriers, to establish through routes and charges applicable thereto and the divisions of such charges, and to establish and provide facilities and regulations for operating such through routes.").

207. Although this description of a "common carrier" would seem to include cable television services, Congress, with Court affirmation, has rejected such classification.

208. *See, The Criminal Practitioner and Knowing the Media Issues: Courts and Trials, supra.*

209. Kevin Werbach, *Digital Tornado: The Internet and Telecommunications Policy, FCC Office of Policy and Planning*, Working Paper Series 29 (March 1997).

210. 47 U.S.C. §1.

There are several other federal laws that affect the use of the Internet. Under most circumstances, laws that apply to offline activity can be applied to online activity as well. The 1996 Telecommunications Act,[211] the Children's Online Protection Act,[212] Children's Internet Protection Act,[213] and Digital Millennium Copyright Act[214] are the primary statutory regimes regulating Internet communications.

Of course, constitutional and regulatory issues come into play when considering the criminal practitioner and the media, due in no small part to the fact that information can be accessed, published, or disseminated at rates unrivaled by traditional media. Moreover, because of its distinctive architecture and dissemination capacity, unique questions arise when prosecuting or defending crimes. A vital consideration for the practitioner is often whether intermediaries that facilitate the communication (e.g., Internet service providers, data routers) can be subject to subpoena to reveal the identities of information disseminated over the Internet.[215]

Defamation, Libel, and Slander

Definition

Defamation occurs when one communicates an unprivileged false statement of or concerning another that harms that individual's reputation. Libel and slander are subcategories of defamation. The former refers to false statements in writing about another that harms reputation; slanders are oral statements that cause the harm. The distinction between libel and slander lies in the type of damages a plaintiff must show when bringing an action.

Redress for defamation is one of the earliest legal actions available. The underlying rationale for the laws protecting reputation was the concern for breaches of the peace and was one of the earliest legal actions avail-

211. Pub. L. No. 104-104, 110 Stat. 56 (1996). Note that the 1996 act was the most significant revision of the 1934 Communications Act to date. Thus, a practitioner should note that although there were many revisions made to the 1934 act too numerous to fully address in this chapter modified or added provisions to the 1934 act will be referred to as part of the 1996 act.

212. 112 Stat. 2681-736, Pub. L. 105-277, 47 U.S.C. § 231.

213. 114 Stat. 2763A-335, 21 U.S.C. § 9131 et seq. (2000).

214. 17 U.S.C. § 1201-1332.

215. 47 U.S.C. § 230.

able. Statements that generate hatred, ridicule, contempt, scorn, shame,[216] or statements that have the effect of "lowering [one's standing] in the estimation of the community or deterring others from associating or dealing with him"[217] are the reputation harms that libel laws seek to vindicate. Criminal defamation actions have seen something of a resurgence with the advent of the Internet.

Defamation can be committed explicitly or by implication. A false statement that "Mr. Smith murdered his wife" is defamatory by its own terms. Often, however, the fact that a statement is defamatory can only be established by implication, insinuation, or innuendo. For example, to state that Mr. Smith is guilty of a crime is to state, by opposition, that Mr. Smith is not guilty of that crime. Photographing a person walking into a courtroom in an orange jumpsuit and handcuffs infers criminality and incarceration (and perhaps guilt). For example, in a libel action, a neighbor is quoted in a news story of a burglary as saying, "The man who lives in the house two doors east of my house was the only person in the Jones home between 7 p.m. and 8 p.m. last night." That statement communicates a possibly actionable statement by communicating three unspoken ideas: It implies that the burglary took place between 7 p.m. and 8 p.m.; it insinuates that the man two doors east committed the burglary; and, for anyone who knows that Mr. Smith lives two doors east, the innuendo is that Mr. Smith burglarized the Jones house.

Defamatory statements fall within two broad categories: libel per se and libel per quod. Libel per se statements are, by their very content, presumed to result in reputational harm. Some categories of per se libel are the imputation of serious crime of moral turpitude (e.g., perjury); the insinuation that one is afflicted with a serious disease; attacks on competency or honesty in a business, trade, or profession; or the charge of unchasteness of a woman. Libel per quod occurs when false statements on other subjects, explicitly or implicitly, cause reputational harm.

Although rarely an issue as a matter of law, the "of and concerning" prong may be relevant to prosecuting defamation cases. More often than not, the allegedly defamatory statement clearly identifies to whom it is re-

---

216. *See, e.g.*, Buckner v. Gilliland, 846 F. Supp. 2d 799 (N.D. Ohio 2012).

217. Restatement (Second) of Torts, §559.

ferring whether explicitly or by extrinsic inferences. False statements lobbied against groups are actionable under narrow circumstances. The issue will turn upon whether the statement lends itself to reflecting upon a definable and identifiable number of individuals. So, to say "all lawyers are crooks" would not be actionable defamation; to say falsely that the lawyers who are employed at law firm X are crooks would be actionable defamation. And although it is an open question as to whether corporations are "people," business entities may bring libel actions in their own names.

Absolute and Conditional Privileges

Certain speakers, and certain speakers in certain settings, enjoy absolute or qualified privilege to make even defamatory statements. For example, members of Congress and state legislators enjoy absolute privilege in making statements on the floor when debating bills.[218] High executive officials, judges, and participants in judicial proceedings also have an absolute privilege to speak on matters relevant to their obligations. Regardless of whether the speaker freely abuses the privilege, no tort liability will flow.[219] With absolute privileges, there is no liability, even if the statement is a deliberate or a knowing lie. The media only has absolute privilege in circumstances in which broadcasters are required to give equal opportunity for political candidates vying for the same office.[220]

Under the doctrine of conditional privilege, the aggrieved party must show that the speaker or communicator abused a privilege. For the media, historically, one who repeats is responsible for the truth of what he or she reports. However, that has evolved into "record libel"—a qualified privilege to allow the press to report upon government affairs even if someone has spoken falsely. Finally, media are entitled to engage in "fair comment" upon matters of public interest. This privilege of fair comment is most commonly applied to literary or artistic criticism.[221] However, the seminal examination of the fair comment privilege offered in a case regarding

218. Tenney v. Brandhove, 341 U.S. 367, 372–375 & n.5 (1951).

219. Barr v. Matteo, 360 U.S. 564 (1959).

220. 1934 Communications Act, § 315 (commonly known as the equal time or equal opportunity provision); Farmers Educational & Cooperative Union of America v. WDAY, Inc., 360 U.S. 525 (1959).

221. Cherry v. Des Moines Leader, 114 Iowa 298, 86 N.W 323 (1901).

sports editorial writing.[222]

There is special privilege for opinion. There are two types of opinion to consider under defamation actions. The first type is "pure" opinion, in which the maker states facts based upon his or her opinion. The opinion might be in the form of a factual statement if it is clear that the maker is not intending to assert another objective fact but only his or her personal comment upon the facts set forth. The second kind of expression of opinion, or the mixed type, is one that, although an opinion in form or context, is apparently based on facts regarding the plaintiff or his or her conduct that have not been stated by the defendant or assumed to exist by the parties to the communication.

To say of a person that he or she is a thief without explaining why may, depending upon the circumstances, be found to imply the assertion that he or she has committed acts that come within the common connotation of thievery. To declare without an indication of the basis for the conclusion that a person is utterly devoid of moral principles may be found to imply the assertion that he or she has been guilty of conduct that would justify the reaching of that conclusion. In *Gertz v. Welch*,[223] the Supreme Court held that the pure type of opinion may not serve as a basis of a defamation action.

"Fair comment" is a special type of opinion statement.[224] It is defined as "a statement based on the writer's or speaker's honest opinion about a matter of public concern."[225] The defense of fair comment was originally recognized at common law as protecting "'expressions of public opinion about public officials, scientists, artists, composers, performers, authors, and other persons who place themselves or their work in the public eye.'"[226] The Supreme Court's decision in *New York Times v. Sullivan*,[227] discussed above, requiring that actual malice be shown, modified the impact of "fair comment"; its decision in *Milkovich v. Lorain Journal Co.*,[228] holding that there was no available separate opinion privilege against libel, limited this scope

222. Milkovich v. Lorain Journal Co., 497 U.S. 1 (1990).
223. 418 U.S. 323 (1974).
224. Black's Law Dictionary 633 (8th ed. 2004).
225. *Id.*
226. Brown v. Kelly Broad. Co., 48 Cal. 3d 711, 732 (Cal. 1989).
227. 376 U.S. 254 (1964).
228. 497 U.S. 1 (1990).

even further. After *Milkovich*, several state courts followed that there could be no "categorical exemption for opinion existing independently" and established that the applicable question is "whether a reasonable fact finder could conclude that the published statements imply a provably false factual assertion."[229]

Truth/Falsity

As defamatory actions turn upon the nature of the statements, what constitutes truth and falsity and who bears the burden of pleading and proof must be assessed. There are circumstances in which a statement, although defamatory on its face, may not be actionable. Because truth is an absolute defense to defamation, if the overall "gist" or "sting" of the statement is true, then the defamation is not actionable.[230] A writer's or speaker's altering syntax or grammar of the original speaker does not prove falsity. However, when the use of devices such as altered syntax or quotations give a different, defamatory meaning to what was actually said, the statement can be deemed actionably false.

In addition, if the statement only causes "incremental harm"[231] or if the subject of the statement is "libel-proof"—that is, possesses such a poor reputation anyhow that the statement can only cause nominal additional reputation harm[232]—such an action will not likely succeed. Some states such as Illinois apply the "innocent construction" rule, in which an initial legal determination as to whether an allegedly defamatory statement remains so after giving the words used their natural and ordinary meaning.[233]

Like pure opinion statements, other assertions are generally not actionable under state laws, judicial interpretations, or federal constitutional law. Statements that are incapable of being proven false; fiction, cartoons, satire, hyperbole, humor, or parody that cannot reasonably be understood as

---

229. Kahn v. Bower, 232 Cal. App. 3d 1599, 1607 (Cal. App. 1st Dist. 1991).

230. Masson v. New Yorker Magazine, 501 U.S. 496 (1991).

231. The incremental harm doctrine reasons that where unchallenged or nonactionable portions of a statement are defamatory, the defamatory statement at issue would not be actionable because of its nominal defamatory impact in the context of the entire statement. *Masson*, 501 U.S. at 522–525.

232. *See, e.g.*, Cardillo v. Doubleday & Co., 518 F.2d 638 (2d Cir. 1975); Urbano v. Sondern, 41 F.R.D. 355, 357 (D. Conn.), *aff'd*, 370 F.2d 13 (2d Cir. 1966), *cert. denied*, 386 U.S. 1034, 18 L. Ed. 2d 596, 87 S. Ct. 1485 (1967); Mattheis v. Hoyt, 136 F. Supp. 119, 124 (W.D. Mich. 1955).

233. Tuite v. Corbitt, 224 Ill. 2d 490 (2006).

stating facts about an individual; and most literary or esthetic reviews are not actionable.

When the defendant is a media actor, a private party suing on a statement of public concern that is allegedly false bears the burden of proving that the statement is false, rather the defendant proving the matter is true.[234]

Public Officials and Figures and Private Figures

In defamation actions, the status of the plaintiff and the status of the defendant impact the burdens of pleading and proofs. Public officials, public figures, and private persons as plaintiffs confront different hurdles in prosecuting defamation actions; by a similar token, different proofs apply if the defendant is a media actor.

Public Officials

A public official is one who serves either by election, appointment, or selection in a public governmental capacity. Yet the Supreme Court has refused to draw clear lines as to who may be considered a "public official," for First Amendment defamation purposes. In *New York Times v. Sullivan*, it was not controverted that the commissioner/plaintiff was a public official being criticized in his conduct as such. The Supreme Court in that case took no occasion "to determine how far down into the lower ranks of government employees the 'public official' designation would extend for purposes of [determining upon whom the actual malice rule would apply], or otherwise to specify categories of persons who would or would not be included."[235] However, the Court has said that the "public official" designation "applies at the very least to those among the hierarchy of government employees who have, or appear to the public to have, substantial responsibility for or control over the conduct of governmental affairs."[236]

Public Figures

Public figures are put on a par with public officials for purposes of defa-

234. Philadelphia Newspapers, Inc. v. Hepps., 475 U.S. 1134 (1986).
235. New York Times v. Sullivan, 376 U.S., at 283, n. 23.
236. Rosenblatt v. Baer, 383 U.S. 75, 85 (1966).

mation actions and the applicability of the actual malice standard. Public figures generally are considered to have "voluntarily put themselves in the spotlight" and clearly possess "general fame or notoriety in the community and pervasive involvement in the affairs of society."[237]

In *Gertz*, the Court set forth two categories of public figures: general-purpose public figures and limited-purpose public figures.[238] In some instances, an individual may achieve such pervasive fame or notoriety that he or she becomes a public figure for all purposes and in all contexts. More commonly, an individual voluntarily injects himself or herself or is drawn into a particular public controversy and thereby becomes a public figure for a limited range of issues. In determining whether a person is a general- or limited-purpose public figure for First Amendment defamation purposes, courts are instructed to look at the nature and extent of the person's participation in a particular controversy.[239] In either case, such persons assume special prominence in the resolution of public questions, and the actual malice standard will apply to both.

In contrast, there are those who have reluctantly been placed into the forefront of controversies. Despite the perhaps public interest and public concern the controversy might engender, the Supreme Court has carved out an exception for those who have been involuntarily thrust into such issues and will consider those persons private figures for First Amendment defamation action purposes.[240]

All states have adopted the classifications set forth by the Supreme Court in *New York Times v. Sullivan*. In that case, the Court held that public officials suing media defendants must prove that the defamatory statement was made with actual malice. Actual malice requires that the plaintiff in a defamation or libel case prove that the publisher of the statement

---

237. Gertz v. Welch, 418 U.S. 323 (1974).

238. *Id.* at 345.

239. *Id.*

240. In Time, Inc. v. Firestone, 424 U.S. 448 (1976), the Supreme Court held that the wife of a "scion of one of America's wealthier industrial families" was not a public figure despite "a few press conferences . . . in an attempt to satisfy inquiring reporters," and that her civil divorce proceedings were not the sort of "public controversy" referred to in *Gertz*. *Id.* at 450, 454. The Court noted that Mrs. Firestone was "compelled to go to court by the State in order to obtain legal release from the bonds of matrimony," rather than freely choosing to publicize issues as to the propriety of her married life, and rejected the proposal to equate "public controversy" with all controversies of interest to the public. *Id.* at 454.

in question knew that the statement was false or acted in reckless disregard of its truth or falsity.[241] Alternatively, some courts will find the existence of actual malice upon a showing that a media defendant entertained serious doubts about the truth of the defamatory statement.[242]

Fault and Burdens of Proof

In general, the defamation plaintiff has the burden of proving each element of the action. That is, the plaintiff must demonstrate (1) the defamatory character of the communication; (2) its publication or communication to a third party; (3) that the statement was "of or concerning" the plaintiff; (4) the defamatory meaning derived by the reader, viewer, or listener and that the recipient understood that the statement was about or concerning the plaintiff; and (5) the harm that resulted. States alternatively require that the defamation cause "significant," "material," or "substantial" harm.[243]

If the plaintiff is a private figure, he must prove that the defamation was made negligently. However, public officials or figures must prove that the defamation was made with the higher standard of actual malice. If the statement made was privileged, such as one made as fair comment, the plaintiff must put forth evidence proving that the privilege was abused.

Media defendants must demonstrate truth as a defense and make the initial case that the statement was privileged. However, burdens shift if the alleged defamation was a matter of public concern. In that case, a private plaintiff has the burden of proving the *falsity* of the statement. The same is true for public officials and figures.

The duties of proving the facts in evidence in defamation actions vary depending on the facts and the litigant involved in the dispute. Most states require that the facts be shown with clear and convincing evidence.[244] However, actual malice must be established with "convincing clarity."[245]

---

241. *Id.*

242. St. Amant v. Thompson, 390 U.S. 727, 731, 88 S. Ct. 1323, 20 L. Ed. 2d 262 (1968).

243. *See, e.g.,*, Cox Broadcasting Corp. v. Cohn, 420 U.S. 469 (1975) (Georgia requires showing of "substantial harm"); Biondi v. Nassimos, 300 N.J. Super. 148, 153, 692 A.2d 103 (App. Div. 1997) ("To establish a slander claim under the common law, a plaintiff is required to show 'special damages,' which is defined as 'harm of a material or pecuniary nature.'") (original citation omitted).

244. *Restatement (Second) of Torts*, §§ 580A, 580B.

245. Bose Corp. v. Consumers Union, 466 U.S. 485 (1984).

Although the Supreme Court expressly holds that proof in this case must be with "convincing clarity" in which public officials or figures are plaintiffs,[246] states such as Texas abide by a clear and convincing evidence standard even as to actual malice.[247]

Damages and Other Remedies

Depending on the status of the injured party—that is, private or public—general or special damages may be had. General damages are harm to reputation presumed or proved to have been sustained. General, or compensatory, damages are given for the demonstrated harm the statement caused to the plaintiff's reputation.[248] A media defendant may also be liable for any special harm the defamatory statement is a substantial factor in bringing the harm and, there is no law relieving the media defendant from liability because of the way in which the publication resulted in the harm.[249]

Special damages may be awarded upon proof that the statement caused particular emotional or physical injury. Nominal damages are awarded when the insignificant character of the defamatory matter, or the plaintiff's bad character, leads the jury to believe that no substantial harm has been done to his reputation and there is no proof that serious harm has resulted from the defendant's attack upon the plaintiff's character and reputation. They are also awarded when they are the only damages claimed, and the action is brought for the purpose of vindicating the plaintiff's character by a verdict of a jury that establishes the falsity of the defamatory matter.[250]

The Supreme Court has held that punitive damages cannot be awarded against a media defendant only upon a showing that the defendant

---

246. New York Times Co. v. Sullivan, 376 U.S. 254, 279-80, 84 S. Ct. 710, 11 L. Ed. 2d 686 (1964); Bose Corp. v. Consumers Union, 466 U.S. 485 (1984). *See, e.g.*, Nelson v. Pagan, 2012 Tex. App. LEXIS 6507 at *22; Lewis v. Rapp, 725 S.E.2d 597, 602 (N.C. Ct. App. 2012); Piper v. Mize, 31 Media L. Rep. 1833 (Tenn. App. 2003); Holtzscheiter v. Thomson Newspapers, 332 S.C. 502 (1998); Chase v. Daily Record, Inc., 83 Wn.2d 37, 515 P.2d 154 (1973).

247. Lynch v. N.J. Educ. Ass'n, 161 N.J. 152, 169, 735 A.2d 1129 (1999); Osak v. University of Mich. Regents, 2012 Mich. App. LEXIS 2069 at *12; Brandom v. Coupled Prods., LLC, 2012 Ind. App. LEXIS 476 at *18; American Chem. Soc'y v. Leadscope, Inc., 2012 Ohio 4193 at *54.

248. Restatement (Second) of Torts, §621.

249. *Id.* at §622A.

250. *Id.* at §620.

negligently communicated the defamatory statement.[251] Punitive damages may be awarded a private plaintiff if he or she is able to demonstrate actual malice. State courts differ as to whether that rule applies to a nonmedia defendant.[252]

Most states have established a one-year statute of limitations for bringing civil defamation actions.[253]

Other remedies to consider for defamation actions are injunctions, rights of reply, and retractions. Injunctions are highly disfavored, especially because they act as a type of prior restraint. A right of reply would allow a defamation victim to respond in his or her own words in the offending publication. States rarely require such a remedy, perhaps because of the serious constitutional problems attendant with requiring a media defendant to "speak" and, specifically, what to speak about.[254] Yet voluntary retractions by media defendants may mitigate if not extinguish any monetary damage determination.

Special Issues In Internet Libel

Traditionally, a prospective plaintiff has little trouble identifying the speaker of the defamatory statement. That idea has been considerably thrown awry in the context of the Internet. Internet defamation now represents the most fervent development of the constitutional contours of defamation.

This is primarily due to the conflicting positions as to whether providers of online services are "publishers" like newspapers, passive distributors, or conduits like libraries or bookstores. This issue was first encountered in *Cubby, Inc. v. CompuServe, Inc.*,[255] in which CompuServe was able to successfully argue that it was a news distributor of the third-

---

251. Gertz v. Welch, 418 U.S. at 349–350.

252. *Compare* Rowe v. Metz, 195 Colo. 424, 579 P.2d 83 (1978); Harley-Davidson Motorsports, Inc. v. Markley, 279 Or. 361(1977) (*Gertz* rule does not apply to nonmedia defendants); Jacron Sales Co. v. Sindorf, 350 A.2d 688 (1976); Rogozinski v. Airstream by Angell, 377 A.2d 807 (1977), *modified in other respects*, 397 A.2d 334 (1979); Ryder Truck Rentals v. Latham, 593 S.W.2d 334 (Tex .Civ. App. 1979) (holding that the *Gertz* rule does apply to nonmedia defendants). Some states, such as Washington, allow no punitive damage recovery under state law unless the law explicitly allows.

253. *See, e.g.*, Arizona, Arkansas, California, Colorado, District of Columbia, Illinois, Kansas, Kentucky, New York, Ohio, Pennsylvania, Texas, and Virginia. Others are two years or, in the rarest of instances, more.

254. Miami Herald Pub. Co. v. Tornillo, 418 U.S. 241 (1974).

255. 776 F.Supp. 135 (S.D.N.Y. 1991).

party newsletter that contained defamatory statements.

By contrast, in *Stratton Oakmont v. Prodigy Services*,[256] the New York Supreme Court found that Prodigy could not hide behind the veil of being a neutral news distributor. In *Stratton*, an unknown user had posted statements on Prodigy's "Money Talk" bulletin alleging that the plaintiff and its president had committed criminal and fraudulent acts in connection with its initial public offering. The court agreed with the plaintiff that Prodigy could be considered a publisher even of an anonymous user's statements because it had widely represented that it exercised editorial control over the content of its servers.

In part as a response to the Hobbesian choice confronting Internet site operators (exercise complete control or no control), Congress passed Section 230 of the Communications Decency Act of 1996.[257] That provision states that "No provider or user of an interactive computer service shall be treated as a publisher or speaker of any information provided by another information content provider."[258] Section 230 also provides that "[n]o cause of action may be brought and no liability may be imposed under any State or local law that is inconsistent with this section."[259]

Seen as a "safe harbor" provision, Section 230 does create liability exceptions. Certainly a service provider may be liable if it creates or develops the offending statements. Furthermore, if the service provider edits provided content in such a way as to make it defamatory, liability may exist.

Criminal Libel

Although criminal libel provisions remain a part of many state statutes, they are sparsely enforced. Criminal libel provisions were part of virtually every state law, but most had fallen into disuse by 1964, when the Supreme Court upheld the constitutionality of Louisiana's criminal libel statute in *Garrison v. Louisiana*.[260] Since 1964, at least 18 states and the District of

256. 23 Media L. Rep. 1794 (1995), superseded by statute, 47 U.S.C. §230.
257. Pub. L. No. 104-104, 110 Stat. 56 (1996), 47 U.S.C. §230.
258. 47 U.S.C. § 230(c)(1).
259. 47 U.S.C. § 230(e)(3).
260. 379 U.S. 64 (1964).

Columbia have repealed criminal libel laws.[261] Courts in 10 other states struck down criminal libel statutes.[262] Nineteen states still have criminal defamation laws in place.[263]

Criminal defamation laws of states went largely repealed, were found unconstitutional, or went unprosecuted for the next 40 years. Over the past several years, criminal libel prosecutions have increased, with the predominant medium of the alleged criminal defamation occurring on the Internet.[264]

According to a recent study, of the 11 threatened and actual libel prosecutions brought between January 2002 and December 2004, seven cases were threatened or brought against speakers who allegedly libeled government employees.[265] It has been surmised that because the majority of recent criminal libel cases appear to be designed primarily to intimidate or prosecute those who speak out against the government rather than to provide compensation to those whose reputations allegedly have been damaged, it is clear that criminal libel is nothing more than seditious libel given a thin veneer of constitutionality.

Criminal libel statutes, which carry the threat of jail time and criminal fines, can have a chilling effect on any speaker. Given that the threat punishment is different than what would result from a civil action, and the fact that it is a content-based/speech-based criminal action, a strong case can be made that criminal libel statutes are facially and ideologically inconsistent with First Amendment principles. Because of the content-based

---

261. Jane E. Kirtley, *Criminal Defamation: An "Instrument of Destruction," in* ENDING THE CHILLING EFFECT: WORKING TO REPEAL CRIMINAL LIBEL AND INSULT LAWS 89–101, 92 (Ana Karlsreiter and Hanna Vuokko eds. 2003); IML. v. State, 61 P.3d 1038 (Utah 2002); Ivey v. Alabama, 821 So.2d 937, 29 Media L. Rep. 2089 (Ala. 2001).

262. Kirtley, *supra* note 261 at 92.

263. ALA. CODE § 13A-11-160 (2012); FLA. STAT. § 836.01 (2012); GA. CODE ANN. § 16-11-40 (2012); IDAHO CODE § 19-1424 (2012); KY. REV. STAT. ANN. § 432.280 (2012); LA. REV. STAT. ANN. 14:47 (2012); MINN. STAT. § 609.765 (2012); MISS. CODE ANN. § 97-3-55 (2012); MONT. CODE ANN., § 45-8-212 (2011); NEV. REV. STAT. ANN. § 200.510 (2012); N.M. STAT. ANN. § 30-11-1 (2012); N.C. GEN. STAT. § 99-1 (2012); N.D. CENT. CODE, § 12.1-15-01 (2012); 22 OKLA. STAT. § 422 (2012); S.C. CODE ANN. § 16-7-150 (2011); TENN. CODE ANN. § 40-13-214 (2012); UTAH CODE ANN. § 76-9-404 (2012); VA. CODE ANN. § 18.2-417 (2012); WIS. STAT. § 942.01 (2012). *See also* Massachusetts, ALM GL ch. 265, § 25 (2012) (extortion by threat of false accusation criminal offense).

264. David Pritchard, *Rethinking Criminal Libel: An Empirical Study*, 14 COMM. L. AND POL'Y 303 (2009) (finding 18 out of 40 criminal libel prosecutions involved material on the Internet); Edward L. Carter, *Outlaw Speech On The Internet: Examining The Link Between Unique Characteristics Of Online Media And Criminal Libel Prosecutions*, 21 SANTA CLARA COMPUTER & HIGH TECH. L.J. 289 (2005).

265. *Developments in Criminal Defamation Law since 2002*, MLRC BULLETIN (Media Law Resource Center), March 2003, at 4–9.

nature of criminal libel violations, there exists a compelling argument that such provisions undergo a strict scrutiny analysis when challenged.[266]

Several years ago, the Supreme Court noted, in the context of online material, that "[c]ontent-based prohibitions, enforced by severe criminal penalties, have the constant potential to be a repressive force in the lives and thoughts of a free people. To guard against that threat the Constitution demands that content-based restrictions on speech be presumed invalid [. . .] and that the Government bear the burden of showing their constitutionality."[267] To be sure, criminal prohibitions on speech are especially suspect when civil remedies covering exactly the same subject matter already exist, as is the case with libel. Consequently, there should be little question as to whether criminal libel statutes are necessary to protect the rights of individuals to their reputation.

Obscenity and Indecency

Section 1464 of Title 18, United States Code, prohibits the broadcast of obscene, indecent, or profane programming.[268] The FCC rules implementing that statute, a subsequent statute establishing a "safe harbor" during certain hours, and the act prohibit radio and television stations from broadcasting obscene material at any time and indecent material between 6 a.m. and 10 p.m.[269] Violators are subject to fine, imprisonment for up to two years, or both.[270] Doing so exposes the broadcaster and content provider to criminal sanction and administrative penalties.[271] For cable television and other subscription services such as direct-to-home satellite, the knowing transmission of "obscene language" and "obscene matter" are proscribed; "indecent" language is not.[272] Forty-

---

266. Sable Communications, Inc. v. FCC, 492 U.S. 115 (1985) (reversing ban on indecent "dial-a-porn" telephone activity).

267. Ashcroft v. American Civil Liberties Union, 124 S.Ct. 2783, 2788 (2004) (citations omitted) (emphasis added).

268. *See* 18 U.S.C. § 1464.

269. *See* 47 C.F.R. § 73.3999; Action for Children's Television v. Federal Communications Commission, 58 F.3d 654 (D.C. Cir. 1995).

270. *See* 18 U.S.C. § 1464.

271. However, television and radio broadcasts have been granted safe harbor time (the hours between 10 p.m.–6 a.m.) during which broadcasts that might otherwise be deemed indecent may be aired. Action for Children's Television v. FCC, 58 F.3d 654, 669–70 (D.C. Cir. 1995) (upholding constitutionality of FCC safe harbor period).

272. 18 U.S.C. § 1468. *See also* 47 U.S.C. § 559 (making it a crime to transmit via cable what is obscene, or any other matter not protected by the United States Constitution over cable).

eight states have laws that criminalize obscene materials.

Enforcement of the provisions restricting the broadcast of indecent, obscene, or profane[273] material is an important component of the FCC's overall responsibility over broadcast and other media except print. At the same time, the First Amendment and Section 326 of the 1934 Communications Act prohibit the Commission from censoring program material or interfering with broadcasters' First Amendment free speech rights.[274]

The Supreme Court stated that "of all forms of communication, it is broadcasting that has received the most limited First Amendment protection" because the broadcast medium is a "uniquely pervasive presence in the lives of all Americans" that extends into the privacy of the home and is "uniquely accessible to children, even those too young to read."[275]

In general, restrictions on First Amendment liberties prompt courts to apply strict scrutiny.[276] Outside the broadcasting context, the Supreme Court has consistently applied strict scrutiny to indecency regulations.[277]

Obscenity

The Supreme Court announced its definition of "obscene" in the 1973 landmark case *Miller v. California*.[278] There, the Court provided the following factors to assess whether content is "obscene":

> (a) whether the average person applying contemporary community standards would find that the work, taken as a whole, appeals to the prurient interest;
> (b) whether the work depicts or describes, in a patently offensive

---

273. The FCC has defined the term *profane* as "blasphemy." Complaints Against Various Broadcast Licensees Regarding Their Airing of the "Golden Globe Awards" Program, 18 F.C.C.R. 19859, at 14.

274. *See* U.S. Const. amend. I; 47 U.S.C. § 326; *see also* United States v. Playboy Entertainment Group, Inc., 529 U.S. 803, 813–15 (2000).

275. Federal Communications Commission v. Pacifica Foundation, 438 U.S. 726, 748–49 (1978).

276. Federal Communications Commission v. League of Women Voters, 468 U.S. 364, 376 (1984).

277. *See, e.g.*, United States v. Playboy Entertainment Group, 529 U.S. 803, 811–13 (2000) (holding that regulation proscribing indecent content on cable television was content-based restriction of speech subject to strict scrutiny); Sable Communications, Inc. v. Federal Communications Commission, 492 U.S. 115, 126 (1985) (holding that indecency regulation of telephone messages was content-based restriction subject to strict scrutiny); Reno v. American Civil Liberties Union, 521 U.S. 844, 868 (1997) (holding that indecency regulation of Internet was a content-based restriction subject to strict scrutiny).

278. 413 U.S. 15 (1973).

way, sexual conduct specifically defined by the applicable law; and (c) whether the work, taken as a whole, lacks serious literary, artistic, political, or scientific value.[279]

Where a court deems content obscene using the Supreme Court's three-prong analysis, such content will not be entitled to First Amendment protection. Indeed, the Court has made it clear that obscene works do not fall within the realm of constitutionally protected speech and may therefore be restricted by state and federal legislatures.[280]

Indecency

The FCC is charged with enforcing anti-indecency through nonprint media. As an initial matter, it is important to appreciate that all speech covered by the FCC's indecency policy is fully protected by the First Amendment.[281] As such, in making indecency determinations, the FCC has been directed to tread lightly in reaching its conclusionS.[282] The Commission defines indecent speech as material that in context depicts or describes sexual or excretory activities or organs in terms patently offensive as measured by contemporary community standards for the broadcast medium.[283]

Indecency determinations involve at least two fundamental findings. First, the material alleged to be indecent must fall within the subject matter scope of the FCC's definition. Second, the broadcast must be *patent-*

---

279. *Id.* at 24.

280. *Id.* at 23 (commenting that obscene material is unprotected by the First Amendment); *see also* Roth v. United States, 354 U.S. 476, 485 (1957) (finding that obscenity lies outside First Amendment protection because it is "utterly without redeeming social importance").

281. *See* Sable Communications. of California, Inc. v. FCC, 492 U.S. 115, 126 (1989) (noting that speech "which is indecent but not obscene is protected by the First Amendment"); *Industry Guidance,* 16 F.C.C.R. 7999, at 3 ("[I]ndecent speech is protected by the First Amendment, and thus, the government must both identify a compelling interest for any regulation it may impose on indecent speech and choose the least restrictive means to further that interest.").

282. *See* Action for Children's Television v. Federal Communications Commission, 852 F.2d 1332, 1344, 1340 n. 14 (1988) (stating that "[b]roadcast material that is indecent but not obscene is protected by the First Amendment; the FCC may regulate such material only with due respect for the high value our Constitution places on freedom and choice in what people may say and hear," and that any "potential chilling effect of the FCC's generic definition of indecency will be tempered by the Commission's restrained enforcement policy.").

283. *See Infinity Broadcasting Corporation of Pennsylvania,* Memorandum Opinion and Order, 2 F.C.C.R. 2705 (1987) (subsequent history omitted) (citing *Pacifica Foundation*, Memorandum Opinion and Order, 56 FCC 2d 94, 98 (1975), *aff'd sub nom.* FCC v. Pacifica Foundation, 438 U.S. 726 (1978)).

ly offensive as measured by contemporary community standards for the broadcast medium.[284]

In assessing whether broadcast material is patently offensive, "the *full context* in which the material appeared is critically important."[285] Three principal factors are significant to that analysis: (1) the explicitness or graphic nature of the material; (2) whether the material dwells on or repeats at length depictions or descriptions of sexual or excretory organs or activities; and (3) whether the material panders to, titillates, or shocks the audience.[286] In examining these three factors, the FCC engages in a balancing test on a case-by-case basis.[287] In particular cases, one or two of the factors may outweigh the others, either rendering the broadcast material patently offensive and consequently indecent[288] or, alternatively, removing the broadcast material from the realm of indecency.

---

284. *Industry Guidance on the Commission's Case Law Interpreting 18 U.S.C. §1464 and Enforcement Policies Regarding Broadcast Indecency*, Policy Statement, 16 F.C.C.R. 7999, 8002 ¶¶ 7-8 (2001) ("*Indecency Policy Statement*") (emphasis in original). In applying the "community standards for the broadcast medium" criterion, the FCC noted that it was not a standard based on geography:

The determination as to whether certain programming is patently offensive is not a local one and does not encompass any particular geographic area. Rather, the standard is that of an average broadcast viewer or listener and not the sensibilities of any individual complainant.

WPBN/WTOM License Subsidiary, Inc., Memorandum Opinion and Order, 15 F.C.C.R. 1838, 1841 ¶ 10 (2000) The FCC's interpretation of the term "contemporary community standards" flows out of the Supreme Court's decision in *Hamling v. United States*, 418 U.S. 87 (1974), *reh'g denied*, 419 U.S. 885 (1974).

285. *Indecency Policy Statement*, 16 F.C.C.R. at 8002 ¶ 9 (emphasis in original).

286. *See id.* at 8002-15 ¶¶ 8-23.

287. *Id.* at 8003 ¶ 10.

288. *See id.* at 8009 ¶ 19 (citations omitted).

5

Media Impact on Trial by Jury

BY NEIL VIDMAR

The deviant act . . . creates a sense of mutuality among the people of a community by supplying a focus for group feeling. Like a war, a flood, or some other emergency, deviance makes people more alert to the interests they share in common and draws attention to those values which constitute the "collective conscience of the community."

—Kai Erikson, *The Wayward Puritans* (1966)

Erikson was referring to the Salem Witch trials, but his observation has an important bearing on any assessment of the effects of contemporary media coverage of criminal trials, namely that responses to crime, or alleged crime, have sociological and sociopsychological underpinnings.[1] Although people and communities have always responded to crime, mass media—newspapers, television, and now the Internet—facilitate that interest, render it vivid through pictures and commentary, and make it salient beyond the immediate locale of the alleged crime, sometimes provoking nationwide interest. Two prominent examples, of many that could be given, are the 1995 O. J. Simpson murder trial[2] and the 2011 murder trial of Casey Anthony involving the death of her two-year-old daughter.[3] Both cases resulted in massive reporting in newspapers

---

1. Erikson's insight was in fact preceded by one of the fathers of modern sociology, who in 1893 drew attention to similar social and social psychological reactions to crime; *see* Emile Durkheim, The Division of Labor in Society (G. Simpson trans. 1967) (1893).

2. *See, e.g.*, *The Trial of O. J. Simpson*, http://www.law2.umkc.edu/faculty/projects/ftrials/simpson/simpson.html.

3. *See, e.g.*, Jeff Ashton, *Imperfect Justice: Prosecuting Casey Anthony* (2011); *see also* http://www.en.wikipedia.org/wiki/Death_of_Caylee_Anthony.

and on television before trial, gavel-to-gavel coverage during the trial, so-called "talking heads" offering commentary on the case, often prejudicially, and continuing coverage after the verdict. The Anthony trial also involved extensive Internet coverage. Both cases are interesting in that each resulted in the defendants being acquitted of murder charges, especially in light of the fact that in Anthony's case the jurors were "death qualified," making them potentially more conviction prone than jurors in other cases.[4] Details of these two cases will not be discussed in this chapter, although the judge's remedy for the massive media coverage of the Anthony case, namely an imported and sequestered jury, will be discussed near the end. My goal is to focus on general issues associated with media coverage and underlying factors in cases that can potentially prejudice jurors. Both empirical research and case studies will be used to illustrate the potential impact of media on trials.

The very substantial literature on media coverage of crime clearly demonstrates that both the quantity and quality of crime news coverage has increased dramatically over the past decades. Both James Hamilton and Sara Beale have documented the fact that media coverage is driven by economics.[5] Crime sells, whether it is fictionalized crime stories or coverage of actual cases. Beale's review of literature on mass media documents the degree to which media coverage of crime—particularly violent crime—has increased dramatically over the last decades.[6] The trends have been documented in network news, on local television news, and in newspapers, both local and national. Moreover, analyses also have shown that news coverage has shifted to a tabloid style of reporting that focuses on the sensational effects of an alleged crime and ignores many of the details that

---

4. *See, e.g.*, Craig Haney, Death by Design 106–12 (2005).

5. James T. Hamilton, Channeling Violence: The Economic Market for Violent Television Programming (1998); Television Violence and Public Policy (James T. Hamilton ed., 1998); *see also* Leo Bogart, Press and Public: Who Reads What, When, Where and Why in American Newspapers (1989); Sara Beale, *The News Media's Influence on Criminal Justice Policy: How Market-Driven News Promotes Punitiveness*, 48 Wm. & Mary L. Rev. 397–482 (2006).

6. Beale, *supra* note 5

might put the event in a broader context.[7]

Mass media help to create public opinion by conveying information to the public, but the influence process is complex. If the readership/viewership sees continuing relevance of a story, media sources continue printing additional stories about the subject on the reasonable premise that the public is interested in the story. The media gauge public interest in part by responses of letters to the editor, online comments, and other informal means.

To be sure, vivid coverage of crime stories in newspapers and on television is not new. Television viewers saw Jack Ruby kill Lee Harvey Oswald, the alleged killer of President Kennedy; attended to the riveting testimony of John Dean testifying before Congress about events preceding and following the Watergate burglary; and witnessed the beatings of Rodney King and truck driver Reginald Denny in Los Angeles. Viewers also saw Patty Hearst in the midst of a bank robbery, and car manufacturer John Z. DeLorean, and, later, former Washington mayor Marion Berry allegedly buying drugs.[8] Often media coverage is highly prejudicial: for example, interviews with the victim or the victim's relatives; reports of the defendant's past criminal record; or pictures of bloody crime scenes.

John Meringolo's account of media coverage of the RICO trial of John A. Gotti III, also known as "Junior" Gotti, provides an illustrative example.[9] Gotti's father was an infamous boss of the Gambino crime family who escaped convictions in three separate trials but finally was convicted in 1992 amid a great deal of media coverage. Six years later, Junior Gotti was indicted, arrested for various crimes, pled guilty, and served about five years in prison. Shortly before his release, Gotti was again indicted. The case ultimately resulted in three hung juries, but Gotti was arrested again in 2008, this time in Florida, but the case was moved to the Southern District of

---

7. *Id. See also* David Altheid, Creating Fear: News and the Construction of Crisis (2002); Jon Bruschke & William Loges, Free Press vs. Fair Trials: Examining Publicity's Role in Trial Outcomes (2004); Mark Geragos, *The Thirteenth Juror: Media Coverage of Supersized Trials*, 39 Loy. L.A. L. Rev. 1167–96 (2006); J. Newton Minnow & Fred H. Cate, *Who is an Impartial Juror in an Age of Mass Media?*, 40 Am. U. L. Rev. 631-64 (1991); V. Hans and J. Dee, *Media Coverage of Law: Its Impact on Juries and the Public*, 35 Am. Behav. Scientist 136–49 (1991); Matthew D. Bunker, Justice and the Media: Reconciling Fair Trials and a Free Press (1997).

8. Robert Hardaway & Douglas L. Tumminello, *Pretrial Publicity in Criminal Cases of National Notoriety: Constructing a Remedy for the Remediless Wrong*, 46 Am. U. L. Rev. 39–90 (1996).

9. John Meringolo, *The Media, the Jury and the High-profile Defendant: A Defense Perspective on the Media Circus*, 55 N.Y.U. Law Rev. 981–1012 (2010–11).

New York. Merlingolo has documented not only the massive amount of media coverage of the case but also the inaccuracy of the reporting. Although Gotti was originally charged with one count of RICO conspiracy, the press reported that he had been charged with three gangland murders. Later the indictment was changed to include *conspiracy* to murder, but the press failed to note the difference and reported the case as involving actual murder charges. The trial was moved from the Southern to the Eastern District of New York consistent with legal rules, but the headlines in one newspaper pejoratively headlined the story as "Team Gotti in Trial Hopscotch." When Gotti's defense team moved for his release on bail, the press selected two small parts from the 20-page bail memorandum: Gotti's medical problem with his kidneys, and his grade point average in prison. The press headlined coverage with "He's Gone from the Most-Wanted List to the Dean's List." Although the judge had ruled that the jury was to be an anonymous jury, the *New York Daily News* released a profile of each juror, reporting each juror's gender, race, and occupation. During the trial, a letter from one juror to the judge complaining about another juror was posted on the websites of the *New York Daily News* and the *New York Post*.

The issue of media exposure and its effects on trial by jury has a number of facets that will be viewed from a social and sociopsychological perspective. As the Junior Gotti case illustrates, media coverage before or during trial can potentially contaminate a jury by providing inadmissible facts, raising issues that impugn a defendant's or witness's character, and/or creating conditions whereby an individual juror or the jury feels the need to reach a verdict consistent with the perceived consensus of a community. Claims also have been made regarding the effects of media on general attitudes toward defendants associated with their racial or ethnic membership (e.g., African American or Muslim defendants). Additionally, claims have been made about the influence on jurors of the so-called "CSI Effect," whereby viewers of crime shows are alleged to be acquittal prone if the prosecution does not have scientific evidence to bolster its case. In recent years, the issue of jurors using the Internet during trial to research inadmissible facts about the case or to make comments during trial on Facebook or other social media also has caused concern to courts.

Not all cases are as dramatic and prejudicial as the coverage in the Simpson, Anthony, and Gotti examples, but potentially prejudicial media effects are fairly common and raise issues about fairness of trials as well as about judicial remedies for potential prejudice. Social context can include the influence on jurors by family members, friends, coworkers, and others who are also exposed to the coverage before or during trial, especially if the verdict is contrary to community consensus. This chapter presents only a partial review of an extensive literature on the effects of media. Instead, greater emphasis will be given to the social and sociopsychological dynamics that make jurors and juries susceptible to the bias that may arise from media coverage. These effects will be considered in the context of judicial remedies, particularly the efficacy of those remedies.

The remainder of this chapter is divided into five sections. The first section deals with general media effects—that is, coverage of crime that often produces widespread community attitudes about criminal defendants and trials. It draws attention to differential effects that may occur among members of subgroups within a community. This section also discusses the so-called "CSI Effect," whereby media have supposedly created juror expectations about the types of evidence needed for a conviction. The next section considers two major cases, *McVeigh* and *Skilling*, in which courts have struggled with the potential impact of media coverage. These two cases set the stage for the next section that reviews research on the social and psychological dynamics of juror decision making. The fourth section provides examples from selected high-profile trials, illustrating how prospective jurors may be contaminated by media publicity but fail to recognize or report their resultant prejudices. The fifth section addresses remedies for media-induced juror prejudices and research approaches to overcome trial judge reluctance to deviate from the remedies of limited *voir dire* and judicial instructions in high-profile cases.

Media Crime Coverage and Community Responses

Kai Erikson's insight about the social context of crime draws attention to the fact that crime not only evokes passion, it causes people to talk and gossip. First consider a case involving the death of a child in which media coverage was minimal. The media absence helps to illustrate the sociopsychological dynamics of responses to crime that in other circumstances are greatly magnified by media coverage.

R. v. Utzi.[10] In 1980, a mother and father were both charged in the death of their two-year-old child in rural Oxford County, Ontario, Canada. Many people throughout the county had at least passing knowledge of the two defendants, their reputations as alcoholics, and their proclivities to sift through trash dumps. The initial death of the child and the parents' arrests were briefly reported in the local weekly newspaper and on a TV station, but that was the extent of the media coverage. In contrast to the United States, Canadian law gives preference to fair trial over free press, and the defense lawyers immediately filed an injunction to prevent any further media coverage. Yet, when the case was coming to trial almost two years later, a community survey bolstered with a small sample of random interviews with inhabitants of Oxford County revealed a great deal of community knowledge and rumor about the case. Some persons reported that they had heard that the child had been killed for insurance money, and others reported that the child had been placed in a washing machine, while still others reported that the Children's Aid Society had taken a previous child away from the mother. None of these rumors were correct. The survey further demonstrated that many members of the community had formed strong opinions that the defendants were definitely guilty and should be punished. The significance of the *Utzi* case, of course, is that it is consistent with Erikson's observation: Rumor and gossip can occur independently of newspaper and television coverage. Next, consider two cases in which media coverage has been shown to amplify differential reactions among subgroups within communities.

Catholics and Mormons. Although the *Utzi* case was somewhat unusual in the sense that there was a near absence of media coverage, consider two examples that further help to illustrate the interaction of media coverage and underlying sociopsychological issues. The first example is another Canadian case in which massive media coverage took place well before

10. *See* N. Vidmar & J. Melnitzer, *Juror Prejudice: An empirical study of a challenge for cause*, 22 Osgoode Hall L.J. 487–511 (1984).

charges were actually laid against the defendants.[11] In 1989, Canadians across the nation were shocked to learn of multiple sex abuse claims made against members of the Irish Christian Brothers of Canada, a Catholic lay order, who ran the Mt. Cashel Orphanage for Boys in St. Johns, Newfoundland. The media exposure in national newspapers and television included interviews with some of some of the former Mt. Cashel boys, now young men, graphically describing the abuse.

In preparing pretrial motions directed toward obtaining a change of venue, defense lawyers conducted a public opinion poll of potential jurors in St. John's. St. John's had an interesting demographic characteristic, namely that it was about evenly divided between Catholics and Protestants. Although the members of the two groups were civil with one another, there was an underlying cultural clash about religion. The clash was manifested in varying ways, but it can be characterized by the perhaps apocryphal story that in the not-distant past when there were only one or two television channels and almost everyone watched Saturday's "Hockey Night in Canada," the Protestants cheered for the Toronto Maple Leafs and the Catholics supported the Montreal Canadiens. Although the defense survey found widespread disgust and hostility against the accused Christian Brothers, the strongest condemnation and hostility came from Catholics. The Catholic respondents perceived the Christian Brothers as bringing shame on all Catholics and providing the Protestants an opportunity to look down on them.

A similar social response was demonstrated in Utah following the 2007 trial of Warren Jeffs, leader of the Fundamentalist Church of Jesus Christ of Latter Day Saints (FLDS), the Mormon group that, among other characteristics, fosters polygamy.[12] Jeffs was found guilty of two felony counts of child sexual abuse for ordering the marriages of underage girls to older men. Subsequently, a young man who had been ordered to marry one of the girls was charged with rape and scheduled to be tried in rural Washington County,

---

11. For a discussion, *see* N. Vidmar, *Retributive Justice: Its Social Context*, in The Justice Motive In Everyday Life, 291 (M. Ross & D.T. Miller eds., 2001).

12. *See, e.g.*, http://www.en.wikipedia.org/wiki/Warren_Jeffs for a discussion of the background to the charges and the trial.

Utah, where the young man and the girls lived in an FLDS community.[13]

Defense lawyers considered asking the court to move the trial to Salt Lake City on the assumption that the city residents would be less hostile. However, survey data showed just the opposite result.[14] Although the mainstream Mormon and other residents of Washington County expressed strong disagreement with the theology and life styles of FLDS members, they also reported that they were familiar with the FLDS inhabitants and often hired them for agricultural and similar jobs because of their strong work ethic. In contrast, the survey found that many residents of the urban Salt Lake City were very hostile toward the defendant. Similar to the Catholics in Newfoundland, they perceived the nationwide publicity surrounding Jeffs and the FLDS as bringing shame on all Mormons.

In summary, in both of these examples media publicity evoked different responses among persons belonging to different social groups, once again emphasizing the interaction between social grouping and attitudes toward criminal defendants.

The McMartin Preschool Case and Media-Inflamed "Social Hysteria" Cases. In 1984, a woman whose son was in the McMartin Preschool in Manhattan Beach, California, alleged that her 18-month-old son had been sexually molested.[15] In the six months following this accusation, almost 400 former students at the school were interviewed; 41 were identified as probably having been sexually abused. The district attorney filed charges against seven persons associated with the school, alleging that the McMartin Preschool was linked to a child pornography ring. Mass media immediately began to report the story. A Los Angeles TV station broadcast the allegations, reporting that 60 children had been sexually abused over a 10-year period and that the children had been frightened into silence by their molesters. The *Los Angeles Times* then reported on the story, repeating and elaborating on the charges. Media reports on the sensational case spread throughout the United States and elsewhere. In March, television

---

13. State of Utah v. Allen Glade Steed, Case No. 07150596 (2007).

14. Unpublished data collected by Neil Vidmar and held on file.

15. *See* Edgar W. Butler et al., Anatomy of the McMartin Child Molestation Case (2001); Paul Eberle & Shirley Eberle, The Abuse of Innocence: The McMartin Preschool Trial (1993); Debbie Nathan & M. Snedeker, Satan's Silence: Ritual Abuse and the Making of a Modern American Witch Hunt (1995).

cameras were allowed to accompany the police when Raymond Buckley and his mother were arrested. Subsequently, charges against five of the accused were dropped on the grounds that the evidence against them was "incredibly weak," but the charges against the two Buckleys remained. As the case progressed, major news sources such as *Newsweek, Time Magazine*, and ABC's *20/20* began to question whether there was ever any basis behind the charges. However, the *Los Angeles Times* continued to write stories that essentially supported the allegations. The case dragged on for almost four years. Shortly before trial, an expert for the defense documented the fact that both print and television coverage were extraordinary in the amount, scope, sensationalism, and negativity toward the two remaining defendants. A public opinion survey found that 96% of those queried had heard of the case and as many as 97% of persons who expressed an opinion thought that the lead defendant, Raymond Buckley, was "definitely or probably guilty." As many as 80% believed that he had mutilated animals to scare the children into silence and, moreover, that the five defendants against whom the charges had been dropped were also guilty. In the light of these and other findings, the judge allowed a lengthy *voir dire*. The trial itself occurred over a period of two and a half years, and, after nine weeks of deliberation, the jury returned not guilty verdicts on 52 of the counts and deadlocked on the remaining 13. Despite the acquittals, a Fox television call-in poll found, by a seven-to-one margin, that respondents believed that justice had not been served.

Media coverage of the *McMartin* case appears at least partially responsible for a wave of similar charges in other locations during the late 1980s and early 1990s. Among the most famous of these cases were the Wee Care Nursery case in Maplewood, New Jersey, involving defendant Kelly Michaels, and the Little Rascals case in Edenton, North Carolina. Interestingly, the media coverage of these and other cases appears to have produced similar charges against day care owners and employees, often involving claims of satanic rituals, in Canada, England, and New Zealand.[16]

16. For references, *see generally* S.J. Ceci & M. Bruck, Jeopardy in the Courtroom (1996); David Hechler, The Battle and the Backlash—The Child Sexual Abuse War (1988); Kathryn Lyon, Witch Hunt: A True Story of Social Hysteria and Abused Justice (1998).

More General Media Effects, Including Perceptions of Racial, Religious, and Ethnic Groups. Media may also produce effects that do not pertain to a specific trial but nevertheless foster and maintain stereotypes about categories of people and associations with the criminal justice system.

Dixon and Linz undertook a content analysis of television news aired in Los Angeles and Orange Counties in 1995, 1996, and 1977.[17] They found that whites were more likely than African Americans and Latinos to be portrayed as victims of crime. Moreover, African Americans and Latinos were more often portrayed as lawbreakers than as victims. The portrayals were substantially out of balance with actual crime statistics and raised issues about public perceptions and stereotypes of both victims and perpetrators. Dixon and Linz were careful to point out that the effects may have been, in some instances, reflections of reality, depending on which index of crime was used as a comparison point. However, research by those authors, as well as studies by Romer et al.[18] and by Sorenson, Manz, and Berk,[19] compared actual incidence of victimization across races and still found that black and Hispanic victims received less media coverage than whites. Dixon and Linz speculated that economic interests of news stations drive the emphasis on racial differences in victimization and perpetrators. We need not concern ourselves with causality in this chapter, but simply note that the imbalanced news coverage helps to reinforce racially tinged public images of crime and its causes and can affect the images that jurors bring to the courtroom.

As mentioned earlier, Beale's review of research drew attention to the fact that commercial pressures have driven the major networks to emphasize crime and violence, which in turn has affected criminal justice policy.[20] For example, despite evidence indicating that certain crime rates have dropped, public opinion surveys have shown greater concerns about crime. Research has also demonstrated that these reports create scripts or

---

17. Travis J. Dixon and Daniel Linz, *Race and Misrepresentation of Victimization on Local Television News*, 27 Communication Research 547–73, Oct. 2000.

18. D. Romer et al., *The Treatment of Persons of Color in Local Television News: Ethnic Blame Discourse or Realistic Group Conflict*, 25 Communication Research 268–305 (1998).

19. S. B. Sorenson, J. P. Manz & R. A. Berk, *News Media Coverage and the Epidemiology of Homicide*, 88 Am. J. Public Health 1510–44 (1998).

20. Beale, *supra* note 5 at 416.

stereotypes in the minds of viewers that affect a wide range of attitudes and beliefs about crime. Empirical findings have shown that people who reported that they watch the news on a daily basis were more likely to have greater fears of crime and to support punitive approaches to crime than those who reported that they did not watch the news on a regular basis.[21] Moreover, frequent viewers were more likely to see African Americans in a negative light. The degree of these reactions were more pronounced for individuals who lived in areas with higher crime rates, among persons who had been victims of crime, and among those who were regular viewers of local news and perceived it as realistically portraying crime.[22]

In this vein, Edith Greene reviewed empirical studies that strongly suggested that general images of crime as portrayed in mass media could affect the perceptions and attitudes that jurors bring to the trial.[23] For example, research on media reports about psychiatrists before and during John Hinckley's trial for shooting President Reagan showed that the psychiatrists who testified in the trial were often denigrated, their fees were described as exorbitant, and their testimony was portrayed as having little merit.[24] Hans and Slater surveyed Delaware residents shortly after Hinkley's trial and found that many respondents believed that psychiatrists were unable to determine legal insanity.[25]

Obviously, causality cannot be determined from such studies; it may be that frequent viewers of television news already have racially biased attitudes and greater tendencies to fear crime because they watch more television news. However, these general attitudes and beliefs are potentially relevant to the way a juror perceives and evaluates evidence presented at trial and how he or she frames the evidence in reaching a verdict. Pretrial surveys of potential jurors, pretrial questionnaires, and *voir dire* questioning should be sensitive to the factors that could potentially influence jurors. Preexisting biases and perceptions could combine with pretrial public-

---

21. *Id.* at 452.

22. Ted Chiricos et al., *Crime, News, and Fear of Crime: Toward an Identification of Audience Effects*, 44 Social Problems 342–47 (1997).

23. Edith Greene, *Media Effects on Jurors*, 14 Law & Hum. Behav. 439–50 (1990).

24. *Id.* at 443.

25. Valerie P. Hans & Dan Slater, *John Hinckley, Jr. and the Insanity Defense: The Public's Verdict*, 47 Public Opinion Quarterly 202–29 (1983).

ity in particular trials, further complicating legal remedies for prejudicial media effects.

Personal or social relevance affects public exposure and interest in potentially prejudicial media coverage. Nietzel and Dillehay, for example, analyzed surveys undertaken for murder trials in three different states. They found that respondents in the original venue counties had read or heard more about the cases than those in alternative venue counties; differences ranged between 40% to 90% of persons having knowledge and attitudes about the cases.[26]

Constantini and King surveyed a sample of jury-eligible persons about their exposure to recent publicity from television and newspapers about either a murder case or a rape case.[27] There was a strong positive correlation between the amount of information that the survey respondents could supply about the case and the respondents' presumption that the defendants were guilty. Their findings were consistent with an earlier study by Simon and Eimermann following a highly publicized murder trial.[28]

Ogloff and Vidmar conducted an experiment that compared the effects of actual television coverage, print coverage, and combined television and print coverage of a major Canadian sex abuse case.[29] Exposure to each form of presentation had a prejudicial impact on the respondents. Television coverage was more prejudicial than print media, but the combination of both produced the strongest biases toward guilt.

Steblay et al. analyzed 44 studies, some involving real cases and others involving experimental simulations, designed to assess the effects of pretrial publicity on juror judgments.[30] The cases in the studies ranged over a wide variety of criminal charges. A meta-analysis of those studies indicated that pretrial publicity had significant negative effects on judg-

---

26. Michael Nietzel and Ronald Dillehay, *Psychologists as Consultants for Changes of Venue: The Use of Public Opinion Surveys*, 7 LAW & HUM. BEHAV. 309–35 (1983); *see also* M. T. NIETZEL & RONALD DILLEHAY, PSYCHOLOGICAL CONSULTATION IN THE COURTROOM (1986).

27. E. Constantini & J. King, *The Partial Juror: Correlates and Causes of Prejudgment*, 15 LAW & SOC'Y REV. 9–40 (1980–81).

28. Rita J. Simon & T. Eimermann, *The Jury Finds not Guilty: Another Look at Media Influences on the Jury*, 48 JOURNALISM QUARTERLY 343–44 (1971).

29. James R. P. Ogloff & N. Vidmar, *The Impact of Pretrial Publicity on Jurors: A Study to Compare the Relative Effects of Television and Print Media in a Child Sex Abuse Case*, 18 LAW & HUM. BEHAV. 507–26 (1994).

30. Nancy Steblay et al., *The Effects of Pretrial Publicity on Juror Verdicts: A Meta-analytic Review*, 23 LAW & HUM. BEHAV. 219–35 (1999).

ments about the guilt of defendants, namely that they were more likely to be viewed as guilty.

There are many more studies and reviews of studies on the effects of pretrial publicity than can be covered in this chapter; however, the above sampling of findings is generally representative of the effects.

The CSI Effect and Jury Acquittal Rates. Although research generally supports the proposition that mass media create widely held beliefs and attitudes that can influence jurors' perceptions and assumptions, some widely believed claims have little empirical support. The most recent example involves the co-called "CSI Effect," in which viewers of popular crime shows involving scientific forensics are asserted to be acquittal prone if the prosecution does not have scientific evidence to bolster its case.

A detailed review of the literature by Cole and Dioso-Villa in 2011[31] reported that a simple Internet search revealed 258 different articles addressed to the CSI Effect—many in newspapers, but others in law reviews or journals intended for judges or other legal practitioners. Indeed, it appears that some judges as well as prosecutors believe the effect is real. Justice Scalia mentioned the effect in passing in a 2006 death penalty case, *Kansas v. Marsh.*[32] Even though some judges strongly believe in the CSI Effect, Cole and Dioso-Villa's examination of acquittal rate data from federal trials and 11 states, before the advent of the CSI programs and after, showed no support for the effect. Their review makes clear that there is no credible evidence supporting a claim of a CSI Effect.

Claims about the CSI Effect are similar to claims made about increasing jury acquittal rates following the 1995 murder trial acquittal of O. J. Simpson. In addition to the Simpson trial, commentators referred to the acquittals of the Menendez brothers; the domestic assault trial of Lorena

31. Simon A. Cole & Rachel Dioso-Villa, *Should Judges Worry About the "CSI Effect"?*, 47 Ct. Rev. 20–31 (2011); *see also* N. J. Schweitzer & Michael J. Saks, *The CSI Effect: Popular Fiction About Forensic Sciences Affects Public Expectations About Real Forensic Science*, 47 Jurimetrics, 357 (Spring 2007). Well before the publicity about the CSI Effect, Haney and Manzolati speculated that television crime dramas might create impressions of certainty in police work and found some modest evidence that frequent viewers of such shows were more likely to endorse theories of crime consistent with television portrayals; *see* Craig Haney & John Manzolati, *Television Criminology: Network Illusions of Criminal Justice Realities, in* Readings on the Social Animal 125–38 (E. Aronson ed., 1977).

32. Kansas v. Marsh, 126 S. Ct. 2516, 2529–39 (2006).

Bobbitt, who used a knife to cut off her husband's penis; the police officers in the Rodney King beating in Los Angeles; the Florida rape trial of William Kennedy Smith; the drug trial acquittal of Mayor Marion Barry in Washington, D.C.; the drug trial of automaker John DeLorean; John Hinckley, who shot President Reagan and successfully pleaded insanity; and the 1979 beating death trial of an African American insurance executive by four Miami police officers. However, Vidmar et al.[33] examined archival data from federal trials and five states and found that conviction rates had actually *increased*, not decreased as the media reports had claimed. Use of conviction/acquittal rates from archival statistics to demonstrate changes in conviction/acquittal rates is subject to methodological problems arising from the fact that changes in plea bargaining practices and other factors could have changed the nature of cases that went to trial, indicating an apples-and-oranges problem in interpreting their findings. The same problem is possible with the findings in the Cole and Dioso-Villa review, but on balance the evidence strongly suggests that the CSI Effect is an invention of prosecutors and the media. This conclusion, however, should not be taken to mean that there are no general media effects, only that in some instances they need to be viewed with a skeptical eye.

Juror Internet Use. In the modern media age, there are many reports of jurors using the Internet to research issues that were not permitted or raised at trial.[34] Although this subject falls generally within the scope of media effects on trials, it will not be considered further in this chapter. Readers, however, may wish to consult a Federal Judicial Center report that indicates that federal judges do not see it as a major problem, primarily because they have taken remedial steps such as issuing instructions and forbidding access to cell phones during trials.[35] Moreover, researchers

---

33. N. Vidmar et al., *Should We Rush to Reform the Criminal Jury? Consider Conviction Rate Data*, 80 JUDICATURE 286–90 (May–June 1997).

34. *See, e.g.*, Steven Wallace, *The Internet Infects the Courtroom*, 93 JUDICATURE, 138–93 (2010); John G. Browning, *The Online Juror*, 93 JUDICATURE 231–35 (2010); Pamela MacLean, *Jurors Gone Wild*, CAL. LAWYER (April 8, 2011), http://www.callalawyer.com/story.cfm?eid=914907&evid=1; Kristen R Brown, *Somebody Poisoned the Jury. Pool: Social Media's Effect on Jury Impartiality*, 19 TEX. WESLEYAN L. REV. 20 (2012–13).

35. *See* MEGHAN DUNN, *Jurors' Use of Social Media During Trials and Deliberations: Report to the Judicial Conference Committee on Court Administration and Case Management*, Federal Judicial Center, November 22, 2011; Miland Simpler III, *The Unjust "Web" We Weave: The Evolution of Social Media and Its Psychological Impact on Impartiality and Fair Trials*, 36 LAW & PSYCHOL. REV. 276 (2012). Additional research by the State Justice Institute was in progress during preparation of this chapter, and it may yield a different conclusion for state courts.

at the National Center for State Courts are also examining the problem.[36] Their initial search of Westlaw found that between 1999 and 2010 at least 90 verdicts were challenged with a claim that there was juror misconduct using the Internet. St. Eve and Zuckerman also discussed the issue, included an informal survey of jurors, and made recommendations on how courts can handle the problem.[37]

Change of Venue: Responses of Courts in *McVeigh* and *Skilling*

U.S. v. McVeigh.[38] In 1996, a change of venue hearing was held in the case of Timothy McVeigh and Terry Nichols, charged with the 1995 Oklahoma City bombing in which 168 were killed. Even though media coverage of the event was nationwide and evoked national outrage, the defense sought a change of venue on the grounds that the terrible event was much more germane and personal to the citizens of Oklahoma, and especially those of Oklahoma City.[39] A systematic content analysis of three Oklahoma newspapers, including the *Oklahoma City Daily*, compared with the *Denver Post* showed that more information was presented in the Oklahoma papers than in Denver. The Oklahoma coverage had more details about emotional suffering and more negative coverage of the defendants.[40] Public opinion surveys also revealed that respondents in cities proximal to the bombing site knew more about the case, were more emotionally affected by the event, and held more negative opinions about the defendants than in cities more distant from Oklahoma City. Compared to Denver, Oklahoma City respondents were more inclined to be confident that McVeigh was guilty. Oklahoma respondents also were more likely to know someone who was killed or injured in the bombing

---

36. Paula Hannaford-Agor et al., *Jurors and Jury Use of New Media: A Baseline Exploration*, paper presented at the Annual Law & Society Meetings, Honolulu, Hawaii, June 6, 2012.

37. A. St. Eve and M. Zuckerman, 11 Duke Law & Technology Rev. 1–29 (2012); *see also* L. Lee, Comment, *Silencing the "Twittering Juror:" The Need to Modernize Pattern Cautionary Jury Instructions to Reflect the Realities of the Electronic Age*, 60 DePaul L. Rev. 181 (2010).

38. United States v. McVeigh, 918 F. Supp. 1467 (1996); United States v. McVeigh, 955 F. Supp. 1281 (1997).

39. *See, e.g.*, Stephen Jones & Holly Hillerman, *McVeigh, McJustice, McMedia*, 53 U. Chi. Legal F. 107–08 (1998).

40. Christina Studebaker and Steven Penrod, *Pretrial Publicity: The Media, the Law and Common Sense*, 3 Psychol. Pub. Pol'y & L. 428–60 (1997).

or have friends who knew someone who was injured or killed.

In responding to this evidence, Judge Richard Matsch asserted:

> Extensive publicity before trial does not, in itself, preclude fairness. In many respects media exposure presents problems not qualitatively different from that experienced in earlier times in small communities where gossip and jurors' personal acquaintances with lawyers, witnesses and even the accused were not uncommon. Properly motivated and carefully instructed jurors can and have exercised the discipline to disregard that kind of prior awareness. Trust in their ability to do so diminishes when the prior exposure is such that it evokes strong emotional responses or such an identification with those directly affected by the conduct at issue that the responses that the jurors feel a personal stake in the outcome. That is also true when there is such identification with a community point of view that jurors feel a sense of obligation to reach a result which will find general acceptance in the relevant audience.[41]

Judge Matsch referenced prior case law, such as *Patton v. Yount* [42] (in which the Supreme Court asserted that jurors are not impartial if "they have such fixed opinions that they [can] not judge impartially the guilt of the defendant.") Quoting from a dictionary, Judge Matsch asserted that prejudice involves an "adverse judgment or opinion formed beforehand or without knowledge or examination of the facts" and went on to state:

> The existence of such a prejudice is difficult to prove. Indeed it may go unrecognized in those who are affected by it. The prejudice that may deny a fair trial is not limited to bias or discriminatory attitude. It includes an impairment of the deliberative process of deductive reasoning from evidentiary facts resulting from an attribution to something not included in the evidence. That something has its

41. United Sates v. McVeigh, 918 F. Supp. 1467–73 (W.D. Okla., 1996).
42. Patton v. Yount, 467 U.S. 1025 (1984).

most powerful effect if it generate[s] strong emotional responses and fits into a pattern of normative values.[43]

Following this thorough analysis, Judge Matsch concluded that the trial should be moved to Denver because the particular facts in the Oklahoma City bombing case were such that "the entire state had become a unified community sharing the emotional trauma of those who had become directly victimized." But his initial caution that extensive publicity does not in itself preclude fairness also needs to be recognized. The task of a defense lawyer is to ascertain and clearly demonstrate with empirical evidence *when* those conditions are present.

Skilling v. United States.[44] The 2009 Supreme Court decision in *Skilling v. United States* provides an interesting contrast to *McVeigh* even though the charges were considerably different. A former CEO of the Enron Corporation that subsequently went bankrupt, Skilling was charged with failure to provide "honest services," 25 counts of fraud-related charges, and insider trading.

Before his 2004 trial, Skilling asked for a change of venue from the Houston area, arguing that extensive publicity in Houston was so pervasive that he could not obtain a fair trial. As in *McVeigh*, hundreds of news reports as well as community surveys comparing the attitudes of the public in Houston to other potential venues were introduced in the change of venue motion. The district court denied the motion on the grounds that despite some intemperate commentary the coverage had been objective and that the facts of the case were neither heinous nor sensational to the degree that *voir dire* could not remedy the issues.

In Skilling's appeal of his conviction, the Supreme Court majority agreed with the trial judge. Although not rejecting the principles in *McVeigh* or other case law involving community prejudice, such as *Rideau v. Louisiana*[45] (1963) and *Murphy v. Florida* (1975)[46] (expressing the totality of circumstances), the court majority concluded that the extensive pretrial questionnaire,

43. United States v McVeigh, 918 F. Supp. 1472
44. (No. 08-1394) 554 F.3d 529 (2010).
45. 373 U.S. 723 (1963).
46. 421 U.S. 794 (1975).

the *voir dire* process, and the highly urbanized nature of the community (Houston) versus the rural community involved in *Rideau* were sufficient for the trial judge to conclude that the selected jury was not prejudiced.

Writing in dissent, Justice Sotomayor, joined in part by Justices Stevens and Breyer, took issue with the conclusion that there was no major effect on the community.[47] Justice Sotomayor emphasized the economic effects that Enron's collapse had on the Houston community, including evidence that the *Houston Chronicle* assigned as many as 12 reporters to the Enron story, resulting in more than 4,000 articles preceding his trial. Although many media stories involved straightforward reporting, others conveyed community outrage at the executives perceived to be responsible for the company's collapse or provided stories about employees and other people who were severely affected by Enron's demise. The pretrial jury questionnaires reflected hostility among many of the prospective jurors. The problems, in Justice Sotomayor's view, were compounded when Richard Causey, another Enron executive, pled guilty. She further noted that during Skilling's trial, the local media coverage was intense and even sarcastic about the defense strategy. Writing in partial concurrence with Justice Sotomayor, Justice Alito agreed that there are circumstances in which pretrial media attention weighs heavily in favor of a change of venue, but that in cases like that of *Skilling*, *voir dire* and trial judge measures to insulate jurors from media coverage during trial could offset media effects.

Although the majority Justices in *Skilling* correctly noted that the dynamics of pretrial prejudice are (probably) different in a large city as opposed to a smaller community, they seemed to ignore, or at least to downgrade, the fact that even members of large communities talk to spouses, relatives, and neighbors, and at work they gossip around the proverbial water cooler about events salient to all. Community members also listen to and engage in radio call-in programs and make comments on Internet sites. We will shortly turn to other case studies involving media-induced prejudice, but first a summary of research findings about jury decision making is in order.

---

47. Skilling v. United States, (No. 08-1394) 554 F.3d 529..

Jury Decision-making Processes

In assessing potential media effects on a trial, it is important to consider the social psychology of how jurors and then juries evaluate evidence and make decisions that lead to their verdicts. Very simply put, the trial is about re-creation of an historical event or events. In the American adversary system, this re-creation is carried out by two opposing sides presenting different versions of the event and the motives or actions of the person or persons who were involved in the event. The stories are supplemented with lay and expert witnesses who provide testimony bearing on certain facts. The trial begins with opening arguments by both sides: the prosecution goes first, followed by the defense; the judge instructs the jurors on the law; and the jurors are sent back to deliberate. The task of the individual juror, as he or she is instructed by the judge, is to listen to the arguments and conflicting evidence but to withhold judgment until the end of trial, closing arguments, and the presentation of judicial instructions. Only then is the juror supposed to begin an evaluation of the evidence in deliberation with fellow jurors to recreate the contested events and arrive at a collective verdict.

However, contrary to this idealized view of trials, jurors do not approach their task as empty receptacles that passively listen to the evidence and decide cases independently of their experience, knowledge, and awareness of community norms and expectations. Rather, they draw upon their prior understandings of human behavior and community norms as the conflicting evidence is presented at trial. They actively select and organize the evidence around preexisting social schemas to construct "stories" about the events in dispute, they fill in gaps in the evidence with inferences based upon their personal knowledge and assumptions about how the world works, and they arrange the evidence in terms of sequences of motivations involved in human actions. These psychological and sociopsychological processes include assumptions about important past events, circumstances in which events took place, inferences about human character, and the motivations of the parties involved.

In 1981, Bennett and Feldman[48] systematically observed a number of trials and noticed that in opening arguments the opposing lawyers frequently began by saying, "Our story is . . . ." The lawyers then attempted to develop facts consistent with their story and that contradicted the story of the opposing lawyer. Bennett and Feldman hypothesized that during the trial the individual jurors processed the information presented in these conflicting narratives in terms of their own life experiences and biases. They further hypothesized that during deliberations the jurors compare their narratives, argue about conflicting perspectives, and then resolve them to reach a verdict. Consistent with Bennett and Feldman's interpretation, a large body of research in social psychology has shown that people intuitively use mental structures, called "schemas" or "scripts," in order to explain how the world about them works.[49] The scripts entail notions about physical and social causality, and what is unusual or abnormal when humans engage in behavior. If facts are missing in a particular setting, people fill in the gaps, relying on what they know about the world. In short, the processes used by people in ordinary life settings *and* as jurors involve the creation of narratives based on past experience and assumptions.

Several years after Bennett and Feldman presented their narrative hypothesis, Hastie, Penrod, and Pennington undertook a series of simulated juror experiments involving a murder trial that contained similar premises about the development of competing trial narratives.[50] Those authors found that jurors made deductions from competing trial evidence that caused them to develop certain conclusions relevant to reconstructing the killing. In a second set of experiments, Pennington and Hastie also found that when factual gaps were purposely left out of the murder story the jurors filled in the gaps by surmising the facts necessary to develop a complete narrative. Their research led them to describe the jury decision-making process as the "story model."

---

48. Lance Bennett & Martha Feldman, Reconstructing Reality in the Courtroom (1981).

49. *See, e.g.*, Richard Wiener et al., *The Psychology of Telling Murder Stories: Do We Think in Scripts, Exemplars, or Prototypes?*, 20 Behav. Sci. & L. 119–30 (2002); *see also* Jessica D. Findley and Bruce D. Sales, The Science of Attorney Advocacy: How Courtroom Behavior Affects Jury Decision Making (2012), at 159–203.

50. *See* Reid Hastie et al., Inside the Jury (1983).

Many subsequent studies by different researchers have lent support to the basic assumptions of the "story model" and expanded on its implications. In essence, jurors enter the jury box with beliefs and expectations about how the world works and, often, how it should work. Evidence is filtered through the jurors' preexisting beliefs. Evidence inconsistent with those beliefs is scrutinized more carefully or apt to be overlooked or rejected. In deliberations, jurors reconcile any competing narratives by sharing life experiences and interpretations. Additional research from the Arizona Jury Project, which videotaped the deliberations of 50 actual civil juries, supported the insights derived from the "story model" research.[51] Other research by social psychologists, not surprisingly, indicates that events or persons that cause strong negative emotions or threaten people's cultural worldview of proper behavior or their direct or indirect interests affect the way that these schemas operate. When strongly negative schemas or impressions are formed prior to hearing the trial evidence, those impressions can, and frequently do, taint the way that trial evidence is perceived and evaluated, thus preventing a fair and objective evaluation of the evidence, ultimately tainting the jury's verdict.[52]

As described above, the sources of juror knowledge and attitudinal perspectives come from preexisting dispositions, from mass media depictions of crime and through means of gossip and rumor from other persons in the jurors' social environments. In ordinary cases, the gossip and rumor may be nugatory or absent, but, in high-profile cases, members of the community frequently discuss the event and make normative statements about its meaning and about the proper outcome of the trial. Judge Matsch, of course, recognized these sociological facts in *McVeigh* to reach his conclusion that the whole citizenry of the state of Oklahoma had become victims.[53]

---

51. *See* Neil Vidmar & Valerie P. Hans, American Juries: The Verdict (2007), at ch. 6–8.

52. *See, e.g.*, M. Miller et al., *How Emotion Affects the Trial Process*, 92 Judicature 56 (2008). Vicki Fishfader et al., *Evidential and Extralegal Factors in Juror Decisions: Presentation Mode, Retention and Level of Emotionality*, 20 Law & Hum. Behav. 565 (1966); Norbert Kerr et al., *On the Effectiveness of Voir Dire in Criminal Cases with Prejudicial Pretrial Publicity: An Empirical Study*, 40 Am. U. L. Rev. 665 (1991); Geoffrey Kramer et al., *Pretrial Publicity, Judicial Remedies and Jury Bias*, 14 Law & Hum. Behav. 409 (1990); James Ogloff & Neil Vidmar, *The Impact Of Pretrial Publicity on Jurors: A Study to Compare the Effects of Television and Print Media in a Child Sex Abuse Case*, 18 Law & Hum. Behav. 507 (1994). On the other hand, there is evidence that strong emotional sympathies for victims also adversely affect rational decision making in verdicts; *see* Neal Feigenson, *Sympathy and Legal Judgment: A Psychological Analysis*, 65 Tenn. L. Rev. 1 (1997) for a review.

53. United States v. McVeigh, 918 F. Supp. 1467 (1996); United States v. McVeigh, 955 F. Supp. 1281 (1997).

The narrative approach to understanding jury behavior is very helpful in understanding media effects. Perhaps well before a juror receives a summons, or after the summons is received, media coverage may, and frequently does, provide the outline of a narrative regarding how and why an alleged crime took place, including the probable motives of the accused person or persons. Of course, much of this information also comes out at trial, but it is in a controlled setting with limiting instructions and arguments about its relevance. However, when the prejudicial media coverage occurs prior to trial, its effect may not only have a direct effect on a potential juror but also on other persons in the juror's social milieu. Spouses, family members, friends, and coworkers may discuss the case with the potential juror, and the discussion helps to shape the narrative before the potential juror arrives at court.

The importance of the brief summary of jury decision making should be apparent. In attempting to assess the effects of mass media on jury trials, we need to consider the dynamics of both juror and jury decision making. But it is also important to consider the insight that can be drawn from Kai Erikson's and from Judge Matsch's observations about community gossip. Mass media stories frequently cause people to gossip and form community opinions prior to receiving a jury summons, and those opinions can affect the way an individual juror thinks about the facts of the case. Gossip creates perceptions that other persons in the juror's social environment may hold similar views. The perceptions may bolster a juror's opinion about a particular case or particular type of crime and may influence him or her to interpret evidence differently or influence how he or she is inclined to vote in reaching a verdict. In short, in some instances media coverage can promote a strong community consensus, or at least the juror's perception of a consensus, that can influence his or her deliberations and ultimate vote on a verdict.

To summarize, the effects of media-induced pretrial publicity can create direct effects on the juror but also can produce indirect effects through rumors and gossip and community expectations about the proper trial outcome. Moreover, the effects can be manifested at various points in the trial process and jeopardize an impartial evaluation of the evidence by

(a) prejudicing jurors' initial assumptions about a defendant's guilt;
(b) improperly influencing the evaluation of evidence through selective attention and weighting of evidence consistent with preexisting biases;
(c) influencing predeliberation preferences of verdicts;
(d) influencing the initial distribution of juror verdicts that lead to the final verdict;
(e) promoting jury deliberations that enhance the initial biases of the jurors;
(f) instigating a "rotten apple" effect, whereby one or more tainted jurors infect other jurors with emotional appeals during deliberation; and
(g) improperly tilting the jury toward an improper verdict in the event that the evidence of guilt is near equipoise at the end of deliberations.

Keeping this social and sociopsychological perspective in mind, we now turn to some illustrative case studies.

Four Case Studies

The American Taliban Case: John Walker Lindh.[54] Shortly after the American invasion of Afghanistan following 9/11, the American public was shocked to learn that a young American was among the captured Taliban fighters. They saw Lindh on CNN being interrogated by CIA agent Johnny Mike Spann. Shortly after renewed fighting began, Lindh and other captives disappeared. Spann was killed in that action. Lindh was wounded and recaptured, interrogated, and then moved to the United States and indicted on multiple charges that included conspiracy to murder U.S. citizens and other charges. Widely publicized statements by officials, including U.S. Attorney General John Ashcroft, were highly condemnatory of Lindh, and some referred to him as a traitor. The media began to portray him as "The American Taliban." Lindh was scheduled to be tried in the

---

54. For a general account and data described about the *Lindh* case, *see* Neil Vidmar, *When All of Us Are Victims: Juror Prejudice and "Terrorist" Trials*, 78 Chi.-Kent L. Rev. 1143–78 (2003).

Eastern District of Virginia. The Eastern District contains the Pentagon within its boundaries, is in close proximity to Washington, D.C., and was the home of Agent Spann who, prior to his death, lived in the District with his family. Although the news coverage of Lindh was nationwide, the local media were especially intense in covering the story. A content analysis of newspaper coverage of the case in northern Virginia showed that it was much more extensive than a control city, namely the Minneapolis metropolitan area.

The defense commissioned surveys of potential jurors in the Northern District of Virginia, where Lindh was scheduled to be tried, and four alternative sites for the trial (San Francisco, Seattle, Chicago, and Minneapolis). The survey, conducted in late April and early May 2002, contained 52 questions. Some of the questions were "close ended" (i.e., multiple choice), and others were "open ended" (i.e., requiring the respondent to state reasons in his or her own words). The survey began by asking a series of questions about the respondent's views of the 9/11 attack and his or her perception of Lindh and his involvement with terrorism. The survey ended with three questions inquiring whether the respondent believed he or she could be a fair and impartial juror for Lindh's trial.[55]

In Virginia, where many residents reported knowing someone killed in the 9/11 attacks, many respondents made strong statements about Lindh's guilt. For example, slightly more than one in four persons believed he was connected to the September 11 attacks and slightly more than one in six believed he was responsible for the death of Agent Spann. In response to another question, 77 percent said Lindh was definitely or probably guilty,

---

55. The wording of the questions was as follows:

Question 50: *I just want to hold your attention for another minute. You have been very patient.*

"I have asked you a lot of questions about the John Walker Lindh case. Here is the most important question. Please visualize the following situation. Please think about it carefully before you give your answer.

Assume that you are called for jury duty in the John Walker Lindh trial. In the courtroom the judge informs you that Mr. Lindh is charged with: conspiracy to murder U.S. citizens; providing material support and resources to al Qaeda, a designated terrorist organization; and supplying services to the Taliban.

The judge states that the burden of proof is on the prosecution to prove Lindh's guilt. The judge also says that it is very important that a juror be able set aside any prejudices and be fair and impartial in deciding his guilt or innocence.

Considering everything—your own feelings, any discussions you have had with other people, and your conscience—do you believe that you could be a fair and impartial juror in the trial of John Walker Lindh as the law requires?"

Question 51: What is your reason for saying that? [Verbatim]

Question 52: Are there any other reasons for saying that? [Verbatim]

and 40 percent said that if Lindh were tried by a judge and jury and found not guilty they would find the verdict unacceptable. After the end of the long interview, Question 50 asked the respondent if he or she could be a fair and impartial juror for Lindh's trial, and Questions 51 and 52 asked the respondent to explain why in his or her own words. Fully 74 percent of Virginia respondents asserted that they could serve as impartial jurors.

However, consider a sample of summary answers by respondents. Responses to Questions 51 and 52, asking why they could be impartial jurors, are presented first, followed by their responses to earlier questions.

Respondent #506: Q51 and Q52: *"I believe in the system and that everyone should have a fair trial."*

> Q23 Strongly unfavorable [perception of Lindh]; Q24 I call him a punk—a traitor; Q25 I think he should be executed if found guilty; Q26 Definitely guilty; Q27 They captured him with a gun in his hand where the CIA agent was killed; Q28 Very unacceptable; Q29 I think they caught him red-handed; Q31 Death; Q32 I believe in capital punishment; Q33 10; Q34 I live 4 miles from the Pentagon; a number of people killed; members in the family were economically affected by the attack; Q36 No; Q37 No; Q42 Definitely a terrorist; Q43 Definitely a traitor; Q46 Yes involved; Q47 He was caught with the people that killed Mr. Spann; Q48 Yes connection; Q49 He worked for them.

Respondent #550: Q51 and Q52: *You never know until you hear all the facts; he still deserves a fair trial.*

> Q23 Somewhat unfavorable; Q24 He was the American who was fighting for the Taliban; I consider him to be a traitor; Q25 He should not have been on the side of the Taliban; Q26 Probably guilty; Q27 He was shooting at American soldiers; Q28 Unacceptable; Q29 He was on the side of the Taliban; a not guilty verdict would not be good for the country; Q31 Life in prison; Q32 To set an example for anybody thinking of doing what he did; Q34 I could see the smoke from

> the Pentagon from where my family and I live; Q36 No; Q37 No; Q42 Definitely a terrorist; Q43 Definitely a traitor; Q46 No opinion; Q47 I don't know all the facts; Q48 No, no connection; Q49 He was a soldier.

Respondent #514: Q51 and Q52: *I feel like it's my Christian duty to be fair, and listen to all of the things set forth in the courtroom. To me that's the most important thing—my responsibility as a citizen and my Christian duty to be fair.*

> Q23 Somewhat unfavorable; Q24 I feel that he was a traitor to our country. And now that he's been caught, he's trying to reverse his decision in order to avoid paying the price; Q25 It's because I feel he was a traitor who embraced the life of terrorism; Q26 Probably guilty; Q27 He has to be tried first but he was with them. He was training with them and didn't have a very good attitude when he was captured; Q28 Acceptable; Q29 I would have to go with the jury because that's our system, but I would be disappointed in it; Q31 I would say at least life in prison, unless he was completely rehabilitated. I wouldn't want him to be able to get back with any terrorists. I don't believe in the death penalty. He should only be paroled, too, after a long period of time if he's [rehabilitated]; Q32 It would be the best punishment because I'm just short of wanting the death penalty for him; Q34 It was just so horrible, the surprise that it happened to our country and that our freedom was threatened. I had total empathy for them; Q36 No; Q37 Yes, know someone; Q42 Probably a terrorist; Q43 Probably a traitor; Q46 No opinion; Q47 I don't have any proof either way. I haven't seen any concrete proof of it; Q48 No, no connection; Q49 I just don't see it. I think this had been planned for a while and would have resulted regardless of him and was planned before he came on the scene.

The *Lindh* case helps to illustrate a number of issues. Although 9/11 was a unique situation, it was an event that threatened the whole country and in effect made all Americans feel that they were victims.[56] The survey data clearly showed major discrepancies between many respondents' assertions that they could be fair and impartial and their expressed underlying beliefs and attitudes. Although Lindh eventually pleaded guilty to some charges, thereby avoiding trial, the examples above strongly suggest problems that *voir dire* would have had in uncovering these prejudices. Seemingly, the respondents did not even recognize the inconsistencies between their answers.

Although prejudice toward Muslims was not explicitly addressed in the survey, it was surely present in most Americans' attitudes at that time. It is quite possible that jurors' underlying beliefs and prejudices about Muslims, especially in the aftermath of 9/11, would have affected the way that trial evidence was built into interpretations of Lindh's actions. It is further very likely that during deliberations the jurors' perceptions of community consensus about his guilt could have preempted judicial instructions about guilt beyond a reasonable doubt in a direction unfavorable to Lindh's defense. The *Lindh* case should be placed alongside another case in which media coverage and Muslim faith were also intertwined.

U.S. v. Al-Arian.[57] Dr. Sami Amin Al-Arian was a tenured computer science professor at the University of South Florida, who retained Palestinian citizenship and had been an outspoken supporter of Palestinian causes since the early 1990s. Al-Arian's strong language about Palestinian causes had been publicly controversial since the early 1990s. His connection to the University of South Florida had played a central role in the 2004 Senate race between Betty Castor, former president of USF, and Mel Martinez. Among other activities, Al-Arian arranged for an ABC interview with Osama bin Laden following the 1998 bombings of U.S. embassies in East Africa, and he had joined with 160 Muslim American activists

56. There were no statistical differences between Virginia residents and the four other venues that were surveyed, *Id.*

57. *See* U.S.A. v. Al-Arian *et. al.* 03 -CR-77 (MI) FL May 1, 2006); Declaration of Neil Vidmar, U.S.A. v. Al-Arian *et al.* 8:03-CR-77-T-30TBM (April 28, 2005). A summary of Professor Al-Arian's background and the charges can be found at http://www.en.wikipedia.org/wiki/samiAl-Arian. The accuracy of parts of the summary is disputed, but the basic outline is correct. The summary and analysis of media coverage of the Al-Arian case is contained in a declaration by Professor Edward Bronson in U.S. v. Sami-Al-Arian, United States Court, Middle District of Florida Case No.8:03-CR-77-T-30TBM (April 28, 2005).

in a briefing with President George W. Bush in June of 2001. Two weeks after the terrorist attack on the World Trade Center, Professor Al-Arian was a guest on *The O'Reilly Factor* talk show and was asked about his connections to alleged terrorist causes. After receiving many death threats following that interview, the University of South Florida put Al-Arian on paid administrative leave.

In 2003, Al-Arian and three other defendants were arrested by the FBI. They remained incarcerated until their 2005 trial in Tampa involving 50 charges (eventually reduced to 17) that included Al-Arian being a leader of the Palestinian Islamic jihad, fundraising for terrorist causes, and conspiring to kill American citizens abroad. Among other media coverage, one local Tampa television station had constructed a website specifically about Al-Arian, including footage of Al-Arian's arrest and prejudicial comments about Al-Arian by Attorney General John Ashcroft.

Analysis of the *Tampa Tribune* and *St. Petersburg Times* revealed that between January 2001 and April 2005, 973 articles were devoted to Al-Arian, compared to 96 articles in Tallahassee and 159 articles in Miami. Surveys undertaken by the defense in Tampa and three other potential venues assessed attitudes toward Al-Arian and his three codefendants. Fully 95.5 percent of Tampa respondents recognized Al-Arian and approximately 58 percent prejudged his guilt. In response to motions regarding the chances of receiving a fair trial in the Tampa venue, the trial judge sent out a pretrial questionnaire containing 83 questions to 500 potential jurors in that venue of which 452 were returned. After some additional exclusions, 319 jury pretrial questionnaires remained.

There are many aspects to the Al-Arian case that are beyond the purview of this chapter, but of particular interest are the responses to the jury questionnaires and the differential impact of print versus television media.[58] Research by Vidmar,[59] and subsequently by McKillop,[60] analyzed the questionnaires using a number of measures of stereotyping and prejudice against

58. The author of this chapter, retains copies of the questionnaires.

59. United States v. Sami-Al-Arian, United States Court, Middle District of Florida Case No.8:03-CR-77-T-30TBM, Declaration by Neil Joseph Vidmar, April 28, 2005.

60. Kara MacKillop, *Psychology in Jury Selection: A Case Study of the Dr. Al-Arian Trial*, Thesis submitted for Master of Sciences Degree, Department of Psychology, Graduate School of Duke University (2005) (copy on file with the author).

Al-Arian as well as against Muslims in general. Respondents were divided into persons who reported that they did not watch TV or read newspapers on a regular basis, those who primarily watched TV, those who primarily read the newspaper, and those who both read papers and watched TV on a regular basis. Compared to persons who were not regularly exposed to either print or television and those who watched or read only one source of news, persons exposed to both forms of media coverage were significantly more likely to stereotype the defendants and judge them guilty.

A sample of typical prospective jurors who expressed bias responded in part as follows:

> **Juror 067:** Q40 Yes. I saw newscasts, read it in the newspaper and heard it on the radio. I did not think it was right for Dr. Al-Arian to remain employed at USF with such serious allegations against him; Q44 Yes. There were allegations that stated that Betty Castor knew Al-Arian was a terrorist supporter. I feel that it was wrong to fund terrorist groups. I don't think I would be impartial because I have heard too much about Dr. Sami Al-Arian. I already have an impression he funded terrorist groups; Q46 Yes. I saw the ads on TV stating that Betty Castor knew Al-Arian funded and was a member of a terrorist group. I have formed the opinion that he funded a terrorist group. Yes, I already have an impression of the defendant; Q48 Yes (biased); Q49 Guilty. The news coverage on the case led me to believe it. Q81 Yes (biased); Q82 Yes. I have heard a lot of media coverage and have the impression Al-Arian funded a terrorist group.

> **Juror 204:** Q42 I wondered why it took so long to build a case against Dr. Al-Arian. It seems like the evidence was there a long time before they arrested him. Q43 I wondered how he could stay and live in this country without being asked to leave. Q44 I believe on what I have seen on TV, he should have been arrested a long time before he was. Yes, I think he is 99.9% likely to be guilty of what he is charged with based on what I have seen heard, and read on TV and in the newspaper; Q45 I believe that Dr. Al-Arian along with his partners helped to

raise money and funnel that money to organizations that are against the U.S. Yes, having lived with the hate that Arabs and Palestinians have for the U.S. makes me wonder why we would give assistance to these types of individuals or countries; Q48 Yes (biased); Q49 Guilty. Everything that I have read and heard about this case has led me to believe that he and his group are guilty. Q81 Yes (biased); Q82 I would have a hard time being fair and impartial to people who take life for granted.

Juror 480: Q40 Too much to state here—read and followed everything I could. I have a daughter attending USF in Tampa and the jerk was a professor there; Q42 Sami Al-Arian looks like a Moslem Radical to me; Q43 Sami is probably one of those "kill the infidels"; Q44 He's probably had a hand in fund raising for terror organizations. . . . What do you think! I saw him all sweaty and screaming with laundry wrapped on his head on those films clips. Looked obvious to me; Q45 Look back at 44d. I think he's guilty of fund raising for terrorists. I would say so. Yes; Q48 Yes; Q49 Guilty. What I've read and seen in the media you can take my vote now and save all that taxpayer money; Q66 Are you kidding? Remember 911?; Q81 Yes (not impartial); Q82 I think Sami is guilty!

Despite the content analyses of newspapers and surveys, and many prejudicial remarks by the jurors on the pretrial questionnaires, the judge refused to move the trial but allowed an extensive *voir dire*.

The prosecution's case took five months, and in the end the defense decided to not call evidence on the grounds that the government's case was weak. Instead, it used closing arguments to describe the social and political history of the Israeli-Palestinian conflict. After 13 days of deliberation, the jury returned a verdict of not guilty on all counts for two of the defendants and found defendant Fasiz not guilty on some counts and deadlocked on others. Defendant Al-Arian was found not guilty on the most serious counts.

In short, despite the massive media publicity, the jury found most of the prosecution evidence wanting. However, the largely favorable defense outcome cannot be divorced from the judicial remedy of extensive *voir dire* that helped the defense to eliminate potential jurors who appeared to be biased by the massive pretrial publicity. Indeed, MacKillop's posttrial analysis of the questionnaires indicated that the defense was able to choose jurors who appeared to be impartial.[61]

U.S. v. Nacchio.[62] Joseph Nacchio was the controversial chairman of the board and CEO of the telecommunications company Qwest Communications from 1997 to 2002. In 2005, Nacchio and six other former employees were indicted on 42 counts of insider trading fraud associated with Qwest stock. Qwest, a major company and employer located in Denver, Colorado, merged with U.S. West during Nacchio's tenure, resulting in the loss of hundreds of jobs. The charges resulted in massive media coverage—some of it highly prejudicial—before, during, and after his trial and conviction, as well as a civil lawsuit filed by the Securities and Exchange Commission (SEC) to recover monies that it alleged were obtained by fraud.

A central defense problem involved the amount of pretrial publicity, and Nacchio's lawyers filed a motion for a change of venue. As part of that motion, the defense retained an expert, Professor Edward Bronson, to assess the media coverage.[63] A partial summary of his findings is useful to place the coverage in perspective. The *Denver Post*, with a circulation over 700,000 on Sundays, contained 643 articles about Nacchio between January 2, 2000, and mid-July 2006. The *Rocky Mountain News* (now defunct), with a weekend circulation of over half a million copies, carried 765 articles. The average length of the downloaded article in the *Post* was 2.74 pages, and in the *Rocky Mountain News* the average was 1.73 pages. Prominence is an indication of the importance given to the news story. In the *Post*, fully 60 percent of the articles were on the front page or on the front page of an interior section, usually the business section. A large per-

---

61. *Id.*

62. United States v. Joseph P Nacchio, U.S. District Court, District of Colorado Criminal Action No.05-cr-00545-EWN, Declaration of Edward Bronson, On Motion for Change of Venue, July 31, 2006. A summary of the news coverage of the Nacchio case may be found in that source.

63. *Id.*

centage of the articles were accompanied by pictures. There were 40 editorials concerning the problems at Qwest in the *Post*. Although many articles in the early years of the coverage could be classified as benign, later articles focused on the loss of jobs from the Qwest and U.S. West merger, and there were also stories about lack of hiring diversity. However, beginning in 2001, many articles had focused on Nacchio, pointing to him as the cause of almost 13,000 lost jobs.

Many other stories were about losses in Qwest share prices. When Nacchio was forced out of the presidency of Qwest by shareholders, the media reported that his pay was nevertheless increased. When the federal criminal probe began, the news coverage and letters to the editor turned vitriolic and suggested that the case against Nacchio and the other defendants was very strong. The *Rocky Mountain News* published a number of sarcastic cartoons about Nacchio. Negative comments about the case by Attorney General John Ashcroft were reported, and comparisons were made to infamous fraud convictions. When the SEC filed its complaint against Nacchio, additional negative commentary appeared in the newspapers urging the government to pursue criminal charges. Later, the guilty pleas of other Qwest employees associated with Nacchio were reported. In summarizing his analysis of the coverage for the defense, Professor Bronson noted that, overall, the publicity was inflammatory, contained inadmissible material, involved inaccurate coverage, and made presumptions of probable guilt.[64]

The defense also planned to undertake an opinion poll to supplement the media analyses, but the hearing was scheduled before a poll could be initiated. The court denied the change of venue motion but did allow an extensive *voir dire* involving questioning of individual venire members. Of 44 persons questioned, 32 of them reported that they were aware of the case from various media or other outside sources. Of the 18 jurors and alternates, 14 had prior knowledge of the case. The media publicity continued throughout the trial. The jury convicted Nacchio on 19 counts of insider trading, sentenced him to six years in prison, and fined him $19 million.

---

64. Bronson, *supra* note 62.

In 2007, during Nacchio's criminal trial, coverage by the *Post* increased dramatically to 188 articles during the 2007 calendar year. This coverage included 16 front-page articles. The average length of an article was 664 words, for a total of 125,442 words in the *Post* in 2007. In 2008, the *Post* contained 30 articles about Nacchio; these articles were an average of 480 words long, for a total of 14,865 words. In 2009, the *Post* carried 39 articles about Nacchio, which averaged 414 words, for a total of 16,151 words.

The verdict of guilty of insider trading, however, did not end media coverage about Mr. Nacchio.[65] His appeal of the verdict and the SEC case kept media attention about the case before the public. Beginning in January 2007 through the conclusion of the trial and sentencing, the *Denver Post* published an additional 160 articles bearing on Nacchio, some as long as 2,000 words; many were on the front page, and some reports involved clearly pejorative casting of Nacchio. One article, for example, headlined "A Straight Up Cure for CEO Hubris," compared Nacchio's case with Enron and other financial scandals. In May, the *Post* set up a website to give the public access to the evidence used in the Nacchio criminal trial, including interviews with jurors regarding their deliberations and an article reporting that Nacchio attempted to shield assets in his wife's name and that Qwest was covering his legal expenses.

In January 2010, the *Post* reported on Nacchio's sentencing hearing with a 171 word article that resulted in 48 blog responses on the *Post*'s website, most of which were very negative, such as:

> "Get this guy into jail before somebody gives him a multi-million dollar bonus!"
>
> "Seriously, I think if he tries any more appeals some whacko is going to off him when he gets out of jail because of how much he made a mockery of the legal system. I'm all for appeals to make sure the innocent don't go to jail but good lordy Naccio you had your hand in the cookie jar!"

---

65. Securities and Exchange Commission v. Joseph P. Nacchio, U.S. District Court, District of Colorado, Civil Action No. 05-cv-00480-MSK-CBS; Exhibit 1: Declaration of Neil Joseph Vidmar in Motion to Transfer Venue March 24, 2010.

> "Joey. First you lose your cushie job, along with all the power-perks, then you get convicted, then you get to wear striped jammies, and now after losing every one of your desperate appeals you get to pay one heck of an attorney fee when you get out of the big house. Don't worry, Joey. I'll bet some Wall Street firm is jonesing for an insider sharpie like you. What a shame you won't get to read my words. Rat spit!"

The Nacchio case helps to demonstrate the degree to which media coverage may not only be extensive but may foster a highly prejudicial atmosphere before, during, and after trial.

People v. Bolin.[66] In 1989, Paul Bolin, who grew marijuana in the rugged mountains of the Walker Basin in Kern County, California (Bakersfield is the county seat), apparently became upset when an acquaintance brought two strangers to the property. A dispute ensued. Two men were shot to death, and the third man escaped, though wounded. After a harrowing night in the forest, the survivor managed to find help. By the time sheriffs arrived at the property, Bolin had disappeared. Bolin, described as "armed and dangerous" in both local newspaper and television coverage, was thought to be hiding in Kern County. News accounts reported that he had once shot a man in the chest with a shotgun, that he had been convicted of manslaughter, that he had been trained as a Navy SEAL, and that pipe bombs that contained "as much explosive power as a hand grenade" were found on the property. These various claims were either completely false or exaggerations. Eventually, the authorities concluded that Bolin had fled the county.

Then, on January 6, 1990, local media reported that the Bolin case would be featured on the *America's Most Wanted* television program as a result of a "national hunt for killer of 2." The program aired on January 7, 1990, and Bolin was arrested outside of Chicago, Illinois, within hours. The local newspaper the *Californian* and local television covered his re-

---

66. *See* Bolin v. Ayers, Case No.1:99-cv-5279-LJO P (filed 03/01/07) for basic details of the case. The declaration of Neil Vidmar in this appeal provides additional details regarding media effects as revealed through a survey and examination of what jurors revealed during the *voir dire* process. (See Appendix D.)

turn to Bakersfield in handcuffs. Bolin was subsequently charged with two counts of first-degree murder, one count of attempted murder, and a felony for marijuana cultivation.

In the last week of September and first week of October 1989, seven months after the last news account, a public opinion survey was taken in Kern County regarding the effect of the publicity on community attitudes. It concluded that 45 percent of respondents were aware of the case through initial news reports and/or from viewing the *America's Most Wanted* program or community gossip. Of those who had viewed the *America's Most Wanted* program, fully 77 percent concluded that Bolin was guilty. Defense counsel moved for a change of venue, but the motion was denied with the caveat that a reapplication could be made following the *voir dire* of prospective jurors. Subsequently, the summoned jurors were asked to fill out a pretrial questionnaire. It indicated an even higher degree of pretrial publicity exposure than the survey. However, during the *voir dire* itself, defense questioning was at best perfunctory, and the motion for a change of venue was not renewed. The jury was sworn on December 3, 1990, and presentation of evidence began the same day. Bolin was found guilty of murder and sentenced to death. The central issue in the appeal of the guilty verdict and sentence involves ineffective assistance of counsel, particularly, but not limited to, the failure of defense counsel to renew the application for a change of venue following *voir dire*.[67]

Aside from clear issues of community gossip and other contamination, the utility of the Bolin case for this chapter is the especial effect of the *America's Most Wanted* program on potential juror contamination. The program drew national attention to Kern County and killings that had occurred in the county, increasing the likelihood of substantial local gossip, but especially important was the content of the program itself. Nine of the jurors or alternates had in varying degrees seen, or thought they had perhaps seen, the *America's Most Wanted* program. The program involved a reenactment of the events, a dramatization blending fact and fiction that characterized the killings as cold-blooded calculation when in fact the ac-

67. The appeal of the Bolin case is still in litigation as this book goes to press.

tual events *could* have occurred in the context of a very heated argument. For example, one of the dead men and the wounded man were portrayed as persons who were at the property mainly for the altruistic goal of providing transportation to the other dead man who lived on the property. In the television portrayal, before the men leave a campsite to the fatal scene of the incident, one of them is portrayed as saying goodbye to his little daughter with the promise that he would be back very shortly. Another scene portrays a caution from the man's dignified father to be careful and come right back. The main climax scene portrays Bolin as carefully taking aim with his pistol and shooting the two men as they plead for their lives.

The essential issue regarding jurors who viewed the program in question is whether the images and fictionalized script tainted their perception of the trial evidence. As described above, research has shown that during the trial and then during deliberations jurors develop narratives about causation and about the personalities and motives of the litigants.[68] In short, the Bolin case helps to demonstrate the strong possibility that prejudicial media exposure can be similar to seeing the movie before you read the book. The prior exposure to the narrative, especially if it is a fictionalized narrative, can create a psychological lens through which subsequent trial evidence is filtered.

Judicial Remedies for Trial Prejudice

The potential judicial remedies for anticipated trial prejudice resulting from media coverage include (1) a continuance, (2) judicial instructions to put prejudices aside, (3) pretrial jury questionnaires, (4) *voir dire*, (5) an increase in the number of peremptory challenges, (6) change of venue, (7) jurors imported from another venue, (8) sequestering the jury, and (9) anonymous juries.

Judges often place great faith in jury instructions and *voir dire* as the primary remedies for potential prejudice induced by intense media coverage and are hesitant to go beyond limited judicial instructions and routine

68. See text at footnotes 48–52 *supra*.

voir dire practices in their jurisdiction.[69] Although these assumptions may often be valid in routine cases,[70] such assumptions can be problematic in trials involving extensive media coverage.

The sample of survey findings from the Lindh, Al-Arian, and Nacchio cases reported above clearly suggest that some potential jurors did not recognize the very major inconsistencies between their answers in the first part of the survey and their stated ability to be impartial as a juror. The inconsistencies should not be surprising. A large body of research in the field of social psychology has demonstrated that people are often unaware of their biases.[71] Additionally, and equally important, they are hesitant to express them to others, especially in public. A large body of sociopsychological research, dating back many decades, has documented the phenomenon of "social desirability" responses to questions, whether in public or in written questionnaires.[72] In brief, people tend to give answers that they think are expected from the questioner or, if answered honestly, will place them in a bad light in the eyes of the questioner (or others privy to the answers). For example, although data show that many persons in contemporary American society harbor prejudices against African Americans or Muslims, many people will not offer those opinions in public. This can be especially true for some persons called to court for jury duty when they are asked about their personal knowledge and preformed attitudes in the presence of a judge, lawyers, other jurors, spectators in the public gallery, and media representatives.

Edward Bronson studied the *voir dire* in a case that had extensive pre-

---

69. *See, e.g.*, Michael Whellan, *What's Happened to Due Process Among the States? Pretrial Publicity and Motions for Change of Venue in Criminal Proceedings*, 17 Am. J. Crim. L. 175 (1990); Gerald Wetherington et al., *Preparing for the High Profile Case: An Omnibus Treatment for Judges and Lawyers*, 51 Fla. L. Rev. 425 (1999).

70. Johnson and Haney, for example, conducted an in-depth investigation of the *voir dire* process in four felony trials that included examination of trial transcripts and posttrial interviews with selected and rejected jurors. They concluded that "the voir dires that we observed were 'effective' at least in terms of each side correctly eliminating jurors who were generally biased against them . . . ." *See* Cathy Johnson & Craig Haney, *Felony Voir Dire: An Exploratory Study of Its Content and Effect*, 18 Law & Hum. Behav. 487–506 (1994). On the other hand, a study by Gregory Mize in the District of Columbia superior court involved post-*voir dire* interviews with jurors who remained silent when the judge asked questions directed to the whole panel. A number of the jurors who had not responded to the questions were subsequently questioned informally and disclosed information suggesting they did have biases bearing on their impartiality. *See* Gregory E. Mize, *On Better Jury Selection: Spotting UFO Jurors Before They Enter the Jury Room*, Ct. Rev. 10–15 (Spring 1999).

71. *See, e.g.*, Richard Nisbett and Timothy Wilson, *Telling More Than We Can Know: Verbal Reports on Mental Process*, 84 Psychol. Rev. 231 (1977); Mahzarin R. Banaji & Larisa Heiphetz, *Attitudes*, *in* 1 Handbook Social Psychology *353–93* (Susan T. Fiske et al. eds., 5th ed. *2010)*.

72. *See* D. P. Crowne & D. Marlowe, *A New Scale of Social Desirability Independent of Psychopathology*, 24 J. Consulting Psychology, 349–54 (1960).

trial publicity and documented what he labeled a "minimization effect" during *voir dire*.[73] In 1978, a brutal killing occurred in a small Florida town. Media reports indicated that a 19-year-old white woman had been abducted from a convenience store where she was a clerk. Residents of the community were frightened. After the victim's body was found, news reports quoted the sheriff as saying she had been raped. Johnny Copeland and two codefendants, all African Americans, were arrested and charged with armed robbery, kidnapping, and first-degree murder. The prosecutor sought the death penalty. Newspaper and television stories carried articles that listed the defendants' prior criminal records, which included burglary, two robberies, an attempted robbery, and possession of a stolen vehicle—all of which had been committed when the accused were under the age of 18. The stories were strongly suggestive of the defendants' guilt.

Public opinion surveys conducted by the defense revealed that the crime had generated a great deal of informal gossip in the community. Hostility was widespread, and many people assumed the defendants were guilty. Comments were often openly racist; for example, "It's a shame all those niggers come down from Tallahassee and commit crimes"; "They ought to lynch those niggers"; "They ought to be hung in front of the courthouse"; and "People are ready to take the jail apart . . . they better not get turned loose." The surveys estimated that 99 percent of the residents had heard of the case. Many residents knew the victim or her family, and nearly three-quarters of the county residents expressed anger, racist attitudes, presumptions of guilt, and other biases. As one respondent said, "Well, people here were very upset. They have very strong feelings about this death and the way the defendants have been handled. They have been handled too good." Despite inflamed community sentiment, the trial judge refused to grant Copeland a change of venue. Copeland was convicted after a four-day trial, and after only one hour of deliberation, the jury recommended the death penalty.

Juror questioning in the Copeland trial took place with the full panel

---

73. Edward J. Bronson, *The effectiveness of voir dire in discovering prejudice in high-profile publicity cases: An archival study of the minimization effect*, Discussion paper series No. 89-1, Department of Political Science, California State University, Chico (1989) (Copeland's sentence was eventually commuted to life in 1992).

present rather than a sequestered individualized *voir dire*. This posed the problem of jurors learning what they were expected to say as they watched other jurors being questioned and challenged. Some jurors conceded their biases, but a striking number displayed what Bronson labeled the "minimization effect"—that is, the use of a vocabulary by the person being questioned to suggest that he or she had little knowledge of the case. One juror said, for example, "*Only* thing I have read is what's in the newspaper," later adding, "I didn't read all of it; I *just* glanced at [the paper]." Another said, "I've heard it discussed and I read some but not a whole lot." Still another said about her exposure to the news, "*Not much*, just newspaper and television coverage" and "*only* what might have been in the *Democrat* [a local newspaper]." Thus, despite almost overwhelming evidence of widespread hostile community feeling about the defendants, Bronson found the questioned jurors continually using words like *just*, *only*, *that's all*, and *nothing but*.

Once again, it should be emphasized that minimization responses, as seen in the Copeland trial, are not necessarily conscious lies. The problem already alluded to is the strong possibility that some jurors may not recognize how their biases—arising from pretrial publicity and community gossip—affect their ability to be fair and impartial. Another explanation, not incompatible with the first, may lie in the fact that many, probably most, jurors are not familiar with a courtroom and find it intimidating. They are sometimes hesitant to state their views, or they perhaps do not understand the questions or their purpose or perhaps do not have insight into their own biases.[74]

Seltzer et al. observed the *voir dire* questioning in 31 criminal trials and subsequently interviewed 190 of the prospective jurors. In the follow-up interviews, roughly 25 percent of prospective jurors did not disclose that they or a family member had been a crime victim, and 30 percent did not disclose that they knew a law enforcement officer.[75]

Of course, *voir dire* has many variations. The judge may conduct all of the questioning, a practice common in many federal courts, or combine judge

74. *See generally* Jeffrey T. Frederick, Mastering Voir Dire and Jury Selection (2012).
75. Richard Seltzer et al., *Juror Honesty During the Voir Dire*, 19 J. Crim. Justice, 451–62 (1991).

questions followed by lawyer questions. In many state courts, the questioning is done primarily by the opposing lawyers. The questioning may be conducted in front of the whole panel, or with a series of 12 jurors seated in the jury box, or with jurors sequestered and brought into the courtroom to undergo questioning individually.

The efficacy of *voir dire* appears to be strongly influenced by its form. Nietzel and Dillehay studied the effects of *voir dire* variations in 13 Kentucky capital murder trials according to whether the venire members were questioned individually or en masse or sequestered. Those authors found that significantly more defense challenges were sustained under conditions of individual sequestration.[76] In a follow-up study involving 18 capital cases in Kentucky, South Carolina, and California, those same researchers found similar results.[77] Research by Moran et al. utilized pretrial survey research for two major drug trials concluding that an extended versus limited *voir dire* would increase accuracy in predicting juror verdicts by 30 to 78 percent.[78]

A substantial number of attempts have been made to study the effects of pretrial publicity and the *voir dire* process via simulations. Simulations inherently have limitations in their ability to mimic the actual conditions in a real trial, but they have the advantage of being capable of controlling factors that are difficult to disentangle in the real world. By and large, the findings support a conclusion that the effects of media-induced prejudice may not be recognized by the persons exposed to the publicity.[79]

Kerr et al. conducted a complex and realistic study of the effectiveness

---

76. Michael T. Nietzel and Ronald C. Dillehay, *The Effects of Variations in Voir Dire Procedures in Capital Murder Trials*, 6 LAW & HUM. BEHAV. 1–13 (1982).

77. Michael T. Nietzel et al., *Effects of Voir Dire Variations in Capital Trials: A Replication and Extension*, 5 BEHAV. SCI. & L. 467–77 (1987).

78. Gary Moran et al., *Jury Selection in Major Controlled Substance Trials: The Need for Extended Voir Dire*, 3 FORENSIC REP. 331–48 (1990).

79. *See, e.g.*, Kramer et al., *Pretrial Publicity, Judicial Remedies and Jury Bias*, 14 LAW & HUM. BEHAV. 409 (1990); Amy L. Otto et al., *The Biasing Impact of Pretrial Publicity on Juror Judgments*, 18 LAW & HUM. BEHAV. 453–69 (1994); Hedy R. Dexter et al. *A Voir Dire for Prejudicial Effects of Pretrial Publicity*, 22 J. APPLIED SOCIAL PSYCHOLOGY 819–32 (1992); Christine Ruva et al. *Effects of Pre-trial Publicity and Jury Deliberation on Juror Bias and Source Memory Errors*, 21 APPLIED COGNITIVE PSYCHOLOGY 45–67 (2007); Steven Fein et al., *Hype and Suspicion: The Effects of Pretrial Publicity, Race and Suspicion on Jurors' Verdicts*, 53 J. SOCIAL ISSUES 487–502 (1997). For additional reviews of this literature and related research, *see* Neal Feigenson, *Sympathy and Legal Judgment: A Psychological Analysis*, 65 TENN. L. REV. 1 (1997); Neil Vidmar, *Case Studies of Pre-and Midtrial Prejudice in Criminal and Civil Litigation*. 26 LAW & HUM. BEHAV. 73 (2002).

of *voir dire* in cases with prejudicial media publicity.[80] It is germane to the issue of whether judges can accurately rule on challenges by legal counsel. In the first phase of the research, simulated jurors were exposed to different amounts and types of pretrial publicity involving the armed robbery of a grocery store: factual publicity, publicity designed to evoke emotional responses, or no publicity. The jurors were subsequently questioned individually about whether they could be fair and impartial in deciding the case. The interviews were videotaped. Next, the jurors were shown a realistic video enactment of the trial resulting from the charges, were given a judicial instruction to disregard the publicity, and then deliberated as jurors. The important finding from this first phase of the experiment was that for persons exposed to emotional publicity, deliberation enhanced prejudices in the direction of conviction. In the second phase of the research, 27 defense lawyers, 29 prosecutors, and 31 judges viewed samples of the videotaped *voir dire* of the jurors and were asked to decide whether each prospective juror was biased and should be challenged. The decisions of these experienced legal experts were compared to how each juror voted in the first phase of the research. For present purposes, the most significant finding was that overall judges were not accurate in assessing which jurors were biased, albeit more experienced judges tended to perform slightly better than less experienced judges.

It is impossible to scientifically determine the degree, if any, that various judicial remedies for media-induced prejudice have been successful—or unsuccessful. O. J. Simpson was acquitted despite a media circus that was not controlled by the trial judge. Timothy McVeigh was found guilty despite venue change to another state, plus an extensive *voir dire*. Joe Nacchio was found guilty of insider trading. The trial judge in Al-Arian refused to move the trial but did allow an extensive pretrial jury questionnaire that research strongly suggests allowed the defense to choose a jury containing members with open minds.[81] Al-Arian was found not guilty of the most serious charges. But the legal issue is not whether defendants are convicted

80. Norbert Kerr et al., *On the Effectiveness of Voir Dire in Criminal Cases with Prejudicial Pretrial Publicity: An Empirical Study*, 40 AM. U. L. REV. 665 (1991).

81. *See* MacKillop, *supra* note 60.

or acquitted, but whether measures were taken to ensure a fair trial. Sometimes the interests of justice require exceptional remedies.

In the Casey Anthony case,[82] the judge engaged in multiple remedies: jurors chosen from a foreign venue (an adjacent county); detailed pretrial jury questionnaires; extensive *voir dire* taking place in the adjacent county, with counsel as well as the judge participating in the questioning; jury instructions; jurors imported back to the original Orlando, Florida, venue; additional jury instructions; sequestering the jury during the entire six-week trial, including monitoring of juror media access during sequestration; and delaying the release of juror names at the conclusion of the trial. Anthony was found not guilty. When some jurors were eventually interviewed by the media, they reported that the evidence presented at trial did not prove guilt beyond a reasonable doubt. Even without the remedial measures, the evidence may have been insufficient to convict, but no one can say. There is no control condition to allow a conclusion that if the trial had been held with Orlando jurors and routine *voir dire* the result would have been a guilty verdict. Although no one can prove a counterfactual outcome, unquestionably the appearance of fairness was enhanced by the remedial measures taken by the trial judge.

Providing Data to Support Requests for Extraordinary Remedies

When faced with concerns about contaminating media coverage, there are a number of steps that can be taken to learn about the extent of contamination of the jury pool and subsequent attempts to convince the trial judge of the need for extraordinary remedies. Both quantitative and qualitative data may be gathered.

The first step is to assess the potential practical remedies, the desired remedy, and alternative remedies, if the preferred remedy is not feasible. Many times, the preferred remedy is a change of venue, but the proclivities of the trial judge, precedent within a jurisdiction, financial resources, and other considerations may affect that choice.

---

82. *See* Jeff Ashton & Lisa Pulitzer, Imperfect Justice: Prosecuting Casey Anthony (2011).

Content analysis of the media coverage is ordinarily the second step. The readership and/or viewership of the media should be ascertained and documented. If the coverage is primarily confined to a particular county or jurisdiction, two or three other jurisdictions should be assessed for comparative purposes. Thus, in assessing media effects, a number of factors need to be considered: (a) the number of articles and their length; (b) the prominence of the articles, including where they are placed (i.e., front page versus inside section), the size of the print used in the headlines, and whether the story is accompanied by photographs; (c) the factual and emotional content of the articles; (d) repetition of the content of the articles over time; (e) repetition of the story content in other media sources; (f) the existence of community interest and formation of community attitudes; (g) the degree of reader exposure to the content of the articles; and (h) the time delay from cessation of the publicity and the start of trial. A fine example of this type of analysis was conducted by Edward Bronson with respect to the Nacchio case discussed above,[83] and additional discussion of how to conduct content analyses is contained in an easily accessible article by Studebaker and Penrod.[84]

A third type of evidence involves a field survey, or public opinion poll such as reported with the discussions of the John Walker Lindh, Sami Al-Arian, and Nacchio cases discussed above. The problems have been briefly summarized in this chapter, but more detailed analyses can be found in several leading handbooks as well as individual articles.[85] The most common obstacle is expense: The costs are high and defense budgets may not accommodate a survey. Telephone surveys are much less expensive than in-person surveys conducted according to a random selection of households. However, although telephone surveys are *relatively* cheap compared to in-person surveys, there are problems affecting representativeness of

---

83. Edward Bronson, Declaration of Edward J. Bronson in support of defendant Joseph P. Nacchio's motion for a change of venue, *in* United States v. Joseph P. Nacchio, United States District Court for the District of Colorado, Case No. 05-CR-00545, July 31, 2006.

84. Christina Studebaker & Steven Penrod, *Pretrial Publicity, the Media, the Law and Common Sense*, 3 PSYCHOL. PUB. POL'Y & L. 428–60 (1997).

85. PETER V. MARSDEN & JAMES D. WRIGHT, HANDBOOK OF SURVEY RESEARCH (2d ed. 2010); DON A. DILLMAN ET AL., INTERNET, MAIL, AND MIXED-MODE SURVEYS: THE TAILORED DESIGN METHOD (3d ed. 2009). *See also* Studebaker & Penrod, supra note 85 at 453–55 for an outline of questionnaire design.

the sample. Many persons have answering machines through which calls are screened by the homeowner in order to avoid solicitations and survey studies. Many households have now switched entirely to cell phones, which are not as easily accessed by survey companies. In many instances, men are less likely to respond to telephone surveys than women, potentially skewing the results. (However, this problem can be addressed by appropriate weighting of the data.) An additional and serious problem is achieving a representative sampling when members of a household work evening or night shifts or are otherwise absent for long periods. A proper survey will have at least five callbacks to a number before attempts to reach that household recipient are abandoned.

There are three basic types of questions that can be asked in either a telephone or in-person survey. "Close-ended" questions ask for yes, no, or "undecided" answers. Surveys sometimes also ask respondents to rate issues on a scale, say from 1 to 10, or to rank various issues. The most useful survey data typically come from "open-ended" questions that ask respondents to state in their own words an opinion or belief. Such questions can provide qualitative richness that is often more persuasive to courts. The Lindh and Nacchio cases, described above, help to demonstrate the utility of inducing respondents to explain responses in their own words. Ideally, surveys should combine all of these techniques.

The particular case facts, of course, will determine the substance of the survey questions. The survey should cover all of the issues that might be germane to prejudicial attitudes and attempt to assess the extent to which the respondent has discussed the case with others because, as discussed earlier, media influence in a high-profile case can not only affect a potential juror directly, it can expose that juror to gossip and exchange of opinions by others in his or her social environment. This issue has often been ignored in survey research, but it can provide valuable information about conformity pressures that might be felt by a prospective juror. For example, in the Nacchio case described above, a question asked:

Have you discussed the Joe Nacchio case with
Members of your family? Yes No

Friends?	Yes	No
Neighbors?	Yes	No
Co-workers?	Yes	No

This question might be followed up with questions requiring verbatim answers, such as "What are their views on Nacchio?" and "Do you agree with them?"[86]

When there are multiple defendants, the survey should attempt to assess attitudes toward them and their perceived responsibility or guilt. For example, although Nacchio was the main focus of media attention, several other persons were named in the suit. Obtaining relative perceptions of shared guilt can shed light on the degree to which the defendant of concern is independent of the others or might be contaminated by them and might provide evidence for a motion to sever the defendant from the others. Research has shown that in comparison to severed trials joined trials increase the chances of conviction.[87]

Survey questionnaires used in the Lindh and Nacchio cases are contained in Appendices A and B. They help to illustrate how the issues discussed above were addressed.

If a field survey is not feasible, or if one is carried out and the judge rules that the data are not persuasive, another approach is to attempt to persuade the judge to at least send out a pretrial questionnaire to members of the jury pool. Jeffrey Frederick's ABA book *Mastering Voir Dire and Jury Selection* provides a number of examples,[88] but an additional example from the Al-Arian trial is contained in Appendix C. The Al-Arian questionnaire, developed in a collaboration between the judge and opposing parties, is unusually long but stands as a model for cases involving complex issues.

Finally, if time and resources permit focus groups or, better still, pretrial jury simulations of the case, they can often produce additional information that will assist in *voir dire*. Even the most detailed survey cannot

---

86. Because of time limitations, these two questions had to be eliminated in the actual survey.

87. *See* Irwin Horowitz et al., *A Comparison of Verdicts Obtained in Severed and Joined Criminal Trials*, 10 J. Applied Social Psychology 445–56 (1980).

88. Jeffery T. Frederich, *Mastering Voir Dire and Jury Selection*, ABA Publishing (2011).

replicate the richness of information obtained by presenting the facts of a case particularly in a simulation that presents both sides of the case: One member of the legal team can play the prosecutor (or plaintiffs lawyer) and other the defense lawyer.[89] After being exposed to the presentations, simulated jurors discuss the case and attempt to reach a verdict.[90]

Summary and Conclusion

Trial prejudice is not a new problem, but there can be little question that both the quantum and types of mass media coverage of criminal cases and subsequent trials have changed rapidly in the past decades and are probably still evolving. This chapter has attempted to summarize the effects that this development can have on trial by jury and explain the social and sociopsychological dynamics that interact with media coverage to produce potential jury prejudice. It provided examples of the results of media coverage on potential jury pool members in three cases and then discussed various remedies for media effects and how to produce research to persuade a judge to implement them.

89. For one large medical malpractice trial conducted by the defendant, the author persuaded the defense lawyer to play the plaintiffs lawyer for the simulation presentation. Reversing the role appeared to be as beneficial as the simulating juror data.

90. *See* JURYWORK: SYSTEMATIC TECHNIQUES (2d ed. 2011–12).

Appendix A
Survey in *United States* v. *John Walker Lindh*

Five District Survey: Eastern District of Virginia: Eastern Division of the Northern District of Illinois, Chicago; Fourth Division of Minnesota, Minneapolis; San Francisco Division of the Northern District of California; Western District of Washington State, Seattle.

_____	Respondent		
_____	SEX	1. Male 2. Female	
_____	SAMPLE	1. Virginia (quota = 400)	2. Illinois (quota = 200)
		3. Minnesota (quota = 200)	4. Washington (quota = 200)
		5. California (quota = 200)	

1st call: Date/time ________________

2nd call: Date/time ________________

3rd call: Date/time ________________

Special Instructions for each district

(Virginia; Chicago, Minneapolis; San Francisco)

(Resume asking everyone)

Before I begin the main questions, let me say that we are seeking opinions and reactions to events. There are no right or wrong answers. If you do not have an opinion on something, you should feel free to simply say that you have no opinion on the matter.

To begin, I am going to read you a list of issues. For each issue please tell me if you are very concerned; concerned; somewhat concerned; not very concerned; or not at all concerned about that issue.

Scale:	1. Very concerned	2. Concerned	3. Somewhat concerned
	4. Not very concerned	5. Not at all concerned	6. Don't know

(Randomize Q19-Q22)

1. The economy

2. The threat of terrorism in the city in which you work or live

3. The costs of medical insurance

4. The environment

Now, I want to turn to some names that have been in the national news.

5. Do you have a strongly favorable, somewhat favorable, somewhat unfavorable or strongly unfavorable opinion of John Walker Lindh (lind)?

1. Strongly favorable	2. Somewhat favorable	3. Somewhat unfavorable
4. Strongly unfavorable	5. (Can't Rate)	6. (Never Heard)

6. What can you tell me about John Walker Lindh. **[Verbatim]**______________

7. Why do you have:
   if Q23=1 or 2, insert "a Favorable"
   if Q23=3 or 4, insert "an Unfavorable"
   if Q23=5 or 6, insert "No"
   Opinion of John Walker Lindh? **[Verbatim]**______________

8. As you may know, John Walker Lindh is charged by the U.S. Government with a number of crimes that include: conspiracy to murder U.S. citizens; providing material support and resources to al Qaeda {all KIE duh}, a designated terrorist organization; and supplying services to the Taliban.

   Based on what you have seen, read or heard about this case, do you think John Walker Lindh is (READ RESPONSES)

1. Definitely guilty	2. Probably guilty	3. Probably not guilty
4. Definitely not guilty	5. [DK/Refused.] Do not read	

9. Why is that? **[Verbatim]**______________

10. Consider this question. Assume that in the near future Mr. Lindh is put on trial before a judge and jury for the crimes that the government alleges that he has committed, and that the jury finds that Mr. Lindh is not guilty of the charges.

Would you personally find a not guilty verdict [READ RESPONSES, randomly reverse order of alternatives, from 1-4 or 4-1]

1. Very acceptable 2. Acceptable 3. Unacceptable
4. Very unacceptable 5. [DK/Refuse] Do not read

11. Why is that? **[Verbatim]**______________

12. Any other reasons? **[Verbatim]**______________

13. If Mr. Lindh is found guilty of the crimes with which he is charged, what do you think his punishment should be? **[Verbatim]**______________

14. Why do you suggest that particular punishment? **[Verbatim]**______________

I need to ask you some questions about the events of September 11 last year.

15. To what extent were you and those close to you affected by the events of September 11th? Please answer on a scale from 1 to 10, with 1 being Not at all affected, and 10 being very much affected. The mid points of the 10-point scale would indicate that you feel moderately affected. Where do you fall on this 10-point scale?

(not at all affected) 1 2 3 4 5 6 7 8 9 10 (Very affected) 11 (Don't Know)

(IF Q33 = 1-5 OR 11, SKIP TO Q36)

16. How were you or those close to you affected? **[Verbatim]**______________
17. How has this impacted your life? **[Verbatim]**______________

(RESUME ASKING EVERYONE)

Thinking specifically about the events related to September 11th…

18. Do you, or does someone close to you, know anyone who was killed or injured at the World Trade Center?
    1. Yes, Know Someone 2. No 3. [DK/Refuse] Do not read

19. Do you, or does someone close to you, know anyone who was killed or injured at the Pentagon?
    1. Yes, Know Someone 2. No 3. [DK/Refuse] Do not read

20. Do you, or does someone close to you, know anyone who was killed or injured in the hijacked plane that crashed in Pennsylvania?
    1. Yes, Know Someone 2. No 3. [DK/Refuse] Do not read

21. Do you, or does someone close to you, know anyone who was killed or injured in the anthrax attack on the postal system?
    1. Yes, Know Someone 2. No 3. [DK/Refuse] Do not read

22. To what extent do you or those close to you feel threatened or fear for the physical safety of your family or friends by the possibility of another event similar to the September 11 events? Please answer on a scale from 1 to 10, with 1 being Not at all threatened, and 10 Very much threatened. Where do you fall on this 10-point scale?
    (not at all threatened) 1 2 3 4 5 6 7 8 9 10 (Very threatened) 11 Don't Know

23. To what degree do you have feelings that you yourself are a victim of the events that occurred in September of last year? Please answer on a 10-point scale with 1 indicating that you don't feel at all like a victim, 10 being that you feel very strongly like a victim. Where do you fall on this 10-point scale?
    (Not at all a victim) 1 2 3 4 5 6 7 8 9 10 (very strongly a victim)
    11 (Don't Know)

Now I want to return for a moment to John Walker Lindh.

Please tell me if you believe the following statements said about John Walker Lindh are definitely true, probably true, probably false or definitely false.

1. Definitely True 2. Probably True 3. Probably False
4. Definitely False 5. (Don't know)

(Randomize Q42-Q45)

24. He is a terrorist

25. He is a traitor

26. He is a confused young man

27. He was on a religious journey

28. Some people have claimed that John Walker Lindh was involved in some way with, or is somehow responsible for, the death of CIA agent Johnny Mike Spann who was killed in Afghanistan. Do you think he was involved with the death of Mr. Spann or do you have no opinion on this matter?

1. Yes, involved 2. No, not involved 3. No opinion

29. Why is that? **[Verbatim]**______________

30. Some people say that there is a connection between John Walker Lindh's actions in Afghanistan and the attacks in New York and Washington last September 11, but other people say that there is no connection to those events. Do you think there is a connection or that there is no connection?

1. Yes, connection 2. No, no connection 3. Don't Know/No Opinion

31. Why is that? **[Verbatim]**______________

32. I just want to hold your attention for another minute. You have been very patient.

I have asked you as lot of questions about the John Walker Lindh case. Here is the most important question. Please visualize the following situation. Please think about it carefully before you give your answer.

Assume that you are called for jury duty in the John Walker Lindh trial. In the courtroom, the judge informs you that Mr. Lindh is charged with: conspiracy to murder U.S. citizens; providing material support and resources to al Qaeda, a designated terrorist organization; and supplying services to the Taliban.

The judge states that the burden of proof is on the prosecution to prove Lindh's guilt. The judge also says that it is very important that a juror be able set aside any prejudices and be fair and impartial in deciding his guilt or innocence.

Considering everything—your own feelings, any discussions you have had with other people, and your conscience—do you believe that you could be a fair and impartial juror in the trial of John Walker Lindh as the law requires?

1. Yes, could be fair and impartial
2. No, could not be fair and impartial
3. Don't Know/Refuse to answer

33. What is your reason for saying that? **[Verbatim]**______________

34. Are there any other reasons for saying that? **[Verbatim]**______________

Those are all the questions that I have for you but before we stop I need to get some general personal information from you to assist us in making sure that we have a representative sample of persons.

35. Do you generally think of yourself as a Democrat, an Independent or a Republican? (IF DEMOCRAT/REPUBLICAN) Would you call yourself a strong (DEMOCRAT/REPUBLICAN) or a not very strong (DEMOCRAT/REPUBLICAN)? (IF INDEPENDENT) Do you think of yourself as closer to the Democratic or Republican party?

1. Strong Democrat	2. Not Strong Democrat	3. Independent Democrat
4. Strong Republican	5. Not Strong Republican	6. Independent Republican
7. Strong Republican	8. (Don't Know)	9. (Some other party)

36. Imagine an ideological scale that runs from 1 to 7, where 1 means very conservative and 7 means very liberal. Where would you place yourself on that scale?

Very Conservative 1 2 3 4 5 6 7 Very Liberal Don't Know

37. Do you have any children age 21 or younger?

1. Yes → CONTINUE
2. No → SKIP TO Q59
3. (Don't know/Refused) → SKIP TO Q59

Do you have any children in each of the following age categories?

1. Yes 2. No 3. Refused

38. Under age 11

39. Ages 11-15

40. Ages 16-21

(RESUME ASKING EVERYONE)

41. What is the last grade you completed in school?

1. Some grade school 2. Some high school 3. Graduated high school
4. Technical/Vocational 5. Some college 6. Graduated college
7. Graduate/Professional 8. Don't Know/Refused

42. In terms of your job status, are you employed, unemployed but looking for work, retired, a homemaker or a student?

1. Employed 2. Unemployed 3. Retired
4. Student 5. Homemaker 6. Other
7. Don't Know

43. Would you consider yourself to be Black/African-American, White, Hispanic/Latino, Asian, bi-racial, multi-racial or something else?

1. Black/African-American 2. White 3. Hispanic/Latino
4. Asian 5. Bi-racial 6. Multi-racial
7. Something Else 8. Refused

44. What is your age? (READ CODES IF NECESSARY)

1. 18-24	2. 25-29	3. 30-34	4. 35-39	5. 40-44 6. 45-49
7. 50-54	8. 55-59	9. 60-64	10. 65+	11. Refused

45. Which of the following categories best describes your total yearly income from all members of your household?

1. Under $20,000	2. $25,000 to $49,000	3. $50,000 to $74,000
4. $75,000 to $100,000	5. $100,000 or over	6. Don't Know
7. Refused		

46. Do you read a daily newspaper? (READ RESPONSES)

1. Every day, almost every day	2. Several times per week
3. Once a week, or	4. Less than once a week
5. Never	6. Varies, Don't Know

(IF Q64=5 or 6, SKIP TO Q66)

47. What is the name of the newspaper or newspapers that you read? (3 responses) **[Verbatim]** ______________

(RESUME ASKING EVERYONE)

48. Do you watch or listen to a news show on television or radio (READ RESPONSES)

1. Every day, almost every day	2. Several times per week
3. Once a week, or	4. Less than once a week
5. (Never)	6. (Varies, Don't Know)

(IF Q66=5 or 6, SKIP TO Q68)

49. Which news show or shows are those? **[Verbatim]**______________ (3 responses)

(RESUME ASKING EVERYONE)

50. Are you or any members of your immediate family members in the military or closely associated with the military?

1. Yes	2. No
3. Don't Know	4. Refused

51. Do you or any members of your immediate family work for the federal government?

1. Yes	2. No
3. Don't Know	4. Refused

52. Since the events of September 11, have you viewed, visited or otherwise been to the site of the World Trade Center?

1. Yes	2. No
3. Don't Know	4. Refused

53. Have you viewed, visited or otherwise been to the Pentagon?

1. Yes	2. No
3. Don't Know	4. Refused

54. Finally, please remember that I am only asking your opinions. I am not recruiting anyone for jury service. In order to serve on a jury in the United States you must be an American citizen, 18 years of age or older; you must not have been convicted of a felony or have pending criminal charges punishable by more than one year in prison, and not have a physical or mental disability that would prevent service as a juror.

Is there anything that would disqualify you from serving on a jury?

1. Yes (can't serve)	2. No (no, disqualifications. Can serve.)
3. Don't Know	4. Refused

Thank you very much for participating in our survey.

Appendix B
NACCHIO SURVEY 2009

(Following Criminal Conviction in Response to Pending SEC Lawsuit)

Start screening section

55. Just to confirm I'm calling in the right area, what county do you live in? **(Do Not Read List)** ______________

  1. Live somewhere else → **TERMINATE**
  2. Don't Know → **TERMINATE**

56. What is your age? **(READ CODES IF NECESSARY)**

1. 18-24	2. 25-29	3. 30-34	4. 35-39	5. 40-44
6. 45-49	7. 50-54	8. 55-59	9. 60-64	10. 65-70
11. 71+	12. Refused			

57. Are you registered to vote in this county?

  1. Yes → Skip to Q5
  2. No → Ask Q4

58. Do you have a valid Colorado driver's license?

  1. Yes → CONTINUE
  2. No → TERMINATE

59. Are you or any member of your household employed in journalism or related mass media employment?

  1. Yes → TERMINATE
  2. No → CONTINUE

60. In your area, if you served on a jury within the last year, if jury duty would cause you hardship, or if you work in the public health or safety field, you can be excused from jury duty. Given what you've heard, would you be automatically

excused from any jury duty?

1. Yes, automatically excused/exempt → TERMINATE
2. No, not exempt → CONTINUE
3. Don't have any exemptions → CONTINUE
4. Don't Know → CONTINUE

---

1. My first questions are about some general issues. For each one, please tell me if you are very concerned; somewhat concerned; not very concerned; or not at all concerned about that issue.

1. Very concerned 2. Somewhat concerned 3. Not very concerned
4. Not at all concerned 5. Don't Know

(Randomize)

a. Taxes in the state of Colorado (Kansas, New Mexico)
b. The costs of local government
c. Corporate corruption
d. Pollution in the local environment

(End Randomize)

2. Do you read a newspaper on a regular basis? *Yes No*
Which newspaper, or newspapers, is that? (Check/report) all that apply:

Denver Post
Durango Herald
Rocky Mountain News (now defunct)
Denver Business Journal
Pueblo Chieftain
Grand Junction Daily Sentinel
Wichita Eagle
Santa Fe New Mexican
New York Times
Wall Street Journal
Other: ______________

3. Have you, or members of your family, or your friends ever worked for any of the following companies—or any subsidiary of that company: (**Randomize)**

a. Walmart *Yes No*
b. Qwest Communications, International *Yes No*
c. U.S. West *Yes No*
d. Mountain Bell *Yes No*
e. Lockheed Martin Corporation *Yes No*

4. I am going to read a list of some persons whose names have been in the news. Tell me if you recognize the name and if you do, tell me in a couple of words who that person is:

(Randomize)

a. Joseph Nacchio (Nashio) *Yes No*
Who is that? (any of these: CEO Qwest; Convicted; in jail) *correct incorrect*
b. Edward W. Nottingham *Yes No*
(judge of Nacchio trial; sex scandal) *correct incorrect*
c. Mark Udall (Colorado Senator)
d. Wilson Chambers (n.b. control name)
e. Afshin Mohebbi (Qwest Officer)
f. Robert S. Woodruff (Qwest officer)

5. I'd like to follow up on the Qwest Communications Company. Would you say that you have a

a. favorable impression of that company,
b. an unfavorable impression, or
c. are you neutral in your feeling toward that company?
Why is that? **Verbatim** ______________

6. Are you familiar with the name of the case of Joe Nacchio, the former Chief Executive Officer of Qwest Communications? *Yes No*

If yes: What is the thing he is known for? **Verbatim**______________

7. In 2007, Joe Nacchio was put on trial and convicted by a jury. Can you tell me in your own words what he was found guilty of doing? **Verbatim**____________

8. Just so we are clear, Joe Nacchio is the former Chief Executive Officer, the CEO, of Qwest Communications. He was charged with insider trading and a jury found him guilty in April of 2007.

To what degree have you followed the court proceedings involving Joe Nacchio? Would you say,

Not at all   A little bit   Closely, or

Very closely

9. Do you recall if Joe Nacchio was sentenced to prison? *Yes No*

If yes: What was the length of his prison sentence?

Verbatim ____________ **or don't recall**

10. How many years in prison do you personally think he should serve as result of his conviction for insider trading? **Verbatim** ____________

11. Have you discussed the Joe Nacchio case with:

Members of your family? *Yes No*

Friends? *Yes No*

Neighbors? *Yes No*

Co-workers? *Yes No*

12. Do you personally know anyone who lost money from an investment in stocks, bonds, an IRA, or 401 K fund associated with Qwest Communications or any of its subsidiaries? *Yes No*

If yes to 12, Was that person or persons:

13. a member of your immediate family, including yourself ? *Yes No*

14. a relative? *Yes No*

15. a friend or neighbor? *Yes No*

16. A co-worker? *Yes No*

17. If Yes to 13: What do you think was the cause of this loss?
Verbatim ____________

18. Some people say that Joe Nacchio, the former CEO of Qwest, was the cause of the fall in the value of Qwest stock and job losses at Qwest, but others say it was a general downturn in the telecommunications market. What is your view? Would you say it was due to:

Joe Nacchio,
a market downturn or
a combination of both, or
some other cause?

19. The Securities and Exchange Commission now has filed a civil lawsuit against Joe Nacchio, Afshin Moehebbi, Robert Woodruff and other former Qwest employees, alleging that during their tenure at Qwest they engaged in multiple acts of fraud under seven sections of the U.S. Securities Act. Unlike a criminal trial, a civil lawsuit may involve an injunction against the defendants from engaging in certain acts and force them to return any money that was gained through fraudulent means. The SEC is asking for a jury trial to force the defendants in this case to return hundreds of millions of dollars in salaries, bonuses, and proceeds from stock sales that resulted from their tenure at Qwest.

Were you aware of this civil lawsuit? *Yes No*

20. Some people say it is unfair to charge Joe Nacchio in a civil lawsuit since he has already been fined and been sentenced to prison What is your view on the civil lawsuit?

Do you think it is generally: *air or unfair?*

21. Why is that ? **Verbatim** ____________

22. Considering everything that you know about the Nacchio case what is your personal view about the SEC lawsuit against Joseph Nacchio? Which of the following best describes your personal view about whether Joe Nacchio engaged in fraud:

Would you say that he:
Very definitely engaged in fraud
Definitely engaged in fraud
Probably engaged in fraud or
Would you have to hear evidence to say one way or another, or
That he probably did not engage in fraud?

23. What is your reason for taking this position? **VERBATIM** ____________

24. Let me ask this question another way. Here are three persons named as defendants in the SEC lawsuit. On a scale from 1 to 100, with 1 being not guilty and 100 being definitely guilty, please indicate the degree to which you currently believe each is guilty of fraud:

Joe Nacchio *or* Don't know *or* refused
Afshin Mohebbi *or* Don't know *or* refused
Robert S. Woodruff *or* Don't know *or* refused

25. Let me ask this question still a different way. Suppose the jury in the upcoming civil case were to find Joe Nacchio and the other defendants to be not legally responsible for fraud during their employment at Qwest. In your opinion, would you find a not legally responsible verdict acceptable or unacceptable?

Would that be:

Very unacceptable	1
Somewhat unacceptable	2
Somewhat acceptable	3
Very acceptable	4
Don't know/refuse	(DO NOT READ)

26. Why do you take this position? **VERBATIM** (accept 3 answers)

1. ____________

2. ____________
3. ____________

27. I have one final question about this case. Please take a moment to reflect before answering this question.

Assume that you were actually called as a juror in this case. The judge would instruct you that it is your duty to be fair and impartial in evaluating the evidence presented by the Securities and Exchange Commission (S.E.C.) and any evidence called by the defendants that is contrary to the S.E.C's claims. The judge will instruct the jury that the S.E.C. has the legal burden of proving its claim against defendants Joe Nacchio, Robert Woodruff and Afshin Moehebbi. However, the judge will further instruct the jury that while the burden of proof in a criminal case is "proof beyond a reasonable doubt" in a civil case the burden is less, namely whether the S.E.C. has proven its case on the balance of probabilities.

Do you believe that you could be a fair and impartial juror in the S.E.C. v. Nacchio civil trial?

1. Yes 2. No 3. Don't Know/Refused

28. Why do you take this position? **VERBATIM** ____________

(RESUME ASKING EVERYONE)

1. What is the last grade you completed in school?

1. Some Grade School	2. Some High School
3. Graduated High School	4. Technical/Vocational
5. Some College	6. Graduated College
7. Graduate/Professional	8. Don't Know/Refused

2. In terms of your job status, are you employed full time, employed part time, unemployed but looking for work, retired, a homemaker or a student?

1. Employed full time	2. Employed part time
3. Unemployed	4. Retired
5. Student	6. Homemaker
7. Other	8. Don't Know

3. Would you consider yourself to be Black/African-American, White, Hispanic/ Latino, Asian, bi-racial, multi-racial or something else?

1. Black/African-American	2. White	3. Hispanic/Latino
4. Asian	5. Bi-racial	6. Multi-racial
7. Something Else	8. Refused	

4. Which of the following categories best describes your total yearly income from all members of your household? **(Read 1-5)**

1. Under $20,000	2. $25,000 to $49,000	3. $50,000 to $74,000
4. $75,000 to $100,000	5. $100,000 or over	6. Don't Know
7. Refused		

Appendix C
JURY PRETRIAL QUESTIONNAIRE IN *UNITED STATES V. AL-ARIAN*

UNITED STATES DISTRICT COURT
MIDDLE DISTRICT OF FLORIDA
TAMPA DIVISION
UNITED STATES OF AMERICA :
:
v. : CASE NO.: 8:03-CR-77-T-30TBM
:
SAMI AMIN Al-Arian :
HATEM NAJI FARIZ :

JUROR QUESTIONNAIRE

General Instructions

The questions on this form are asked to help the Court and the attorneys learn about your views on issues that may be related to this case. Its use will expedite the process of selecting a jury. The questions are not meant to invade your privacy, but to help select the best possible jury for this case. If there is any reason why you might not be able to give both sides a fair trial in this case, it is important to say so. Please answer each question as fully as you can. Your complete honesty is essential. Because the questionnaire is part of the jury selection process, the questionnaires are to be answered under your oath as a prospective juror to tell the truth. If you think an answer is too personal, please say so in the space provided. You will have an opportunity to discuss your answer privately. If a question does not apply to you in any way, write N/A (Not Applicable), rather than leave the question blank.

Please keep in mind that there are no right or wrong answers, only complete and incomplete answers. If you do not understand a question, need more space for your response, or wish to make further comments about any question, please use the extra sheet attached to the back of the questionnaire. You are instructed not to discuss this case or questionnaire with anyone, including your family or fellow jurors. It is important that your answers be your own. The case for which you are being questioned is United States of America v. Sami Al-Arian, et al. In this case there are two defendants against whom the government has brought charges of conspiracy to provide material support to or for the benefit of designated terrorists and other federal crimes. Of course, the bringing of charges is not evidence of guilt. Each of the accused is entitled to a presumption of innocence and the case against each must be decided individually.

Because there has been a high degree of publicity about this case and some of its participants, the court has directed that this juror questionnaire be sent to you. Thank you for your cooperation.

Participant No. _________
Juror No. _________

(Please PRINT your answers in INK)

JUROR'S OATH:

I declare under penalty of perjury that the information which I have provided in this juror questionnaire and any attachments is true and correct. I further declare that I have completed this questionnaire without anyone's assistance.

____

Juror Number (not your name)

____

Date

HARDSHIP QUESTION:

The Court and the parties estimate that the trial in this case will last approximately two (2) months. Jurors will be paid an attendance fee of $40.00 per day for the first thirty (30) days of trial, and $50.00 per day thereafter. You will be reimbursed for mileage expense for use of your private vehicle.

Jury service is one of the highest duties and privileges of a citizen. The participation of people like yourself is essential to the proper administration of justice. The Court recognizes that not everyone can serve on a case of this length. However, mere inconvenience or the usual financial hardships of jury service will not be enough to excuse you. You must show that service in this case would cause an unacceptable amount of personal hardship.

Would you have a serious hardship if chosen for this case?
_____ YES, I would have a serious hardship if chosen for this case. Please answer the questions below, and fully explain your hardship. You must still complete the entire questionnaire.
_____ NO, I would not have a serious hardship if chosen for this case. Please move onto the next section of the questionnaire.

If YES, please explain the hardship, and list your current occupation. Describe the type of job and business without giving details of your employer's name or address. For example, simply list "receptionis," "business executive," "school teacher," or "self-employed/freelance". If you are retired or unemployed, please indicate that fact and list your previous occupation. Please write legibly.

Occupation: ______________________________ **Your Age:** ________ **Sex:** ________
Please do not list the name of your employer.

Are you self-employed? *Yes No* Are you retired? *Yes No*
Will you be paid a salary while you serve jury duty? *Yes No*
What is your hardship? ____
What arrangements can you make to alleviate your hardship? __________________
____

1. Do you have any problem with your hearing or vision that would make it difficult for you to serve as a juror? *Yes No*

2. Do you have any medical condition that would make it difficult for you to serve as a juror on this case? *Yes No* If Yes, **briefly** list the condition(s):

____

3. Are you taking any prescription medication or have any other condition that may interfere with your ability to concentrate or serve as a juror in any way?
Yes No

4. Is there anything the Court should know about your ability to concentrate for long periods of time? *Yes No I'm not sure*
Please explain: ____

5. Have you had any problems or concerns about your ability to remember complex information? *Yes No I'm not sure*
Please explain:____

6. What is your place of birth? (Please list only the **city and state**, and, if outside the United States, the country.) __________________________________

7. Are you (check one):

Married _____

Single _____

Living with another person as a couple _____

Divorced/Separated _____

Widow/Widower _____

(a) What is your racial/ethnic background?

(b) If married, what is the racial/ethnic background of your spouse?

(c) What is your religion? ________________________________

(d) If married, what is your spouse's religion? __________________

8. In what Florida county do you reside? _____________________________

(a) How long have you lived in this area?___________________________

(b) What other places have you lived? ____________________________

9. Do you read a newspaper regularly (at least two or three times a week)? *Yes No*

If Yes, list the names of the newspapers you read and indicate how often you read each newspaper.

Name of Newspaper: ________________

Once a Week   2-3 times a week   More than 4 times a week

Daily   Sunday Only

10. Do you watch any television newscasts on a regular basis? *Yes* *No*

(a) If Yes, which ones? ____

(b) Do you consider the television newscasts you watch to be:

_______ always biased

_______ sometimes biased

_______ not at all biased

Please explain the kind of bias you find and any concerns you have about those biases:

11. What, if any, talk shows do you listen to or watch? ____________________

12. Do you use the internet as a source of news? *Yes* *No*

13. If Yes, which web pages do you view? ____________________

14. Do you have a personal computer at home, or do you have daily access to a personal computer outside your home (e.g. at work, library, etc.)?

_______ Yes, I have a computer at home

_______ Yes, I have daily access outside my home

_______ Yes, both

_______ No

How often do you log onto the internet?

_______ Several times a day

_______ At least once a day

_______ At least two or three days a week

_______ Once a week or less

How much time do you spend on the internet daily?

________More than five hours a day
________Three to five hours a day
________One to three hours a day
________Less than one hour per day
________Do not spend time on the internet daily

Which of the following activities do you spend the *most* internet time on? Please check all that apply:

________E-mail/Chatting/Instant messaging
________Entertainment (games, cards, puzzles)
________Shopping/Auctioning
________Stock trading
________Banking/Paying bills
________Research/Information gathering
________Reading the news/Current events
________Fantasy sports
________Gambling
________Downloading music
________Blogging
________Other: SPECIFY____________________________________
________None

15. Is English your first language? *Yes No*

16. What other languages do you speak, read or understand? ________________

17. Are you, your spouse or a former spouse a naturalized U.S. Citizen? *Yes No*
If Yes, please tell us who and when they became a citizen. ________________

18. Do you speak, read, write or understand any of the following languages?

Yes, speak	*Yes, read*	*Yes, understand*	*No*
Arabic	Any	Arabic dialect	Hebrew
Any Hebrew dialect			

(a) Did you grow up in, or have you spent substantial time in, households or other environments where Arabic, any Arabic dialect, Hebrew or any Hebrew dialect was spoken, written or read?

_______ Yes, I grew up in, or have spent substantial time in an environment where Arabic/Arabic dialect(s) were spoken, written or read.

_______ Yes, I grew up in, or have spent substantial time in an environment where Hebrew/Hebrew dialect(s) were spoken, written or read.

_______ No, I did not grow up in and have not spent substantial time in an environment where any of these languages/dialect(s) were spoken, written or read.

(b) If you answered "Yes" to any part of Question 15 or 15(a), would you have any difficulty relying solely upon a translator's translation of the evidence? *Yes* *No*

19. Are you:

( ) Employed full-time ( ) Retired

( ) Employed part-time ( ) Student

( ) Homemaker ( ) Disabled & unable to work

( ) Unemployed/laid off

(a) Without telling us the name of your employer (or if self-employed), what kind of work do you do? (For example: electric utility, maintenance; teacher/high school.)

(b) If retired or unemployed, what was your primary vocation?

(c) If homemaker or student, please tell us what jobs outside the home (if any) you have had in the past year:

20. What is (was) your job title? ______________________________

(a) What are (were) your duties on that job? ________________

(b) Do (did) you supervise others in that job? ________________

Yes *No* If Yes, how many? ______________________________

21. Do you have a second job? *Yes* *No*

If Yes, what do you do?___________________________________

22. What other jobs have you held as an adult? ______________________

23. Please tell us the following about your children, stepchildren, foster children and/or grandchildren:

Relationship Gender Age Level of

Education

Occupation

(a) Which of these, if any, presently live with you? ______________________

24. If you have ever been married, list your spouse's and/or former spouse's most recent type of work: ______________________

25. Parents (or stepparents) occupations: If retired or deceased, what did they do before?

Father: ______________________

Mother: ______________________

26. Have you ever filled in, or helped someone else fill in, any immigration or visa documents with the Immigration and Naturalization Service (INS) or the Bureau of Immigration and Customs Enforcement (BICE)? *Yes No*

________ Yes, I have filled in INS/BICE immigration or visa documents.

________ Yes, I have helped someone else fill in INS/BICE immigration or visa documents.

________ No. Please briefly describe the circumstances: ______________

When filling in INS/BICE immigration or visa documents, do you believe that it is important to disclose the whole truth, no matter what the consequences might be? *Yes No*

Please explain: ____

Do you believe that INS/BICE immigration or visa documents are too complicated for the average person to understand or accurately fill out?

Yes No I am not sure

Do you believe that INS/BICE immigration or visa documents ask too many personal questions?

Yes No I am not sure

Which of the following best describes your opinion?

_______ The INS/BICE is too strict in enforcing immigration policy.

_______ The INS/BICE aims to protect Americans from potential threats and harm.

_______ The INS/BICE is too lenient in enforcing immigration policy.

Is there anything about your views on the INS/BICE or immigration policy that you believe may affect your ability to be fair and impartial to either the defendants or the government in this case?

Yes No I am not sure

Please explain: ____

26. What is the highest grade of schooling you have completed?

( ) 8th grade or less ( ) Community college
( ) Some high school ( ) Some four-year college
( ) High school graduate ( ) College graduate
( ) Post graduate

(a) Major area(s) of study: ________________________________

(b) Degrees or certificates: ________________________________

27. What civic, social, union, professional, fraternal, political, recreational, churches, synagogues, temples, mosques, or other religious organizations do you belong to or participate in, and what offices, if any, have you held in any of these organizations?

28. (a) Have you ever donated money/goods to, or volunteered to work at, charitable causes or organizations?

Yes No I am not sure

If "NO," SKIP to Question #29.

(b) Please list the causes or organizations to which you have donated money/goods or at which you have volunteered.

(c) Did any of these organizations represent to you that they provided aid to people outside the United States? ______________________________

(d) When you donate money to a charitable organization how carefully do you investigate how the organization spends that money?

CHECK ALL THAT APPLY:

_______ I always check where the organization is spending the money.

_______ I mostly check where the organization is spending the money.

_______ I don't usually check where the organization is spending the money because I trust the organization or never thought about it.

_______ I don't usually check where the organization is spending the money because I don't want to know or don't need to know.

_______ Other: PLEASE EXPLAIN: ____________________________

(e) Is there anything about your practices of donating money to charity or investigating where money goes that would affect your ability to be fair and impartial in this case?

Yes *No* *I am not sure*

If "Yes" or "I am not sure," please explain: __________________________

29. Have you ever served in the military? *Yes* *No*

Branch and highest rank: ______________________________________

30. Has your spouse or children ever served in the military? *Yes* *No*

Branch and highest rank: ______________________________________

31. Have you or any children or relatives served in the recent war in Iraq, in Desert Storm or in military operations in Afghanistan and other areas of the Middle East?

Iraq: *Yes* *No*

Branch and highest rank: ______________________________________

Desert Storm: *Yes* *No*

Branch and highest rank: ______________________________________

Afghanistan: *Yes* *No*

Branch and highest rank: ________________________________

Other areas of the Middle East: *Yes No*

Branch and highest rank: ________________________________

If Yes, where is, or was that person stationed? ____________________

32. Were any such persons ever in a combat situation?

Yes No I am not sure

If Yes, please tell us where and when: ________________________

(a) Have you, a family member, close friend or acquaintance been injured or killed while serving in a combat or military zone? *Yes No*

33. In what contexts have you had personal contact with people who are Muslims, Palestinian or Arab descent? (Please check all answers that apply.)

_______ in the family

_______ in the neighborhood

_______ in organizations

_______ through work/business

_______ in place of worship

_______ in school

_______ none

_______ other: ____

34. Have you had any unpleasant experiences with Muslims, Palestinians or Arabs?

Yes No

If Yes, please explain: ___________________________

35. Have you or any member of your family or friends had any experience which would cause you to be biased against a Muslim defendant in a case where there are allegations of support for people and/or organizations the government has designated as terrorists?

Yes No

If Yes, please explain: ___________________________

36. Have you had any particularly pleasant experiences with Muslims, Palestinians or Arabs or associated organizations?

Yes No I am not sure

If Yes or I'm not sure, please explain: ______________________________

37. Do you feel that any of your experiences with or feelings towards Muslims, Palestinians or Arabs, or associated organizations, would cause you to be biased in favor of or against a Muslim, Palestinian or Arab defendant or biased in favor of or against the government in a case involving a Muslim, Palestinian or Arab defendant.

Yes No I am not sure

If Yes or I'm not sure, please explain: ______________________________

38. Have you had any negative experiences with Jewish people or Israelis?

Yes No I am not sure

If Yes or I'm not sure, please explain: ______________________________

39. Do you feel that any of your experiences with, or feelings or impressions about, Jewish people or Israelis would cause you to be biased for or against a Muslim, Palestinian, or Arab defendant or biased for or against the government in a case involving a Muslim, Palestinian, or Arab defendant allegedly committing crimes against Jewish people or Israelis?

Yes No I am not sure

Please explain: ______________________________

40. Do you believe that Muslims, Palestinians, Arabs or Israelis are disproportionately more violent than other religious or ethnic groups?

Yes No I am not sure

If Yes, what gives you that impression? ______________________________

41. Do you believe that Muslims, Israelis, Palestinians or Arabs commit disproportionately more crimes than other ethnic groups?

Yes No I am not sure

If Yes, what gives you that impression? ______________________________

42. Do you have any experiences, feelings or impressions about Palestinians, Arabs or Muslims that would make it difficult for you to listen to the evidence with an open mind and render a verdict based solely on the evidence presented in court when the case involves Palestinian, Arab, or Muslim men charged with various acts of terrorism?

Yes No Don't know

If Yes, please explain: ______________________________

43. Do you think Palestinians were responsible for the attack on the United States on September 11, 2001?

Yes No Don't know

If Yes, please explain: ______________________________

44. Do you or does any relative or close friend know or have any connection with any of the defendants?

Sami Amin Al-Arian *Yes No*

Hatem Naji Fariz *Yes No*

(a) Please explain in detail who has the connection and the nature of the connection for each individual: ___________________________

(b) Have you seen, heard or read anything about any of the defendants? This includes not only the media, but anything you may have heard from friends, relatives, or co-workers. *Yes No*

(c) What have you seen, heard or read? ___________________________

(d) Do you, or does anyone close to you, know or have any connection with either of the following individuals or their family members:

Sameeh Taha Hammoudeh *Yes No*

Ghassan Zayed Ballut *Yes No*

(e) For each individual (or individual's family member), please explain in detail who has the connection and the nature of the connection:

____

(f) Have you, or has anyone close to you, seen, heard or read anything about any of the above defendants or individuals from any source whatsoever? This includes not only from the media (television, radio or internet), but anything you may have heard from friends, relatives, co-workers, or other people. *Yes No*

45. Several individuals have been charged in the indictment in this case but will not be defendants in this trial. Do you or does any relative or close friend know or have any connection with any of these individuals?

Ramadan Abdullah Shallah *Yes No*

Bashir Musa Mohammed Nafi *Yes No*

Muhammed Tasir Hassan Al-Khatib *Yes No*

Abd Al Aziz Awda *Yes No*

Mazen Al-Najjar *Yes No*

(a) Have you seen, heard or read anything about any of these defendants? This includes not only the media, but anything you may have heard from friends, relatives, or co-workers. *Yes No*

(b) What have you seen, heard or read? ______________________________

46. Have you, or has anyone close to you, seen, heard, or read anything about this case or Dr. Sami Al-Arian, Hatem Naji Fariz, Sameeh Taha Hammoudeh, Ghassan Zayed Ballut, or Mazen Al-Najjar, or have you discussed this case or these individuals with anyone?

_______Yes, self

_______Yes, someone close

_______No

IF "NO," SKIP SUBSECTIONS (a) - (c).

(a) Please explain what information you have or have heard, the source of the information, and with whom you may have discussed the case and what was discussed. ______________________________

(b) What were your reactions, thoughts, feelings or impressions about what you saw, heard, read or discussed? ______________________________

(c) Have you formed any opinion about this case or Dr. Sami Al-Arian, Hatem Naji Fariz, Sameeh Taha Hammoudeh, Ghassan Zayed Ballut, or Mazen Al-Najjar? ______________________________

Yes No I am not sure

If Yes or I'm not sure, please explain: ______________________________

47. Have you, or has anyone close to you, seen, heard, or read anything about the prior federal criminal trial involving Dr. Sami Al-Arian and Hatem Naji Fariz that was held from June through December 2005, or have you discussed the prior criminal trial with anyone?

_______ Yes, self

_______ Yes, someone close

_______ No

IF "NO," SKIP SUBSECTIONS (a) - (d).

(a) Please explain what information you have or have heard, the source of the information, and with whom you may have discussed the case and what was discussed. ______________________________

(b) What were your reactions, thoughts, feelings or impressions about what you saw, heard, read or discussed? ______________________

(c) Have you formed any opinion about any aspect of the prior federal criminal trial (e.g., the attorneys, the Court, the evidence, etc.)?

Yes No I am not sure

If Yes or I'm not sure, please explain: ______________________________

(d) What was your reaction to the verdict? ______________________

48. (a) If the United States government brought a case against a criminal defendant and the case resulted in a mistrial because the jury could not reach a verdict, do you think it is unfair for the government to bring the case a second time?

_______ Yes, it is unfair

_______ No, it is fair

If "Yes," please describe your views and why you think it is unfair. _____

____

(b) If the United States government brought a case against a criminal defendant and the case resulted in a mistrial because the jury could not reach a verdict, do you think it is a waste of taxpayer dollars for the government to bring the case a second time?

________ Yes, it is a waste of taxpayer dollars

________ No, it is not a waste of taxpayer dollars

If "Yes," please describe your views and why you think it is a waste of taxpayer dollars. ________________________________

(c) If the United States government brought a case against a criminal defendant and the case resulted in a mistrial because the jury could not reach a verdict, do you think that it means that the defendant is:

________ More likely to be not guilty

________ More likely to be guilty

________ The findings of the previous jury have no bearing on my opinions of this case.

Please explain your view: ________________________________

(d) Other than the views you have expressed above, do you have any other concerns about the United States government bringing a case against a criminal defendant when a prior case resulted in a mistrial because the jury could not reach a verdict)?

________ Yes, I have concerns

________ No, I do not have concerns

If "Yes," please describe your concerns: ________________________________

49. Have you heard or read about any statements attributable to Dr. Al-Arian?

Yes No

(a) Were any described as critical of the United States?

Yes No

(b) What were your reactions or impressions based on what you read or heard? ________________________________

50. Have you seen, heard or read anything about Dr. Sami Al-Arian in the past Senatorial Primary Race that involved Mrs. Betty Castor and Mr. Peter Deutsch? This includes not only the media, but anything you may have heard from friends, relatives or coworkers: *Yes No*

(a) What did you see, hear or read?

(b) What was your reaction to what you heard or read?

(c) Based on what you have heard, read or saw, please tell us what feelings or opinions you have formed about this case or about Dr. Sami Al-Arian?

(d) Based on this opinion, would it make it difficult for you to sit as a fair and impartial juror in this type of case?

51. Have you seen, heard, or read media accounts in the past coverage of the Senatorial Race between Mrs. Betty Castor and Mr. Mel Martinez? This includes not only the media, but also anything you may have heard from friends, relatives or co-workers? *Yes No*

(a) What did you see, hear or read? ______________________________

(b) What was your reaction to what you heard or read? ______________

(c) Based on what you have heard, read or seen, please tell us what your feelings or opinions you have formed about this case or about Dr. Sami Al-Arian. ____

(d) Based on this opinion, would it make it difficult for you to sit as a fair and impartial juror in this type of case? ____________________________

52. Have you seen, read or heard anything concerning Mazen Al-Najjar's immigration case? If so, what were your reactions or impressions based on what you read or heard? ____

53. Is there anything you have seen, heard, or read about that would interfere with your ability to render a fair verdict in this case based solely on the evidence presented in court? *Yes No*

54. Have you formed an opinion as to the innocence or guilt of any of the defendants in this case before hearing the evidence?

________Guilty

________Innocent

________No decision

Please explain what led to your position: ____________________________

55. This case is likely to receive ongoing media attention. The Court wants to make sure that this case is decided solely on the evidence in the courtroom and not based on things that are said outside the courtroom. Accordingly, the Court

will be instructing you periodically that you must avoid reading about the case in the newspapers or on the internet, or listening to any radio or television reports about the case. The Court will also instruct you periodically that you must avoid discussing this case with friends or family during the course of the trial. Would these requirements pose any difficulty for you? *Yes No*

56. How closely have you followed the media coverage of the conflict between Israel and the Palestinians?

________Very closely

________ Somewhat closely

________ Not too closely

(a) If you have followed the media coverage of this event, based on what you have heard or read, have you formed any opinions about the nature of this conflict? *Yes No*

(b) Have you formed an opinion or belief about the nature of the conflict? *Yes No*

If you answered "Yes" to (a) and/or (b), please explain: ________________

(c) Have you formed any opinion about which side of the conflict is right or wrong? *Yes No I'm not sure*

(d) Have you formed any opinion about any other aspect of the conflict? *Yes No I'm not sure*

(e) If you answered Yes to (a), (b), (c), or (d), please explain: ____________

____

(f) Would this opinion make it difficult for you to sit as a fair and impartial juror in this type of case? *Yes No I'm not sure*

57. Do you believe that the United States should not be involved in any way in conflicts in the Middle East? *Yes No I'm not sure*

Please explain: ____

58. Do you believe that the United States should not be involved in any way in the conflict between Israel and the Palestinians? *Yes No I'm not sure*

Please explain: ______________________________

59. Do you believe that the United States offers too much sympathy or support for either side of the conflict? *Yes No I'm not sure*

Please explain: ______________________________

60. Have you ever served on a jury? *Yes No*

_______ Civil Date(s): ______________________________

Nature of case(s): ______________________________

Criminal Date(s): ______________________________

Nature of case(s): ______________________________

_______ Grand Jury Date(s): ______________________________

Nature of case(s): ______________________________

(a) If Yes, did the jury reach a verdict? ______________________________

(b) Was there anything about your jury experience that would make it difficult to serve again? *Yes No*

Please explain: ______________________________

61. Have you, any member of your family, or a close friend studied at the University of South Florida? *Yes No*

If Yes, when? ______________________________

Course of study? ______________________________

62. Have you, any member of your family, or a close friend been employed at USF? *Yes No*

If Yes, when? ______________________________

In what capacity? ______________________________

63. Have you read or heard the media accounts of Dr. Al-Arian's involvement with USF? *Yes No*

If Yes, what did you learn and from what source? ______________________________

64. What were your reactions or impressions based on what you saw, read or heard? ______________________________

65. Have you read or heard media accounts or other reports regarding Mazen Al-Najjar's involvement with USF? *Yes No*

66. Do you, any member of your family, or a close friend know the current president of USF, Ms. Judy Genshaft? *Yes No*

67. Have you or anyone close to you worked for, applied to or had training with: (check all that apply)

________ a. Any law enforcement, security or investigative agency, including but not limited to the FBI, CIA, INS, Department of Homeland Security and the Department of Justice?

________ b. A prison, jail, detention center or probation service?

________ c. Any city or town attorney, Attorney General, state or federal prosecutor, or court?

________ d. Any law firm that practices criminal defense?

________ e. Any accounting, banking, financial institutions?

________ f. Any newspaper, radio, television, or other media outlet?

If Yes to any of the above, please state who (relation to you), where, when and circumstances. ________________________________

68. Have you or anyone close to you ever worked in an effort to change a law or the enforcement of a law? *Yes No*

If Yes, please briefly describe that effort and your level of participation:

____

69. Have you or a member of your family had any legal action, dispute or negative experience with the United States or any of its agencies, or any officer, agents or employees of the United States? *Yes No*

If Yes, please explain the nature of your interest in such proceedings:

____

70. Are you a vendor or a contractor for the United States Government or do you work for one? *Yes No*

71. Not all of the defendants are citizens of the United States. Would you afford each of the defendants the same consideration? *Yes* *No*

72. What are your feelings about the criminal justice system? ______________

73. Do you believe that you, a member of your family, or a close friend, has ever been directly or indirectly affected in any way by a terrorist act or threat?

Yes *No*

If Yes, please explain the event: ______________________________

74. Have you or any family members or close friends had any personal experience with acts of terrorism? *Yes* *No*

If Yes, please explain the event: ______________________________

75. Have you or anyone close to you ever had an experience involving the police, FBI, or any other law enforcement agency, including being interviewed by or making a report to a law enforcement officer? *Yes* *No*

If Yes, please explain the event: ______________________________

(a) Was your overall experience positive, negative or mixed:

_______ Positive

_______ Negative

_______ A mix - some positive, some negative

_______ Not sure

(b) Did the agency/officer deal with you/their issue appropriately?

Yes *No* *I don't know*

76. Have you or has a family member or close friend ever been the victim of an act of violence (or abuse), reported or not? *Yes* *No*

If Yes, please explain who (relation to you) and circumstances: _______

____

Was there an arrest? *Yes* *No*

What was the outcome? ________________

77. Have you, or has anyone close to you, been discriminated against in any way?

________ Yes, self
________ Yes, someone close
________ No

IF "NO," SKIP SUBSECTIONS (a) - (e).

(a) Was the discrimination on the basis of:
Please check all that apply
________ Age
________ Disability
________ Ethnicity
________ Gender
________ Marital status
________ Race
________ Religious beliefs
________ Socio-economic status
________ Other: SPECIFY ________________________________

(b) Do you think that discrimination happens in the United States:
________ All the time
________ Some of the time
________ Not often
________ Never

(c) Do you think that groups that have been victimized or discriminated against should have the same rights as other groups under the law?
Yes No I'm not sure

(d) Do you think that groups that have been victimized or discriminated against should have to live up to the same laws and standards as other groups, or do you think that groups that have been victimized or discriminated againstshould be given special consideration?
________ Live up to the same laws and standards as other groups
________ Given special consideration
Please explain: ________________________________

(e) Do you think that your experiences with discrimination or your views on discrimination would affect your ability to be fair and impartial in this case?

Yes No I'm not sure
Please explain: ______________________________

78. Have you or anyone close to you ever been arrested, charged or convicted for a crime other than a traffic ticket? *Yes No*
If Yes, please explain who (relation to you), when, nature of the charge and circumstances: ______________________________

79. Have you or has a family member or close friend ever been falsely accused of a crime? *Yes No*
If Yes, please explain: ______________________________
(a) Were you satisfied with the outcome? Please explain: ______________

80. Do you believe that the protections of free speech in a democracy extend both to citizens and non-citizens? *Yes No*
If Yes, please explain: ______________________________

81. Do you believe that the criticism of United States foreign policy is protected free speech under the First Amendment to the U.S. Constitution? *Yes No*
If Yes, please explain: ______________________________
82. Can a person criticize the United States government and still be patriotic?
Yes No
If Yes, please explain: ______________________________

83. Under the United States Constitution, a person accused of a crime does not have to testify in his defense, and his silence may not be used against him. What are your feelings about that?

84. If a person does not tell his side of the story, do you feel he is more likely guilty? *Yes No*
Why or why not? ______________________________

85. There may be evidence in this case consisting of tape recordings of conversations taking place over the telephone through the use of electronic devices com-

monly known as "wiretaps." Before received in evidence, the Court will have ruled that this evidence is lawfully before you and you may give it the weight you deem appropriate. How do you feel about electronic surveillance of private conversations?

(a) Do you feel that electronic surveillance of private conversations is an invasion of privacy that should never happen regardless of the circumstances? *Yes No I'm not sure*

Explain: ____

86. There may also be evidence obtained from photographic and physical surveillance as well as evidence seized pursuant to lawful searches of various places, including the homes of some of the defendants. How do you feel about surveillance or searches of private property?

(a) Do you feel that surveillance or searches of private property is an invasion of privacy that should never happen regardless of the circumstances? *Yes No I'm not sure*

Explain: ____

87. Some of the evidence that you will hear about in this case is more than ten years old.

Which of the following statements describes your views on older evidence:

________ Older evidence is always less reliable than more recent evidence.

________ Older evidence is sometimes less reliable than more recent evidence.

________ Older evidence is as reliable as more recent evidence.

________ Older evidence is sometimes more reliable than more recent evidence.

________ Older evidence is always more reliable than more recent evidence.

________ None of the above.

Explain: ____

Appendix D
DECLARATION OF NEIL VIDMAR IN *BOLIN V. AYERS*, 2012

I, Neil Vidmar, declare as follows:

1. I am a social psychologist and professor of psychology and law whose research focuses on the empirical study of law, including jury behavior. At the request of habeas counsel for Paul C. Bolin, I submit this declaration regarding the effects of pretrial publicity on Mr. Bolin's trial.

QUALIFICATIONS

2. I am presently the Russell M. Robinson II Professor of Law at Duke Law School and Professor of Psychology at Duke University. I earned my Ph.D. in Psychology at the University of Illinois in 1967 and joined the Duke Law faculty in 1987. I have served as the Research Director of Duke Law's Center for Criminal Justice and Ethical Responsibility since 2009. I am a Fellow of the Association for Psychological Science and an active member of the Law and Society Association, the American Psychology – Law Society (a division of the American Psychological Association), and the Society for Empirical Legal Studies. My curriculum vitae is attached to this Declaration as Appendix A.

3. I have researched juries and jury decision-making for over four decades. I have extensively studied malpractice litigation, punitive damages, dispute resolution, and the social psychology of retribution and revenge. I was co-principal investigator of the Arizona Jury Project, which taped and analyzed the actual deliberation of 50 civil juries. In addition to many articles, I am the co-author of *American Juries: The Verdict* (Prometheus

Books, 2007) and *Judging the Jury* (Plenum Press, 1986), and the author of *Medical Malpractice and the American Jury: Confronting the Myths About Jury Incompetence, Deep Pockets and Outrageous Damage Awards* (University of Michigan Press, 1995). I am the editor of *World Jury Systems* (Oxford University Press, 2000).

4. My scholarly interests extend to criminal law and jury behavior in criminal cases. I have conducted research and published articles in major law reviews and peer-reviewed psychology journals on the issue of pre- and mid-trial prejudice. I have published on topics including public opinion and the death penalty; jury bias in high-profile criminal cases; jury selection and the quest for impartial jurors; the use of survey research in litigating venue; and the impact of pretrial publicity on jurors. These publications and others are listed in my curriculum vitae, attached.

5. I have testified about jury prejudice and related issues in criminal and civil trials, including cases involving charges of terrorism. I conducted research on pretrial publicity for the trial of John Walker Lindh, the so-called "American Taliban," and subsequently tendered expert opinion for the Florida trial of Sami-Al-Arian, accused of supporting terrorism. I have testified or consulted about juries in Canada, England, Australia, New Zealand, and Hong Kong, and have testified before the United States Senate on issues relating to medical malpractice reform and damage awards. I have drafted amicus briefs on criminal matters before the U.S. Supreme Court and elsewhere.

6. I am thoroughly familiar with the state of social scientific knowledge about jury pretrial prejudice that existed at the time of Paul C. Bolin's 1990 capital murder trial. Current understanding of jury behavior and jury bias is based on psychological and sociological principles that were well-established at the time of the Bolin trial. Emile Durkheim, the father of modern sociology, pioneered the study of community responses to crimes in 1893. Modern social science research about trial prejudice began in the 1960s and early 1970s in response to trials involving the "Chicago Seven" and

subsequent trials involving protests against the war in Vietnam. My own involvement in studying trial prejudice predates the Bolin trial. *See, e.g.*, Rokeach, M. and Vidmar, N. *Testimony Concerning Possible Jury Bias in a Black Panther Murder Trial*, 3 Journal of Applied Social Psychology 19-29 (1973); Vidmar, N. and Ellsworth, P., *Public opinion and the death penalty*, 26 Stanford Law Review, 1245-1270 (1974); Berg, K., and Vidmar, N., *Authoritarianism and recall of evidence about Criminal Behavior*, 9 Journal of Research in Personality 147-157 (1975). Trial prejudice was the subject of a chapter in my co-authored book *Judging the Jury* (1986). As a researcher, scholar and teacher, I have maintained a thorough working knowledge of developments in this field since the 1970s.

PEOPLE V. PAUL C. BOLIN

7. At the request of habeas counsel, I have reviewed the following materials related to pretrial publicity and jury selection in the Kern County, California case of *People v. Paul C. Bolin*:

(1) the transcript of the November 1, 1990, hearing on change of venue motion;
(2) the Community Attitudes Survey prepared in relation to the change of venue motion;
(3) newspaper articles submitted as an exhibit to the venue motion (Petitioner's Exh. 53);
(4) the *America's Most Wanted* episode of January 7, 2990
(5) the Bakersfield Channel 29 report of January 8, 1990, regarding Mr. Bolin's arrest;
(6) the FOX broadcast of January 14, 1990, regarding Mr. Bolin's capture;
(7) a blank copy of the pretrial questionnaire;
(8) all of the pretrial questionnaires returned to the Court by prospective jurors, as provided to habeas counsel by Respondent (3368 pages);
(9) the transcripts of jury voir dire conducted for Mr. Bolin's trial;

(10) Petitioner's Opening Brief in Support of Writ of Habeas Corpus, pages 3-10 (Statement of Facts) and 19-63 (pretrial publicity and jury selection issues); and
(11) the Order Re: Petitioner's Request for an Evidentiary Hearing (dated 4/27/12).

8. I reviewed this material through the lens of what was known about the effects of pre-trial publicity in 1990.

Summary of Opinion

9. It is my professional opinion that the pretrial publicity in this case, including the *America's Most Wanted* ("*AMW*") television program of January 7, 1990, likely prejudiced the Kern County jury pool and prevented the selection of an impartial jury. The combination of factors in this case—media coverage portraying a dangerous Mr. Bolin as a threat to the residents of Kern County, national attention centered on the Bolin case through the *AMW* program, local news coverage of Mr. Bolin's case before and after the *AMW* program, the extent of community bias indicated by the Varinsky survey, and, especially important, the extent of bias uncovered during the *voir dire* process itself—casts serious doubt on the impartiality of the jury.

10. Had I been retained as an expert consultant at the time of jury selection, I would have advised defense counsel at the conclusion of voir dire that individual jurors' assurances of impartiality should not be accepted at face value. Because of the unacceptable level of exposure to pretrial publicity in Kern County and the likelihood of continuing bias among jurors, I would have advised defense counsel to renew the change of venue motion rather than accept the jury that was seated for Mr. Bolin's trial.

Analysis Underlying Opinion

Media Coverage About the Manhunt for Mr. Bolin

11. The newspaper, local television and radio reports regarding the man-

hunt for Mr. Bolin shortly after the shootings would unquestionably have caused gossip and concern among members of Kern County regarding their own safety and that of their families.

a. The September 4, 1989, issue of *The Californian* carried a report on the front page that was headlined, "Armed pair sought in deaths," followed by a heading on page A2, "Police seek armed and dangerous men."
b. On September 6, 1989, a *Californian* article was sub-headlined "Slayings: Suspect at large called Dangerous." That article also asserted that Mr. Bolin had been previously convicted of manslaughter; that he was trained as a Navy SEAL and was an explosives expert; that "pipe bombs were found in his cabin" and that the pipe bombs "had as much explosive power as a hand grenade."
c. The September 7, 1989, *Californian* article was headlined: "Murder suspect once convicted in shooting," and contained the assertion that Mr. Bolin had once shot a man in the chest with a shotgun and had been convicted of manslaughter. It also reported again that pipe bombs were found on the property where two men had been killed.
d. The September 8, 1989, article in *The Californian* was sub-headlined: "Tract near scene of double slaying."
e. A September 9, 1989, article in *The Californian* reported a police belief that Mr. Bolin might have fled the area. However, that report plus the initial reports had raised the specter of a very dangerous man being at large in the community—and implicitly posing a threat to the Kern County community.
f. Although no survey data of community awareness of the case at that time is available, it would be a rare community in which many of its citizens did not discuss a killer in their midst over the breakfast table and/or at work. Indeed, in 1893, Emile Durkheim, the father of modern sociology, drew attention to the effects of crime and the threat of crime on community gossip, *see* E. Durkheim, *The Division of Labor in Society* (G. Simpson Trans, 1967) (1893). Gordon Allport and Leo Postman elaborated these social and social psycho-

logical dynamics in a classic study in 1948. G. Allport and L. Postman, *The Psychology of Rumor* (1947).

12. My professional experience and research with community gossip and rumor in response to the effects of criminal events and alleged crimes goes back many decades and is consistent with the Durkheim and Allport and Postman analyses. *See, e.g.* Vidmar, N. and Melnitzer, J., *Juror Prejudice: An empirical study of a challenge for cause, 22* Osgoode Hall Law Journal 487-511 (1984); Hans and Vidmar, *Judging the Jury,* Chapter 5 (1986); and my peer-reviewed article, Vidmar, N., *Case Studies of Pre-and Midtrial Prejudice in Criminal and Civil Litigation* 26 Law and Human Behavior 73 (2002). Although *Case Studies of Pre-and Midtrial Prejudice in Criminal and Civil Litigation* was published subsequent to the Bolin case, it reviews many of my earlier professional experiences with pre-trial publicity. The Bolin case, in my professional opinion, falls clearly within the genre of cases that cause a high level of community concern and that result in substantial prejudice against the accused prior to trial.

13. Although important news events sometimes fade from public attention and discussion over time, something like the perceived threat to the community posed by the allegations against Mr. Bolin would not have faded even if intense discussion had stopped. Such threats are present in community memory and can be revived, especially when they are publicized by mass media. On January 6, 1990, *The Californian* drew attention to the fact that the *America's Most Wanted* program would focus on the "national hunt for killer of 2." The disclosure of the upcoming program would have, in my professional opinion, revived discussion of the Bolin manhunt among members of the community and caused more discussion, especially as it identified Mr. Bolin, a Kern County resident, as the center of a nationwide manhunt. Put bluntly, this had to be big news to the residents of Kern County.

The *America's Most Wanted* Program

14. It is especially important to emphasize the obvious fact that the *America's*

Most Wanted program (hereinafter *AMW*) was not a true depiction of how the events happened, but rather a dramatization that was, to say the least, highly unfavorable to Mr. Bolin. I will not analyze all the fact and fiction components of the *AMW* program here as they are analyzed in detail in Petitioner's Opening Brief in Support of Petition of Habeas Corpus (filed on *03/01107)* at pages 19 to 24. Having viewed the *AMW* program four times in preparation of this report, I am in complete agreement with that analysis, namely that it blends fact and fiction in a direction favorable to the deceased and highly unfavorable to Mr. Bolin. The entire narrative assumes Mr. Bolin's guilt, and portrays him as a coldblooded executioner. The program inspires fear and loathing of Mr. Bolin and sympathy for and identification with the victims. The fact that the real Mr. Wilson actually comments on the incident in the episode and in subsequent follow-up newscasts fosters the impression that the dramatization is accurate and should be accepted as fact.

15. *Primacy Effects: Seeing the Movie before Reading the Book.* For many viewers of the *AMW* episode, including the jurors on Mr. Bolin's jury, the highly likely effect of the AMW program was the equivalent of seeing a movie before reading the book—it is difficult to separate prior impressions drawn from the dramatization and subsequent evidence at trial. Further, in the Bolin case the effect cannot be separated from background impressions initially created during the manhunt for Mr. Bolin.

16. A large body of social psychological research on what is called the "primacy effect," first formulated in 1925 by Frederick Lund and demonstrated in hundreds and hundreds of subsequent studies, has found that the side of an issue presented first will very often cause subsequent information to be filtered through that first impression. *See, e.g.,* C. Hoveland, *The Role of Primacy and Recency in Persuasive Communication,* in S. Himmelfarb and A. Eagly, eds., *Readings in Attitude Change* (1974) at 262-274. In this instance, the fact that the *AMW* program presented an emotional picture of the victims, and portrayed Mr. Bolin as having a callous disregard for human life and having a propensity for violence, raises a very real possibility that the *AMW* program served as a lens through which trial evidence bearing on

guilt and on sentencing were filtered by the images held by the jurors who were exposed to the program. As I will discuss infra, at least seven of the jurors who served on Mr. Bolin's trial admitted that they had either seen the *AMW* program or had otherwise been exposed to publicity about the program or media reports about the manhunt preceding Mr. Bolin's arrest. Further, it is likely that their biased view had influence on the remaining jurors when deliberations began.

The Extent and Impact of Pre-trial Publicity in the Bolin Case, Especially Among those Persons Chosen as Jurors

17. The San Diego State University (SDSU) community attitudes survey of Kern County for the Bolin case, undertaken during the last week of September and first week of October 1990, provides additional insight about the combined impact of the initial (1989) newspaper coverage of the killings and the search for Mr. Bolin, the *AMW* program of January 1990, subsequent coverage of the program on local TV and of Mr. Bolin's arrest and his March 3, 1990, bail hearing. Although the survey was conducted approximately seven months after the last news account, it found that 45% of respondents reported that they were aware of the case and that half of these persons reported that they had seen the *AMW* program, with fully 66% reporting that they had seen or heard other media stories about the case. The SDSU report also found that of persons who had viewed the *AMW* program fully 77% had concluded that Mr. Bolin was guilty.

18. An examination of the actual voir dire proceedings in the Bolin case supports the SDSU survey figure regarding pretrial exposure to the case. A brief summary of the responses of prospective jurors during voir dire is contained in Appendix B, along with examples of some of the responses given to the court. Even though the voir dire resulted in a number of jurors being excused without any questioning about media exposure, fully 76 of 160 total persons (or 47.5% of all persons) admitted that they had seen the *AMW* program or had learned about it through the newspaper and or gossip with other persons (not to mention some who were reminded of it by the pretrial jury questionnaire that specifically drew attention

to the *AMW* program.)

19. The prospective juror questionnaire responses reflect an even greater level of exposure to pretrial publicity. (As noted above, not all jurors who completed questionnaires were asked about pretrial publicity on voir dire.) A tally of questionnaire responses is attached as Appendix C. Out of 161 completed questionnaires, 39 prospective jurors reported that they had seen the *AMW* episode about Mr. Bolin. Twenty-four out of those 39 had learned about the case from news reports as well as viewing *AMW*. Twenty-five of the same 39 had formed the opinion that Mr. Bolin was probably or definitely guilty. In addition to those 39, 24 other prospective jurors indicated they "maybe" had seen the program. Of those 24, 11 had also learned about the case from sources other than *AMW*. Of the jurors who had *not* seen the *AMW* episode, 35 had seen, heard, or read about the case from other sources. All told, 85 out of 161 questionnaires indicated awareness of the case from pretrial publicity. When these numbers are adjusted to include jurors whose questionnaires are not available but whose voir dire was transcribed, the number of media-exposed jurors rises to 87 out of 164, or 52% of respondents. If those who "maybe" saw *AMW* are included, the exposure rate may be as high as 101 out of 164, that is, 62% of respondents.

20. In my professional opinion the likely prejudicial impact of the AMW program was exacerbated by the structure of the questionnaire, which drew attention to the *AMW* program before jurors were even questioned by the judge. Such forewarning emphasized the fact and significance of the program and likely had the effect of causing the assembled jurors to talk about the case before being subjected to voir dire. Many trial lawyers, in my experience, are very aware of potential juror discussions in the jury assembly room when high profile cases are involved, and ask about whether such discussions have taken place prior to being questioned. That did not happen in this case. As a result, the pretrial questionnaire had the rough effect of what is known as a "push-pull" survey—that is, the questions themselves helped to push at least some of the jurors in a particular direction, namely to favor

the prosecution over the defense. *See generally,* P. Marsden and J. Wright, eds., *Handbook of Survey Research,* 2nd ed. (2010) at 20. Any assembly room discussion would have contaminated other jurors.

21. The most relevant and striking finding regarding the pretrial publicity can be gleaned from the voir dire responses of persons who actually were chosen and served as the jurors for Mr. Bolin's trial.

a. Juror Gilbert Barnes, RT 93, said he believed Mr. Bolin was definitely guilty "because of the write up in the paper."
b. Juror Jeannie Lee, RT 238, indicated that she had heard about the case and believed she had seen the *AMW* episode or someone told her about it. Strikingly, instead of following up on what Ms. Lee knew and her opinions about it, the Court's next question began, "Right now I don't think you do know much about this case, and what you know may be wrong ...." RT 240. In my professional opinion, this very likely put Juror Lee in a difficult position in which she felt she had to concede that she had no biases, even if that was not the state of her mind.
c. Juror Michael Vaughn stated that he had seen the *AMW* broadcast about the Bolin case. The reason that he was interested in the program was that it was in Kern County. RT 362. He had also read about the case in the newspaper. RT 363. Mr. Vaughn further conceded that in the pretrial questionnaire he had written that Mr. Bolin was "probably guilty" and that "they wouldn't have arrested him if he probably—you know, it is evident that they have something to believe that he is guilty. It doesn't mean he is guilty but -." He subsequently conceded his belief in Mr. Bolin's guilt stemmed from a combination of the fact that Bolin had been arrested and the television segment he had seen. RT 363-365.
d. Juror Dale Eyraud Cambbell remembered seeing the *AMW* program and also saw something about the case on TV and knew something about the case from the newspaper, but she stated that she believed that she could be impartial. RT 1005-1006. Defense counsel

did not follow up with further questions about her initial concession. (A subsequent defense challenge for cause was denied.)
e. Juror Julie Hanson, RT 1092, saw the *AMW* episode and also saw the case reported on local television news and "probably" in the newspaper. She was not questioned about whether and how this fact might have influenced her opinion prior to hearing evidence.
f. Juror Patricia Hinson, RT 1011, reported that she saw the *AMW* episode. She recalled it contained information about a "homicide and another shooting" and "marijuana farming and that "One suspect in the case had fled." Upon examination by Mr. Soria, RT 1120, Juror Hinson stated that some of her knowledge about the case also came from the *Californian*. However, then she stated that she remembered nothing from the TV episode itself. (A defense challenge for cause was denied, but again defense counsel failed to follow up on her initial concession.)
g. Juror Beverley Lauer, RT 1142, heard about the case "when it happened," but did not see the *AMW* program. She was asked if she read the newspapers and said yes, but was not asked specifically about whether she had read about the Bolin case or if she had formed any opinions about the case.
h. Juror Robert Bowles testified that he had seen the *AMW* program, RT 1396, but stated that he did not pay much attention to it because it was his kids who were watching the show. But he also recalled reading about it in the newspaper and seeing television reports, including seeing television reports of Mr. Bolin being returned to California "when they were escorting him." However, Juror Bowles also stated that "everybody has their day in court and if a person has not been convicted or proven guilty, I don't feel that they should be shown on that program because it's exactly what they are saying." Again, there was no attempt by the Court or by defense counsel to follow up on this ambiguous statement by a juror.
i. Juror John Medina said he did see the *AMW* program on his questionnaire, but in voir dire said he thought he did not. RT 1422. Juror Medina then said he recognized the Bolin name from what he saw

in the paper or on TV, but believed he could put whatever he heard in the media out of his mind.

22. Despite these obvious flags about lack of impartiality, all of the above jurors were coached by the judge or the prosecutor into saying that they could be fair despite the impact of the pretrial publicity. For example, Juror Gilbert Barnes RT 91):

Q. Now, do you believe everything you read in the newspaper?

A. No, your honor.

Q. Do you even believe everything you see on television?

A. No, your Honor.

And at RT 92:

Q. We do not want to try this case in the courtroom. We don't want to try it in the newspaper or the television for the very reasons that you suggest. Do you have any quarrel with trying a case in the courtroom and not in the newspaper?

A. That is where it is supposed to be tried.

And at RT 94:

Q. And is that—is that because you have now reflected and don't know anything about this case except what you have read or heard?

A. Basically, yes.

Q. You, see, it would be wrong for you to compare what you read or heard in the newspaper or the television with what you heard and saw in this courtroom, because that's not evidence at all. That's some reporter's view of this, and they like to sell newspapers. We want you to decide this case in the courtroom. Do you think you can do that?

A. I think I could, yes.

Juror Michael Vaughn provides another example (at RT 366):

Q. [from the Court]: Let me ask you this question: If you were down here where

Mr. Bolin is charged with these crimes, keeping in mind what you have seen on the television and read in the newspaper, would you be satisfied to have a person with your present frame of mind sitting on your jury?

A. I suppose so.

23. These examples are typical of the process by which media-exposed jurors were led to assert that they would be impartial. Given the nature and extent of the pretrial publicity in this case, it is not a process by which actual impartiality can be assured. Be clear that I am not asserting that the judge did something wrong; part of the judge's job is to be hortatory to the jurors. However, this process of juror rehabilitation, in my professional opinion as a social psychologist, exerted psychological pressures on each of the jurors to state they could be impartial, even if they had personal doubts. In a slightly different context the exchange between the Court and the juror would be characterized as subjecting a witness to leading questions.

24. Social psychologists have long recognized what is labeled "socially desirable" responses to questions—that is, the tendency of people to respond with answers that are consistent with what they believe is the appropriate response, even when it does not reflect their true attitudes and beliefs. *See, e.g.,* Crowne and Marlowe, *The Approval Motive: Studies in Evaluative Dependence* (1964). Especially in public settings, people often provide "socially desirable" responses when they may not be consciously aware of their actual beliefs. *See* Nisbett and Wilson, *Telling More Than We Can Know: Verbal Reports on Mental Process,* 84 Psychological Review 231 (1977). In my professional opinion, those social psychological conditions were especially likely to be prevalent when a layperson, inexperienced and uncomfortable in a courtroom, was seated alone and questioned by a robed judge in front of other court personnel.

25. In my experience observing the voir dire process over many years, and on some occasions interviewing jurors afterward, it is clear that prospective jurors for high profile cases are often not forthcoming about their true beliefs simply because they are intimidated by the courtroom setting or are unaware of why it is important to express their true attitudes and beliefs to the court. Indeed, I am not the only social scientist to draw this conclusion. Other examples are collected in my review article: Vidmar, *Case Studies of Pre-and Midtrial Prejudice in Criminal and Civil Litiga-*

tion, 26 Law & Human Behavior 73 (2002). Although that article was published more than a decade after the Bolin trial, it relied heavily on research from the 1980s and 1990s *(see, e.g.,* references to Bronson, 1989; Graham et al, 1997; Greene and Loftus, 1984; Mullin et al. 1996; Nietzel and Dillehay, 1982; Studebaker and Penrod, 1997; Vidmar and Judson, 1981; Vidmar and Melnitzer, 1984).

26. As a law professor and jury expert I recognize that voir dire questioning, including hortatory questioning, by judges and lawyers, is a necessary part of the legal process going back centuries. However, provisions for changes of venue have an equally long legal history. Sometimes, the law recognizes pretrial publicity and local public interests in the outcome of a trial are so powerful that hortatory questioning is insufficient to remove the taint of prejudice; the goal of a fair trial requires moving the proceedings to a venue other than the community where the alleged crime occurred.

27. As noted above, the transcript of the voir dire process in this case reveals almost no attempt by defense counsel to follow-up and explore the originally stated biases of the jurors. In my professional experience working with defense lawyers over many years, I find this omission mystifying and inexcusable.

28. Furthermore, in my professional opinion, that defense counsel failed to renew the motion for a change of venue is mystifying—especially in light of the fact that the Court indicated that such a motion would be considered after the voir dire process.

29. There is a line of cases dating back to the 1960s that outlines standards bearing on jury taints from pretrial publicity. Jury experts like myself are always conscious of the guidelines set forth in *Irvin v. Dowd,* 366 U.S. 717 (1961) and *Rideau v. State of Louisiana,* 373 U.S. 723 (1963). Judge Nancy Gertner and Judith H. Mizner have summarized these two cases in *The Law of Juries,* 5th ed. (2011) at 75-82, as follows:

"*Irvin* emphasized the quantitative aspect of the publicity, namely that it was so pervasive and so intensive as to disqualify the whole community and to require a change of venue. *Rideau* emphasized the qualitative aspect of the publicity, holding that the circulation in a given community of certain information, like a defendant's detailed confession, disqualified the community from serving on the jury ....

"In the face of exposure to publicity of this sort, *Irvin*-like or *Rideau*-like jurors' disclaimers of partiality would not be conclusive."

30. Gertner and Mizner's assertion is consistent with social science research regarding juror behavior. Several social and psychological mechanisms have been identified to explain the fact that a juror may profess impartiality while harboring actual bias: the juror may not be aware of his or her prejudices; the juror may be aware but uncomfortable in admitting biases in public or just simply downplay them in what has been labeled a "minimization effect;" or the juror may not admit them because he or she wants to be chosen as a juror in order to "do justice." The relevant literature is reviewed in my *Case Studies* article, *supra,* at 92-99.

31. In summary, a majority of members of the Bolin jury began to hear trial evidence filtered through their expressed biases and/or through the lens of a biased narrative provided by pretrial publicity. It is quite possible that some of the other jurors in the Bolin trial may have had similar biased views, but their true attitudes were not explored by defense counsel during voir dire. In any event, the Bolin jury began deliberations with a majority of members biased by these influences, and they very likely contaminated the remaining jurors during deliberations. Social psychologists who study group behavior have long documented what is.called the "polarization effect." To wit, when a substantial number of members of a group begin with biases leaning in a particular direction, rather than averaging their biases they reinforce each other's beliefs, and as a group make decisions that are more extreme than the statistical average of the individual members' biases. *See, e.g.,* Isenberg, D.I., *Group Polarization: A Critical Review and Meta-Analysis,* Journal of Personality and Social Psychology 50 (6): 1141-1151 (1986). This process can and

does take place in the jury context. *See* Kalven and Zeisel, *The American Jury* (1966), pp. 488-489. In Mr. Bolin's case, it is likely that instead of weighing the issues of guilt and of punishment as separate individuals, the group dynamics moved jurors to weight inculpating evidence more heavily than any exonerating evidence.

32. This effect of bias on the jury's deliberative process was entirely predictable in light of the pretrial publicity in this case, the degree to which the jury pool was exposed to *America's Most Wanted* and local news coverage, and the extent of bias expressed in prospective jurors' questionnaires and during voir dire. Given these circumstances, and in light of social psychological principles that were well-established at the time of the Bolin trial, the assurances of individual jurors that they would set aside the influence of the media and/or their own initial biases should not have been credited.

33. In my professional opinion, the views expressed by the jurors on their questionnaires and during the voir dire process, long-standing case law, the Court's earlier invitation to renew the change of venue motion following voir dire, and just plain lawyer common sense, should have caused Mr. Bolin's defense counsel to renew the application for a change of venue to a neutral community. Had I been retained as a jury consultant for the defense at the time of trial, I would have so advised.

CONCLUSION

34. For all the reasons explained above, it is my professional opinion that the pretrial publicity in this case likely prejudiced the Kern County jury pool and prevented the selection of an impartial jury. Had I been retained as an expert consultant at the time of jury selection, I would have strongly advised defense counsel at the conclusion of voir dire that individual jurors' assurances of impartiality should not be accepted at face value. Because of the unacceptable level of exposure to prejudicial publicity and the likelihood of continuing bias among the jurors, I would have advised defense counsel to renew the change of venue motion rather than accept the jury that was seated for Mr. Bolin's trial.

I declare under penalty of perjury that the foregoing is true and correct. Signed this __ day of ________, 2012.

Neil Vidmar, Ph.D.

6

Law Professors

BY LAURIE L. LEVENSON

"Grab Levenson, she's all we've got."

—CBS News Producer
Rodney King Trial 1994

Introduction

In my wildest dreams, I never thought I would be a television commentator. I left trial practice for academia secure in the belief that I would be sheltered from the spotlight of the public and courtroom, safe to ponder great thoughts behind the ivy walls. But, as they say, "People plan, God laughs." When the Rodney King trial hit Los Angeles, the ivy walls came crashing down. I went from nerdy law professor to legal expert overnight. How? I was there. I showed up to watch the federal trial of four Los Angeles Police Department officers charged with beating African American motorist Rodney King. As soon as I arrived, reporting started to ask questions. Because I was willing to answer them, I became an instant legal commentator. Although I thought the experience would be one of a kind, once my phone number made it into the reporters' Rolodexes, I was asked to comment on many other trials. Legal commentators never die; they just become too old for television. Then we move to radio and print.

In the last twenty years, law professors have found their niche as commentators on some of the country's most high-profile cases. Whether it is the murder trial of O. J. Simpson or the impeachment trial of former president Bill Clinton, the airwaves have teemed with professors offering their insights on legal and quasi-legal proceedings. Reporters rarely report on legal matters without seeking insights from law professors. Some professors just provide background for the reporters; others are on-air commentators covering a case gavel to gavel. Even those professors who have never practiced law may be asked to comment on a case. For today's law professors, a phone call from the press has become nearly as routine as a question from a student.

Initially, professors may be fascinated or intimidated by this very public role. There is little or no training in law school for lawyers, let alone professors, as to how to interact with the media. Professors are thrust into a milieu in which they do not necessarily control the message that is conveyed. Their thoughts are reduced to sound bites, rather than 100-page law review articles. There is little time to research issues, and the information provided may be relied upon by literally millions of individuals.

Yet, despite the challenges, law professors have become critical to accurate reporting of legal proceedings. Most journalists have never attended law school. Their understanding of the law derives from basic government and civics class. Television law dramas dominate the public's understanding of how the justice system works. Public polls have repeatedly shown that the public is remarkably ignorant about the legal system. One such poll indicates that less than 50 percent of Americans can name even one U.S. Supreme Court Justice.[1] Law professors have an important role to play in educating the public on all aspects of the legal system, from the Supreme Court to the most basic cases in criminal and civil trial courts.

This chapter will focus on the history and role of law professors in interacting with the media—how they contribute to the reporting of cases and what their proper role is. Then, it will discuss the pros and cons of a professor serving in this role. The chapter will then offer some practical advice for professors who choose to serve as legal commentators. Finally, the chapter offers some ethical guidelines for professors who choose to serve as legal commentators and new avenues for professors to influence the public's understanding of the law.

---

1. *The Invisible Court*, Pew Research Center (Aug. 3, 2010).

The History and Role of Legal Commentators

The role of legal commentators can be traced back to the time of Sir William Blackstone. Blackstone, who was not himself a star of the bar, developed his famous Commentaries on the Laws of England based upon his observations of other lawyers' cases. Yet, the current practice of legal commentators is a relatively new phenomenon. In 1984, Harvard Law professors Arthur R. Miller and Charles R. Nesson made headlines when they agreed to moderate roundtable discussions on legal topics for the Public Broadcasting System. These two professors embraced a confrontational style that made "it possible to stop people who are very important (from providing) baloney answers" to critical questions."[2] The roundtables focused more on important legal issues than ongoing cases, but their television segments did engage legal experts on a range of topics, from the death penalty to the insanity plea to a defendant's right to a fair trial.

The 1990s marked the birth of the modern-day era of law professors serving as legal commentators. As the media expanded and television stations focused on ongoing trials, law professors were asked to help reporters cover high-profile cases. Within five years, the media covered the two Rodney King beating trials, the prosecution of the Menendez brothers for killing their parents, and the infamous O. J. Simpson murder trial and companion civil trial. Over 1,400 journalists received credentials to cover these cases, and they began to rely regularly on professors as legal commentators.

The specific role of a professor as a legal commentator has never been firmly established. Law professors can interact with the media in a myriad of ways. On the most basic level, nearly all law professors have had the occasion to answer their phone and answer a question for a reporter. Professors may be asked to explain the applicable law, anticipate litigation strategy, critique a court's ruling, or explain the court's procedures. Sometimes, the professor will provide information "on background" (that is, not for attribution); other times, the professor's quoted comments may play a prominent role in the story.

---

2. The Harvard Crimson, *Two Law Professors Host TV Show*, www.crimson.com/article/1984/10/17two-law-professors-host (last visited June 16, 2013).

Yet, the role of professors as legal commentators that has garnered the most attention has been professors appearing on television, or radio, or as a regular columnist to cover an ongoing legal proceeding. Today, law professors are regularly called upon to appear as on-air guests to discuss highly visible trials. The professor may be a co-anchor with a journalist or one of a panel of experts. The show may be edited or live. The program may be an in-depth examination of a legal issue or the programmatic equivalent of a food fight in which the professor is set up to spar with another guest with contrary opinions.

The role of a professor as a legal commentator that has sparked the most criticism has been professors who provide the equivalent of play-by-play commentary regarding a case. Although some commentators just seek to interpret the proceedings for the viewing or listening audience, others are akin to sideline quarterbacks willing to skewer the judge or lawyers for their missteps. Their so-called analysis of a case suggests that the outcome of a case can be measured by the number of objections sustained or the fury with which a lawyer attacks a witness. Of course, legal proceedings, especially trials, are more than just the sum of their parts. Litigants who are successful one day may ultimately lose a case because of developments the very next day. Yet, the professor is used to keep the public informed as to how effectively each side is presenting its case. The professor may be retained by a specific media outlet or make himself available to a sea of journalists who attend proceedings and want the professor's analysis.

Finally, there is a growing role for law professors to comment on cases by writing legal blogs, op-eds, or even agreeing to contemporaneously tweet their comments regarding a case. The explosion of information outlets has created unlimited options for professors to disseminate their opinions on legal matters. Professors can comment instantaneously on a range of legal issues or use these outlets to write more in-depth analyses of timely legal issues.

The specific role of a professor as a legal commentator will depend on the setting in which that professor is providing commentary. However, there are some basic functions and responsibilities that all commentators share. First, legal commentators are expected to know the law. This may be tougher than it sounds. Professors tend to be experts in specific areas. Even the most brilliant contracts professor is unlikely to be versed in the intricacies of the criminal justice system. Moreover, even a criminal law professor is unlikely to know the laws of all jurisdictions or the strategy for trying every type of criminal case. Journalists, who themselves have never been to law school, are unlikely to appreciate the fact that a law professor is not an expert on all matters. Thus, the responsibility falls on the professor to serve as a legal commentator only on matters for which he or she is actually an expert.

Next, legal commentators are expected to be good teachers. Much of the job of serving as a legal commentator is to put into layperson's language the workings of the law. One of the key reasons law professors are selected as legal commentators is that they generally have the ability to take difficult concepts and break them down for the listener. Yet, it still requires a particular skill for any commentator to sum up complicated matters in a sound bite or two.

Legal commentators are also expected to perform the role of being a guide to the journalists covering a case. For many journalists, the most difficult challenge in covering a legal matter is to know what questions to ask. Legal commentators can quickly assess a legal issue, explain to the reporter what will be important to its outcome, and direct the reporter to sources that will help in the coverage of the case.

Finally, legal commentators are expected to be a voice other than those of the adversaries involved in a case. What that means is that there is often an assumption that the law professor covering a case will be objective in his or her evaluation. In practice, this may not prove to be true, but commentators are perceived as experts who have little or no stake in the outcome of a case other than to see that "justice is done."

Although the specific functions of professors as legal commentators may vary, the basic role is to be the voice of knowledge and reason during the coverage of a case. The only difference is that their media audience may be a class of millions.

Pros and Cons of Serving as a Legal Commentator

It is open for debate whether it is appropriate and worthwhile for professors to serve as legal commentators. Colleagues' reactions may range from curiosity to jealousy. For some, it is beneath the stature of a professor to serve as a "pundit" for the press. Others recognize legal commentary as an important way in which professors can have an impact on the actual workings of our legal system.

As with other types of endeavors, some professors are better suited to provide legal commentary than others, and one's opinion of legal commentators can be influenced greatly by the commentator he or she has seen in action. Take, for example, the legal commentators who covered the O. J. Simpson murder trial. Each of the major networks selected commentators to assist with their coverage. Most chose professors and practitioners with established legal reputations. CNN, however, selected Patty Hearst, the heiress who was convicted of committing bank robberies with the Symbionese Liberation Army, to provide its color commentary on Simpson's preliminary hearing. What was her in-depth analysis of the case? Ignorant of the actual workings of the law, she opined that the judge looked terrible in her robe and "nattily draped scarf and pearls." Anyone can be Chyroned as a legal commentator, but the title alone does not make a person a legal expert. It is how that person performs the role.

Reasons for Professors to Serve as Legal Commentators

Most professors accidentally fall into the role of a legal commentator. It starts by answering questions, and then the next thing the professor knows, he or she is doing so on radio or television. Yet, if one were actually to think carefully about whether this is a role a professor should perform, there are many arguments in support of having professors as legal commentators.

Providing objective, honest commentary

First, professors generally have the freedom to provide an objective perspective on the case. Unlike counsel for the parties who are expected to be zealous advocates for their clients, professors have the luxury to "call them as they see them." In doing so, professors can give the viewer or reader an honest assessment of a case. The freedom to tell the truth should never be underestimated. Unless a professor is anticipating a judicial confirmation hearing, he or she can criticize individuals and institutions in a way that is rare for others in society. A professor has the background and liberty to let the public know when the search for justice has gone off track. Professors can make the most of the First Amendment right to critically report on and examine our government institutions, including our courts. It will be up to the individual professor how candid to be about a judge's ruling, but the professor will certainly have more leeway than others involved in the case.

Keeping one foot in the real world

Second, providing legal commentary allows professors to keep one foot in the real world, which can enhance the professor's work in the so-called ivory tower. There are relatively few legal issues that can be viewed completely in the abstract. Even those professors who stick to the most esoteric aspects of the law must regularly do a reality check to determine whether abstract principles are relevant to our legal processes. Providing legal commentary not only allows professors to provide the legal standards that are supposed to govern the outcome of a case, it reminds professors how their theoretical work will have an impact on the legal world. Some of the most renowned professors have written entire books on high-profile cases they have observed. Moreover, the issues that arise in current cases help professors focus on issues for further study both in and out of the courtroom. Abstract principles come alive for students, and, together with the professor, students can follow the development of the law.

Developing new teaching skills

Third, the job of a professor is to teach. For many professors, the size of their classes will range from a seminar of a dozen students to a lecture hall of over 100 students. Legal commentary is still teaching; it is just that the camera lens expands the size of the classroom to millions of viewers. The best commentators are those who can boil down complex legal issues into concepts that can be grasped by those who are unschooled in the law. Unlike in law school where legal concepts are often deconstructed and thereby made more complex, the process of legal commentary is to deconstruct concepts and make them simpler. As a legal commentator, a law professor must present the black letter law while still giving the listening audience an appreciation of the subtleties and contingencies in the law. The discipline of serving as a legal commentator can often help a professor fine-tune lessons inside the classroom and anticipate where students will be confused and challenged.

Raising a professor's and a law school's visibility

Fourth, law professors enjoy providing legal commentary because it is often more exciting than the daily rigor of classes and faculty committees. Professors who engage in legal commentary typically garner a great deal of recognition. Of course, it is unlikely that anyone will confuse a law professor with a movie star, but a professor's ego is undoubtedly stroked by the "Hey, aren't you Professor So-and-So" while standing in the grocery checkout line. Everyone, including professors, craves public recognition. In the media realm, the professor is transformed from the legal geek to the legal star. Some professors will also profit financially from providing legal commentary. Although most legal commentators are not paid, those who are hired to provide regular legal commentary or have an exclusive arrangement with a media outlet can receive very tangible rewards for their efforts. Lastly, a professor's role as a legal commentator may help bring greater notoriety to his or her institution. Relatively unknown legal institutions can become household names once a professor from that law school provides regular commentary.

Impacting outcome of cases

Fifth, professors can actually make an impact on a case or the law by providing legal commentary. It is not unheard of for judges to read the comments of professors regarding a pending legal issue and pay attention to those opinions when reaching their decisions. During a trial, judges are inundated with decisions to make and little time (and sometimes little expertise) to make those decisions. On the other hand, a professor may be very familiar with an issue and can offer instantaneous guidance on a complex legal issue. Judges and their clerks may rely on this information in reaching their decisions.

A professor's comments can also lead to legal reforms, including legislative changes. For example, recent changes in the ABA Standards for Criminal Justice, DNA testing protocols, and prosecution discovery rules have all been sparked by legal commentary. More importantly, the willingness of professors who have provided such commentary to continue working toward these legal reforms has been critical to leading to substantive changes in the law. It is no secret that the media provides a professor with a bully pulpit from which to call for changes in the courts and the law. Law professors who understand this have an important vehicle for actualizing their ideas for legal reform.

Engaging in professional dialogue

Finally, the most recent type of legal commentary—such as that found on legal blogs and social networking sites—offers professors an avenue to engage in legal discourse with other professors interested in similar issues. Today, there are legal blogs that cover everything from constitutional law to tax law reform. This form of legal commentary is the modern-day equivalent of legal colloquia without participants having to travel long distances to engage each other in discussion.

As described, there are many benefits to both society and the professor in serving as a legal commentator. Of course, whether any individual professor enjoys such benefits will depend on the nature of his or her commentary and the specific arrangements the professor has made with the media. Increasingly, professors are recognizing these benefits and making themselves available to do legal commentary.

Perils of Law Professors Serving as Legal Commentators

Although having law professors serve as legal commentators provides many advantages to the professor and the media, there are downsides as well. Before jumping into the world of the Fourth Estate, it is best to know the downsides of serving in such a role. There can be significant personal and professional costs when entering the very visible world of legal commentary.

"But I Have Real Work To Do"

Perhaps the foremost peril of becoming a legal commentator is losing a substantial amount of control over your life. The media works on deadlines, and those deadlines can interfere with other work of the law professor. Coordinating teaching and legal commentary can be a Herculean task. When working on a high-profile case, a professor may end up working from approximately 5:00 a.m. (to cover the morning shows) to 11:00 p.m. (to cover the late-night news). If the media finds a commentator they like, they will be relentless in seeking commentary from that individual, and there will be very little time for the professor to enjoy other pursuits, at least during the period of that case.

Once engaging with the media, it can be difficult to set limits. These limits include both time of availability and what subject matter the commentator will address. An unsophisticated reporter may call upon a professor to answer questions regarding areas of the law way beyond the professor's expertise. It is the responsibility of the professors to let the media know both when they can answer questions about a case and what kinds of questions they cannot answer.

"But That Is Not What I Said"

One of the greatest challenges in serving as a legal commentator is that the law professor does not necessarily control the content of his or her remarks. Unless a professor is offering live commentary, some editor—who has absolutely no legal training at all and who may be far more interested in ratings than accuracy—has the final power to edit the professor's statements. Misquotations in newspapers are not unusual. A professor's verbal remarks may be edited to a sound bite that may actually contradict what the professor originally said. Consider, for example, the media editing a professor's statement, "It is better that 12 guilty men go free than that one innocent man be convicted," to "It is better that 12 guilty men go free."

Professor Michael Mogill accurately warned:

> Most of us strive for some degree of control over our daily lives. . . . As law professors, we tend to have more control over our envi-

> ronment than practitioners, except for the occasional "zinger" of a question, which can sometimes be mirrored back for possible "answers." The call from a reporter can easily move us from our comfort zone. We are asked to answer questions at that very moment or soon thereafter, with our pronouncements then being carried live over the airwaves. . . . How does the commentator cope with giving up such control?[3]

Professors do not have much way to control an editor who wishes to alter their remarks, nor is it easy for professors to retract a comment given in a live broadcast once they realize that their opinion was based upon inadequate information from the reporter. The nature of news does not provide for the luxury of time or retakes. Given the constant crush of deadlines, professors are on the hot seat to provide instantaneous and hopefully accurate commentary.

"That's The Wrong Question"

Professors are used to asking questions, but as a legal commentator, the roles are reversed. One of the most difficult things for a professor to do is to answer a dumb question without making the questioner sound or feel dumb. For example, during the O. J. Simpson case, one network anchor asked a law professor, "So, how will this case affect the situation in Bosnia?" Other than saying, "Gee, that's a fascinating question," there is not much else the professor can say. One of the key roles that professors can and should be playing as commentators is to guide the reporters to the right questions.

During my years as a commentator, I have kept track of the 10 worst questions asked by reporters. (Hopefully, they have not been keeping track of the 10 worst answers I have provided.) Here they are:

> Which side is winning? (asked before any evidence was presented)

---

3. Michael A. Mogill, *Academic TROs: How to Prevail in the Court of Public Opinion*, 27 N.M. L. Rev. 473, 479 (1997).

What are the jurors thinking?
Why would the witness say that if it weren't true?
Why is the judge so impatient?
Why is the witness wearing chiffon?
How many of the 12 jurors do you need for a unanimous verdict?
Will the government appeal?
Would you help us contact the jurors? (while the case is still pending)
Is there justice?
In the next 10 seconds, can you sum up this 10-month long case for us?

The best legal commentators control the questions as well as the answers. They let the reporters know ahead of time what issues should be explored and how questions should be phrased. Without such guidance, interviews can often run amok.

"You Have A Face For Radio"

Face it, not every professor has the looks that the media wants for television coverage. Television worships the young and beautiful. Some professors may fit that description, but others may not. The media wants professors who fit the image that they are trying to create. They want attractive yet studious. Young but seasoned. Approachable but distinguished. Therefore, it is not unheard of for the media to ask a professor to don glasses (instead of contact lens) so that the professor looks the role of a studious expert. It is also common for the media to seek out a "young, fresh face," even if that individual has relatively little actual legal experience. For many professors, it is considered demeaning to be judged more on one's appearance than the content of one's remarks. However, that is very much the nature and reality of at least television commentary.

"I Sound Like An Idiot"

Many professors are not used to speaking in sound bites and find it challenging, to say the least, to answer complex questions in seven to nine seconds. Professors may resort to legalese and lose the audience altogether. Worse yet, they may try to answer a question without really understanding what is being asked. The resulting answer then sounds like an out-of-touch pontification by an out-of-touch academic. It takes practice to answer questions, and professors do not regularly receive practice or training in doing legal commentary. Rather, they are thrown in and learn only by practice (and mistakes).

"I Thought That Is What They Wanted"

Professors are not above sensationalizing a case, especially once they recognize that is what the reporters want. The professor who uses inflammatory language or quickly predicts the outcome of a case is more likely to be invited to be a guest on a program than one who appears too deliberative or cautious. Perhaps this can be referred to as the "Nancy Grace Phenomenon," but there are professors, just like other legal commentators, who are more interested in being seen and heard than being respected.

"My Colleagues All Hate Me"

Professors who becomes legal commentators should not assume that their fellow faculty members will praise their work. Whether it is jealousy or a genuine belief that it is inappropriate for professors to engage in legal commentary, some professors come under criticism by their colleagues for venturing into the world of the media. Professors who would not give a second thought to a professor needing a semester free to research and write on an obscure issue of the law will readily scoff at the proposal that a professor be given a lighter teaching load in order to provide legal commentary. Legal commentary is generally not viewed as a scholarly pursuit, and a professor who provides too much of it may be deemed a lightweight in academic circles.

"Why Do All Of These People Hate Me?"

I have a special drawer in my office that is labeled "Look Here First If I Am Killed." The drawer is brimming with hate letters from people who have seen my commentary. Perhaps the most notable one reads as follows:

> *To Laurie Levenson*
>
> *Every time I saw your face on t.v., I felt like shooting you. How do you feel about two decent policemen being in prison, while a criminal—Rodney King, is free.*
>
> *Anyone who drives 110 miles an hour, on drugs, drunk, lunges at police, resists arrest deserves to be beaten to a pulp. I pray every day that one of these drunks hits you, and kills or injures you. Or one rapes you. . . .*
>
> *Wait till you need the police. I think all the police should quit and see how . . . jerks like you get along. I hope God punishes you.*

Public figures are targets for anyone in society who does not like their opinions. Professors are no different. In fact, we are much easier to locate because we are affiliated with particular teaching institutions. Although most of those who call or write with negative comments are completely harmless, it only takes one obsessive opponent to put a professor at risk. I try not to let this worry affect my commentary, but it is yet another peril of being a legal commentator.

"You Are A Disgrace to the Profession"

Finally, there is the criticism that it is demeaning to the role of a professor to opine regarding ongoing legal matters. Some people prefer for their professors to remain "above the fray," by staying out of the public limelight. Professors become "talking heads" or "pundits" when they move from the classroom to the media's spotlight. Some of the most vehement attacks come from judges who are uncomfortable with law professors second-guessing their decisions. In high-profile cases, legal commentators have been called "jackals" or worse.

Notwithstanding these perils, it is probably a public service for professors to continue to interact with the media. The truth is that professors frequently know more about the law than even the judges presiding over the cases. Moreover, professors have the resources to quickly research legal issues, and many are experts in areas of the law that are rarely handled by judges. If professors view their interactions with the media as a form of teaching, and one that demands excellence, then the benefits of providing such commentary are likely to outweigh the detriments.

Dealing Effectively with the Media

How, then, should professors most effectively deal with the media? Assuming that the professor's goal is to provide the most accurate commentary possible, there are a few key rules to remember:

Rule 1: Be Honest, Be Competent, Be Fair

This seems like such a basic rule, but it is one that commentators appear to compromise every day. The duty to be honest begins with admitting to reporters whether one is indeed knowledgeable enough about a topic to comment intelligently on it. Professors are not used to saying, "I don't know," but the truth is that they may not know more about a topic than even the reporter who calls. The basic duty to be honest includes a professor only offering commentary if he or she is competent to do so.

To be competent, commentators must possess the substantive knowledge and practical experience necessary to comment accurately regarding a proceeding. There are many ways professors can become competent to comment on a matter. They may attend or watch the proceedings, read pleadings, or even get third-hand reports regarding a case. But it is imperative that the commentators actually know both the facts and laws at issue. This means that if a professor is from another jurisdiction he or she must study the laws of the jurisdiction in which the action is taking place. Pontificating about law in the abstract rarely provides the type of commentary that will be helpful to the public.

One criticism frequently made of legal commentators is that they do not have extensive trial practice in the same type of case for which they are providing commentary. Experience as a practicing lawyer can certainly be helpful in providing commentary, but is not always a prerequisite. A commentator can certainly discuss the meaning of a legal code without having served for years as a trial lawyer. However, before a commentator remarks regarding legal strategy, that person should at least be expected to know the actual operations of the courts.

Finally, there is the responsibility to be fair. Being fair does not necessarily mean that the commentator must give equal credence to both sides of a case. However, it does mean considering counterarguments before presenting his or her opinions to the media. The advocates always have an opportunity to spin their views of the case to the media. The most helpful role of a professor as a commentator is to consider all views before offering an opinion.

Rule 2: Reveal Conflicts of Interests

Although professors should strive to be objective in their comments, they should also recognize that they might have a conflict of interest that will influence their commentary. This conflict does not necessarily disqualify a professor from serving as a legal commentator, but the conflict should be disclosed so that those relying on the legal commentary know how to judge its credibility.

Conflicts of interest can take several forms. First, there are the conflicts that may be created by the commentator's relationship with any of the lawyers or a judge in a case. To the extent that a professor is consulting on the side with one of the parties in an action, that relationship should be disclosed to the public and the reporter. The public assumes that the law professor is assessing a case fairly because that individual does not have a stake in the outcome of the case. If the commentator has another agenda, the audience should know.

Second, commentators may develop a conflict because they have other types of stakes in the outcome of a proceeding or ruling on a legal issue. Although academic freedom can help alleviate some of these concerns, a professor needs to think about the possible impact of the professor's commentary on his or her own institution. Consider, for example, a professor who teaches at a law school who is asked about a legal matter affecting that school. Should that professor serve as a "legal commentator" on that case? That can be a difficult question to answer because the professor is often thrust into the position of being a spokesperson for the institution.

A professor may also have other types of conflicts with a case. For example, a professor may have an intellectual or financial stake in the outcome of the case. Professors are known to be amici or strategic consultants on cases. In these situations, it is misleading for the professor to provide legal commentary without disclosing his or her interest in the case.

Sixteen years ago, a voluntary Code of Ethics for Legal Commentators was proposed to address these types of concerns.[4] That code recognizes numerous scenarios in which a commentator may have a conflict of interest that should be disclosed, including the following: (1) conflicts created by a commentator's personal relationships with a case, (2) conflicts created by a commentator's stake in the outcome of the proceedings, (3) conflicts created by a commentator's political or organizational affiliations, (4) conflicts created when speaking to more than one media outlet, (5) conflicts created by contacting represented parties, and (6) conflicts created by assisting the court. By and large, the solution to most of these conflicts is recognition of the conflict, disclosure to the media and the public as much as possible, and an effort by the commentator to be aware of how these conflicts are impacting the professor's commentary.

Rule 3: Be a Good Teacher

It is amazing how quickly professors forget why they were asked to provide legal commentary in the first place. Professors are asked because they have perspective and information that the layperson does not have. The professor understands how individual legal proceedings or principles operate. They can appreciate the complexities of a case. They know how courts are likely to rule and what the consequences may be to the parties. They have this ability because they have invested the time and energy to learn the law and evaluate how to present it. The same should be true for legal commentary. In advance of providing commentary, a professor must learn what he or she is being asked to comment on, do the necessary research to be

---

4. *See* Erwin Chemerinsky & Laurie Levenson, *The Ethics of Being a Commentator*, 9 S. CAL. L. REV. 1303 (1996); Erwin Chemerinsky & Laurie Levenson, *The Ethics of Being a Commentator II*, 37 SANTA CLARA L. REV. 913 (1997); Erwin Chemerinsky & Laurie Levenson, *The Ethics of Being a Commentator III*, 40 MERCER L. REV. 737 (1999).

prepared on the subject, help guide the media as to what questions he or she should ask, and assess the most effective way of providing information to the public. As professors do in their other work, they should be ready to credit others for their contributions to the field, direct the media to persons who might have better information, and be open to changing opinions should circumstances warrant.

Practical Advice for Professors as Legal Commentators

Some of the most difficult challenges for professors becoming legal commentators are just the logistics of dealing with the media. How does one break into this field? On a day-to-day, minute-to-minute basis, how does one actually do the job? Here are some basic tips for the uninitiated:

How to Become a Legal Commentator

So, you want to be a legal commentator? How does one enter this field? The simple answer is, generally, "Don't call the media. The media will call you!"

Typically, the media will initiate contact with a professor to be a legal commentator. For years, this was an informal process in which media would hear which professors would be helpful with their particular type of question. Yet, with the explosion of media outlets, there has also been an effort to draw new commentators into the mix. The media may be looking for someone with not only the right expertise but also the right demographics and look for their programming.

Additionally, professors can be proactive in reaching out to the media and advertising their services as legal commentators. Almost every law school today has some type of public or media relations officials who will let the media know which professors are available for commentary and help arrange for their contact.

Moreover, nowadays it is simple enough for the media to search the Internet and find professors who have commented on cases or written regarding the legal issue at hand. The media's search generally does not involve researching the law review citations. Rather, popular media turns to popular sources, like op-eds in newspapers or commentaries in legal magazines or online publications. Some law schools are even working toward having ongoing relations with media sources by hosting Journalist Law Schools at which journalists are given cram courses in the basics of the legal system and then maintaining contact with the professors at the school who have proven knowledgeable and interested in speaking to the media.

Finally, there is another way professors can become legal commentators. As Woody Allen once quipped, "Eighty percent of life is just showing up."[5] It is not unheard of for law professors to show up at a trial just to observe the proceedings. Once there, it is almost inevitable that the professor will be asked questions and, like it or not, be launched into the role of legal commentator.

If a professor is thinking of making legal commentary a second profession, there are more formal steps that need to be taken. In addition to financial agreements, the professor would be well advised to find out who has content control over the programming. If a professor is looking for independence, he or she should set rules as to how, when, and with whose approval the professor's remarks will be edited.

Accessing Information for Legal Commentary

Although generally very smart, law professors cannot just divine all information relevant to their commentary. They must get the underlying facts to make intelligent comments and assessments regarding the case. Being a successful legal commentator means knowing how to quickly access information relevant to a case.

The quickest and most reliable sources for information tend to be the pleadings filed in the case, the court transcript, wire service stories, and, if possible, a quick conversation with the individuals involved in the case. Relying on journalists to share with the commentator what is important to know about a case is extremely risky. Most journalists have never attended law school. Even most of the journalists who cover the highest court of the land have never had a single day of formal legal education. Thus, it is un-

5. Brainy Quotes, Woody Allen Quotes, http://www.brainyquote.com/quotes/authors/w/woody_allen.html (last visited June 16, 2013).

realistic to expect that these individuals will know precisely which facts a professor needs to provide legal commentary.

Online sources, such as FindLaw, now frequently provide copies of key legal pleadings in a case. Many firms will also create a litigation site that can be accessed to follow court proceedings. Finally, law professors and their assistants should be accustomed to research. To be a competent legal commentator, one must research the facts and law applicable to the case. Although some questions will seem very basic, it is usually the twist in the case that the reporter really wants to know about and that can lead a professor to revise his or her opinion.

It is best to keep in mind one caution before leaving this topic. Law professors tend to fixate on rankings, such as the ranking of law reviews and law schools. This elitism can lead to false assumptions regarding the most reliable sources of information. For example, during the O. J. Simpson murder trial, *The National Enquirer*'s information was sometimes more reliable than that of major newspapers. In fact, the *New York Times* actually quoted the *Enquirer* during the trial.

A law professor has the responsibility of finding the most accurate information as quickly as possible before providing commentary. If this information is not obtained, opining about a matter may be treacherous, indeed.

Deciding When Not to Comment

Although knowing when to comment about a case is important, it can be equally important to know when it is a good idea not to comment about a matter. The media may know no boundaries, but law professors should exercise some judgment in deciding how and when to comment on a matter. Law professors should be particularly sensitive to their responsibility to ensure that the public receives accurate information but also that the defendant has the opportunity for a fair trial.

The most misleading and dangerous type of commentary is that which resembles sports commentary. For example, reporters want to know minute to minute who is "winning" a case. Rather than answering the question of who is winning, a professor may be providing a greater service by explaining how a development fits into an overall case. Giving the audience a more sophisticated approach to analyzing a legal proceeding may be the best commentary of all.

Professor Samuel Pillsbury has sagely remarked:

> The expert has a powerful defense against all forms of media trivialization: refusing to play the game. The expert can resist the temptation to assume total intellectual authority and admit to limitations of knowledge and insight. When the media insists on a simplistic question, the expert may respond by emphasizing the complexities involved. When conflict is sought, the expert may emphasize points of agreement as well as points of disagreement. When the law is presented as a game, the expert may remind viewers of the real stakes involved. Sometimes, the expert must be willing to take more drastic action. The expert must be willing to walk—ready to walk off the network set, away from the talk show appearance, or to decline to answer the reporter's inquiry.[6]

Out of ignorance or intentionally, the media may even seek to have the expert help them with unethical or illegal conduct. For example, the media always wants to know what they don't know. Accordingly, one of their greatest fascinations is with the grand jury because of laws of grand jury secrecy. It is perfectly fine for a professor to explain grand jury workings to the media and how one can access other avenues of information. However, professors should draw the line at improper behavior such as staking out and trying to contact sitting grand jurors. The same is true, of course, for jurors in ongoing trials.

Commentators must also be sensitive to the ethical issues that arise when they are asked to reach out to participants who may be under a court gag order. When a law professor assumes the responsibilities of a legal commentator, he must live in two worlds: the media world where access to information is always at a premium, and the lawyer's world where there is an ongoing

---

6. Samuel H. Pillsbury, *Why Are We Ignored? The Peculiar Place of Experts in the Current Debate About Crime and Justice*, Crim. L. Bull. July–Aug. 1995, at 305, 335.

duty to act as an officer of the court. Although the propriety of gag orders is open to debate, law professors must carefully consider whether they want to engage in activities that are designed to circumvent court orders.

Framing the Interview

The best kind of commentator is the one who helps the media understand the most important questions to ask. To do this, the commentator needs to talk to the interviewer before the actual interview. The reporter will still have control over the questions, but an educated question will provide better coverage of a matter and allow the commentator to provide more pertinent information. If a professor wants to help frame an interview, he or she can suggest to the reporter that the reporter ask about the significance of a ruling, what is the applicable law, how much discretion the court has, and what strategies are at play.

Even during an interview, a commentator can answer the question he or she thinks the reporter should have asked rather than the one actually asked. Crucial to any commentary is incorporating the question into the commentator's answer. By incorporating a different question into his or her answer, the commentator can have a substantial impact on the nature of the coverage. It is also important to integrate any necessary caveats into one's opinion. In other words, if a professor's opinion is based upon a critical fact provided by the reporter, that fact should be integrated into the answer.

Speaking in Sound Bites

The biggest challenge for many law professors is speaking in sound bites. Most professors have had little or no formal media training. In the classroom, professors can dominate the discussion. However, during media interviews, professors must boil down the essence of their remarks into a few, hopefully cogent, sound bites.

What is a sound bite? A "short" sound bite, such as the kind used routinely for news programs, is usually around seven seconds. In that time, a professor is expected to sum up an entire legal ruling or summarize a day's worth of action in court. A "medium" sound bite, often used for more in-depth news programming, will be around twice as long (approximately fifteen seconds). A professor will rarely be given more than this amount of time to explain even the most complicated issues in the law. When professors serve as panelists on television or radio, they must ordinarily answer in short, pithy sound bites.

Speaking to print journalists gives a commentator greater leeway, but the ultimate quotations the reporter uses will likely be the print version of a sound bite. Therefore, when providing commentary, it is often helpful to remember that "less is more." The less verbose a professor's statements, the more likely they are to be quoted and not edited by the journalist.

It is also important to remember that the media and public prefer someone who speaks confidently without sounding rehearsed. A professor who speaks in "plain English," who avoids legal jargon, will be more effective than one who sounds like he or she is presenting a formal paper to an academic symposium.

Finally, if a commentator is interacting with a listening audience by, for example, taking live phone calls, the professor will be most effective by speaking politely and with tact and civility, regardless of the position of the caller. "The commentator should remember the level of her audience and respond in an interesting and understanding manner, possibly disarming hostile callers with the use of humor."[7]

"What Will I Wear?"

Professors often do not give much thought to what they will wear to teach class. Attire ranges from coat and tie to extremely casual. Television, however, is much more about appearances. Commentators' credibility can depend on what they wear or how they present themselves. If truth be told, professors worry about appearances much more than they will admit. Yet, they too often are reluctant to ask the journalists what guidance they can provide. It will not make a professor seem any less scholarly if he asks what the dress code is for the interview. Once that issue is resolved, the professor can focus on what really counts: a correct, cogent analysis of the legal issues in the case.

---

7. Mogill, *supra note 3* at 482.

"Can I Really Say the Judge Made a Mistake?"

It is remarkable that professors who are more than willing to write an entire law review article criticizing a court's decision become shy and compliant when asked about the appropriateness of a court's ruling. Just as in academic writing, in legal commentary there are respectful ways to criticize a court's decision. Part of being an objective commentator is to be able to critically analyze the conduct of others in the justice system. Commentators have a responsibility to be honest in their analysis, regardless of whether they agree with the court's decision.

A separate question is whether a legal commentator should have off-the-record conversations with a judge about the judge's rulings. As members of the legal community, it is not uncommon for law professors to actually know judges handling cases being covered by the media. At minimum, a commentator must be willing to respect the confidences of the court and not to engage in ex parte communications on behalf of one party or another. In many jurisdictions, including federal courts, professors who are used as a sounding board by the court are considered experts, and their relationship to the court must be disclosed to the parties.[8]

"How Do I Deal With Other Commentators?"

Two of the most frustrating things for many commentators can be realizing that they are not the only voice on a subject and that they do not control what other voices the media airs. Yet, a professor can distinguish himself or herself by being respectful to those other voices, much as one would be in the classroom, and attack ideas, not people. One way to keep commentary on the professional level is to reach out to an opposing commentator after an interview to share ideas and find out the basis for the commentator's remarks.

It is also helpful to keep in mind that providing legal commentary is not a competition. Those who view it as a competition often lapse into sensationalism and name-calling. As professors teach their students, the power in legal argument is in the power of the ideas, not the antics of the speaker.

---

8. Fed. R. Evid. 706(c).

"Should I Get Paid?"

The question of whether to be paid for legal commentary is an individual decision. Many professors see legal commentary as a form of community service. Most print reporters do not pay for commentary, and even electronic media rarely pays for isolated coverage of a legal matter.

However, in high-profile cases, the pay can be substantial. For instance, during the O. J. Simpson case, some consultants were paid $4,000 per day to provide legal commentary.[9] Thus, for the professor who has the time, inclination, and talent to enlist with the media to cover a case, there can be very tangible rewards. In determining whether to accept such fees, professors must first consider whether their home institutions permit such arrangements. Another consideration should also be whether the financial arrangements come with any conditions that may affect the content of the professor's remarks. Media censoring is a reality, even in the United States, and can be a rude awakening for many professors.

Integrating Legal Commentary into Teaching and Keep Teaching Yourself

The intangibles of providing legal commentary can be greater than the formal pay. The types of issues commentators are often asked to discuss can be on the cutting edge of the law, precisely the same kinds of issues that can spark the best discussion in classes. Professors should consider getting permission from the beginning to use tapes of their commentary as teaching aids or even access to the entire tape of a case. Likewise, professors should collect the documents obtained by journalists during a case. Once reported on, reporters will frequently discard such documents. However, for a professor, they are often ready-made teaching materials.

It is too bad that most law schools have not yet incorporated speaking to the press into their curriculum to train prospective lawyers. Thus, law professors are a bit on their own to learn the tricks of the trade as they provide their commentary. Although it may be painful, one of the quick-

9. Deborah Graham, *In the Simpson Spotlight*, A.B.A. J. Nov. 1995, at 49.

est ways to improve one's legal commentary is to watch or listen to oneself or read a transcript of one's remarks. It may be too late to salvage that particular interview, but learning from one's mistakes is an effective way of improving one's commentary.

New Avenues of Legal Commentary by Law Professors

Professors now have more avenues than ever to influence the public debate on legal issues. They can provide commentary through blogs, Facebook, YouTube, Twitter, and countless new forms of communication.[10] It is simple enough for the media to access professors' blawgs and assess a range of opinions on legal issues.

Although blawgs provide an easy means to disseminate information, there are no standards that control their accuracy. As an informal form of expression, the blawg can lull a professor into a false sense that their commentary will be seen for what it is—an initial impression regarding an issue that is published to spark further debate. It is easy for a professor's comments on a blawg to be misinterpreted and used by the media. Thus, it is critical that a professor posting a blawg comment assume that his or her remarks will be published exactly as stated. Professors may appreciate the differences between their commentary in a law review article and on a blawg, but it is not at all certain that the media or public will.

The blogosphere also poses the challenge of responding to "media" inquiries from individuals who are far afield from the mainstream press. As one commentator put it, "I don't think the blogosphere is breeding cannibals. But it looks to me as if the world of blogs may be filling up with people who for the previous 200 millennia of human existence kept their weird thoughts more or less to themselves. Now, they don't have to. They've got the Web. Now they can share."

In using modern electronic media to disseminate legal commentary, law professors are joining a virtual Hyde Park. To distinguish their opinions from those who have little background in the law but present them-

---

10. For an overview on the role of legal blogs, *see* Brian A. Craddock, *2009: A Blawg Odyssey: Exploring How the Legal Community Is Using Blogs and How Blogs Are Changing the Legal Community*, 60 Mercer L. Rev. 1353 (2009).

selves as legal experts, professors must be careful as to both where they publish and how they present their ideas and commentary.

Conclusion

In this era, it is nearly impossible for law professors not to find themselves serving as legal commentators at some point. Commenting comes with responsibilities and challenges. It is not beneath the dignity of professors to share their knowledge with the public, but it is important that they approach their commentary work with the same commitment and professionalism as their other academic responsibilities. After the makeup is removed and the studio lights are dimmed, commentators are in essence teachers. Teaching is one thing that law professors should know how to do.

Index